PIETIST AND WESLEYAN STUDIES

Editors: David Bundy and J. Steven O'Malley

This monograph series will publish volumes in two areas of scholarly research: Pietism and Methodism (broadly understood). The focus will be Pietism, its history and development, and the influence of this socioreligious tradition in modern culture, especially within the Wesleyan religious traditions.

Consideration will be given to scholarly works on classical and neo-Pietism, on English and American Methodism, as well as on the social and ecclesiastical institutions shaped by Pietism (e.g., Evangelicals, United Brethren, and the Pietist traditions among the Lutherans, Reformed, and Anabaptists). Works focusing on leaders within the Pietist and Wesleyan traditions will also be included in the series, as well as occasional translations and/or editions of Pietist texts. It is anticipated that the monographs will emphasize theological developments, but with close attention to the interaction of Pietism with other cultural forces and to the sociocultural identity of the Pietist and Wesleyan movements.

1. Gregory S. Clapper, *John Wesley on Religious Affections.* 1989.
2. Peter Erb, *Gottfried Arnold.* 1989.

PIETISTS, PROTESTANTS, AND MYSTICISM:

The Use of Late Medieval Spiritual Texts in the Work of Gottfried Arnold (1666-1714)

by

Peter C. Erb

Pietist and Wesleyan Studies, No. 2

The Scarecrow Press, Inc.
Metuchen, N.J., & London
1989

Research for this publication was aided by grants from the Social Sciences and Humanities Research Council of Canada, Schwenkfelder Library, Pennsburg, Pennsylvania, and Wilfrid Laurier University, Waterloo, Ontario.

British Library Cataloguing-in-Publication data available

Library of Congress Cataloging-in-Publication Data

Erb, Peter C., 1943-
    Pietists, Protestants, and mysticism : the use of late Medieval spiritual texts in the work of Gottfried Arnold (1666-1714) / by Peter C. Erb.
        p.   cm. -- (Pietist and Wesleyan studies ; no. 2)
    Includes bibliographical references.
    ISBN 0-8108-2281-4 (alk. paper)
    1. Arnold, Gottfried, 1666-1714.   2. Pietism--Germany--History of doctrines--17th century.   3. Pietism--Germany--History of doctrines--18th century.   4. Mysticism--History--Middle Ages, 600-1500.   5. Mysticism--Germany--History--17th century.
6. Mysticism--Germany--History--18th century.   I. Title.   II. Series.
BR1653.A75E72   •1989
273'.7--dc20   89-29185

In Memory of
Lloyd Erb
1919-1983

Table of Contents

Editors' Foreword

European Pietism and its leaders have remained a sort of *terra incognita* in the study of North American religion and culture, despite their central role in the definition of American religious culture through interaction at the level of both person and text over a period of two centuries. It can be argued that the structures of piety within American Reformed, Methodist, and Anabaptist churches as well as those of the nineteenth- and twentieth-century "evangelical" denominations trace their character to that influence. The Roman Catholic tradition also drank deeply at that well, especially in the Western-European mystical and American Paulist contexts. During the twentieth century, building on the base of earlier mission efforts, Pentecostal denominations have taken the pietist impulse throughout the world.

The Pietist and Wesleyan Studies series is committed to increasing our understanding of Pietism and Pietists. Peter Erb's analysis of Gottfried Arnold (1666-1714) is a significant inaugural contribution on Pietism for Pietist and Wesleyan Studies. Arnold is arguably the most important figure of "radical Pietism" and was justifiably renowned for his erudition. However, he has been little known or studied outside the orb of German scholarship.

Erb's study holds promise for several reasons. Previous research has focused on Arnold's role as a church historian who pioneered an inclusive "non-sectarian" historiography, especially as developed in his *Unparteiische Kirchen- und Ketzer Historie*, published 1699-1700. Other scholars had examined his influence on the development of Northern European ecclesiology. What has been less understood is Arnold's engagement with medieval writers, especially as points of dependency and interaction in the formation of his soteriology and ecclesiology. Erb documents and analyzes these relationships.

Another contribution is the presentation of Arnold as an independent and creative scholar who seriously engaged and challenged the major thinkers of the Christian tradition. Finally, Erb develops these foci within the framework of the theological biography of Arnold. As such, he points toward several avenues of potential research in Arnold and Pietist studies, whose nurture we trust this volume will hasten.

Peter Erb is uniquely qualified to write this volume, which is a revised and updated presentation of research presented in his dissertation at the University of Toronto (1976). His is the author of *Schwenckfeld in his Reformation Setting* (1977), *The Spiritual Diary of Christopher Wiegner* (1977), *Jacob Boehme: The Way to Christ* (1978), *Johann Arndt: True Christianity* (1979), *Pietists* (1983), and *Schwenckfeld and Early Schwenkfeldianism* (1985), as well as numerous scholarly articles and essays. Erb is Professor of English and Religion and Culture at Wilfrid Laurier University, Waterloo, Ontario, Canada.

We are pleased to publish his study as the second volume of Pietist and Wesleyan Studies.

David Bundy
Assoc. Prof. of
    Christian Origins
Collection Development
    Librarian
Asbury Theological Seminary
Wilmore, KY

J. Stephen O'Malley
Professor of Church
    History and
Historical Theology

Asbury Theological Seminary
Wilmore, KY

Introduction

In opening his discussion of the most significant awakening
within Protestantism since the sixteenth century, Emil Brunner wrote, 'Squeezed in between rationalism and orthodoxy,
and mediating between them at the same time as it was marked
off from both, a place was found for Pietism, a mode of understanding faith, the deepest roots of which must be sought in
medieval mysticism.'[1] Brunner's conclusion provides a fitting
introduction to this study, for although the Swiss theologian
often offers penetrating insights into the development of Christian thought, he is not the first scholar to link the mysticism
of the late Middle Ages and Pietist spirituality without doc-
umentation. His statement on the ties between the two is,
in fact, a commonplace in the literature on Pietism. Already
in 1676, Joachim Stoll, a close adherent to Pietist theory, expressed his concern with the use of medieval mystical materials
by Protestants,[2] and contemporary opponents of the awakening continually stated their reservations concerning its mystical
orientation.[3]

Among the first modern students of Pietism, only Albrecht
Ritschl in his *Geschichte des Pietismus* attempted an analysis of the influence late medieval mysticism exercised on the
movement.[4] His work was marred, however, by his antagonism
to the tradition he chronicled, and by a number of serious
shortcomings in his attempt to document what he believed was
an essentially unified sequence of piety extending back from
Pietism to Anabaptism, and from Anabaptism to late medieval
Franciscan spirituality.[5] Nevertheless, despite its obvious negativism, Ritschl's study rapidly became the authority for all
students of Pietism, and its discussion of the medieval background, in addition to the fact that individual Pietists often
cited medieval mystical texts,[6] led many subsequent writers
to accept the premise that late medieval mysticism played a

major role in the development of Pietist thought.[7] A reaction
against this approach was inevitable, but, when it did come,
scholars who rejected the premise that late medieval mysticism
played an important role in the development of Pietism, like
those who accepted it, did so for the most part without closely
examining the morphological or generic relationships between
the two movements.[8]

Among those Pietists who afford the best insights into these
relationships, the most important was the Lutheran historian,
poet, theologian, and pastor, Gottfried Arnold (1666-1714).
He stands at the close of the seventeenth century, in many
ways summing it up. His life spans almost exactly that critical period in European development, aptly designated by Paul
Hazard as 'the crisis of European consciousness.' In Arnold
almost all the traits of the period are found: its authoritarian
framework and its strivings for individual freedom, its baroque
lyricism and scientific inquiry, its sectarian and established theologies, and, above all, its eclectic interest in mysticism, including that of the late Middle Ages.[9]

It is the primary purpose of this study to determine the
role late medieval spirituality played in Arnold's work. Such
an investigation is of value beyond the interest it has for students of Arnold, however. As a case study it casts light on the
larger question of the relationship between late medieval piety
and Pietism generally. Arnold, rather than another Pietist,
is a particularly apt subject for study in this regard. He was
by far the most learned of all the Pietists and made the most
extensive use of late medieval texts. Moreover, with the exception of August Hermann Francke, Arnold's works were the
most influential of those by first generation Pietists.[10] Again,
Arnold unlike any other writer of his day, best reflects both
conservative and radical wings within the Pietist awakening,
and, finally, his historical and theological studies mirror in a
striking manner the place of medieval texts and mystical theology among his Protestant forebears and contemporaries.

Part One of this study offers a general guide to Arnold's
Protestant and Pietist heritage and a brief review of his life
and work.[11] The first chapter which surveys Arnold's religious
background is somewhat general, and readers well acquainted
with the period may wish to begin with the biography in Chap-

ter Two. The writing of a full Arnold biography is not yet
possible, complicated as it is by the lack of detailed studies
on his extensive literary production and the precise nature of
theological influences on his development.[12] Part Two takes up
one aspect of the latter problem and discusses the growth of
Arnold's interest in late medieval texts within the context of
the use of those texts by the theological sources from which
he drew. Besides the approach of the Lutheran tradition to
medieval materials—and it is within Lutheranism that Arnold
must always be interpreted—the use of such sources in three
other theological streams (Mystical Spiritualism, Boehmism,
and Quietism) is treated. Whereas Part Two is concerned with
tracing Arnold's growing use of medieval texts in relation to
his developing personal and theological concerns, Part Three
discusses his mature view of those texts and compares and
contrasts Arnold's spirituality with certain medieval spiritual-
ities from which he selected source material, in particular with
Tauler and Ruusbroec. Part Two describes Arnold's relationship to late medieval spirituality generically (diachronically);
Part Three treats the same topic morphologically (synchroni-
cally).

The study which follows is based on my Ph. D. dissertation,
*The Role of Late Medieval Spirituality in the Life and Work
of Gottfried Arnold*, submitted to the University of Toronto
well over a decade ago (1976), and it is with some reluctance
that I offer it in its present form. Like any such study it is
dated, although I have considered recent scholarly work in the
notes and bibliography, have edited and shortened the piece,
and have done some necessary rewriting. Other than this I
have not made major changes.

The central focus of the dissertation remains: The original
work was initiated in the context of discussions concerning the
use of late medieval German mystics such as Tauler and the author of the *Theologia deutsch* among the Protestant Reformers,
and since the later Arnold had been particularly interested in
the Taulerian materials and Ruusbroec, the concluding chapter
outlining his mature theology treated him in this framework.
But such an approach limits our view of Arnold. For a complete treatment of his 'mystical' theology a study of his use
of Macarius and of the relationships between his thought and

that of Augustinian-Cistercian spirituality (particularly that of Bernard of Clairvaux) on the image-likeness theme remains essential.

A number of matters have kept me from rewriting the piece accordingly. Teaching and administrative responsibilities are among these, but more significant is a shift in interest: The work on Arnold initially directed my attention to the wider problem of Christian historiography, theologies of Scripture and tradition, and, in particular, the use of Patristic materials by theologians after Arnold. Among these I have been especially attracted to the work of the early nineteenth century Roman Catholic Tübingen theologian, Johann Adam Möhler (who may have been stimulated by Arnold's work[13]), and through Möhler to nineteenth-century Catholic theology generally.

If I were to take up the study of Arnold again, I would do so *ab ovo*, and my attention would then be directed to the writing of an intellectual biography. Such a biography would of necessity include discussion of previously unknown manuscript materials related to Arnold.[14] Were I to take up such a biography, however, it is unlikely that the new work would stand in opposition to the findings of the present study. Review of Arnold's use of Patristic texts supports the conclusions reached in this work. I continue to see more theological and 'spiritual' continuity in Arnold's career than discontinuity and to read the whole of his work, including his separatistic rhetoric of 1699-1701, within, rather than aside from or in opposition to, the established (and, indeed 'Orthodox') Lutheran context. As a result, I understand his decision to marry and his acceptance of a pastorate in 1701 more as a tactical shift on the part of a Pietist reformer whose primary concern was pastoral than a 'reversal' on the part of a radical separatist or a Baroque 'disjuncture' in his career.

Thus, while much earlier scholarship has tended to accent the radical aspects of Arnold's work and has emphasised as a result his Boehmist, Quietist, and to a lesser degree Radical Reformation ties, a study of the texts he quotes throughout his life and of those with which he seems best acquainted points away from such a conclusion. Next to early Christian and Patristic texts he refers most frequently to medieval sources, and his interest in these latter sources increases throughout his life.

As extensive as Arnold's use of late medieval mystical texts is, however, there is no indication that he was directly influenced by medieval thought. His use of these writers is always within the context of his Lutheran Pietism.

As a typical Pietist, his first concern was with directing the individual to new birth and to growth in the Christian life. It was for purposes of edification, then, that he found late medieval texts valuable, and for this reason he edited selections from late medieval mystics, wrote poetry based on their work, and regularly quoted them as authorities. In his use of these mystics Arnold was one with his Pietist contemporaries. He approached history as a pastor; as a pastor, too, he wrote and edited poetry and theological works.

It is this pastoral concern, as well, which must be primarily considered in any discussion of Arnold's theological and ecclesiological dualism and his interest in religious experience. His individualism Arnold shared with his Pietist colleagues.[15] Like them he called the believer to live responsibly before God; final responsibility for Christian life rested with the believer and was not mediated by any ecclesiastical institution or religious rite. Yet Arnold's individualism was not that of the mystical Spiritualists, nor was his interest in the life of solitude an extension of their demand that one progress by an interior journey toward the inner word.[16] He was Pietist, but also fully Lutheran. The Scripture, creeds, theological formulations, and, above all, the church, were for him, as for his Protestant associates, guides to a proper Christian life, and in spite of his attacks on the Lutheran scholasticism of his day, he used its theological method, particularly its doctrine of the *ordo salutis*, according to which he interpreted the mystical texts he used.

Arnold's interest in and concern for Christian community, both as Pietist conventicle and larger denominational structure, explain his moral and ecclesiological dualism. Because of the hermeneutical function of the community, both in the interpretation of the word as spoken outwardly in the pulpit and Scripture and in the validation of the interior word spoken to the individual believer, it was important, for Arnold, that the

Christian community of which he was a member be pure, or
as pure as possible. In this he had much in common with the
earlier Anabaptists, but he was not an Anabaptist despite his
insistence on an adult, considered decision of faith. For Arnold
an act of faith was not the first step in uniting with a purified
community—his notion of the new birth was not narrowed in
this way—but, in Lutheran fashion, an acceptance of God's
power of redemption and presence in baptism and the Supper. Nor must Arnold's early interest in visions[17] and direct
religious experience be interpreted as that of a Boehmist visionary or mystical Spiritualist. Certainly in his demand that
religious experience bring warmth, joy, and consolation, he was
no Quietist.

Although it was his pastoral interest which was the primary
reason for his attraction to late medieval mystics, writers prior
to the Reformation also provided apologetic materials for him,
and he used these to support his own specific emphases in the
same way as did many Protestants. Forerunners of the Reformation and witnesses to the truth were one and the same for
him; both designations were in his historiography the result
of personal apologetic in the same way as they were for those
nineteenth-century scholars such as Wilhelm Preger who stood
with his opponent, Heinrich Suso Denifle, at the beginning of
the modern study of late medieval mysticism.[18] Had the intellectual climate been different in Arnold's own day, had his
interest in medieval writers been taken with as much seriousness as was his Patristic study, the beginning of scientific study
into late medieval mysticism might well have been initiated a
century and a half earlier and in an atmosphere of much less
invective.

That Arnold and his Pietist colleagues had a significant effect on later Christian separatistic groups and that fascinating
parallels can be drawn between him and contemporary North
American Evangelicals is obvious, but care must always be
taken that the concerns of later developments, whether or not
they owe something directly to his work, not be read back
into his life. Although, for example, early members of the
church of the Brethren may have found inspiration in his writings, Arnold must not be interpreted as a 'proto' member of
that or any other denomination,[19] any more than his religious

concern and that of Pietists generally with 'new birth' forces him and the movement of which he was a part into the role of 'forerunners' of American revivalism, or 'participants' in an 'Evangelical tradition', shaped as the latter is by a particular historiographical interest of a period long after the demise of the classic form of Pietism in the late 1720s. His rejection of an academic post in the late seventeenth century has no direct parallels with the anti-intellectualism of late nineteenth-century American sectarian piety[20] and should not be read within that context, nor should his separatistic rhetoric and call for non-partisanship be understood in the framework of an Enlightenment culture which prides itself on its idiosyncratic form of the separation of church and state.

* * * * * *

Some sections of the original thesis were reworked on the basis of study done in Germany (under the support of the Social Sciences and Humanities Research Council of Canada) and were published in my translations and editions for the Paulist Press 'Classics of Western Spirituality' series (Jacob Boehme, *The Way to Christ* [1978]; Johann Arndt, *True Christianity* [1979]; *Pietists* [1983]), two book chapters ('Pietist Spirituality: Some Aspects of Present Research' and 'The Medieval Sources of Pietism: A Case Study') in E. Rozanne Elder (ed.), *The Roots of the Modern Christian Tradition* (Kalamzoo, Mich.: Cistercian Publications, 1984) and a paper presented at the sixth centenary of Ruusbroec's death held in Belgium in 1981 and published as 'The Use of Ruusbroec among German Protestants' in P. Mommaers and N. de Paepe (eds.), *Jan van Ruusbroec: The sources, content and sequels of his mysticism* (Leuven: Leuven University Press, 1984). I thank Carlotte Cox for typing the thesis draft into the computer and Benedict Sheehy for compiling the index.

To Father Edmund Colledge, O.S.A. I owe special thanks; his personal interest in my work, his skills as an academic director and teacher, and his extensive studies in medieval spirituality continue to shape me long after the completion of a doctorate and licentiate.

I am particularly thankful as well to the many friends who have come to me and my family through Schwenkfelder Library, and for the Library's continuing support of my work: to Fred A. Grater (now of Pitts Theology Library, Atlanta) and to Claire Conway who first introduced me to the collection in 1970, to Dennis Moyer, the Director, and to Lib Dewey, to Arlene and Paul Bieler for a 'home away from home', to Claude A. Schultz, Jr., who has served as President of the Library Board during the greater part of my tenure there, and to W. Kyrel and Barbara Meschter, whose encouragement of my work has always been exactly placed at the time it was needed most. The usefulness of Schwenkfelder Library's holdings for a study such as this has been without equal, but many other collections in Pennsylvania, the Federal Republic of Germany, and the German Democratic Republic were of importance to me as well.

To my wife, Betty, and our daughters, Catharine and Suzanne, I owe more than a mere note of thanks can ever reach.

Peter C. Erb
Department of Religion and Culture
Wilfrid Laurier University
Waterloo, Ont.

Associate Director
Schwenkfelder Library
Pennsburg, Pa.

Part One
Historical Background

Chapter One:
Arnold's Protestant Heritage

What is commonly called Protestantism is a highly diversified religious movement, embracing those many Christian traditions which arose in opposition to Catholicism and separated from it in the early sixteenth century. Popularly interpreted as a single reformation of the late medieval church, it was, in fact, two movements. One, the Magisterial Reformation—so named because it spread under the dictates of political *magisteria*— embraced the work of Martin Luther, (1483-1546), Hulderich Zwingli (1484-1531), Martin Butzer (1491-1551), John Calvin (1509-1564), and the Anglicans among others.[1] A second, the Radical or Left-Wing Reformation, was distinct sociologically and theologically from the first and included within its parameters many loosely connected, yet separate and independent units, including Revolutionaries, Anabaptists, and Spiritualists.[2]

Unlike any earlier writer, Gottfried Arnold incorporated within his work many of the diverse doctrines and traditions of both Magisterial and Radical Protestantism. His historical works chart Protestant development with such completeness that for some aspects they remain our most reliable guides to much of its history. Not unfittingly, modern scholars have praised Arnold for the breadth and tolerance with which he treated his subject and have described him as the first modern historian of the Christian Church.[3] It is true that Arnold was the first historian to attempt to outline Protestantism in its full dimensions, but it is equally true that he was not always aware of the precise nature or of the complex inter-dependency of the denominations he chronicled. His method was eclectic; he chose what suited his purpose and, fortunately for later students, he found much that was suitable. He read widely and had great knowledge, but he fitted his facts into the categories specified by his own theological perspective.

His approach is well exemplified in his treatment of Lutheran controversies in the sixteenth century. In his *Unparteiische Kirchen- und Ketzer-Historie*, Arnold's antagonism to Protestant scholasticism or Orthodoxy, defined by its opponents as the theology of the schools (*Schultheologie*), is ever present.[4] The young Luther is hero. Philip Melanchthon (1497-1560), a catalyst in the doctrinal disputes of mid-century Lutheranism, is viewed negatively as the initiator of the Orthodox concern with theoretical dogmatics. Major opponents of Lutheranism are treated with respect. Little attention is directed to the rise of scholasticism in the late sixteenth century; it is simply viewed negatively. No attempt is made to analyse the real reason for its development or the nature of its mature form, and the practical interests of men like Johann Arndt (1555-1621) and the prophetic visions of more radical spirits are treated as the sole expressions of truth in a declining age.

Magisterial Protestantism's growth cannot be so naively delineated. The intense theological debates within Lutheranism in the sixteenth century, for example, were attempts to deal with theoretical issues which had not been solved earlier.[5] For Lutherans the questions raised by these controversies were eventually resolved in the *Formula of Concord* (1580). In their attempts to support their various positions and in the polemical inter-denominational literature which grew up, the debating theologians, both Lutheran and Calvinist, developed a precise theological method and vocabulary known as Protestant Orthodoxy or scholasticism.[6] Its method was rooted in that of Melanchthon's *Loci Communes*[7] and was particularly influenced by the Spanish-Jesuit scholastics of the sixteenth century.[8] Aside from its method Orthodoxy is difficult to define. To its enemies such as Arnold it was seen as a dry, polemical, intolerant defence of a single denomination's position, lacking any concern with issues relevant to religious life or the practice of Christian virtue and devotion. Yet, Orthodoxy's opponents often owed much to its form and matter. Interest in personal piety was not neglected by the greater orthodox theologians, who were important sources for Pietism's own teaching.[9]

Orthodoxy is commonly categorised according to three his-

torical periods.[10] The first, a Golden Age, extended from the
Formula of Concord to 1618; the second, High Orthodoxy, covered the period of the Thirty Years' War; a third, the Silver
Age, lasted to the early eighteenth century. The major figure
in the second was Johann Gerhard (1582-1637). In the third
Johann Andreas Quenstedt (1617-1688), David Hollatz (1648-
1713), and the eirenic George Calixtus (1586-1656) were the
most significant authors.

From its beginnings Lutheran Orthodoxy was opposed by
individuals who were primarily interested in the practice of
piety: personal renewal, individual growth in the holiness,
and religious experience.[11] This practically-oriented opposition
found a spokesman in the Lutheran pastor and author, Johann Arndt, who, in his *Wahres Christentum* and devotional
works,[12] established the direction of this moment which grew
under his followers, and eventually blossomed into Pietism
at the end of the seventeenth century.[13] Arndt was fiercely
denounced for heresy by contemporary theologians and, although defended by many, including Johann Gerhard, he did
leave himself open to charges of unorthodoxy.[14] One of his
chief sources, for example, was the speculative mystic Valentine Weigel (1533-1588).[15]

Contemporary with Arndt, and equally as significant in
establishing the milieu in which Pietism flourished, was the
Görlitz shoemaker and visionary Jacob Boehme (1575-1624).[16]
Boehme's influence has been traced with some reliability
through the seventeenth century and came to Arnold in
two ways.[17] Boehme's immediate disciples, Abraham von
Franckenburg (1593-1653) and Johann Theodor von Tschesch
(1595-1649), were active missionaries. Through their efforts,
by the end of the century Boehmist materials had pene-
trated west to the Lowlands where they were used by the
Quietists Antoniette Bourignon (1616-1680) and Pierre Poiret
(1646-1719), to England where they were reworked by Jane
Leade (1623-1704) and her Philadelphian Society and reintro-
duced into Germany through such Philadelphians as Johann
Petersen (1649-1727) and his wife Johanna Eleonora. In Holland Boehme's works were edited by his greatest disciple, Johann Conrad Gichtel (1638-1710). Secondly, Boehme's influence reached Arnold through the mysticism of such baroque

poets as Angelus Silesius (1624-1677), and Quirinus Kuhlmann
(1652-1689/90).

Calvinist theology underwent much the same development as did Lutheranism.[18] Calvinism, too, developed a
scholasticism, equally as rigorous as the Lutheran variety
and, from Arnold's point of view, equally as pernicious.[19]
In Calvinist scholasticism, as well, antagonism quickly developed. No better can this be seen than in Holland. There a
proto-Pietist position rapidly gained ground.[20] A similar direction was taken by English Puritans who, following William
Perkins (1558-1602), penned doctrinal and devotional works
which rapidly made their way to the continent in German and
Dutch translations.[21]

The basic premises of all practically-directed reform groups
in seventeenth-century Protestantism found expression in a
single treatise issued in 1675. In that year Philipp Jakob
Spener (1635-1705),[22] *senior* of the *ministerium* in Frankfurt am Main, published an introduction to the postills of
Johann Arndt. The treatise, reissued separately a year
later under the title *Pia Desideria: oder Hertzliches Verlan-
gen Nach Gottgefälliger Besserung der wahren Evangelischen
Kirche*[23] was to spur a concern for the practice of piety within
Protestantism and, before the author's death in 1705, it had
passed through four editions and was translated into Latin to
make it more widely available.[24] As Lutheran pastor to a community which had known the turmoil and disillusionment of the
Thirty Years War,[25] Spener was sadly aware of the low ebb of
Christian life in his city and throughout Germany. Pressing
the need for repentance and rebirth on the part of individual
believers, he attempted to remedy the situation in 1670 by the
introduction of small prayer and study groups or conventicles
of awakened Christians, who met for mutual encouragement in
individual faith and practice.[26]

Spener's *Pia Desideria* outlined his hopes and intentions
under five headings. After noting the decline in moral life at
the time, it detailed at length the defects of political and clerical authorities as well as those of the populace, clarified the
possibility of reform, and set down proposals to enact it.[27]
New attention was first to be given to the revitalisation of
the Word within individuals.[28] Scripture reading by individuals was emphasised and a call made for sermons which would

treat the biblical text in context and progress through a book rather than centering on themes chosen according to the church year.[29] It was at this point in the argument that Spener outlined his proposal for the use of group meetings to stimulate Christian growth:

> It would perhaps not be inexpedient to reintroduce the ancient and apostolic kind of church meetings. In addition to our customary services with preaching, other assemblies would also be held in the manner in which Paul describes them in I Corinthians 14:26-40. One person would not rise to preach (although this practice would be continued at other times), but others who have been blessed with gifts and knowledge would also speak and present their pious opinions on all the proposed subject to the judgment of the rest, doing all this in such a way as to avoid disorder and strife. This might conveniently be done by having several ministers meet together or by having several members of a congregation who have a fair knowledge of God or desire to increase their knowledge meet under the leadership of a minister, take up the Holy Scriptures, read aloud from them, and fraternally discuss each verse in order to discover its simple meaning and whatever may be useful for the edification of all. Anybody who is not satisfied with his understanding of a matter should be permitted to express his doubts and seek further explanation. Everything should be arranged with an eye to the glory of God, to the spiritual growth of the participants, and therefore also to their limitations. Any threat of meddlesomeness, quarrelsomeness, self-seeking, or something else of this sort should be guarded against and tactfully cut off especially by the preachers who retain leadership in these meetings.[30]

Discussion of such conventicles led Spener to his second proposal: the necessity of practising the spiritual priesthood of all believers.[31] Two years after the publication of the *Pia Desideria*, Spener drew his ideas on this doctrine into catechetical form. In that work, *Das Geistliche Priestertum*, he defined the spiritual priesthood as:

> The right which our Saviour Jesus Christ has purchased for all men, and for which he anoints all believers with his Holy Spirit, in virtue of which they may and shall bring sacrifices acceptable to God, pray for themselves and others, and severally edify themselves and their neighbours.[32]

The definition sums up his vision. Each Christian and not only ministers are to function as priests. All Christians are to fulfill the office of sacrifice by offering their bodies, free of sin, to God. Likewise, their spiritual natures are to be tamed and submitted in passive obedience. The tongue and mind are to be offered in prayer and meditation on the Scriptural text. If this is done the Holy Spirit will illumine the mind of each committed believer. Study is to be assiduously undertaken and to be directed to the conversion of the erring and the comfort of the weak.[33]

A demand for the practice of piety is the substance of the *Pia Desideria's* third proposal, and the specific characteristic of this piety is developed in the last three proposals. Rather than maintain polemical attack, Christians should endeavour to come to agreement through dedicated prayer, examples of moral well-being, and heartfelt love.[34] Antagonistic scholastic disputation must be ended. The role of the pastor must be reemphasised and pastoral education revamped with greater attention given to the daily life of a pastor in its devotional and moral aspects, and less on superfluous learning.[35] Sermons must likewise be considered for their practical advice for living the Christian life and not for rhetorical display.[36] As guides for all such reforms, Spener concludes, late medieval mystical texts are of particular value:

> It might also be useful to make more effort to put into the hands of students and recommend to them the use of such simple little books as the *Theologia Germanica* and the writings of Tauler, which, next to the Scriptures, probably made our dear Luther what he was. Such was the advice of Luther himself, who in a letter to Spalatin wrote thus of the man of God (as he called Tauler elsewhere): 'If you desire to read the old, pure theology in German, you can obtain the sermons of the Dominican friar, John Tauler. Neither in the Latin nor in the German language have I found a purer, more wholesome theology or one that agrees more with the Gospel.' Again Luther wrote: 'Once again I beg you, believe me in this case, follow me, and buy Tauler's book. I have admonished you before to get it wherever you can. You will have no trouble finding a copy. It is a book in which you will find such a skillful presentation of pure and wholesome doctrine that in comparison all other books, whether written in Greek, Latin, or Hebrew, are like iron or clay.' Elsewhere Luther said: 'I have found more of pure, divine teaching in it than I have found or am likely to find in all the books of the scholastics in all the universities.' Concerning *Theologia Germanica* (which Luther also ascribed to Tauler, although it was written later, and which I look upon as a particular honor to this city inasmuch as it is supposed to have been written here in Frankfurt) Luther expressed this opinion: 'No book except the Bible and St. Augustine has come to my attention from which I have learned more about God, Christ and man, and all things.' Hence this little book was republished and furnished with a foreword by our dear Arndt in the interest of

Christian edification. Moreover, it is in order to praise him rather than criticize him that we mention that the dear man often made use of Tauler and extolled him in his *True Christianity*. Thomas à Kempis' *Imitation of Christ* is to be placed beside these other two books; a few years ago it was republished for the common good together with a guide....

There is no doubt that such little books, to which something of the darkness of their age still clings, can and may easily be esteemed too highly, but an intelligent reader will not go astray in them. In any case, if diligently used they will accomplish much more good in students and give them a better taste of true piety than other writings which are often filled with useless subtleties and provide a good deal of easily digested fodder for the ego of the old Adam. Hopefully the reading of such books would, for many students, fulfill the ardent longing of the frequently mentioned Chytraeus, 'We show ourselves to be Christians and theologians by our godly faith, holy living, and love of God and neighbors rather than by our subtle and sophistical argumentation.[37]

Principles exclusively developed from such a statement as that of the Lutheran David Chytraeus (1531-1600) seemed to many of Spener's contemporaries to be based on a questionable theology, which relegated doctrine to a secondary position and elevated experiential piety, personal assurance, and a high moral and devotional life, in practice, if not in theory to the rank of saving graces. For those whose thought moved within the *simul justus et peccator* paradox of Luther, such a theology was seen as a return to a concept of justification based on merit, and the use of conventicles (*ecclesiolae in ecclesia*) was viewed as a base for the development of separatism. To emphasise both these dangers, its enemies maligned the movement with the designation 'Pietism,'[38] the chief characteristics of which can be outlined as follows:

The need for, and the possiblity of, an authentic and vitally significant experience of God on the part of individual Christians; the religious life as a life of love for God and man, which is marked by social sensitivity and ethical concern; utter confidence, with respect to the issues of both life and death, in the experientially verifiable authenticity of God's revelation in Christ, as found in the biblical witness; the church as a community of God's people, which must ever be renewed through the transformation of individuals, and which necessarily transcends all organizationally required boundaries; the need for the implementation of the Reformation understanding of the priesthood of all believers through responsible lay participation in the varied concerns of the Christian enterprise; a ministry

which is sensitized, trained, and oriented to respond to the needs
and problems of a given age; and finally, the continual adaptation
of ecclesiastical structures, practices, and verbal definitions to the
mission of the church.[39]

Such Pietist concerns spread rapidly and by the close of the
century had affected Protestant denominations in Germany,
Holland, and Switzerland, and were carried to the Germanic-
speaking areas of North America.[40] Many of the adherents of
the movement, often called church Pietists, remained within
the organised churches of their birth and saw in the Pietist
spirit, the form and power by which their various congrega-
tions and traditions might be revitalised. Many others, however, conveniently designated radical Pietists, moved in the
direction towards which Spener's enemies saw the whole re-
vival oriented. Some of these, in fact, separated themselves
from the churches with which they had initially been associated, forming new sectarian bodies as they did. In some cases
this movement to separation was furthered by Spiritualist and
Anabaptist communities in the areas, in others by the theo-
sophic tradition of Jacob Boehme.

A brief history of Pietism is useful in illustrating the relationships between church and radical Pietists. Early in his
career Spener had met the radical pastor Jean de Labadie
(1610-1674)[41] and had refused to take up a position against
Boehme.[42] It is little wonder as a result that he raised antagonisms during his life at Frankfurt am Main (1666-1668),
Dresden (1668-1691), and Berlin (1691-1705). Supporters such
as Heinrich Horb (1645-1695), Joachim Stoll (1615-1678), and
Johann G. Pritius (1662-1732) came quickly to his side in all
German cities. Controversy began immediately. In Hamburg
under Johann Friedrich Mayer (1650-1712), in Wittenberg under Valentine Ernst Loescher (1673-1749), and in Gotha under
Ernst Salomon Cyprian (1673-1745) opposition was especially
strong.[43]

Chief among Spener's defenders was August Hermann
Franck (1663-1727).[44] An avid and pious student, Francke
studied first at Kiel, and after entering the university at
Leipzig in 1684, he took a leading role in a *collegium bib-
licum* there which was formed on the model and under the
inspiration of Spener's conventicles. In 1687 he experienced

a conversion, and in several pastoral offices thereafter supported Spenerian reforms. On the latter's recommendation he was appointed to the newly established university at Halle in 1692.[45] Under his direction Halle rapidly became the centre for Pietist study. Francke's emphasis on conversion (*Wiedergeburt*), repentance (*Busse*), religious experience, and growth in grace were keynotes in Halle's theology.[46] There a new interest was taken in pastoral training and education at all levels, an orphanage was built,[47] and an extensive foreign mission work undertaken.[48] Francke's work with its mystical orientation and ecumenical concern[49] was quickly broadcast through an active printing program,[50] sponsored with other institutions at Halle during the reigns of Friedrich I, King of Prussia (1701-1713) and his son Friedrich Wilhelm I (1713-1740).[51]

Supported by the political leadership of Prussia and defended in its orthodoxy by men such as Joachim Lange (1670-1744),[52] the Halle Pietists had, nevertheless, much in common with those Pietists later labelled 'Radical'. Francke and Arnold after him were interested in Quietism; both published Molinos' *Spiritual Guide.*[53] At Halle, too, taught Christian Thomasius (1655-1728), whose liberal attitude to church history influenced the young Arnold,[54] and Joachim Justius Breithaupt (1658-1732) who in a treatise *De heresi* redefined the term heresy (as had the earlier work of George Calixtus[55]) so as to make it applicable only to those who rejected basic Christian truths (*Hauptwahrheiten*), that is those truths which directed one to a full experiential relationship with God.[56] Assent to Lutheran symbolic books was thereby set aside. Under such a principle Boehme could be defended, the Reformed Church praised, and Roman Catholics accepted as fellow believers; in addition, radicals such as Johann Kaspar Schade (1666-1698) were seen as spiritual brethren,[57] and Halle could play an important role in aiding the Quedlinburg radical, Gottfried Arnold, and, through Arnold, all radicals who came under his influence.

Arnold's concern with his role in the development of radical Pietism grew in his later life. During his last days, he is said to have regretted his use of Boehmist themes and to have expressed the wish he had been more circumspect in his early historical work.[58] His later works are not, however, to be discounted in the development of radicalism. Many of them, as well, were avidly read and appreciated by the sectarians, despite the fact their author had returned to the traditional forms of the church. Thus, radicals like Heinrich Horche (1652-1729), Johann Heinrich Reitz (d. 1721), as well as the Swiss separatists associated with Samuel Koenig (d. 1750), found a stimulation in Arnold's work.[59] Perhaps his thought and career also played a role in the formation of the more revolutionary bodies aligned to the radical Pietists, the Eva von Buttlar flock, and the Inspirationalists.[60] Certainly Arnold was of major importance in the career of Johann Conrad Dippel (1673-1734),[61] whose peregrinations throughout Germany, Denmark, and Sweden, strengthened the radical Pietist bodies in those countries, and of Ernst Christian Hochmann von Hochenau (1670- 1721),[62] a central figure in the establishment of the Church of the Brethren which in America was parent to the first significant Protestant monastic community, the Ephrata Cloister.[63] Both these bodies returned to Arnold's writings at numerous times in their history. So too his influence continued on in the Berleberg Bible (1726-1742)[64] and the periodical *Geistliche* Fama (1730-1744).[65] In the thought of Gerhard Tersteegen (1697-1769),[66] the last of the great radical Pietists in Germany, Arnold's interest in medieval mysticism in particular, reached its climatic conclusion.

One must not distinguish between the two poles in Pietism too strongly or the movement at large will be misrepresented. Pietism is best understood as a spiritual continuum, extending from established religious frameworks to those of the separatist radical communities. At several points in history members of the movement who had travelled farthest along that continuum did separate from the established churches and develop into sectarian units. Again, members of sectarian traditions were often drawn into Pietist conventicles and served as radicalising agents within them, although not always as forces of separation. Arnold must be interpreted within the latter situation. He was always on the continuum moving first toward the sectarian end, pressing the need for radical change in individuals and communities, and then returning again towards the centre, as he came to understand more fully the value of pastoral care. It is against such background then, of both church and radical Pietism, that his theology and the role of late medieval spirituality within it is to be understood.

Chapter Two:
The Shape of Arnold's Career

Gottfried Arnold was born on September 5, 1666 in the Saxon town of Annaberg.[1] Of his childhood little is known. His father, also Gottfried, was an instructor in the local school, having been called to that position from his native Schlettau a year before his son's birth. Shortly after his arrival in June of 1665, the elder Arnold married a local widow, on whose death eight years later[2] he married again. Although poverty troubled the family, the younger Arnold was able to attend the gymnasium at Gera (1682-1685) and the university at Wittenberg (1685-1689).

Arnold's concern with practical piety seems to have been inculcated at an early age and his years in Wittenberg strengthened it.[3] He felt isolated during his residence at the university, both from his teachers, who, as he later expressed it, offered him only a knowledge of polemics and dead scholastic orthodoxy,[4] and from his fellow students whose behaviour he deplored. In this situation he turned to study. Three years later he had completed three dissertations, which indicate the early importance historical demonstration as an apologetic tool had for him.[5]

a. Tutor at Dresden (1689-1693)

The development of Arnold's spirituality during his period of studies at Wittenberg and his first years as a tutor at Dresden following his matriculation is difficult to document since his publications at the time offer little of a personal nature and his later comments on that stage of his life do not properly distinguish the specific direction of his growth. That these later comments were made during periods of controversy and bear the inevitable marks of such increases the difficulty.[6] Nevertheless, certain statements can be made with some assurance. Arnold was a deeply pious youth and the scope of that piety

can be seen in the intensity with which he faced his choice of
vocation, a choice directed by his spiritual concerns towards a
pastoral career, in his introspection and resulting battle with
personal pride, and, finally, in his dissatisfaction with the contemporary church. These three concerns were augmented by
his social isolation from his peers at Wittenberg.

Arnold was early attracted to the Pietist movement, and
twice in 1688 Spener visited him in Wittenberg to persuade
him to enter the pastorate. The vocational question was the
first he had to solve on completion of his studies, but his dissatisfaction with the church and, one suspects, his love of privacy,
led him to reject the role of pastor and choose to become a
tutor in Dresden.[7] In spite of this decision, all his later activities, whether directly related to the institutional church or not,
bear the marks of one primarily interested in the care of souls.

At a later period Arnold was to look back in dismay on
his life at Wittenberg during which, having overcome the
temptations which plagued his peers, he fell into pride. As
the *Gedoppelter Lebenslauf,* the biography composed after his
death by his friends in Perleberg, describes the situation, he
often recalled the kindness of God to him during his student
days in that his passionate desire for knowledge protected him
from the transgressions of his fellows.

> Yet the vice of ambition swelled up strongly in him through the
> inducement of his instructors who counseled him as early as 1686
> to become a Master. But God in his great mercy had resolved on
> a more salutary life for him; through his gracious Spirit and in a
> hidden fashion, God had incited Arnold from his childhood to prayer
> and piety. For this reason he tore him unexpectedly and against his
> will out of his deceptive circumstances. He was requested [through
> the mediation of Spener] by the Saxon Hofrath Christopher Ritter
> to come to Dresden in 1689 to serve as tutor to the son of the
> Oberst of Goetz. Shortly after he would have the same position in
> the household of General Birckholtz.
>
> In Dresden he had the opportunity for the first time to immerse
> himself in practical theological issues.[8]

Arnold's initial contacts with Spener at Wittenberg were
furthered on his arrival in Dresden where he immediately joined
the pastor's conventicle. Through it he met August Hermann
Francke. Arnold's piety deepened in this situation and he experienced an awakening shortly after he began to meet at Spener's

home.[9]

The hagiographical intent of the *Gedoppelter Lebenslauf* calls its interpretation into question at numerous places, but the passages describing Arnold's Wittenberg experience and his removal to Dresden help to clarify an important aspect of his developing thought.   Arnold was drawn to the challenge of historical research, and understood his academic abilities as tools for service to God and humanity. In them he took pride, but within the framework of his thought, any form of pride stood first among the sins; it was the mark of an individual totally involved in self rather than in God.[10] As a result his piety grew in opposition to his studies and led the young scholar to publish his first works in total or partial anonymity;[11] it eventually constrained him to give up the practice of acknowledging his degree;[12] it would finally necessitate his resignation from an academic position.[13] Yet, it was through his dedication to historical study that he first considered the life of the early church, which served for him and his Pietist brethren as the best standard of judgement on questions of Christian life and dogma. Some ten years after this period, Arnold formulated his own description of the dual attractions during his life as a student and tutor and of his initial rejection of a pastoral career:

> Since my tenderest years I have always been remarkably stirred and drawn by divine wisdom.... When out of natural blindness I faithfully followed lesser values, the Holy Spirit in many guiding ways always protected me in my simplicity from the desires of youth and other expressions of evil. He drew me to himself with great love. In the same manner, the true shepherd, Christ Jesus, untiringly followed after me, a poor sheep, and allowed me to be loaded down with difficulties, under many impulses of the law and other human directives, as well as hopeless striving after one's own righteousness and holiness ... until at last I was truly grasped by him and brought to a living experiential knowledge of Christ through the power of his transcendent spirit. I had earlier searched for the most part in [dead] letters, in much reading, studying, listening, and consultations (all which in themselves were good), as well as in other ecclesiastical and academic practices. These things were a path and witness to Christ Jesus in that the Scriptures as a light in the dark recesses of my heart, gave witness to him. But to him I did not come....

> In the meantime, the devil, who did not wish my salvation, attemped to hinder me in a thousand different ways from achieving my goal. In the first place, I was drawn by my natural desire and inclination to gain much knowledge, especially in philology, antiq-

uity and secular and critical history. In this, under great difficulty
the spirit suffered much danger and shame. The love of God often
drew me by continual opposition and witness powerfully away from
such interests and towards the one thing necessary. So real was this,
in fact, that at times I thought not only to give up all useless study
but also to cast aside all my books except a few, for I was concerned
by the outer fearfulness of my heart and the witness to the great
vanity of my present concerns. My natural desire was inclined to
diversions and was greatly attracted by human praise. Because of
this I always leaned to my clear desire of learning. In his divine
foresight, God allowed this until I filled myself to the highest point
of disgust and boredom....

   Likewise, my mind was directed to a single good goal, in that,
after much exertion in other disciplines and languages, I came to
church history. Now according to my knowledge of the deep fall of
so-called Christendom, I had had no intention of taking a regular
church position, nor did I find myself trained in nor inclined towards
external ceremonies and the ideas necessarily associated with them.
Accordingly, the thought came to me that I might most profitably
spend my whole life [outside of the regular pastorate] in researching
and publicising among us Germans the highly falsified and unknown
history of the church.[14]

The difficulty the young graduate faced was not one of his
own making; it lay at the basis of the Pietist vision he had
inherited in which the call for reform of both individuals and
community and the practical ecclesiology of the movement had
never been properly assimilated within the established religious
setting. These two characteristics were in fact contradictory,
demanding on the one hand a concerned relationship with the
corrupted church in an effort to purify it, and on the other distinguishing in a very practical way, in conventicles, reformed
members of the church from and against Christians at large.
It would take Arnold more than a dozen years to solve this
contradiction, which the choice of career immediately thrust
upon him, and to bring under control each of the forces which
drew him in its own direction to opposing ends of the Pietist
continuum. Basic to his understanding of his role, however,
was his belief that he was called as a scholarly prophet and
pastor to direct the established ecclesial community to return
to its pure source.[15] His difficulty, struggle, and partial solution were those of Pietism as a whole, and if Spener can be
said to have inaugurated that awakening, and August Hermann
Francke to have given it physical form, Arnold, in his agonising

personal choices, provided for it its historical and theological justification.

That Arnold had not openly espoused separatism from the established church by 1693 is clear. In that year Spener again recommended him for a tutorial position, this time with the family of Adrian Adam von Stammler in Quedlinburg. There Arnold lived for the next four years. Spener seems not to have feared that the atmosphere of the town would affect his protegé in a negative way, in spite of the reputation for radicalism the area had already gained. However, Arnold's intolerance with the spiritual laxness of nominal Christians, which eventually led him toward the radical camp, was increasing during the years following his awakening, and Spener was called to Berlin in 1691. With his moderating influence at a distance, Arnold spoke out fiercely against members of the household of General Birckholtz, the head of the second family by whom he was employed as instructor, and was dismissed.

b. The Radical Milieu of Quedlinburg (1693-1697)

The Quedlinburg to which Arnold came in 1693 was, and would for some years remain, a centre of political, social, and religious upheaval.[16] In 1690 Christian Scriver (1629-1693)[17] was called there as pastor and had soon gathered about him a body of awakened laity, many of whom experienced revelations and ecstasies. A local women sweated blood; others prophesied. A centre of disturbance was the home of Arnold's future father-in-law, the Hofdiakon Johann Heinrich Sproegel.[18] With Scriver's death in 1693, these manifestations increased, encouraged to a degree perhaps by Francke and the Pietists at nearby Halle.[19] Especially significant was the case of the goldsmith, Heinrich Kratzenstein,[20] who desired a second wife after a revelation which told him to leave his first. A Spiritualist, Kratzenstein rejected infant baptism, the validity of the sacraments, and the necessity of legal marriages. He was also strongly opposed to the use of images, altars, and baptismal founts which he considered idols. Imprisoned, he languished and died, and the radicals of the area published a volume of poems in his honour.[21]

Almost all these radicals tended to separatism, often refusing to attend regular worship services or to receive the Lord's

Supper. Their commitment appealed to Arnold and within a
short time after his arrival in the city he was attending meetings in Sproegel's home.[22] Among these believers he found for
the first time in his life kindred spirits and a seeming solution to
his vocational concerns. As he grew more and more estranged
from the existing church, his sense of a call to an established
pastorate faded. In radical circles he was able to make use of
his gifts as an historian and to see them bearing direct results.
Paradoxically, his relationship to the group, while leading him
away from a normal pastoral position, placed him in a situation in which practical academic leadership of a semi-pastoral
nature fell to him and must have convinced him that his initial
vocational choice was correct.

During his first year in Quedlinburg, Arnold was already associated with the more radical stance of the Pietists at Halle,
and he published a lengthy article in Christian Thomasius'
Geschichte der Weiszheit und Thorheit on the life of the early
church,[23] and another on martyrdom in the early church in the
Latin equivalent of the *Geschichte*.[24] The editor's comments to
the first work describe the shape of Arnold's thought at this
time, indicating his conclusions regarding the decline of the
early church, the shortcomings of previous church histories,
and the necessity of using primitive Christianity as a model
for contemporary religious life. Here already, although not in
Arnold's own words, are the themes that he would develop
over the next twelve years. His chief purpose in the article was
to point to the corruption of the contemporary church.[25] This
study of Arndt's on the life of the early church was extracted
from his larger Latin work, the *Fratrum sororumque appelatio*,[26] and was based on the theory of the Constantinian corruption of the church. The journal in which Arnold's treatise is included contains a discussion of the opposition between mystical
and scholastic theology[27] and lengthy studies of the radical reformer David Joris[28] and the seventeenth-century Protestant
mystics Eziechel Meth and Esaiah Stieffel.[29] Thus, already in
his first studies Arnold was associated closely with the party
which looked with tolerance and admiration on heretics of the
past.

c. Historical Offensive (1696)

Not long after Arnold's initial association with the Sproegel conventicle, the group found itself attacked by the local pastors who upheld the Orthodox position on the need for regular, ordered worship. The secular authorities intervened and Sproegel came to the defence of his friends.[30] Arnold was indicted and brought before the authorities on August 27, 1695, but was immediately released.

Despite the upheaval these occurrences must have caused in his personal life, Arnold was able to pursue extensive research and writing. He continued to compose poetry. In the year of his indictment he published his *Erstes Martyrtum*[31] and released his edition of the epistles of Clement and Barnabas.[32] The year after, he completed an edition of Sebastian Castellio's *De calumnia* (in which he praised its author in his call for Christian tolerance[33]) and the *Fratrum sororumque appelatio...*, a bulky Latin description of the life of the early church.[34] To this he appended the earlier essay on martyrdom.[35]

Shortly before 1695 Arnold once again took up the homilies of Macarius, which he had read for the first time at Wittenberg,[36] and in 1696 he published his translation of them.[37] Their emphasis on the shortcomings of institutional Christianity, the invisible church, Christ's role in human justification, the role of the Spirit in Christian growth, the possibility of Christian perfection, and the value of the ascetic ideal,[38] all of which could be interpreted within his Pietist theology, immediately attracted him and directed him toward mystical theology. This attraction would last to the end of his career.[39] Macarius was for him a chief witness to divine truth[40] and in the 'Vorrede' to the edition, Arnold sketched an order of redemption which he claimed to have found in the homilies, not surprisingly the same order as that outlined in *Die Erste Liebe*, his major historical work of the same year.[41]

The intention and structure of *Die Erste Liebe* was firmly rooted within the Protestant tradition. Faced as they were with the proclamation and defence of novel theological systems, the emerging Protestant communities of the early sixteenth century had been constrained to establish authoritative bases for their teachings[42] and, following general principles employed by Christians from earliest times, they sought their solutions to the question in reanalyses of the concepts of Scripture and tradition.[43] Distinctive Protestant emphases on the primacy of Scriptural authority, and the clear separation of that authority from whatever rights Christian tradition might have in the institution of dogmas, were not unique; the Middle Ages provided numerous precedents.[44] What was unique, however, was that in Protestantism, the Word of God was reduced in practice to the words of Scripture (*sola scriptura*), and their authority, in turn, to that central hermeneutical principle of the Reformation, justification by grace through faith alone (*sola fide*).[45] The material principle (*sola fide*), as Melanchthon and later Lutheran Orthodoxy developed the topic, was at all times to be considered side by side with the formal principle (*sola scriptura*).[46] Even for the sects of the Radical Reformation this held true, although among such groups other additional principles of interpretation often played major roles.[47]

The subjective dangers inherent in this approach to the Scripture are obvious, and all groups, though in varying degrees, were aware of the difficulties. Each reaffirmed, therefore, a concept of tradition which would support its respective position. As a result, a narrowing, similar to that which had occurred in the case of biblical interpretation, occurred in the use of tradition. The Church of Christ was, henceforth, defined by Protestants according to the standards established by their biblical exegesis. These standards described the early purity of the church. That a decline from this original purity had occurred at the time of Constantine had been taught by some groups in the Middle Ages,[48] and this teaching was used by Protestant historians.[49] After the Constantinian decline, only those Christians were of interest to Protestants who could be proven in some manner to support the doctrines or polities of the particular church or sect for which historical support was being sought. These Christians were understood as witnesses to the Reformation truth (*Zeugen der Wahrheit*).[50] From this principle the historiographic defence of the new teaching was built, and in that defence the mystics of the late Middle Ages as witnesses to the truth or as forerunners of the Reformation played an important role.

Protestant historiography had a long history, and Arnold was closely acquainted with much of it.[51] It is not likely that

he had studied Luther from this point of view,[52] but the initiator of the Lutheran approach to church history, Flacius
Illyricus, was well known to him as were later Lutheran histories and handbooks of church history by Johann Sleidanus
(1506?-1556), Johann Gerhard, Johann Andreas Quenstedt,
Christian Thomasius, Veit Ludwig von Seckendorf (1626-1692)
and others, including those by Reformed authors such as Andreas Rivet (1577-1647 or 1651), Pierre Daille (1594-1670)
and Friedrich Spanheim (1600-1649).[53] The radical historians
Sebastian Franck and Pierre Poiret were also important sources
for him.[54] These latter scholars shared with those historians
who wrote from a Magisterial point of view in providing for
him both historical form and content, although one ought not
to forget the significance ascribed by him in many of his works
to Roman Catholic historians such as Caesar Baronius (1538-
1607) and Robert Bellarmine (1542-1621).

Arnold's *Die Erste Liebe: Wahre Abbildung der Ersten
Christen* was published in 1696 at Frankfurt am Main. According to the title, the volume was intended as a true portrayal
of the practical faith and life of the first Christians according
to the authentic documents of the period, and was written to
call Christians back to their forsaken 'first love' (Revelation
2:4), the love manifested prior to the Constantinian decline.
In methodology, it was non-partisan (*unparteyisch*). As such,
the study was to serve as a corrective to the interpretation of
early church history presented in *Primitive Christianity: or,
The religion of the ancient Christians in the first age of the
Gospel* by the English historian William Cave (1637-1713).[55]
Arnold's study was not partisan in the way Cave's was, but
it did have its biases.[56] As the 'Zuschrift' indicates, the work
was intended as an aid to those reborn Christians who wish
to understand God's will for the church. The clearest indications of the concerns of that will are found in those persecuted
and suffering witnesses to the truth (*Zeugen der Wahrheit*) in
the early church and thereafter. They are to serve as models
for all Christian endeavours.[57] The writer or reader of history,
Arnold contends, as he did in the 'Erinnerung' to the Macarius
edition, must be open to the leading of the Spirit in the interpretation of the texts, for it is the divine which is working in
history and it is the divine, as a result, which is the best guide

to history's meaning.[58] Despite his premises, however, scientific procedures are not set aside, and in a lengthy 'Vorbericht' which introduces the authors to be treated, Arnold clarifies the nature of those procedures by which texts were chosen and authenticated.[59]

Cave had studied the first four centuries of the Christian era as well, but placed greatest emphasis on the fourth century, thereby finding ample material to uphold the Anglican teaching on ecclesiastical hierarchy and the liturgy. For Arnold such a conclusion was untenable. In his mind the church of the Constantinian period had corrupted the spirituality of the first-century Christians, and any attempt to support later practices from fourth-century examples was therefore in error.[60]

Book One of *Die Erste Liebe* was devoted to outlining the theology of the early Christians. Having thus established his foundation, Arnold went on, after discussing the relatively pure life of the primitive church,[61] to describe the relationships of the first Christians to God,[62] to each other, and to non-Christians,[63] and having reported the various facets of their worship,[64] private life,[65] and miraculous achievements,[66] he discussed in detail the decline under Constantine,[67] laying particular emphasis on the fall of earlier leadership and the growth of a powerful but unenlightened and immoral clergy.[68] His discussion of the decline in leadership filled almost one-fifth of the final segment of his work and provided the basis for his *Unparteiische Kirchen- und Ketzer-Historie* begun in the same year in which *Die Erste Liebe* was published.[69]

d. The Professional Historian (1697-1698)

In its interpretation Arnold's *Erste Liebe* kept within and provided corroborating material for Pietist principles on the new birth, inner piety, and the practice of Christian love. By so doing, it gained immediate popularity. Spener and Francke, among others, praised the work loudly.[70] One of the individuals particularly impressed with it was Ernst Ludwig von Hessen-Darmstadt, who had opened his lands to Pietist conventicles a year earlier. On May 24, 1697, he offered Arnold a position as professor of history at the university of Giessen, where a number of vacancies had occurred with the purging of the Orthodox party in 1696.[71] Despite his reservations, Arnold accepted the honour on August 24, and shortly after held his inaugural lecture, *De corrupto historiarum studio*, in which he re-emphasised the need for spiritually reborn, committed Christian scholars, and for careful scientific historical work by them.[72] Immediately after his inaugural address, he began his work and during the fall semester offered a seminar in civil history and one in church history the next. It was during this year that he met for the first time the radicals Johann Conrad Dippel and Ernst Hochmann von Hochenau.

Arnold's initial reservations regarding his academic position grew as his life at the university proceeded. A solitary, earnest Christian, he found his time absorbed by the demands of students, lectures, and colleagues, and by administrative duties, among which were those convivial obligations so distasteful to the Pietist. The demands placed before him by the life of the primitive church as revealed through his study of that period of history accentuated his sense of dissatisfaction with the established church. In addition, he found himself open once again to the temptations of pride in position and academic prowess which had plagued him at Wittenberg. His scholarship continued to play its paradoxical role in his life, and the inner turmoil which resulted was viewed by his colleagues as melancholia.[73] Early in 1698, unable to deal effectively with the issues as they faced him, he decided to resign. The date of his resignation is unknown but in May he was back in Quedlinburg writing his apology, *Offenhertziges Bekänntnüsz*. The preface is dated June 10 and suggests that his resignation took place shortly before its composition.[74]

Arnold's defence of his resignation shocked his contemporaries. Some praised his move; others attacked it as the mark of a foolishly scrupulous man. Spener's reaction is of particular interest. Admitting the difficulty of Arnold's situation, he saw the resignation as a judgement on the whole church. Yet he could not accept Arnold's action. In Spener's opinion, the true Christian must take great risks, even risk sin, for the good of others.[75] It was this premise, unacceptable to Arnold at the time, which would eventually lead him back to the traditional forms of the established church.

e. The History of Church and Heresy (1698-1700)

Most important among Arnold's works written at the time
was his *Unparteiische Kirchen- und Ketzer-Historie*. The first
part, describing the history of the Christian church from its
earliest beginnings to 1688, was published in 1699; the second, which included separate discussions of specific facets of
church history with extensive source materials, appeared in
1700. That he began work on the *Kirchen- und Ketzer-Historie*
immediately after *Die Erste Liebe* there is no doubt—he had,
indeed, outlined the great history while completing his study
on the early church[76]—yet the preface to the first volume indicates that that part was finished[77] but was dated March 1,
1697, a date too early for the completion of so large a study.
That the volume was first printed two years later indicates, as
well, that some research and writing probably yet remained to
be done in 1697. In all likelihood, the preface, written in that
year, was reworked just before the volume was brought to press
in 1699.[78]

The principles of the *Kirchen- und Ketzer-Historie* were
those of *Die Erste Liebe*, but the later work is much more radically oriented in its approach. This is already to be noted in
the 'Vorrede,' which reiterates many of the earlier themes and
deepens them. There the same concerns with God's revelation
in history, with proper sources, with the example of the early
church, the practical intention of history, toleration, and *un-
parteilichkeit* are all displayed. There, too, his concern is with
the true definition of the church, but that definition incorpo-
rates greater invective than previously, distinguishing clearly
between the true church of Christ and the false, fallen, and
corrupted church of the clerics.[79]

This particular distinction forms the basis of the 'Allgemeine Anmerckungen' which introduce the *Historie* and on
which the whole work is constructed. In the first section of his
'Anmerckungen,' Arnold outlines the change which took place
in the approach to, treatment of, and resulting redefinition of
heresy in the first four centuries. Early Christian leaders attacked evil teaching where they found it, Arnold taught, but
as time went on they extended the definition to teachings they
did not understand. These they attacked with great ferocity,
driving the persecuted into greater error. This process grew

during the second and third centuries, and with the growth in persecution there was a parallel growth in the power abrogated by the persecutors from the communities over which they were in charge. The result was a battle for even more power and position, and tyrannous action on the part of the clergy. In their arrogance, these powerful, hypocritical clerics came to believe that only they upheld the truth, and that anyone who spoke against them, or against their manifest crimes, was automatically defined as a heretic. Such orthodoxy was built on sand, however; it made use of heathen philosophy to support its position and wrote history based on these false premises. Although defined as heretics, those who stood against the institution, those who upheld the simplicity of Christ's Gospel, were the true witnesses to the truth, the true church. Actual heresy was that teaching pressed by the so-called Orthodox.[80]

For Arnold, the witnesses to the truth (*Zeugen der Wahrheit*) were the true followers of Christ, the true successors to his apostles, and were to be recognised by the persecution they suffered. Their faults were only that they did not learn and parrot the concepts and definitions of scholastic theology. They had been taught by God and protected by him in their previous battle against pharisaic, institutional Christianity; they continue to be so.[81] At the beginning, the truth of God was immediately available to the reborn. As time went on the clerics forced their definitions into narrow confines, building not only the scriptural canon but the symbols and conciliar statements by which they insisted all truth must be judged,[82] although the work of the Holy Spirit in renewing the image of God in the human person ought to have been followed.[83] The true witnesses experienced the working of the divine and, established as the true church, they witnessed against the institutional heresy about them.[84]

The final sections of the 'Anmerckungen' go on to attack this institutional heresy in Arnold's own day, although the possibility of the church's renewal is also suggested.[85] The theology Arnold believed was taught by the *Zeugen der Wahrheit*, is that outlined in Book One of *Die Erste Liebe*.[86] Faith in Christ is the ground of salvation,[87] and justification is by him alone;[88] with faith comes power for holiness and the growth to perfection.[89] Union with Christ is described in terms of the beginning and end of the Christian life, of the point from which one moves and to the fulfillment and experience of which, one progresses in discipleship (*Nachfolge*).[90]

f. Attack and Counter-attack (1700-1701)

The ideas of the *Kirchen- und Ketzer-Historie* were not to go uncontested. Not only did the volume oppose the practice of the Lutheran church and offer material for the Reformed and Roman Catholic attack on that denomination,[91] but it provided, as well, an historical foundation for a defence of radical Pietist practice.[92] Foremost among those who came to the defence of the established church were Ernst Salomon Cyprian of Gotha and the learned theologian of Wittenberg, Valentin Ernst Loescher. Lesser figures joined with them. The concentrated attack on Arnold's historical principles continued throughout his life and well beyond his death. So fierce did the onslaught become during his life, and so much did he weary of defence, that Arnold regretted having written the *Historie*, expressing his reservations concerning the composition on his deathbed in words which expressed more distaste with the turmoil caused by its publication, than with the actual radicalism expressed by its pages.[93]

The prelude to this controversy began with his initial support of the Sproegel group in Quedlinburg. With the publication of *Die Erste Liebe*, a basis for opposition on a broader scale was available but little was made of this until after the publication of the *Kirchen- und Ketzer-Historie*.[94] At Giessen, he early and clearly marked himself off from the churchly Pietists, but how far his resignation immediately affected the religious world is somewhat difficult to say. His defence of the resignation, the *Offenhertziges Bekänntnüsz*, certainly made a major impact. It was in circulation at least by the end of 1698 when Spener read it, and its publication in 1699 was given added significance, since it appeared in its more widely available printed form in the same year as the first volume of the *Unparteiische Kirchen- und Ketzer-Historie*. Its attacks on religious institutions[95] were read, as a result, in light of the principles of the great history. Such poems as 'Babels Grablied' in the *Göttliche Liebes-Funcken* of the same year provided even more incentive for attack,[96] and, however one might wish to explain away the negative aspects of his work at the time, when viewed by a student outraged by the *Kirchen- und Ketzer-Historie*, Arnold's publication in 1688 seemed to reject the authority of the state church. Moreover, the second edition of the Macarius homilies in 1699 included a treatise *Erinnerung von Brauch und Missbrauch Böser Exempel* which questioned the practical implications of the *simul justus et peccator* stance among Protestants and thereby added to its author's offence. The edition of Molinos' *Spiritual Guide* in 1699 was a further indication to Arnold's enemies of his unorthodoxy, as were his selected editions of medieval and sixteenth-century Catholic, Radical, and Quietist authors in the years following.[97]

Not everyone was antagonistic, however, and Arnold was concerned with the practical effects of his writings vis-a-vis the organised church. His concern in this regard does not allow one to describe him as a dedicated separatist. Sometime after the publication of the *Offenhertziges Bekänntnüsz* a pastor, who had taken the principles of the piece seriously, wrote Arnold expressing his scruples. Arnold's answer was sent on October 14, 1699.[98] In it he suggests to the pastor the manner to function properly within the established church, despite the evils of the day, and, in words which must have served in an important way to direct him to a pastorate two years later, he delineates the need for dedicated humble pastoral love in the service of the weak members of the body of Christ.

But Arnold's answer to this pastor was not circulated at the time, and the year 1700 with its publications and answers to attacks continued to add incentive to opposition. The concluding part of the *Kirchen- und Ketzer-Historie* appeared in that year. Although its 'Nachwort' was an attempt to tone down the implications of the work as a whole,[99] its contents detailing the activities of sectarians and other radicals did nothing to ease the tension.

One other highly significant development in the controversy must be outlined at this point in the narrative. At the same time as readers were being angered by the contents of Volume II of the *Kirchen- und Ketzer-Historie*, they were presented with a collection of prose and poetic treatments, seemingly upholding Boehmist themes. Although this volume, *Das Geheimnisz der Göttlichen Sophia*, and its supplements, the *Poetische Lob-*

und Liebes-Sprüche and the *Neue Göttliche Liebes-Funcken*,
did not necessarily support a belief in Boehmist theosophy,[100]
they did use terminology frequently quoted by the Görlitz shoemaker's disciples, and the volume was accompanied by a second
publication, the *Erbauliche Theosophische Sendschreiben*, containing pieces by the foremost Boehmist of the day, Johann
George Gichtel, with whom Arnold was corresponding.

It was against such a threat that Ernst Salomon Cyprian re-
sponded early in 1700. On March 24, he completed the preface
to his *Allgemeine Anmerckungen*,[101] in which the Orthodox
disapprobation of Pietism comes most clearly alive. What was
at stake for him was God's honour.[102] God can be properly
honoured, he felt, only if properly known,[103] but such knowledge is impossible in Arnold's thought, which he saw as indifferent to, that is, not concerned with, dogmatic formulae.[104] The
result of this indifference is Universalism,[105] Arianism,[106] and
a negative approach to Scripture,[107] the church,[108] baptism,[109]
and communion.[110] After a personal attack on Arnold,[111] the
author then proceeded to detail the shortcomings in Arnold's
position regarding symbolic books,[112] the relationship between
spirit and letter in Scriptural hermeneutics,[113] the church
as a mother,[114] and universal redemption,[115] and to question specific aspects of his historical work both factually and
historiographically.[116]

Arnold's answer to Cyprian came in the most radical of his
works, the *Erklärung von gemeinen Secktenwesen*, the preface
to which is dated June 6, 1700.[117] The piece opens with an
attack on the pharisaic, hypocritical practices of the learned
(*Schriftgelehrten*, that is, the opposite of *Gottesgelehrten*),[118]
emphasising the need of the inner reign of Christ for true worship against Cyprian's call for proper knowledge.[119] A strong
appeal is made to political leaders for religious tolerance,[120]
which is stated within the general context of Spener's position
on the same question.[121] In the work, Arnold defends himself against personal attacks made upon him,[122] and attempts
to clarify his position on church attendance,[123] presence at
the Supper,[124] and the role of the church in the life of the
believer.[125] A highly separatistic tone runs through the work,
emphasising the mature Christian's freedom, church organisa-
tion, and ceremony,[126] and calling for a rejection of the evil

tendencies in Christendom.[127]

But this tone must be interpreted in its proper context. Firstly, Arnold maintains the distinction between mature and weak Christians which he had considered in his answer to the perplexed pastor and in *Die Erste Liebe*. When speaking of Christian freedom in regard to institutional Christianity, he is directing his words to the mature believer, not the beginner.[128] Secondly, he insists on his loyalty to the Lutheran cause,[129] and on his concern with church attendance and Christian community,[130] and he rejects any Weigelian tendencies ascribed to him,[131] or any intention on his part to found a new sect.[132] Finally, the *Erklärung* is best understood if read in light of Luther's two-fold premise at the centre of *The Freedom of a Christian*: 'A Christian is a perfectly free lord of all, subject to none; a Christian is a perfectly dutiful servant of all, subject to all.'[133] In his work, Arnold affirms the first of these statements before corrupt ecclesiastical control, and, although he tends to omit discussion of the second, it was in his mind and was the basis of his acceptance of a pastorate the following year. The *Erklärung* was accompanied by the considerations of a friend defending Arnold against Cyprian's attack by subjecting the latter's treatment to a minute point by point criticism.[134] In June a second anonymous author came to Cyprian's defence, but his treatment was brief and merits little close consideration.[135]

On July 31, 1700, an edict was published in Quedlinburg against all separatists, ordering them to attend communion within four weeks. It was read from the church chancels the following day.[136] Arnold allowed the month to pass and, despite a formal protest, was ordered to leave the city in three days' time. He and his landlord Sproegel remained firm. On October 23, notice was received from the Elector of Brandenburg, a Pietist sympathiser to whom Arnold had dedicated the *Kirchen- und Ketzer-Historie*. The Elector vetoed the former decision and on October 31 ordered von Stammler, Arnold's employer, to protect him.[137] A committee of two Halle professors and one local authority was struck to investigate the matter, but it was firmly opposed by the Orthodox party, and on November 5, it was forced to call for military help in the face of a public uprising. On November 12, Arnold expressed willingness to conform. The next day a second order came from the Elector repeating the earlier one, but seven days later Sproegel made a public complaint, stating that he had been threatened with a fine of 20 Thalers if he allowed Arnold to remain in his home. The commission issued a counter-fine of 30 Thalers against anyone who would force Arnold out.

Public statements against the separatists continued and the commission finally disallowed these. Arnold published at this time his *Richtigste Weg durch Christum zu Gott* in which, although with harsh criticism of contemporary Christendom, he once again pointed out his ties with the established church.[138] The statement was to no avail in the city, however, and on December 3, 1700, Sproegel was again ordered by the local authorities to dismiss Arnold from his home. Sproegel complained once more, and once more the Elector sent an ultimatum to the consistory, noting that nothing had been proven against Arnold's character which warranted such exile, and that he had never been formally charged and prosecuted. The members of the consistory were charged with overstepping their authority, the commission was revived, and in January, 1701, with the election of the Elector of Brandenburg as King of Prussia, Arnold's protection, although not his peace, was assured.[139] Arnold was weary of the controversy and by early 1701 must have been searching for a possibility of peace with honour.[140]

Late in 1700 Arnold saw in manuscript a second major attack against the *Kirchen- und Ketzer-Historie*, Tobias Pfanner's *Unparteiisches Bedencken*, and answered it briefly. Both the work and Arnold's answer were published early in 1701.[141] In the letter to Spener, written October 31, 1700, he commented on his orthodoxy regarding the doctrine of justification by faith, and the sacraments of baptism and the Supper. The letter to Pfanner (November 1, 1700) maintained the same stance, although the defensive position Arnold was forced to take in it, necessitated a somewhat colder style.[142]

Despite his attempts to explain and defend his work, however, criticism continued to be made. Elias Veiel, the Superintendent at Ulm, pronounced a negative judgement on the *Kirchen- und Ketzer-Historie*[143] and released his *Theologisches Sendschreiben* on the work,[144] along with his edition of scholarly notes indicating the mistakes in Arnold's treatment of the Valentinian fragments.[145] The situation must have caused Arnold great dismay. Spener, from whom he had some reason to hope he might receive a favourable response, did not speak openly for his protégé's work, and wrote on January 25, 1701, that he had not so much as read it and did not intend to.[146]

In February the leader of the Orthodox party, Gebhardt Mayer, penned an attack against the Pietists,[147] whom he associated with the sectarian *Stille im Lande*.[148] The volume referred specifically to Arnold, charging him not only as a heretic but as a political revolutionary. When permission to publish the work was denied, the pastor made use of the situation to stir up unrest, and on Sunday, February 27, he bade farewell to religious freedom in the city. So much stir did his words cause that five days later, Arnold and Sproegel requested the commission to lift the ban on Mayer, but to allow a work on their defence. On March 1, Arnold wrote the preface to his second defence, the *Fernere Erläuterung*, with a further reply to Pfanner,[149] which the latter felt bound to answer.[150] In May additional explanations appeared in his *Endliche Vorstellung*,[151] but the opposition, enraged perhaps even more by Arnold's editions of Quietist and Catholic mystics,[152] continued, despite the peaceful overtures to established Lutheranism made by Arnold in his two defences.

Not all the learned stood against Arnold, of course, and among those who came to his defence were Christian Thomasius,[153] Joachim Lange[154] and the erratic chiliast Johann Wilhelm Petersen.[155] Petersen's piece defending Arnold from the charge of Arianism only prolonged the struggle, calling, as it did, his own enemy Johann Corvinus into the fray.[156] Cyprian came into the foreground once again in August, 1701 with a third edition of his *Allgemeine Anmerckungen*, and a number of additional treatises.[157] Lesser authors followed his lead.[158]

In Quedlinburg, consistory and commission continued fully at odds, each nullifying the other's actions. The commission was powerless to prevent the suspension of Sproegel from his office on the grounds that he had not submitted to the just rule of the consistory, but the consistory would not exile Sproegel or Arnold from the town. At this point Mayer departed for Bremen. The commission realised that an opportunity now

existed to settle the turmoil, if Sproegel were to be given a
position other than the one he had earlier held and if Arnold
could modify his stance.

Other occurrences in the Sproegel household had already
laid the groundwork for a solution in keeping with the commission's hope. Some time earlier Sproegel took a traveller
into his home who stole jewellry. The thief was captured
in Allstedt. Sproegel's wife and youngest daughter, Anna
Marie, travelled there as witnesses and to recover the prop-
erty, and Arnold went with them as a protector. The journey
had two major consequences. The first was apprehended by
Gichtel, when he heard that Arnold, the chaste lover of the
virgin Sophia, was travelling in the company of an unmarried
woman. He feared it would end Arnold's celibate life.[159] It did.
Arnold and Sproegel's daughter were married September 5,
1701, in Quedlinburg. The second consequence of the journey
was equally significant. On Arnold's earlier arrival in Allstedt,
Sophie Charlotte, the widowed Duchess of Sachsen-Eisenach,
had called Arnold to her castle to preach. So impressed was
she with his words that she offered him a position as court
pastor which he accepted.

g. The Later Arnold (1701-1714)

Arnold's marriage and his acceptance of a regular pastoral
position helped to lessen the tension in Quedlinburg, but did
not release Arnold himself from personal trials. Gichtel refused
to answer his letters and privately expressed the hope that the
marriage would remain spiritual.[160] His hope was soon to be
dashed with the birth of Arnold's first child.[161]

Unfortunately difficulties ensued with the Allstedt appoint-
ment almost immediately on Arnold's acceptance of it. He had
understood that he might have the position without submit-
ting to the oath of loyalty to the *Formula of Concord*. The
Duke, however, refused to break established custom and set
new precedents. In August of 1701, prior to his marriage,
Arnold travelled to Berlin, where he renewed his friendship
with Spener and received the support of King Friedrich, who
wrote letters to the young Duke of Sachsen-Eisenach, assuring
him of Arnold's orthodoxy.[162] The matter was still not settled
in December of the same year, but early in 1702, Arnold trav-

elled to Allstedt and undertook his duties at the insistence of the Duchess.

On his arrival in Allstedt, he was instantly the centre of contention. Despite his promise not to interfere in established church matters, the authorities demanded his removal, by force if necessary. The Duchess and her Pietist friends appealed to the King. On January 17, both she and Arnold submitted requests to him. Arnold simply stated his position. The Duchess put forth a proposal: If the King would provide Arnold with a royal post—she suggested royal historian—the problems would cease.[163] The idea was accepted, and on January 27, Arnold was appointed the first royal historian of the Prussian State.

Tension in the city did not ease, however, and Arnold removed himself for a time. When he returned, the conflict began anew. On October 4, he was ordered from the area forever and given six weeks to leave. His appeals for a theological examination or colloquy forced negotiations, and the matter dragged on. In September, 1703, a possibility for peace opened when a call was offered to him from Ascherleben, but turmoil in that area and the wishes of the Duchess at Allstedt did not permit acceptance. With the protection of the Prussian King, Arnold was able to remain in Allstedt through 1704, but the situation was certainly not satisfactory either for him or his patron, although he was able to preach and write.

Arnold was always fully capable of composing while controversy raged around him, and the years following his arrival in Allstedt were no more troublesome to him than any others had been. Thus, in 1702 he was able to complete the apologetic *Das Eheliche und Unverehelichte Leben der ersten Christen*,[164] compose forewords for editions of the letters of Petrucci,[165] the *Confessio Amantis* of Gertrude More,[166] and the Pseudo-Clementine *Recognitions*,[167] as well as to write additions for, and supervise the publication of, the third edition of his Macarius translation. The same year saw the appearance of the Latin edition of the *Historie und Beschreibung der Mystischen Theologie*, which appeared in German the following year and introduced the reader both to the theology and history of mysticism as Arnold understood them.[168] In 1703, as well, the *Supplementa*[169] to his *Kirchen- und Ketzer Historie* appeared, and in the year following, the *Neuer Kern wahrer Geistesge-*

bete,[170] *Die Geistliche Gestalt eines evangelischen Lehrers*[171] and a collection of sermons and meditations, *Die Verklärung Christi in der Seele,*[172] were issued.

Despite the removal of Arnold from Quedlinburg, peace had been reestablished there only on the departure of the second major figure in the controversy, Sproegel, who received the position of Inspector in Werben (Altmark). In 1704 he was called to Stolpe (Hinterpommern), and suggested to both Spener and King Friedrich that Arnold succeed him at Werben. The succession was arranged with some difficulty, but by early spring, 1705, Arnold was able to move. He arrived in Werben on March 6. The days of turmoil were past. Two years later he was called to Perleberg as Inspector and first pastor, and he accepted the post. He remained there to his death. The only complaint on his arrival in the latter city was that his voice was weak and that it was difficult to hear him. During his life there he took the initiative to reform both religious and secular life, and continued to write, completing numerous editions, writing forewords to others,[173] and publishing several collections of sermons and theological essays,[174] a prayer book, *Paradiesische Lustgärtlein* (1709),[175] an educational tract (1711),[176] a lengthy theological study, *Theologia Experimentalis, Das ist Geistliche Erfahrungs-Lehre* (posthumous publication),[177] the apologetic *Historische-Theologische Betrachtungen* (1702ff.),[178] *Die Abwege oder Irrungen und versuchungen gutwilliger und frommer Menschen* (1708)[179] and historical works,[180] among which the most important was a companion volume to *Die Erste Liebe*, the *Wahre Abbildung des inwendigen Christentums*[181] which supported the claims enunciated in his earlier works. The *Abwege* and *Wahre Abbildung* made special use of the late medieval mystics.

In 1713, Arnold was seriously ill. Throughout the year his health waned. Weakness did not hinder him in his duties, however, which he continued until his death. On Ascension Day, 1714, he preached, and while distributing the Supper, was shocked to see his church invaded by Prussian soldiers, who, to the sound of drumbeats, dragged communicants from the altar to serve in the army. The experience was his death blow. He preached a funeral sermon several days later but in such a weakened condition that he had to be held in the chancel by a parishioner. For the next three days he sat quietly at home in deep meditation, briefly, but pleasantly answering any who came to visit. He died among friends on May 30, 1714, and on June 1, was buried.

Part Two
Arnold's Use of
Late Medieval Spiritual Texts

Chapter Three:
Arnold's Initial Contacts
with the Medieval World

Too often influential aspects of a person's thought are interpreted as the whole of that thought. This is especially true in the case of Gottfried Arnold. The furor raised by his *Unparteiische Kirchen- und Ketzer-Historie* focussed attention on the radical period of Arnold's theological development, and, following his contemporaries, future scholars read all his later works either as apologies for the *Historie* or as partial retractions of that work, thereby effectively ignoring over sixty percent of his publications. Total attention, thus, is often given to Arnold's early thirties, and this period of his life is considered the climax of his career. Climactic the events of those years were for Arnold, as well as for the future of Protestant historiography, but Arnold's creativity was not concluded with their passing. Fortunately, some recent scholarship has reacted against this restrictive approach,[1] although no full attempt has yet been made to evaluate the development of Arnold's work throughout the last fourteen years of his life or to document the continuity between his earlier and later career. An analysis of his use of late medieval spiritual texts serves as a contribution toward such an evaluation.

a. The Early Works

Prior to his completion of the *Unparteiische Kirchen- und Ketzer-Historie*, Arnold displayed almost no knowledge of late medieval spirituality, his attention being fully devoted to Patristic sources. His attraction to certain of these, particularly to the Pseudo-Macarian corpus,[2] indicates his early interest in ascetic and mystical theology rather than in purely dogmatic questions, but there are few suggestions in these writings that he had seriously investigated the continuation of spiritual theology in the Middle Ages.

The one exception to his early lack of interest in medieval

writers is his use of Bernard of Clairvaux. In *Von der Bruder-
und Schwester-Namen*, amidst a mass of Patristic citations,
Bernard is mentioned, but is cited only three times and quoted
only once. No specific locations are given, and the topics under discussion in support of which Bernard is cited are so general that it is difficult to know to which passages or works of
the Cistercian abbot Arnold is referring.[3] The *Fratrum sororumque appelatio* displays a closer knowledge of Bernard on
Arnold's part, but the number of citations is not striking; only
five percent of the pages contain references to him. The locations of all are clearly indicated, however. Three-quarters of
these are to the letters,[4] almost all the rest are to the sermons
on Canticles.[5] Additional references are made to *De diligendo
deo*,[6] and to a few sermons.[7] In no part of the *Fratrum sororumque appelatio* can a major influence from Bernard be detected; his works are simply called upon to provide yet further
proof texts for Arnold's contentions.[8] The overwhelming majority of these quotations and references, in keeping with the
theme of the work, treat spiritual friendship,[9] but there is no
sign that he was aware of the significance of this theme for the
Cistercians and other medieval writers.[10]

The use of Bernard to support this theme of friendship is
not maintained in *Die Erste Liebe*, although this work makes
more extensive use of the abbot, doubling the proportion of
references to him over that of the *Fratrum sororumque appelatio*. One-third of these references occur in Book One of *Die
Erste Liebe*,[11] in which spiritual friendship is seldom noted.
The remaining citations occur regularly throughout the rest of
the volume, where Bernard is called upon to support whatever
particular point Arnold wishes to emphasise.[12] Once again,
Bernard's epistles and his sermons on Canticles are the sources
for a majority of these citations. Arnold's admiration of the
Cistercian is also enunciated in his 'Vorbericht' to *Die Erste
Liebe*.[13] In it, following the normal patterns of Protestant historiography, he states that Bernard was a 'dear witness of much
truth' and was trusted by Luther and others. Bernard, according to Arnold, was a pious, understanding, and suffering
witness of God's glory, who, despite the darkness around him,
would allow no truth to remain unspoken, and was divinely
assisted in his opposition to contemporary hypocrisy and the

evil of papal and clerical domination.

b. The Theological Context of Arnold's Work

Except for reference to Bernard, *Die Erste Liebe* does not make any extensive use of late medieval writing, but its theological structure does provide the context in which Arnold's later use of mystical texts is firmly set. During the seventeenth-century Lutheran theologians developed in detail that sector of their dogmatic system known as the *ordo salutis*, in which they discussed the process by which the merits of Christ's redemption were applied to a faithful, individual believer. Book One of *Die Erste Liebe* follows this *ordo*, and failure to recognise this fact has resulted in misrepresentation of Arnold's position in this and in his later work. Of particular interest for the present study is that aspect of the *ordo* known as the *unio mystica*.

Although no full history of the doctrine of the *unio mystica* in Protestantism exists, a general outline can be drawn, and the roots of the teaching traced to Luther.[14] That the reformer was deeply impressed (*beeindruckt*, rather than *beeinflusst*[15]) by late medieval mysticism, there is no doubt.[16] It seems certain that his attitude to mysticism remained essentially the same throughout his career,[17] suffering no change in nature, although it did grow in intensity after his battles with the radicals in 1525.[18]

Luther's concern with a practical and pious Biblicism[19] was of great importance in his thought, and lies at the basis of many of his warnings against speculative mysticism. To the practical directions in mystical writing he was always open; they assured him that his teachings were not startling innovations, and provided for him a simple, popular, religious vocabulary.[20] For speculation which suggested the possibility of human spiritual achievement, of a person reaching beyond Christ to the divine darkness—for speculation which replaced a *theologia crucis* with a *theologia gloriae*[21]—Luther afforded no opportunity at any point in his mature thought.

Luther's opposition to mysticism was rooted in much more than his practical concerns. For him much of the speculative mysticism of the late middle ages enunciated the central theological problem which he considered to be in need of reform.

Emphasising the bondage of the human will to its own limited desires and the primal sinfullness of the creature, Luther insisted that any attempts at salvation on the part of the individual alone are doomed to failure. Without grace no one can be saved; salvation is possible only by grace and grace is through faith 'alone,' Luther taught, emphasising that over against Galatians 5:6 which taught that what counted for redemption was 'faith working through love' (*fides charitate formata*) the word 'faith' stood alone in Ephesians 2:8, indicating that acts of love did not in any way 'merit' salvation.

Luther thus opposed the traditional medical model of salvation. That model viewed individuals as sick unto death; without proper medical care they would inevitably die. Under this model grace comes with Christ the physician who through his body, the church, offers the necessary medicine through the sacraments and the directives for a return to health. According to the medical model human beings can improve. 'Working through love,' the faith they have placed in the proffered grace can lead them to higher degrees of holiness. The image of God in which they where originally created was not lost in the fall; that image is best reflected in the human intellect (by which one seeks to know the highest truth) and the will (by which one seeks to love the highest good). What was lost was the 'likeness,' graciously returned in baptism and 'increased' by participation in the body of Christ, the church.

Luther rejected this model in whole and replaced it with a forensic or legal model according to which human beings are understood as criminals, deserving of the death sentence. According to this forensic model God is a judge who declares the guilty person free from the sentence deserved. By faith such a person accepts the promise of life and freedom in this divine declaration, is justified, but remains always a sinner (*simul justus et peccator*). One can never atone on one's own for the crime committed. As a result Luther opposed every form of religious life which suggested that an individual could improve his or her position before the righteous God, and the practice of a spiritual life such as what he understood was taught by many mystics, he rejected.

For him there could be no 'progression' through a life of purgation (the overcoming of sin), illumination (the practice of the virtues) to a mystical union with the divine in which the two would become, as it were, one. The supposition that such a three-fold life was possible, was for Luther the heights of human pride. Theological treatments of the three-fold life did have their influence on his thought, however. Throughout the fifteenth century there had been a growing movement to 'democratise' the final, unitive stage. Whereas earlier this mystical union had been understood to be a special grace offered to a very few, by the late fifteenth century the imagery of mystical union was often applied to believers generally, and Luther made use of such an approach to enunciate his doctrine of forensic justification, turning the three-fold path on its head in a sense. For him the life of faith begins with union with God in Christ, and thereafter follow acts of purgation and illumination, although these acts are, in an important sense, meaningless over against the initial faith union.[22]

Warning against speculative mysticism early in his career,[23] the Saxon reformer continued his monitions during the first years of his attack on Rome. 'Many labor and dream many things regarding mystical theology,' he wrote. 'They are ignorant, knowing not of what they speak or what they affirm.'[24] This same attitude is expressed in a sermon of 1525, in which he discusses his own experience with such speculation,[25] and is still apparent in his later life.[26]

One must not suppose, however, that these negative attitudes were applied by Luther to all mystical writing. Mystical theology was, he believed, a legitimate topic for theological study,[27] and as a young man he praised the life of contemplation.[28] Mysticism he understood with Bernard of Clairvaux as 'the experience of God,'[29] but for Luther this was the immediate experience of every believer and not the experience of chosen souls who had reached the highest rung on a ladder stretched toward the divine. It was not Luther's concern to set aside mystical literature; rather he wished to point out the theological and spiritual dangers involved in speculation on mystical union.[30] His aim was first to clarify the role of faith in the life of a Christian, a role which he continuously discussed in terms borrowed from late medieval mystical writings.

> Moreover faith is that light above our every achievement. Nothing other than the light of faith can lift us to it because it itself is most high; it pours forth over us; by it we are raised up. From this it is able to be described as closed and incomprehensible to us although

it comprehends us.[31]

This selection strikes the keynote of Luther's theology. Every possibility of gaining access to the divine on one's own merit is closed. God works all in the individual. He strips the soul, effecting faith in it, and in the stripping one experiences the wrath of God, God's 'No.' Yet, in this turmoil, faith grasps God's 'yes'; it clings to the experiential knowledge of the fact that although a sinner, one is justified. Before death one can never hope to rise above this paradoxical situation. An individual can know God's love only through the torment of the cross. Any other attempt on one's own to comprehend the glory of the divine is in reality the flaunting of one's own supposed abilities, an act of idolatry. Luther's statement is directed against speculative mysticism which suggested, as he believed, that an individual can achieve a superlative holiness. Nevertheless, it makes use of vocabulary and images borrowed from that same mysticism. It refers to divine illumination, to elevation, to heights closed and incomprehensible to the creature.

Elsewhere Luther treats the same theme with texts from the Song of Songs, so popular among medieval mystics, and in explicitly mystical vocabulary,[32] although he reshapes that vocabulary to suit his particular needs. This reshaping is best seen in his use of the word *exstasis*. Luther was influenced in his use of this term by Augustine, in whose works it has both positive and negative connotations; *exstasis* can describe the panic in the fear of death or the experience of revelation, much in the same way as Luther's word 'faith' does.[33] Luther, then, had little difficulty in associating *exstasis*, so popular among medieval mystics, with *fides*, thereby changing the denotation ascribed to *exstasis* by those mystics who applied the term to the experience of mystical union. His meaning is particularly clear in his commentary on Psalm 115:

> *Exstasis* is in the first place the sense of faith which literally exceeds the sense in which the unfaithful remain. In the second place, it is a rapture of the mind into the clear cognition of faith and this is properly *exstasis*. In the third place, it is alienation or trembling of the mind in persecution. In the fourth, it is that transfiguration (*excessus*) which martyrs achieve just as the transfiguration of Christ, Moses, and Elijah as discussed in Luke 9.[34]

Here the word *excessus*, similarly popular among medieval mystics, is also drawn into his treatment of faith, and shortly after, in the same commentary, he draws parallels between *ex-cessus* and *fides* in explicitly mystical terminology: 'That is *ex-cessus* when one is elevated above oneself ... and illuminated, sees that one is nothing. One looks down, as it were, from above into oneself, into one's own shadows and darkness. Nevertheless one is looking down from a mountain.'[35]

Leaving aside those references to union between God and the individual in Luther's works which are textually questionable,[36] a number of related terms and images remain which describe a union of the believer with Christ in faith[37] so close that the two become as it were (*quasi*)[38] one thing. As he had made use of the mystical terms *exstasis* and *excessus* to describe the experience of faith, so too Luther used other medieval images related to mystical union. In his treatise *On the Freedom of a Christian*, for example, referring to Ephesians 5:31-33 he wrote, 'The third incomprehensible gift of faith is this, that the soul is joined with Christ just as a bride with a bridegroom and by this sacrament ... Christ and the soul are made one flesh.'[39] This same image occurs in greater detail in a sermon on marriage written two years later.[40] In it, once again, Luther points out that Christ and the believer are one just as the bridal couple are one. That union, like the mystical, is real, but in it no confusion of persons occurs. Nor does such an image endanger the doctrine of forensic justification. 'Faith makes it that Christ becomes us; his love makes it that we become him.'[41]

It is Christ's love alone which brings about holy actions in the believer. In it one loves one's neighbour.[42] The love of God does not lie dormant; it is effective. It gives the Son, and having done so, draws the believer back to the source in love.[43]

In describing the reality of this union, then, Luther found some of the vocabulary of late medieval mysticism such as *exstasis* and *excessus* useful, but he always took care to distinguish his meaning from that of his medieval predecessors. Nevertheless, there was one aspect of his teaching which allowed later Lutherans to re-emphasise earlier mystical notions on the ascetical ascent and the mystical union.[44] As already noted, the union of a believer in faith with Christ is, for Luther, effected and made effective by God's love. Faith receives that love and acts in accordance with it. It is manifested in reciprocal love for God and neighbour, and only in it is there a possibility for a human, experimental, loving, knowledge of God.[45] For Luther, however, it must always be emphasised, the love which is experienced for God is the individual's psychological love; it is the action of a thankful soul, not 'ontological change' as the result of an infusion of grace.

In teaching this Luther was followed closely by his immediate disciples such as Flacius Illyricus and the Gnesio-Lutherans, who consistently opposed the form and content of Melanchthon's theological system. Melanchthon's influence remained strong, however, and his methodology shaped later Lutheran statements on the *unio mystica* in the *Formula of Concord*,[46] Martin Chemnitz,[47] and Philip Nicolai.[48] In the work of these men the various aspects of the application of saving grace to the believer, chief among which is the mystical union, tend to be formed into a progressive order, the *ordo salutis*.

The exact role played by the proto-Pietist Johann Arndt[49] in the development of the orthodox Lutheran doctrine on the *unio mystica* and its place in the *ordo salutis* has not yet been properly determined, but there is no doubt as to Arndt's significance in this, nor to his continuing direct influence on theology and piety throughout the seventeenth century.[50] The impact of his thought on Arnold is especially strong.[51]

Arndt opens his major work, *Wahres Christentum*,[52] with a description of the individual created in the image of God, the Holy Trinity.[53] Lost in the fall,[54] the one who is redeemed in Christ[55] lives toward full renewal of that image in the world to come.[56] Without such renewal one remains lost,[57] yet of oneself, fallen, one has no power to correct the situation. One must in faith experience a new birth and be justified and sanctified according to the image of God in the person of Jesus.[58]

The gift of faith at the basis of the new birth brings with it repentance, true sorrow for all past sins, and an unwillingness to commit them further.[59] But faith brings much more. In it and with repentance comes the mystical union of the believer with Christ[60] and all Christ's attendant merits.[61] Out of the mystical union, the newborn creature directs his or her steps in imitation of the life of Christ,[62] dying to personal wishes[63] in daily amendment of life.[64] All of these activities lead to the full renewal of the divine image.[65] The most significant among them is love.[66] For each, union with Christ is an absolute necessity.[67]

Arndt treats the doctrine of the *unio mystica* in greater depth in a treatise later included in his fifth book of the *Wahres Christentum*.[68] In it he insists, with Luther, that God has freely intended the union from the beginning;[69] that it is announced to the individual believer through God's word, externally in Scripture and internally in the heart;[70] that it is totally a gift of grace;[71] and that it is primarily union with Christ[72] in his body, the church.[73] Like Luther, as well, he interprets it in close relationship with purification[74] and repentance,[75] describes it in nuptial[76] and sacramental images,[77] and sees it as the root of continuing love of God[78] and full renovation of life,[79] finally completed in glory.[80]

The differences between Arndt and Luther must not be overlooked. Over half a century separates them and their attitudes are consequently different. The agonising terror experienced by Luther is presented in polished, balanced phrases in Arndt's discussion of repentance. Arndt insists on the need for divine election and proffered grace, but tends to take it for granted, pointing out that grace will do its part if one places nothing in its way.[81] Whereas Luther is concerned with faith first and shifts the meanings inherent in mystical terms such as *exstasis* to bring them completely under the rule of his doctrine on justification, for Arndt faith and union are broken apart and becomes separate stages in an ordered movement leading from birth to rebirth and a new life thereafter. The theological density in Luther's use of the word 'faith' is diffused by Arndt into an *ordo salutis*.

This *ordo* changed little throughout the seventeenth century, and in David Hollatz, the Pietistically influenced Lutheran scholastic, reached its fullest development at the beginning of the eighteenth century. The similarities between Arndt and Hollatz— and, as we shall see, between them and Arnold—are apparent when one parallels the chapters of Arndt's treatise on union with the respective sections in Hollatz's *Examen Theologicum*,[82] as follows:

Arndt	Hollatz
I, II	*electio*

III	*vocatio*
IV	*illuminatio*
V	*conversio*
VI (Busse)	*regeneratio*
VI (Glaube)	*justificatio*
VII	*unio*
VIII, IX	*renovatio*
X	*conservatio*
XIV	*glorificatio*

One other major difference between Luther and Arndt must be treated. In Luther's work the love described as growing out of faith toward God is closely tied to faith throughout the believer's life as are all other stages later included in the *ordo*. Arndt, as noted, tends to let this centrality of faith fade; at the same time he emphasises the importance of love, and by so doing, in a theological setting initiated and concluded by a concern with the restoration of the image of God in the fallen person, he changes the tone of Luther's position.

Love, for Arndt, is the ultimate manifestation of a unitive life of faith in imitation of Christ. It is directed toward neighbour and God;[83] its end is perfect patience[84] and praise.[85] Now, the only object worthy of the individual's love or praise is the chief good, God.[86] To Him, one is directed throughout life.[87] In all this there is little one cannot find in Luther, but in Arndt the emphasis on the life of love allows a much larger scope for a mystical interpretation of progression toward the completion of the renewal of the image of God,[88] and of contemplative prayer,[89] than exists in the thought of Luther.

Arndt agrees fully with Luther's accentuation of faith, but in his work the possibility for a perfected experience of the faith union is continually expressed in words which might well have sounded to Luther like those of the speculative mystics he so vehemently attacked. Often, in fact, Arndt paraphrases or quotes directly from earlier mystical texts.[90] He is no longer describing a union of the type discussed by Luther. Rather, the believer is directed to explore the nature of his or her union with Christ, is admonished to cast aside all love for creatures, and to learn progressively to love, in fullness, the God who has united himself with the believer. Spiritual joy, Arndt believes, will crown the fulfillment of this unitive experience.[91]

When one considers such a position in the light of Arndt's

extensive use of medieval texts,[92] one can better understand
why the antagonisms against him were so fierce.[93] Nevertheless, one must always remember that Arndt never intended his
words to be used outside of the Lutheran dogmatic framework.
He did accent the justified person rather than the sinner and
he did reduce faith to a mere part in the process of justification
and sanctification; and he did schematise the Christian life so
as to suggest that at the end of it there was a possibility for the
viator of an experienced mystical union. The union of which
he speaks, however, is always that of a soul united in faith to
Christ and the experience of that union is one of human psychological love for God in Christ in that love. Nor does Arndt
interpret such an experience as the ultimate point in Christian
life. It is ever a new beginning for the expression of yet greater
love for God and neighbour.

Arndt's mystical orientation was rejected in later Lutheran scholastic treatises, although they did make use of his *ordo*
and his treatment of the *unio mystica*. Among these treatises
the *Theologia Didactico-Polemica* (1685) by Arnold's teacher,
Johann Andreas Quenstedt,[94] is the most exhaustive and best
represents the culmination of orthodox teaching on the subject
of mystical union.

In his work, Quenstedt initiates his discussion of the *ordo*
with a treatment of redemption,[95] and then outlines questions relating to the call,[96] regeneration,[97] and conversion,[98]
before developing an article on justification.[99] It is only after this article that he treats penance and confession,[100] the
unio mystica,[101] and renovation,[102] changing, to a degree,
Arndt's order. By making regeneration precede conversion,
and penitence grow out of justification, Quenstedt is able to insist more strongly that the process of salvation is totally God's
work and human power has no part in it. Regeneration by
the Spirit's guidance leads to a quickening, a conversion.[103]
Penitence is possible only for those who are justified in Christ
and thereby know their shortcomings; it is, therefore, closely
related to renovation.

In addition, Quenstedt points out that the whole process
occurs in a moment (*in instantu*), in a mathematical point
of time from God's point of view.[104] All parts of the *ordo*
are bound together in the act of faith, the agent by which

Christ's merits are ascribed to the individual.[105] From the human point of view, however, the *unio* can be seen as growing out of justification.[106] This union can be understood in two ways. It can refer to that general union of the individual in creation,[107] but in the *ordo* it is understood as a special union, generously given to be fully enjoyed in glory.[108] It is a spiritual union as distinguished from a physical union,[109] and one of substances, but not a substantial union.[110] It is initiated by the entire Trinity,[111] its instrumental cause is the Word and sacraments,[112] its medium the faith of the believer.[113]

Just as, from a human point of view, the *unio mystica* grows out of justification, so renovation rises from the union.[114] Elsewhere in his work, Quenstedt outlines the exact relationship between renovation and this union,[115] but in no way does he allow for the possibility of growth toward a union in love of God on the part of the *viator*. For Quenstedt, renovation is dependent on the cooperation of the individual, *justus* indeed—and thereby able to play a role in such renewal—but always *peccator*, a fact which Arndt, and Arnold after him, sometimes neglected to note specifically.

c. The Theology of *Die Erste Liebe*

Book One of Arnold's *Die Erste Liebe*, although intended as a presentation of early Christian theology, is based on the Lutheran *ordo salutis*, and the structure of the book is invigorated by direct contact with the works of Arndt. The argument of this first book is carefully outlined. It progresses through three major movements, the first of which is recapitulated and more deeply developed in the second. The first is primarily concerned with establishing the general progression of the *ordo* according to its external manifestations; the second treats of inner spiritual change and growth. Two final sections comprise a third movement; each review the *ordo* once more, adding depth and breadth according to their differing emphases, the renewal of God's image in the individual and the union of the human person and God in love.

Arnold begins the first section of his argument in proper Lutheran fashion with a statement on God's call to the sinner. Faith comes through preaching[116] which announces the word of grace in Christ,[117] and directs the individual to turn from self and the world to God (vocatio).[118] Illumination by the Holy Spirit follows; this gives knowledge of sin[119] and of the punishment necessitated by God's law.[120] The result is that past wrongs are admitted and rejected (conversio),[121] and a new regenerated life[122] is undertaken by that faith in Christ which justifies and leads to knowledge and certainty of the mercy of God.[123] All this is solely a gift of God for which one merits nothing.[124] Renovation of life follows upon this changed attitude; sin is hated and truth sought without hypocrisy.[125] Renovation is experienced by the Christian within the Christian community to which he or she is led by the Holy Spirit.[126] It grows out of a mystical union of the believer with Christ, understood in the first instance, as in Luther and Arndt, as a union into Christ's body, the church, through baptism.[127] Like his predecessors, Arnold insists that the union is directed toward God in love.[128]

Having thus presented the general pattern of redemption, portrayed, as he believed, in the primitive church, Arnold returns to an earlier stage of the redemptive process, the stage of illumination, and begins to work through the ordo salutis again, this time in greater detail, placing emphasis more directly on the inner person, rather than on the external manifestations of inner change that he chronicled in the first section of his work. Under the topic illumination, he calls his readers' attention to this change of emphasis, noting the role of the inner spiritual voice which will continue in the believer to death. This inner voice he opposes to the outer dead letter,[129] but in proper Lutheran fashion he also indicates the necessary use of the outer word of Scripture.[130]

A discussion of the new birth (Wiedergeburt, conversio) follows, as expected, the treatment of illumination. The new birth is the sine qua non of Christian life, a supernatural act worked solely by the divine[131] to the increase of a holy life[132] and the renewal of the image of God in the individual (regeneratio).[133] Borrowing heavily from Arndt,[134] Arnold developed the latter's teaching within a three-fold anthropology. A Christian is body, soul, and spirit. The spirit is God's gift, his image and likeness received in faith (justificatio).

> The early Christians distinguished clearly between the natural and new born person. They knew that the Holy Scripture spoke of three different things, namely, body, soul, and spirit ... And ...

they discovered that this power of the new birth was placed in their
souls by the Holy Spirit and that it would rise over all of human
nature and human reason.[135]

It is through this spirit that the image of God is renewed at
conversion, and it is toward the fulfillment of that image that
the soul is directed for final perfect renewal in heaven.

This supernatural power [the spirit] is from the Holy Spirit. It is,
by the Holy Spirit, able to grow according to the image and likeness
of God and to partake of the divine nature. This, it is believed, is
not a carnal pursuit of an inheritance, but a gracious communion
in adoption. The Spirit makes those who were strangers, children
through the new birth from above.... The Spirit manifests itself in
reality among them in a renewal of the divine image, a perfection
of the mind, an improvement of the soul.[136]

Through the spirit as well, one is made like the angels and
united with God (*unio mystica*). The believer thus becomes
a participant in the very nature of God, but pantheism is
avoided:

This communion with God [the early Christians] considered high
and powerful, but they had no thoughts of defining the new birth
as a divinisation in the purest sense from 2 Peter 1:4. They did not
believe that the individual became God in nature when renewed to
the image of God.... 'The person who clings to God is one spirit with
him; this occurs when one is swallowed up in faith....' This and similar passages the ancients made use of to explain their understanding
not of a change into the divine being but a divine illumination or
enlightenment, the goal of the divine mystery through which one
comes near to God and is divinised.[137]

In such participation the believer receives the gifts of the
Spirit,[138] chief among which is faith.[139] Arndt's emphasis on
the fruits of faith as love for God and neighbour[140] and patient
endurance[141] preserved in hope for a blessed eternity[142] then
follows.

In this second development of his theme, Arnold has made
use of the scholastic teaching on the union of the major stages
in the *ordo* 'in one moment of time.' By faith the believer
is reborn and regenerated; by faith he or she is renewed toward the image of God and united with the divine. In this
way the believer is complete in the new birth 'in a moment of
time' in that he or she knows and loves the maker, but such
love naturally seeks its object, and in a renewed life,[143] a pious walk according to the teachings and example of Jesus,[144]
obedience to God's will and law,[145] and the shunning of sin,[146]

it progresses to ultimate perfection[147] lived out in full love,[148] trust,[149] hope,[150] humility,[151] and praise toward God,[152] both here, and finally and completely in glory.[153]

Faith is for Arnold an act which progresses experientially in love from the time of the new birth through to its completion, full renovation, and perfect union.[154]

> [The early Christians] knew that human nature, even in its sinfulness, always desires something upon which it can cast its love; that the heart moves according to certain stirrings and affections; that one desire always overcomes another and one grows out of another. After they had known the true and only life-giving source in their enlightenment and had begun to enjoy it, the love and inclination of their spirit had to rest in that source and become a true piece and witness of true Christianity. Love for God was, for them, a living being in the soul which joined together two things in the closest way ... namely the loving heart of the child and the loving Father in heaven.[155]

Such love gains its end only in heaven, but it can achieve ecstatic insights while on earth, although its ultimate goal here is peace and joy in the Holy Spirit.[156]

> The person who has reached a high grade of love, discovers that the Lord's promises are true for those who love him, those whom he yet at this time fills according to his wisdom. He will be overcome and almost drunken, indeed, swallowed up and imprisoned in another world as if that person were not able any longer to know his or her own nature.[157]

With this emphasis, Arnold was able to uphold a strongly mystical approach. His approach, however, was always stated in terms of incomplete or fuller psychological love for God in Christ.[158] In his system, as in Arndt's and Luther's before them, mystical union was already present for those in whom Christ dwelt[159] and who dwelt in him by faith;[160] it defined, in fact, only that indwelling. It was marked by the fruits of faith[161] and was completed in heaven whither Christians were drawn as chaste brides of Christ.[162] Nevertheless, in this union the possibility was ever open for ecstatic sensations of the divine in love, for mystical experience possibly accompanied by praeternatural charismata such as visions and prophetic utterances. The possibility of such ecstacy had been opened but guarded against in Arndt; in Arnold it is a practicality for Christian life. For both, the *unum necessarium* (Luke 10:42) is the mystical union wrought solely by God, but in Arnold

even more than in Arndt, the Lutheran emphasis tends to be
set aside by his practical spiritual teaching, in which 'the one
thing necessary' is much more the fulfillment of acts of piety
and love for God than the initial justifying *unio* itself. Lutheran principles are not in any way rejected by Arnold, however,
as the final two chapters in Book One of *Die Erste Liebe* make
clear. In both it is emphasised that the renewal of God's image
in the believer and God's union with the individual is fulfilled
in the act of faith itself, and that thereafter the activities of
purgation and the life of virtue are to be carried out.

d. Medieval Spiritual Writers in Lutheranism: The Background of Arnold's Historiography

The systematic theological orientation of Book One of *Die
Erste Liebe* is not continued throughout the work. This does
not mean it is neglected; it is, indeed, an active force throughout all of Arnold's work. But, once having established his
theological position, Arnold seems to have felt it unnecessary
to develop it any further and was able to direct his attention to
his chief interest: The portrayal of earlier periods of church history as models for his contemporaries. His antagonism to the
church of his day grew as he proceeded with *Die Erste Liebe*,
and reached a climax in the final three hundred page chapter
of that book. In this chapter he described the decline of early
Christian spirituality prior to, and during the Constantinian
era. This antagonism to a Christianity centred on external
forms increased in the *Kirchen- und Ketzer-Historie*; it is the
principal explanatory factor for the inclusion of topics on medieval spirituality and for the peculiar treatment medieval authors receive. Such treatment was not Arnold's own, however;
it was, to a large extent, derived from earlier Lutheran histo-
riograhy.

'The entrance of medieval mysticism into Lutheranism begins neither with the adoption of medieval and Jesuitical subject matter by way of Lutheran prayer literature,[163] nor particularly with Johann Arndt,[164]' wrote Werner Elert in his
Structure of Lutheranism. 'It begins with Luther.'[165] Of this
fact Arnold was well aware, and he looked back throughout
his career to the young Luther.[166] The importance of late medieval mysticism for Luther's concept of the *unio mystica* has

already been discussed. It remains only to outline briefly the reformer's view of medieval mystics and their writings as historical entities.

Those medieval mystical writings which particularly attracted Luther's interest can be conveniently treated under three main headings: the Pseudo-Dionysian corpus, the 'Romance' mystics, especially Bernard of Clairvaux, and fourteenth-century German mysticism, including Tauler and the Theologia deutsch, among others.[167] Of these, German mysticism is of primary interest to this study, but a brief survey of the first two is of value in interpreting its significance.

Throughout his writings, Luther's antagonism to Pseudo-Dionysius is frequently and vociferously expressed. No words of disdain seem strong enough for him.[168] These writings are in error, he claims;[169] they are filled with curiosities and superstition and are the sources of pernicious doctrine.[170] They fabricate foolish dreams[171] and are, as a result, rightfully derided.[172] Their garrulous author[173] was not the disciple of Paul as some pretend him to be.[174] Among all his other crimes, he was responsible for the perpetuation of the allegorical method of exegesis.[175]

Yet, there are passages in which Luther does not react negatively to the Dionysian corpus. Twice in 1518,[176] he uses the works of Denis as authorities to lend credence to his argument, and in the debate with Eck in 1519 he accepts their authority.[177] Other instances of this use can be found as well, although all were written in 1520 or earlier.[178] The proposal by some scholars to establish a pro-Dionysian period early in Luther's life,[179] as distinct from his maturity, during which he attacked the same material, does not explain the dichotomy, since several of the passages favouring Denis are nearer to 1520. What Luther was against was not the Dionysian corpus in itself, but the speculative mysticism in it which directed one from the practical concerns of a *viator* into the treacherous paths intended to lead to mystical union, paths which presupposed, according to Luther, the idolatrous claim of human merit.[180]

When one turns to Luther's discussions of the 'Romance' mystics, to Bernard, Bonaventure, and Gerson in particular, the same principles can be seen, but, on the whole,

more positive statements are made regarding them. Although
Luther attacks Bonaventure's fantasising,[181] complains that
his speculative writings 'drove me completely mad,'[182] and describes him as a poor sophist,[183] he quotes him at the same
time positively,[184] designates him an incomparable man,[185]
best among the scholastics,[186] and a true Christian.[187] It is
Bonaventure's simple faith in and confession of Christ that are
the most praiseworthy, yet the dangers in his approbation of
mysticism are manifest.

To Bernard and Gerson, Luther owed particular debts.[188]
What captured his attention in the works of Bernard, first of
all, was the monk's Christocentric piety, which rested solely
on the grace of God.[189] The great abbot's concern for his
fellows,[190] only one of the fruits of his salvation[191] through
which God was glorified[192] and the church strengthened,[193]
was rooted in his deep love of the incarnate Christ.[194] It was
this Christocentricity along with Bernard's love and use of the
Scriptures[195] which accounts for Luther's praise of his life and
preaching[196] and for the number of specific quotations from
and reflections on Bernard in his writings. Although these
are not numerous and are limited to mere epigrammatic statements and exempla, they are significant when one considers
that none appear from Tauler or the *Theologia deutsch*, both
of which Luther praised extensively.[197]

Luther was well aware that Bernard did not agree with
him on all points, however,[198] that he sometimes twisted the
word of the Scriptures,[199] that he was more deeply immersed
in Marian theology than Luther himself,[200] that he was dedicated to the perpetuation of the monastic life[201] and of questionable church festivals,[202] and that Bernard's concept of *Anfechtung* was not his.[203] Nor, in Luther's mind, were Bernard's
vocabulary and emphases at all points proper.[204] Luther was
like Bernard, he said, in that he drank from the same source,
although not the same stream.[205] When Bernard preached
Christ, he had no equal; when he disputed concerning Christ,
he was lost.[206]

The relationship between the theologies of Bernard and
Luther must not be over-emphasised. Yet Luther's concern
with the incarnate rather than the glorified Christ[207] must have
attracted him to Bernard's works. The latter's devotion to the

historical Jesus must have been a major factor as well.[208] In Bernard, Luther found a pious attention to the cross and a personal (*für mich*) salvation.[209] From Bernard too he gained significant insights into spiritual development and hermeneutical principles.[210]

Although the writings of the Abbot of Clairvaux remained important for him throughout his life,[211] a cooling can be detected in his use of that author after the confrontation with Eck, which opened Luther's eyes more fully to the clear differences between his own thought and that of the medieval monk.[212]

The same 'yes and no' attitude of Luther to Bernard and to speculative mysticism is to be seen in his use of Gerson,[213] and it may have been through Gerson[214] that he first saw the dangers in the mystical approach to salvation.[215] First among the characteristics which Luther admired in the French author was the latter's attention to the atoning role of the historical Christ.[216] Only he, Luther said, properly understood the role of grace in the economy of salvation[217] and realised that in reducing things to their first principles, one was led to the Scriptures and to a theology of Law and Gospel.[218]

Besides these considerations, Gerson's interest in practical church reform, his work on the conciliar movement, and his comments on indulgences, for example, were matters of secondary interest to Luther, although he did note them at numerous times.[219] That the French theologian could be deceived, Luther was ready to admit, but he is more positive in speaking of Gerson than he is in discussing any other writer, with the exception of Tauler and the author of the *Theologia deutsch*.[220] Gerson was not a speculator according to Luther's understanding; he was the finest of the theologians of conscience,[221] a writer who dealt firmly and rationally with temptation (*Anfechtung*)[222] and the problems of a scrupulous soul.[223] There are manifold distinctions between Luther and Gerson regarding *Anfechtung*, however. For Luther, spiritual temptation is not simply dealing with others, as in Gerson. For Luther, it is a subjective condition, the experience of God's wrath, and cannot be overcome by one's own striving.[224]

Despite Luther's antagonism to speculative mysticism, he did find great value in German speculation and visionary experience.[225] Seemingly, he had read Mechthild of Magdeburg,[226] and, in 1528, he published the material on Nicolas von der Flue.[227] His interest in Flue was, however, polemical: his sole purpose in publishing it was to place his own anti-papalism on a firmer historical footing.[228] The Brethren of the Common Life seemed to hold little attraction for him, although he had positive comments to make about Gerhard Zerbolt of Zutphen and Pupper von Goch.[229]

Despite his great praise for the *Theologia deutsch* in the prefaces of 1516 and 1518,[230] the influence of the work itself on Luther's thought is difficult to ascertain.[231] Certainly it had nothing like the impact Tauler's sermons had (although Luther never directly quotes Tauler either[232]), and in later life he tended to neglect its use.[233] What were particularly of interest to him were its practical aspects,[234] not its speculation,[235] and, above all, its lack of rhetorical ornament and the fact that it was in German.[236]

In 1515, in all likelihood before he came to his insight on justification,[237] Luther began to annotate the 1508 Augsburg edition of Tauler,[238] an author he greatly admired.[239] The exact nature of his annotations can best be understood by interpreting his comments in light of a roughly contemporanious passage from his commentary on Romans, in which he refers the reader to Tauler in support of his own theological position. Discussing Romans 8:26 on one's incapacity for proper prayer, Luther notes that it is necessary that God's Spirit help our spirit, and that one suffer and endure the work of God.[240] Salvation can come only from God. We understand human problems in their beginnings, but the great works of God we can appreciate only in their conclusion. No possibility exists for individuals to so much as desire the correct end. In the Spirit's operation one experiences the grasp of God, in which the very form of his thought perishes,[241] in which an individual's very substance is eradicated.[242] The experience is that of perdition and annihilation; it must be suffered with patient resignation, for, although painful, in it one finds one's deepest consolation.

Later in the commentary Luther describes this resignation as the willing acceptance of damnation if God so wills.[243] In all likelihood, it was Tauler's sermon 'Ascendens Jesus in naviculum'[244] Luther had in mind on this point. In his Tauler marginalia, it is this sermon which receives the most attention, and his annotations to it make statements similar to those in the Romans commentary.[245] Here again, God's work in the individual is emphasised, a work not understood by human reason.[246] All individual attempts to obtain salvation by one's own strength must be crushed. One must suffer this action and must accept reshaping at the potter's hands. Only faith can endure such a renewal.[247]

The significance of Luther's use of late medieval mystical materials for a study of Arnold is threefold. As indicated earlier, Arnold's *sic et non* attitude to mystical texts was shaped by Luther's distinctive approach to the *unio mystica*. In the second place, Luther's 'implicit' view of Christian history,[248] teaching a fall of the church from its pristine purity, and the continuity of true teaching by a small band of Christians through the ages,[249] was of decisive importance in Lutheran historiography. Its effects can be noted in the Melanchthonian school,[250] and in the works of Flacius Illyricus, they continued to be felt through the seventeenth century to Arnold.[251] Thirdly, Luther approved of medieval mystical texts for their significance as directives in morality or devotional practice,[252] an approach which was passed on to Arnold by Johann Arndt, in particular.

Arndt, too, was deeply interested in the German mystics of the late middle ages, published the *Theologia deutsch*, following Luther's 1518 edition in 1597 with his own introduction, and reprinted the full work in an improved edition, with the *Imitation of Christ*, in 1605, 1606, 1617, and 1621.[253] From 1605[254] onward, he published the six books of *Wahres Christentum*, in which medieval authors are basic sources, and the *Theologia deutsch* is again defended. In 1621, his edition of the sermons of Tauler appeared.[255]

Arndt's *Wahres Christentum* made extensive use of medieval authors. To protect himself from the charge of heresy, he stated his position at the outset of his first book, co-opting the medieval mystics to support Lutheran theology:

> Now this Book which I have written, specially treats of such sincere and earnest repentance of the heart, of the exhibition of faith in the life and conduct, and of the spirit of love which should animate all the acts of the Christian; for that which proceeds from Christian

love, is, at the same time, the fruit of faith. It is true that I have
referred to some earlier writers, such as Tauler, Thomas à Kempis,
and others, who may seem to ascribe more than is due to human
ability and works; but my whole Book is designed to counteract such
an error. I would, therefore, kindly request the Christian reader to
remember the great object for which I wrote this Book. He will find
that its main purpose is this: To teach the reader how to perceive
the hidden and innate abomination of Original Sin; to set forth
distinctly our misery and helplessness; to teach us to put no trust
in ourselves or our ability; to take away everything from ourselves
and to ascribe all to Christ, so that he alone may dwell in us, and
create all things in us, because he is the beginning, middle, and end
of our conversion and salvation.[256]

The place of the *Theologia deutsch* in the *Wahres Christentum* is interesting, but its influence is not extensive. Verbal and theological similarities have been noted at only eight
points.[257] Two of these are highly questionable,[258] and of the
remaining six, the citations are extremely brief and of little
significance for Arndt's theology as a whole.[259] In many cases
Arndt, like Luther, deliberately ignored any statements in the
original which referred to ecstatic mystical union at the end
of a graduated progress toward the divine and reshaped them
according to his understanding of a union of all believers with
Christ in faith. This intentional rethinking of medieval texts
is especially apparent in his preface to the *Theologia deutsch*
and the *Imitation of Christ* where he considers the teaching of
both works within the framework of the Lutheran theological
structure:

> The end of all theology and Christianity is union with God ... mar-
> riage with the heavenly bridegroom, Jesus Christ... the life-giving
> faith, the new birth, Christ's dwelling in us, Christ's noble life
> in us, the fruits of the Holy Spirit in us, the enlightenment and
> sanctification, the kingdom of God in us. This is all one thing
> since where true faith is, there is Christ with all his justification ...
> Christ and faith unite themselves with one another so that every-
> thing which is Christ's is ours through faith. Where Christ dwells in
> faith, he brings forth a holy life, and this is the noble life of Christ
> in us.[260]

As a guide for this 'noble life of Christ' in the believer the
Imitation of Christ was of special value and might be easily
read as a handbook directing one from repentance through
conversion into the activities of a renovated life. This was
the understanding Arndt had of the piece. The only sections
from it which he used directly were from Book One, sections

19-22 treating of Godly exercises, prayer, compunction, and human misery[261] and, in their context in Arndt's work, they are perfectly consistent with his Lutheranism.

Nevertheless, unlike Luther, Arndt was willing to make use of medieval portrayals of ecstatic mystical transport to describe experiences of love for God possible for believers during intense prayer or devotion. In the second book of his *Wahres Christentum*, for example, Arndt makes use of Angela of Foligno's second treatise in support of this possibility. A parallel printing of Arndt's work[262] and his source[263] helps to indicate how important such experience was for Arndt, elucidating as it does his expansion of the source on the subject of affective devotion (see Addendum to this chapter).

In spite of Arndt's interest in Angela of Foligno, Tauler was for him first among the medieval mystics. He is quoted at numerous times in Books One and Two of *Wahres Christentum* and is heavily relied upon in Book Three:[264]

> But that thou mayest more fully and distinctly apprehend in the commencement of this Third Book, which relates entirely to the inward man, how the children of God are to be drawn from the exterior to the interior man, or the ground of the heart; that they may search, know, purify, and change it, and keep their spiritual eyes fixed upon God, and his kingdom in the inmost recesses of the soul; that the reader, I say, may more fully understand this, I shall first of all more generally in this chapter, and then more particularly, touch upon and explain the several heads of this doctrine, referring occasionally to the Theology of Dr. John Tauler, and quoting him as often as possible in his own words. And here I may remark, that as the Holy Scripture, great and sacred as it is, regards the heart of man; so likewise, the whole divinity of Tauler aims at the inward man, the ground of the heart, and deepest recesses of the soul. Hence it is, that he again and again inculcates, 'that God and the kingdom of God, are purely to be enjoyed, sought for, and found in the ground of the heart:' that is, whatsoever the Holy Scripture and its true interpretation, discover outwardly, all that ought to be really, spiritually, and truly felt and experienced in the ground of the soul.[265]

Arndt's final comment here on the passage he quotes from Tauler makes his approach clear. The profundity of Tauler's doctrine of 'the ground of the soul' cannot be simplistically paralleled with Arndt's Lutheran doctrine on the 'inner person,' nor can Tauler's reworked version of Eckhart's concept of 'the birth of Christ in the soul' be equated with the Lutheran

'inner, spiritual experience' of an 'outward' form. The 'truth'
of the interpretation of Scripture which Arndt calls in to his
defence is in this light Lutheran, but not that of a medieval
Catholic. The medieval book is only for those already united
in the Lutheran sense, for those who have become one with
Christ in faith. It is for these, for their continuance in renovation of character and love of God, Arndt believes, that Tauler's
theology, despite its shortcomings, is particularly well suited.

Unlike Luther, Arndt saw little need to rethink his source
radically. He took what was before him as fitting his own
theology nearly perfectly. Tauler's emphasis on *Gelassenheit*
worked easily into Arndt's *ordo salutis*, and Tauler's statements on ecstatic mystical experience could be reinterpreted
in terms of a developing progression in the love for God of
a believer who is already united by faith in Christ in typical
Lutheran fashion and whose love is focussed not on the divinity
itself, but at all times on the divinity in the person of Jesus.

> The true way of attaining this divine inward treasure is by a true
> and living faith. Though we have already in Books I and II treated
> largely of faith, with all its powers and properties, how it cleaves
> unto Christ, rests and depends upon him; yet we must here return
> to it, and show of what use and advantage it is, in the matter
> before us. The property of a true and living faith is, to cleave unto
> God with our whole heart; to put our whole trust in him; to depend
> upon him; to dedicate and resign ourselves entirely to his mercy and
> goodness; to be united to God; and to enjoy him in the internal rest
> of the soul. True faith prefers nothing to God; it makes him the true
> object of all its desires, by unfeigned abstraction from all earthly
> comforts. In a word, it places its chief, eternal, infinite, and perfect
> good in Him alone, who is the true fountain of all good whether in
> heaven or earth, in time or eternity, and all through Jesus Christ,
> who is 'the author and finisher of our faith.' Heb. 12:2. This is
> that faith which leads us to our inward treasure, which is our chief
> good.[266]

In some cases the union of essences suggested in Arndt's
sources is rejected,[267] but in others even this language is
retained for Arndt's own purposes.[268] Tauler's influence is
strongest in Arndt's chapter which discusses the direction of a
soul searching this union in love:

> There are two ways of seeking after God, the one external, and the
> other internal. The first is the active way, when man seeks after
> God; the second is the passive, when God seeks after man. In the
> outward way, we seek God by various exercises of a Christian life; as
> fasting, prayer, retirement, meekness, accordingly as we are moved

by God, or led by devout people. In the inward, we enter into the ground of our heart's attending upon the revelation of the kingdom of God which is within us. Luke 17:21. For if the kingdom of God be in us, then God himself is in us, and more intimately united to the soul than she is to herself: and such a treasure as this within us, ought carefully to be attended to. The soul that desires to enter into this inward way, must entirely resign and submit itself to all the dispensations of Providence, both inward and outward; must perfectly rest in God, and be content to be, as God shall appoint, poor or rich, cheerful or sad, peaceful or joyless.[269]

Tauler's sermon 'Que mulier dragmas,' the source for this selection, outlines in general the same movement,[270] but, although following Tauler, Arndt is never unaware of his Lutheranism and immediately places his words in an eschatological context, insisting at the same time that no possibility exists for one to work one's way to such a union; even the experience of the union already granted is a gift of grace.

And now if man could with his bodily eyes take a view of such a soul in this, he would see the most beautiful creature in the world, shining forth in all the transcendent beauties of holiness; for such a soul is united to God, and by consequence is a partaker of his glory, not by nature, but by grace.... On the other hand, could we but see with our bodily eyes a soul sunk in the love of itself and the creatures, wholly polluted with the lust of the flesh, the lust of the eyes, and pride of life; and all its corrupt thoughts and imaginations externally figured by visible characters and impressions; neither earth nor hell could furnish a more dreadful monster than this. But in the last great day, when the hearts and consciences of all men shall be laid open (1 Cor. 4:5), and the inward eye shall be unclosed, so that every one shall have a full view of himself, then shall such an impure soul see its secret abominations, and find in itself an eternal source of sorrow, misery, and torment.[271]

Similar protective measures are not taken in a later chapter, possibly influenced by Eckhart's 'Beati pauperi,'[272] but there, too, Arndt's debt to his Lutheran tradition rises to the fore, and he insists on the Christocentric nature of the union and its psychological rather than its ontological dimension:

This nobility of the soul is but little known to the men of this world, even those that are accounted wise and learned: and they that have written volumes about the soul and its faculties, have never come to the fundamental point. For Christ is the true strength of the soul, its understanding, will, and memory; that is, light in its understanding; pleasure in its will; and joy in its memory. So Christ is the true sanctification, glory, and ornament of the soul; so that a man, for the love of Christ, which he experiences in himself, does

not desire to sin. Thus we are told, 'Whoso abideth in him sinneth
not. Whosoever is born of God doth not commit sin; for his seed
remaineth in him and he cannot sin.' 1 John 3: 6, 9. Yea, from
this love of Christ arises often joy so great as to make crosses and
afflictions not only tolerable, but even desirable for Christ's sake
(Acts 5:41); so that the cross is turned into joy, which is continually
springing up from its eternal fountain in the centre of the soul.[273]

Arndt's use of late medieval mystics grew out of Luther's
use of them, and it differed from his predecessor's approach
to the same extent as his teaching on the *unio mystica* did.
Whereas Luther's democratisation of that principle shaped the
way in which he saw medieval texts on the subject and his use
of them, the tensions inherent in Arndt's teaching—his desire
to maintain orthodox Lutheranism and his attraction to the
possibility of mystical insight in this life—manifested themselves in his use of medieval mystical texts. The historiography of Flacius Illyricus had also influenced, but undergone
a change, in Arndt's work. Whereas Illyricus had been concerned with establishing a tradition of *Zeugen der Wahrheit*
to uphold Lutheran teachings in the face of Roman Catholic
polemics, Arndt marks the beginning of a tradition in Lutheranism in which the medieval mystics are used as *Zeugen* in
support of a specific wing within Lutheranism. It is in this,
above all, that Arndt is followed by Philipp Jacob Spener and
the Pietists in their use of late medieval mystical texts.

Spener's first important statement on the subject occurs
in his discussion of scholastic polemical theology in his *Pia
desideria* of 1675.[274] Proposing that religious controversies be
brought to an end, and that a return to apostolic simplicity in
theological discussion be sought by a careful re-evaluation of
teaching approaches and texts, he suggests that the *Theologia
deutsch*, Tauler, and the *Imitation of Christ* might be of particular use. There is no doubt that he sees them as witnesses
to the truth, but equally no doubt that for him they support
a very specific truth: Evangelical theology is a *habitus practi-
cus*.[275] In support of this, he draws up a list of *Zeugen* to the
Zeugen, as it were. Luther's words to Spalatin on Tauler are
quoted, as is a selection from his introduction to the *Theologia
deutsch*. Arndt's extensive use of both medieval authors and
Johann Olearius' words of praise for the *Imitation* are quoted,
although Olearius' lengthy reservations regarding the work are

not mentioned.[276] The medieval works have their shortcomings, Spener notes; they were written during a time of darkness, but are still of value.

In 1680 Spener wrote a forward to an edition of Tauler's sermons, the *Nachfolgung des armen Lebens Christi*, the *Medulla Tauleri*, the *Theologia deutsch*, the *Imitation of Christ*, and Staupitz's treatises on the love of God and Christian faith.[277] The last four were reprints of Arndt's editions.[278] Although Spener was not himself responsible for the edition, it came to be closely associated with his name, particularly in the later 1703 reprint.[279] In his foreword, as is normal for formal requested prefaces, Spener follows the editor's preface to a large degree, outlining once again, after the fashion of Flacius Illyricus, its emphasis on Tauler as a witness to the truth against Roman Catholicism, and listing Luther's and Arndt's praise of these medieval works. Spener's individual concerns are manifest, however. Tauler is a witness to Lutheran teaching against Roman doctrines, but one must understand him particularly in his battle against scholasticism. In his discussion, not specifically treated in the editorial preface, which is in the Illyrican tradition, Spener is paralleling his understanding of the corrupt church in Tauler's day and the Lutheran church of his own.

> It is a special and precious grace of merciful God that although at times because of thanklessness for divine truth, he allows the church to fall into a very corrupt state, and much darkness to manifest itself ... yet he allows a beam of grace to remain.... At all times he supports witnesses to the truth who oppose the errors and corruptions [of their time], and guard against them.... This happened to the papacy.... There was no light, but cold and frost. It was corrupted with men's opinions and traditions, through superstition, self-chosen worship, and similar things. This had particularly arisen through scholastic theology which insisted that spiritual mysteries must be explained with Aristotelean teaching.... Out of this arose disputes, antagonisms, and contentions ... which darkened the majesty of the ancient theology, indeed set it aside, and what is worse, led many astray from the Word of God which alone can make one holy. It is contained in the Scriptures and follows from a true and living knowledge of God.... But the Lord allowed seeds to remain not only among the children and the simple ... but also among the learned.[280]

Spener's knowledge of medieval mysticism was not deep, despite the association of his name with the large edition of medieval texts. Spener does not, for the most part, quote from these sources, and his references are not as extensive as either

Luther's or Arndt's. To his *Natur und Gnade* of 1687 he added passages selected by an associate from Tauler, the *Theologia deutsch*, and the *Imitation of Christ*. They uphold, he claimed, not only the Lutheran doctrine of justification, but also Spener's own emphasis on sanctification. They serve as good practical guides for the Christian life.

> The reason [for including the material] is this: to point out how at a time when the light of the Gospel and the power of the grace of God was not so clear and was much more darkened, these dear people were led not only by the doctrine of justification and holiness (available only by the grace of God and not out of works.... We may also say that our dear Luther learned much from Tauler as well as others ...) but also of sanctification.... I hope that seeing the light of God in these Christian men will also bring joy to other God-loving souls. I believe that the reader will gain through these texts ... a firmer basis from these ancient teachers than I could establish with my own words.[281]

The selections published by Spener at the end of his work were in some cases paraphrastic renderings of the original, in others, edited, abbreviated compilations from longer passages.[282] All follow the pattern expected. Spener's work is concerned with emphasising the need for a renewed life of virtue in faith, love toward God in obedience to his commandments and toward neighbour in service, humility, patience, self-denial, joy, and prayer, rather than a false life of pretended sanctity. The Tauler sections distinguish between divine and natural love, speak of wrongful selfish desire for divine love, and distinguish the carnal, hypocritical, pharisaic life, from the life of the friends of God.[283] The selections from the *Medulla Tauleri* reject the possibility of salvation by human power and disparage any attempts at it.[284] A short selection compiled from the *Theologia deutsch* upholds the same theme of true and false Christianity,[285] as do the passages taken from the *Imitation of Christ*.[286]

In 1691, in his foreward to Dannhauer's *Tabulae hodosophicae* Spener concerned himself with the impediments to theological study in his day.[287] His treatment of mystical theology in that tract brings together a body of material which reflects Arnold's later approach to the same subject. Mystical theology, Spener claims, was a term used since earliest times and has always been directed against the philosophical falsehoods of scholastic theology.[288] As such it cannot be set aside, although its claims for direct revelation must be.[289] Dogmatics teaches intellectual truth; mystical theology leads to experiential change.[290] Of the two, mystical theology is the more important.[291] Excellent guides into its subject matter are the works of Tauler, à Kempis, Gerson, and the author of the *Theologia deutsch*.[292] In their simplicity they move the spirit, although in their enthusiasm, obscure vocabulary, and popery— Spener's anti-Catholicism and negativeness with regard to medieval texts on this point is always to be noted[293]—they are to be avoided by the enlightened reader.[294] The end of mystical theology is to direct the believer closer to God.[295]

In his concept of the *unio mystica*, Spener is in full agreement with the Lutheran scholastics of the late seventeenth century. The union between the believer and Christ in his church exists only by faith.[296] Out of this union, the fruits of faith proceed.[297] In Spener the 'democratisation' of mystical terminology has reached its expected conclusion. The mystical ascent is completely reversed, the unitive stage coming first, the illuminative and purgative stages following thereupon. The end of life (*in via*) is the perfection of practical morality. Any direct experience or knowledge of God is possible only hereafter (*in patria*).[298] Meditation and prayer are aids in the furtherance and perfection of such a life. Spener's emphasis on subjective piety is not that of the medieval mystics he quotes to support it. Prayer, for him, directs human attention to God's will and away from one's own. It provides the believer with strength to bear patiently the burdens of this world by drawing one's attention ever more closely to joy in the assurance of present righteousness and the hope of future reconciliation.[299] The same theological patterns emerge in the work of August Hermann Francke.[300] Except for Tauler, neither Spener nor Francke refer to medieval mystics extensively,[301] although both use the word *Gelassenheit* much more frequently than does Arnold.[302]

e. Arnold's Preliminary Research on Medieval Authors in the *Unparteiische Kirchen- und Ketzer-Historie*

Conceived primarily as a moralisation of institutional Christianity's history, Arnold's *Kirchen- und Ketzer-Historie* is an extended historical attack on what he considers religious

hypocrisy, pharisaic practice, scholastic debate, and polemical
theology. The strength of the *Historie* is in its discussions of
the first five, the sixteenth, and the seventeenth centuries of
the Christian church; the Middle Ages and medieval spirituality are poorly treated. The major interest of this section is to
reject scholastically oriented theology.[303] Only in one significant place does Arnold refer to mystical theology, in a passage
which is preceded by a discussion of the 'wretched' formulations of Bonaventure and Aquinas,[304] and this is followed by
an attack on the role of Aristotelean philosophy in theological
disputes.[305] The setting of the passage shapes its intent, but
what is of particular interest is that even though Arnold had
reached the thirteenth century in his study, the term mystical
theology leads him immediately to Pseudo-Dionysius. Nor is
his attitude to mystical theology completely positive.

> Some have much to say on how mystical theology came into the
> foreground in this century. Yet, prior to Richard and Hugh of
> St. Victor, John Scotus Erigena, already in the ninth century, had
> made the books of Dionysius the Areopagite known in a Latin
> translation.... There is clearly much good and useful in these writ-
> ings. Indeed, on one page there is more than in all the great fo-
> lios of the scholastics.... Only an experienced Christian is able to
> know truly how much impurity, human, and useless material are in
> these. They do urge [men to follow] the good, that is full union with
> God, but they are not clear on the true means [to this union] and
> spend time describing legalities.... Among the mystics are counted
> Joh. Ruusbroec, Bernardino of Siena, Laurence Giustiniani, Hein-
> rich Harphius, and the two well known men Tauler and Thomas à
> Kempis. Of these more will be said at a later point.[306]

One has the sense in reading the passage that, although he
notes the names of later medieval mystics, they are, perhaps
with the exception of Tauler and Thomas à Kempis, merely
names for him, gleaned at the moment from books he had
at hand. That he does not refer to two of these authors,
Bernardino of Siena and Giustiniani, again in the *Kirchen-
und Ketzer-Historie*, corroborates this assumption.

When one considers his treatment of late medieval mystics
in the *Kirchen- und Ketzer-Historie* generally, it is difficult to
say which, of the many he mentions, he knew in depth, but
when he relies on secondary sources for facts of biography or
bibliography, it is a good indication that he is unsure of himself. Of twelfth century mystics, other than Bernard,[307] Arnold
seems to have had fair acquaintance with the Victorine school.

For Hugh of St. Victor he had little use, interpreting his work within the scholastic tradition as he saw it, but he praises the mystic Richard.[308] He knew of Hildegard of Bingen, Mechthild of Magdeburg, and Elizabeth of Schönau, but to how great a degree is questionable. The section devoted to them contains little of an interpretive nature and suggests that he knew them only from secondary sources.[309] There is a characteristic note regarding Hildegard's protest against institutional authority. Certainly, that all three were visionaries must have added to his respect for them. Among thirteenth century mystics, he had read Angela of Foligno, as a brief note indicates;[310] however, his greatest interest in this century is devoted to St. Francis, whom he understood to have fiercely denounced the decadent monasticism of his day,[311] and to the Waldensian heresy.[312] Bonaventure, surprisingly enough, receives almost no consideration.[313]

In all, Arnold's discussion of earlier medieval mystics is governed as much by a need to list writers who attacked institutional Christianity as by any other concern; this purpose is continued in his treatment of the fourteenth century. In his review of that period, he distinguishes between the witnesses of the truth (*Zeugen der Wahrheit*) and the practical theologians. The former are those whose central importance, for Arnold, was their attack on clerical and papal power; among them are Marsilius of Padua, Occam, and Petrarch.[314] As practical theologians, Gerhard Zerbolt of Zutphen, Jan van Ruusbroec, Johann Tauler, Bridget of Sweden, and Catherine of Siena are discussed. Arnold was also aware of the existence of Christine Ebner;[315] of the great mystics, Eckhart and Suso are surprisingly missing.

Arnold's discussion of Gerhard Zerbolt is brief but accurate; he knows of two works by him: one on inner renewal, possibly the *Exercises*, and the *De spiritualibus ascensionibus*. Arnold felt positively toward him, since Zerbolt's concern with church renewal began with the renewal of individuals.[316] More details are given regarding Ruusbroec.[317] Arnold's acquaintance with the Surius' translation from which he lists thirteen titles[318] accounts for his knowledge of Jordaens' translation, Gerson's attack, and the various defences of Ruusbroec, all of which facts were documented in the Surius introduction.[319] Arnold accepts the positive statements made regarding Ruusbroec, that he was completely given to the contemplation of God, and notes, in addition, that his writings give witness of this love. The attacks on him, Arnold felt, were initiated by the causes of all attacks on mystics, that is, by a refusal on the part of the learned to understand the mystics' intentions.[320] It is this last point, the fact that Ruusbroec was charged with heresy, which may well be the most significant reason for Arnold's praise.

Arnold was likely well acquainted with Tauler's sermons,[321] and like all students of the Dominican preacher at the time, he believed in the authenticity of the *Meisterbuch*.[322] He also thought Tauler died in 1376. The major part of his discussion is dedicated to praises of the German mystic, not to the man himself. A comment of Luther's is quoted, those of Melanchthon and Matthias Lauterwelt (fl. 1553) noted, and a number of other Lutheran, Reformed, and Roman Catholic positive evaluations are stated; the negative positions of Nicolaus Hunnius (1585-1643) and Johannes Himmel (1581-1642) are rejected. He was also aware of Tauler's influence on Caspar Schwenckfeld and Valentine Weigel, although there is no indication of how closely he studied the problem.[323]

Bridget of Sweden and Catherine of Siena[324] interested Arnold in all likelihood because of their concern with ecclesiastical corruption, rather than for their specific spiritual writings, although he did know of the revelations of Bridget and of Catherine's letters. Of fifteenth century writers he knew of Geiler von Kaisersberg, Johann de Wesalia, Johann Capistrano, and Savonarola.[325] His interest in Nicolas de Clemangiis[326] was probably increased by the fact that the author was a solitary, and he quotes the titles of a number of his works. Catherine of Bologna is mentioned but receives negative treatment, corrupted as her revelations are, he believes, by 'papal superstition.'[327] Several of Vincent Ferrer's works are listed,[328] his miracles noted, and his oratory praised. Harphius too is treated and his works listed, but the interest in him seems primarily to be that of an historian attempting to establish a tradition of witnesses against the established church.[329]

With Thomas à Kempis, Arnold is on somewhat firmer ground. He knew of his sermons, the *Imitation*, à Kempis' autograph of that work, and the controversy concerning its authorship. He also had heard of translations of the work into English, French, Spanish, Italian, Czech, Hungarian, Turkish, Arabic, and a German translation by Lutheran theologians.[330] It is the question of authorship also which is of major importance in his discussion of the *Theologia deutsch*.[331] He notes the Luther edition and leaves the possibility of authorship open to three persons: Johann Theophilus of Frankfurt, Tauler, and Schwenckfeld.[332] The works of Dionysius von Rijckel are listed but little is said regarding him.[333] The main interest in the discussion of Gerson, whom Arnold had read, is his attack on the papacy. Gerson's book of mystical theology is not noted.[334]

Although scholars have previously devoted the closest study to Arnold's *Kirchen- und Ketzer-Historie*, the work is not seminal in the present study nor is it so from the point of view of Arnold's career as a whole. In the development of his theology first outlined in *Die Erste Liebe*, the mysticism of the late Middle Ages played only a small role and, if its themes reached Arnold, they did so most probably only in an indirect way through Arndt and other similar writers. The *Kirchen- und Ketzer-Historie* marks no real change in this. Arnold's attitude to the medieval past at this time is like Spener's. Like him, Arnold calls upon *Zeugen* to support his own distinctive doctrines and, like his, Arnold's interest in late medieval authors is in individuals who represented, for him, opposition to scholastic theology. Spener's negativism with respect to medieval and Roman Catholic writers is also paralleled in Arnold. Arnold treated the Middle Ages in the *Kirchen- und Ketzer-Historie* only because his subject demanded it. He did not display the same care in his treatment of that period as he did in the case of Patristic and Reformation eras. Nevertheless, the *Kirchen- und Ketzer-Historie* forced him to consider late medieval mysticism seriously for the first time. The contact was of great importance, for having once taken regard of the materials, he began to study them in depth. IIis study of medieval texts grew in the years thereafter, until it reached its climax near the end of his career, when it was no longer the early church or the Reformation on which he focused his greatest attention, but the spirituality of the late middle ages.

Addendum: Arndt and Angela of Foligno

Arndt

Since the living knowledge
of God and of Christ crucified is not to be attain-
ed unless we keep our eye
constantly fixed upon the
innocent and holy life of
Jesus Christ our Lord; and
since we cannot arrive at
this elevation of mind,
but by devout, humble,
believing and earnest
prayer, it is, therefore,
highly necessary to make
some further inquiry into
the nature of prayer. It
consists not so much in an
utterance of words, as in
a meditation or inter-
course of the believing
heart with God, and in a
lifting up of the soul,
and of all her faculties
and powers, to our Heavenly
Father. Ps. 19:14; 25:1.
As it is impossible to
find God without prayer,
so prayer is a means for
seeking and finding him.
Matt. 7:7, 8.
2. And as it falls under a
threefold denomination, it
being either oral, internal,
or supernatural (according
to St. Paul: 'I will pray
with the spirit, and I will
pray with the understanding
also;' 1 Cor. 14:15), so we
shall now consider each of
these in order.
3. Oral prayer is an
humble address to God and
an external exercise which
conducts the soul to the
internal duty of prayer,

Angela

Forasmuch, therefore, as the
knowledge of God uncreate and
of Christ crucified is need-
ful, and seeing that without
it we cannot transform our
minds in His love, it behov-
eth us to read diligently in
that aforesaid Book of Life,
that is to say, the life and
death of Jesus Christ. and
whereas this reading, or
rather knowledge, cannot
possibly be acquired without
devout, pure, humble, fervent,
attentive, and constant
prayer (not with the lips
alone, but with the heart and
mind and all the strength),
something must be said of
prayer, as well as of the
Book of Life.

It is through prayer and in
prayer that we find God.
There are divers kinds of
prayer, but in these three
kinds alone is God to be
found. The first is corporal,
the second mental, and the
third supernatural.

Corporal prayer is that which
is always accompanied by the
sound of words and by bodily
exercises, such as kneeling
down, asking pardon, and bow-

and leads man into the interior recesses of his own heart, especially if the words uttered be digested in faith, and if, by attentive application, they be well pondered and considered. This often proves a means of elevating the spirit and soul so near unto God, as to enjoy with faith a truly filial intercourse with Him, our heavenly Father.

ing oneself. This kind do I continually perform; and the reason thereof is, that, desiring to exercise myself in mental prayer, I was sometimes deceived and hindered therefrom by idleness and sleep, and thus lost time. For this reason do I exercise myself in corporal prayer, and this corporal prayer leadeth me unto the mental. But this must be done very attentively. Therefore when thou sayest the Paternoster, thou must consider well that which thou sayest and not repeat it in haste in order to say it a certain number of times, as do those vain women who perform good deeds for a reward.

4. Internal prayer is offered up without intermission, in faith, spirit, and mind, according to the words of our Saviour: 'The true worshippers shall worship the Father in spirit and in truth' (John 4:23); also those of David: 'Let the meditation of my heart be acceptable in thy sight, O Lord,' Ps. 19:14. And again: 'I commune with mine own heart, and my spirit made diligent search.' Ps. 77:6. Hereby, says St. Paul (speaking of the Spirit of adoption), we cry, Abba, Father. Rom. 8:15. By this internal prayer, we are led on gradually to that which is supernatural; which, according to Tauler,

Mental prayer is when the meditation of God filleth the mind so entirely that it thinketh on naught else save on God. But when some other reflection entereth into the mind it asketh not that it should be mental prayer because that prayer doth hinder the tongue from performing its office and it cannot speak. So completely is the mind filled with God that it can concern itself with naught else, neither think of anything save of God. Hence from this mental prayer proceedeth the supernatural.

Supernatural prayer is that during which the soul is so exalted by this knowledge, or

'consists in a true union
with God by faith, when our
created spirit dissolves,
as it were, and sinks away
in the uncreated Spirit of
God. It is then that all
is transacted in a moment,
which in words or deeds has
been done by all the saints
from the beginning of the
world.' For this reason
this supernatural prayer is
unspeakably more excellent
than that which is chiefly
external; for therein the
soul is by true faith so
replenished with the divine
love, that it can think
nothing else but of God
only. Or if another
thought should enter inad-
vertently into the heart,
it proves but an occasion
of trouble and sorrow; and
the soul cannot be at ease
till the intruding thought
has again vanished. A
soul that has once arrived
at this happy state gives
but little or no employ-
ment to the tongue: it is
silent before the Lord; it
panteth and thirsteth after
God (Ps. 42:1, 2); it long-
eth, yea, even fainteth for
him (Ps. 63:1, 84:2). It
loves him only; it rests in
him alone, not at all mind-
ing the world, nor worldly
affairs. Whence it is
still more and more filled
with an experimental knowledge of God, and with such
love and joy as no tongue
is able to utter. Whatever
the soul then perceives, is

meditation, or fulness of God
that it is uplifted above its
own nature and understandeth
more of God than it otherwise
could naturally. And understanding, it knoweth; but
that which it knoweth it cannot explain, because all that
it perceiveth and feeleth is
above its own nature.

beyond all possibility of
being expressed in words.
If one should ask a soul
under these contemplations:
What dost thou perceive?
the answer would be: A
good that is above all
good. What seest thou? A
perfection of beauty,
transcending all other
beauty. What feelest
thou? A joy surpassing
all joys. What does thou
taste? The inexpressible
delight of love. Nay, such
a one would tell you that
all the words that possibly
could be framed were but a
shadow, and came infinitely
short of the inward delight
which was experienced.
This is the voice of the
eternal Word; this His
speech to a loving soul,
according to that saying of
the Lord: 'He that loveth
me—I will manifest myself
unto him.' John 14:21.
Whatever is felt here,
whatever is seen here, is
above nature. Here voices
are heard, and words per-
ceived that are termed
words of the understanding
and the mind.

5. This is the school in
which the soul learns to
know God aright, and, as it
were, to taste him. Ps.
34:8. Whilst she knows him,
she loves him: and whilst
she loves him, she longs
for the full enjoyment of
him. This is the true sign
of love, to desire wholly
to possess the beloved

In these three degrees of
prayer, therefore, man learn-
eth to know God and himself.
And knowing Him, he loveth
Him, and loving Him he desir-
eth to possess Him; and this
is the sign of love, for he
who loveth not only a part of
himself, but the whole, trans-
formeth himself in the thing
beloved.

object, to be intimately
united with, and altogether
transformed into it.
6. This the soul now and
then perceives in a glance,
which lasts for a moment,
and then vanishes again;
but it puts the soul upon
fervent desires, to recover,
if possible, that beam of
heavenly joy which darted
upon her, and to regain
this divine taste, which so
lovingly moved her. And
she desires all this, in
order to be more intimately
united to her beloved.
From this affectionate
desire spring up both
internal and oral prayer;
the soul being fully con-
vinced that these heavenly
pleasures and visitations
are to be attained only by
prayer. And in all this,
the wonderful wisdom of God
appears, by which every-
thing is managed in the
most pefect order.
7. Thus none is permitted
to attain unto mental prayer but he who begins with
that which is oral; and
none can have an access to
the supernatural prayer, or
to a union with the highest
and most delightful Good,
but by mental prayer. But
this highest can only be
known by an experimental
perception, not expressible
by words.
8. And this is the cause
why God so strictly, so frequently, and so earnestly
enjoins prayer (Ps. 50:14),

But because this transformation endureth not for ever,
the soul seeketh and examin-
eth all other means whereby
it may transform itself in its
Beloved, in order that this
union may be repeated. Where-
for must it be known that
the divine wisdom hath ordered
all things and given unto each
its appointed place.

For this reason hath the
ineffable wisdom ordained that
no man should attain unto mental prayer who hath not previously exercised himself in
corporal prayer, neither doth
it permit the supernatural to
be vouchsafed unto any person
who hath not first performed
both corporal and mental prayer.

This orderly wisdom doth further desire that the prayers
set apart for certain hours
should be offered at the hours

because it is a sacred pledge and bond, by which God draws us up to himself, and by elevating us into his immediate presence, detains us there a while, and unites us with himself, who is the source of all that is good. And thus we are always reminded of him, without this gracious order, we would think less frequently on him, and would not share in the gifts of his mercy.[262]

appointed, as is seemly and due. Excepting only if we be so hindered by the great joy of mental or supernatural prayer that the tongue is absolved from performing its office, or if because of grievous infirmity we are not able. In such a case satisfaction may be offered, if possible, in mental quiet, with solicitude, according as we are able. And God doth further desire that when we pray, we should do so with our whole attention.[263]

Chapter Four:
Late Medieval Mysticism
and the Sources of Arnold's Poetry

It was not only as an historian but also as a poet that Arnold became acquainted with late medieval mystical texts. The Baroque poetic tradition within which he worked was highly influenced by mystical materials, including those of the late Middle Ages, but other spiritual traditions which Arnold studied at the time, and which were influential in his work, also mediated medieval texts to him. Chief among these were Boehmism, Quietism, and the mystical Spiritualism of the Schwenkfelder Daniel Sudermann, whose poetry depended on Eckhart, Tauler, and other fourteenth and fifteenth-century authors.

a. The Setting of Arnold's Poetry

Although Arnold's poetry cannot be defined within Baroque categories alone, many characteristics of this literature suited his thought well.[1] Baroque pessimism complemented Arnold's Pietistic reaction against the church and world of his day, and butressed his ethical rigorism.[2] Consideration of the vanity of human endeavours and the inevitability of death, themes so constant in seventeenth-century German poetry, are not explicitly stated in Arnold's work, but they help to establish a literary setting within which a demand for mystical fulfillment and a life lived totally for God can be made.[3] The same is true for the Baroque use of macrocosm-microcosm images as for the *vanitas vanitatum*, *de contemptu mundi*, and *memento mori* themes.[4] With other writers of his day, Arnold's interest in the parallels between microcosm and macrocosm led him to use emblematic books[5] and to develop extended conceits within individual poems.[6] He followed the Baroque style in other ways as well: he used encyclopedic lists, periphrasis, and hyperbole;[7] he developed prothematic introductions to many poems;[8] he was fond of epigrams and intensified concluding phrases;[9] and above all, he demonstrated a love of juxtaposition, antithesis, and paradox, all of which must be carefully considered in interpreting his verbal distinctions between the church and Babel, the church and the world, and true and false Christians.[10] The love of the dialogue genre is loosely related to this interest,[11] and Arnold's nature imagery,[12] as well as his attraction to the *Nosce teipsum* theme is also Baroque.[13]

Formed in the Counter Reformation,[14] Baroque style had developed a mystical vocabulary which it passed on to its Protestant practitioners. Thus, for example, the Lutheran Johann Georg Albini (1624-1679), using the images of medieval *Brautmystik*, called for the soul to leave the vanity of this life and rise toward eternity,[15] and his work was not considered by his fellow-believers as heretical. Arnold, too, had studied the poetic handbooks (he lists their authors[16]), but the Baroque mystical vocabulary and themes he used were in all likelihood influenced directly by his reading of the poets, above all Quirinus Kuhlmann(1651-1689)[17] and Angelus Silesius (Johann Scheffler, 1624-1677).[18]

With Silesius and many other Baroque writers, Arnold was interested in the source of poetic inspiration. Only the reborn person, he believed, could properly interpret the Scriptures, Christian tradition, or theology, and only the reborn person could write true religious poetry.[19] In describing his own experience, Arnold remarks that poems often came to him while on walks, during quiet mediation, or when his mind was raised in praise to God. The best poem for him was in the language of angels. It was a vision revealed directly by God to the poet; poets, visionaries, and mystics had much in common.[20] Yet, paradoxically, Arnold's poetry is derivative. Like other Baroque authors, he rewrites earlier literature. Several of the emblems printed in the *Göttliche Liebes-Funcken* were originally used by the Lutheran Johann Michael Dilherr (1604-1669)[21] whose influence on Arnold's book is significant.[22] And the whole of the *Poetische Lob- und Liebes-Sprüche* is a reworking of the Schwenkfelder, Daniel Sudermann's *Hohe Geistreiche Lehren*.[23] From others, Arnold's borrowings are less extensive, but not less important.[24] How far Silesius and Kuhlmann shaped the structure of Arnold's poetry cannot be said. He had close knowledge of both. Nevertheless, as his treatment of Kuhlmann in the *Kirchen- und Ketzer-Historie* shows, despite his extensive knowledge of the erratic prophet, he did not fully understand or face the implications of Kuhlmann's thought, which he narrowed into his own Pietist framework.[25] The *Historie* includes a detailed account of Kuhlmann's life (Arnold had available manuscript sources of the poet's final days in Russia[26]), lists his major works, but does not treat his theology. It is noted only generally for its rejection of the moral shortcomings of the Lutheran pastorate.

His treatment of Angelus Silesius is similar. In the introduction to his 1701 edition of Silesius' *Cherubinischer Wandersmann* Arnold praised the poet as a mystical theologian who was loved within the Roman Catholic Church for his righteous life and his useful spiritual writings and translations.[27] The greater part of the introduction is devoted to mystical theology in general, not to Silesius specifically. The Silesian poet is defended primarily as a proponent of a spirituality which stood in opposition to scholastic theology,[28] and the argument of the introduction is patterned after Arnold's earlier work and has much in common with the Spenerian use of *Zeugen*: Silesius' writing can be understood only by those who are enlightened by the Holy Spirit.[29] His compositions, Arnold suggests, follow the teachings of the *Theologia deutsch* and Tauler, whose authority, it is pointed out, is supported by Luther and Spener among others.[30] The words of Silesius and other mystics may be paradoxical and difficult to understand, Arnold notes, but this is because of the nature of the mystical experience—in any event, those words are primarily intended as guides in the practice of piety.[31]

There is little doubt that Silesius had medieval texts directly available to him.[32] He was associated with a Silesian Boehmist circle which made extensive use of them,[33] although how closely Boehme himself knew earlier mystical thought has still not been established.[34] Seventeenth-century Silesia did, however, provide an intellectual and literary milieu in which medieval mysticism was studied,[35] and in the establishment of this milieu, Boehme's greatest disciples, Abraham von Franckenburg (1593-1652)[36] and Johann Theodor von Tschesch (1595-1649),[37] played an important part. They used medieval mystical vocabulary in their writing and translated

and published medieval texts.[38] Some idea of the significance
of their role is evident, for example, in a manuscript of Silesian Boehmist and Quietist materials which contains extensive translations by von Tschesch from Thomas à Kempis'
works.[39] Boehmist circles, like Pietist groups, produced numerous manuscripts.   Neither thought solely in terms of
printed books, and Arnold, too, continued this practice, using manuscript sources for information on the sixteenth and
seventeenth centuries and perhaps as well for his study of medieval writers.[40]

Boehmism and Quietism have been suggested most often
as the chief theological influences in Arnold's poetry.[41] His detailed defence of the Boehmist movement in the *Kirchen- und
Ketzer-Historie*,[42] his interest in poets like Kuhlmann and Silesius, who are often treated as Boehmists, and above all, his use
of Boehmist motifs in his poetry, together with the publication
of *Das Geheimnisz der Göttlichen Sophia* as an introduction
to his verse, make an examination of this factor, in particular,
imperative.

The *Göttliche Liebes-Funcken* of 1698 was written in an orthodox Lutheran perspective. The 'Zuschrift' emphasises that
it is through grace alone that human love is raised toward God,
and the whole of the section is formed on the Lutheran theme
of Law and Gospel.[43] This theological commonplace is used to
clarify Arnold's concept of *unio mystica* in the 'Vorrede' to the
work as well. The Law is a guide, directing the individual to
Christ. With him, one is united by accepting the promise in the
Gospel. Following the union, Christ will live in the believer,
directing him or her to fuller spiritual awareness and greater
virtue.[44] Both contemplative and active lives are considered
as important, but Arnold here places greater emphasis on the
contemplative.[45] All trials will not be lifted suddenly in the
joy of mystic union; the believer must continue to strive with
suffering and to climb toward fuller holiness.[46] Suffering will be
made easier by remembrances of the 'sweet love of Christ.'[47]
By directing his attention to the love which lies united within,
the believer comes to experience a psychological transport in
love and praise.[48]

The tract, *Von der Stuffen der Christen*, appended to the
Göttliche Liebes-Funcken, upholds the same theological po-

sition. Typically Pietistic, it insists initially that growth in Christian life is necessary[49] and possible in and through Christ alone.[50] Growth comes only after the new birth,[51] the reality of which can be known by the presence in the believer of the gifts of the Holy Spirit.[52] Hindrances to their effectiveness are not indications that the new birth has not taken place, but rather that the new person is striving to improve.[53] The various stages of Christian growth (babes, youth, and adults) are listed, with the difficulties to be faced at each stage.[54] Birth pains are experienced in the chastisement of the law and repentance.[55] Initially weak, the new Christian must beware of pride,[56] pretension,[57] and self-deceit.[58] Such a Christian must live humbly under Christ,[59] be innocent in faith[60] and practical piety.[61] Living faith will direct the individual's attention ever more closely to the union the individual has with Christ.[62] The experience of this unity and growth in that experience can occur only if one's own Martha, one's activity, is set aside.[63] In greater knowledge of this union, the believer seeks rest and peace,[64] learns wisdom,[65] and, in wisdom, renovates his or her life more perfectly[66] in the fruits of patience,[67] purity,[68] strength,[69] and love for Christ.[70] As is the case in *Die Erste Liebe*, the fullness of love, described by Arnold as the mystic marriage,[71] is not a union of essences or of wills. It is an experience of joy in glimpsing the reality of that union, an experience which develops,[72] the more the mature adult believer purifies his or her life.[73]

Arnold's poetry in the *Göttliche Liebes-Funcken*, too, follows the theological pattern established in *Die Erste Liebe*. Christians are pilgrims on their way to heaven.[74] They experience God's mercy in a knowledge of their own evil.[75] Love incites them to repentance.[76] New birth is necessary for all; the old Adam must die.[77] The believer finds new life in a union with Christ in whom all unrighteousness is lost.[78] To Christ the believer is united as in marriage,[79] and Christ sustains[80] and directs the believer's life.[81] Toward the fullness of the image of God, Christ, every believer is directed.[82] But one can never rise completely above the flesh while on earth;[83] the crosses and pains of life must be accepted,[84] and the battle against sin continued.[85] Nevertheless, the battle will cease in death, and the faithful soul will be accepted as a bride of Christ.[86] But all worldly desires must be rejected,[87] both in individuals and in the Christian community.[88] The desire for a holy life progressively increases in the faithful Christian who seeks to rise above disunity to the unity of God,[89] to be filled with joyous knowledge of divine love,[90] and to be perfected after the image of Christ.[91] In the mature believer's heart Christ speaks his intentions directly.[92] The eye of faith in God's light may look toward the deep ground of the soul.[93] The result is an experience and knowledge which can be gradually developed and conditioned and graciously furthered through time, of the reality of a union previously consummated by faith in Christ. As such, the experience is a foretaste of heaven,[94] for there it will be complete.[95]

In the writing of his poetry, as in his other work, Arnold's primary aim is pastoral. His poems, he states, are intended to aid the weak sparks of new life in the believer as they long for their sun,[96] to direct them toward full experience with Christ, on whom they may feed;[97] in the depths of the soul to which Christ leads the believer, he speaks his counsel.[98] To fulfill his pastoral aim, Arnold used whatever materials he felt practical. Among those materials were Boehmist and Quietest texts, but Arnold must not be charged with holding either theological position. His inclusion of a translation from the seventeenth-century English Boehmist Thomas Bromley's *Way to the Sabbath of Rest*[99] is no proof of Boehmism, and the section, appended by Arnold immediately after his *Von der Stuffen der Christen*, includes nothing which could be read in the theological context of the earlier work. In addition, Arnold explicitly denied agreement with the Philadelphian Society.[100] None of Boehme's alchemical imagery is used by Arnold. The Sophia theme is used only twice in the *Göttliche Liebes-Funcken*, and, in both cases, its use is openly Christocentric.[101] In his later poetry, this theme is used to a greater degree, but even in these cases it is used in the same way.

Moreover, although Arnold treated Boehme and his followers at length in his *Kirchen- und Ketzer-Historie*, there is little in that work which suggests that he saw the thought of the Silesian shoemaker in any light other than that in which he saw the medieval mystics, Kuhlmann, or Silesius. Like that of many other individuals, Arnold's discussion of Boehme is

moulded by his presuppositions. Boehme is one of those orthodox, practically-oriented, Christian souls, according to Arnold,
whose work was directly inspired by the Spirit, who intended
no separation from the church, and whose greatest fault was
a refusal to use the terms of the scholastics, replacing them
instead with a language which he hoped would offer greater
insight into divine reality.[102] For this he suffered the persecution of the powerful and was charged with heresy. Boehme's
life and work provide yet another example for Arnold of the
unjust attacks of polemically-oriented Christianity against the
divinely-inspired practical theology of the children of God.

Despite the title of Arnold's *Geheimnisz der Göttlichen
Sophia*, there is little in the book which suggests a dramatic
reconstruction in Arnold's thought. Boehmist themes in it are
discontinuous; they are used as rhetorical techniques better to
call the lost to a new creation and the redeemed to mature
Christian life. Although the treatise is not tightly composed,
it is constructed according to a model, similar in many ways
to that of *Die Erste Liebe*.

The work falls into five sections; the first of these treats the
nature of Sophia from a metaphysical point of view (Chapters
1-7). The next three divisions discuss the practical implications
of Christian life, outlining first the relationship of Sophia to
the individual (Chapters 8-12), then her life in the individual
(Chapters 13-17), and finally, the fruits which result from that
association (Chapters 18-22). These three central sections are
strongly influenced by the *ordo salutis*. The first two stages of
the *ordo* are roughly parallel to the first two divisions of that
book, in that they work through the *ordo* first from an external,
physical and then from an internal, spiritual point of view. The
scholastic doctrine of the *ordo*, occurring *in instantu*, is again
seemingly accepted as axiomatic. The three central sections
are each composed of five chapters, all of which are parallel.
The fifth section of the work treats in greater depth, as does the
third section of *Die Erste Liebe*, Book One, some theological
implications and problems relating to the unitive life.[103]

Like his earlier works, Arnold's *Sophia* supports a dualism between true and false Christianity, in this case defined as
true and false wisdom.[104] But Arnold's perspective has shifted
somewhat. The ecclesiological interest of the *Kirchen- und*

Ketzer-Historie is not primary in the *Sophia*. Its concern is soteriological. It calls upon the believer to follow the call of the spark of life within and seek inner contemplation.[105] Christians have left the search for true wisdom; they have fallen from their earlier purity.[106] True wisdom is a gracious gift and is synonymous with Christ.[107] The life in wisdom is the life in Christ.[108] Growth in wisdom is growth in his love.[109]

Sophia, Arnold tells his reader, reworking the popular Augustinian adage,[110] is nearer to one than one is to oneself.[111] Human beings were created in this divine image, but fell from it.[112] Sophia continues to call in a hidden manner.[113] Youths hear the call best, untrained as they still are in the evil lusts of the world.[114] Human possession of free will is emphasised throughout the *Sophia*, yet the role of grace is always insisted upon.[115] Two aspects of love are understood throughout: (1) the gracious stimulation to love and wisdom is from God and (2) growth in that love will result eventually in the full love in marriage to the virgin Sophia.[116] Desire leads to love, love to obedience, and obedience brings one near to God, who is Wisdom itself.[117] In initial love, the believer, having repented and been born again,[118] is united with Christ by his Wisdom,[119] and in that union the believer continues the search. God the Father and Wisdom as Mother bear Christ in the believer, Arnold declares,[120] but his image is intended purely rhetorically. Elsewhere, he insists that the birth which occurs is that of Wisdom itself in the soul,[121] which in turn bears the seven gifts of the Spirit,[122] but in all these cases he does not intend his words to be understood ontologically. Throughout, his argument is fashioned according to the Lutheran *ordo*.

Three premises maintained in the *Sophia* may lead students of the piece to question its Lutheranism: its insistence on celibacy, its use of terms such as *substantie* and *wesentlich* to describe the *unio*, its lengthy and detailed description of the mystical marriage. The first and the third may be conveniently discussed together. The second is the most problematic, jeopardising as it does the Lutheran position on forensic justification. At times, God's life in the soul is described as a 'life-giving, essential seed of his eternal work';[123] at others, the word 'substance'[124] is used to describe the union. Other images are equally questionable, suggesting as they do that

Arnold maintained that an essential justification existed for
the believer, much in the way Osiander had.[125] That Arnold
had not been circumspect enough in his use of language in the
Sophia, even he was willing to admit. His intention is ascer-
tainable, nevertheless. His description of the *unio* is always
from the believer's point of view.[126] Never does he teach that
righteousness and its progress in the Christian, belong properly
to the believer; it is God's gift, living with human beings, not
an individual's own work.[127] Finally, as will be demonstrated
below, Arnold was concerned to guard himself in his poetry
against the doctrine of essential justification as taught by the
Schwenkfelder, Daniel Sudermann, for example.

The images in *Sophia* are in flux. Both mother and child,
Sophia is also the Virgin loved by and betrothed to the soul,
with whom the soul will be united in marriage. The early
experience of life in Christ is like Jacob's marriage to Lea; the
joy of spiritual marriage is union with Rachel.[128] The spiritual
marriage is experienced in a way which cannot be described
in words.[129] One grows in love toward it; Sophia first grants
kisses, then fuller favours.[130] The marriage is not an end in
itself. It, too, directs one in one's life on earth and in one's
Christian work.[131] It is not human work in any way.[132]

Only the pure can claim such an experience, and Arnold,
making use of the Boehmist image of an androgynous Adam
who fell into male and female,[133] was encouraged by this doctrine to insist that only celibate lovers of the virgin Sophia
might gain access to the marriage chamber.[134] His defence
of celibacy possibly owed much to his own reclusive tendencies, manifested among both his fellow students at Wittenberg, and his colleagues at Giessen. Nevertheless, as a doctrine, celibacy was not part of his system in either *Die Erste
Liebe* or the *Kirchen- und Ketzer-Historie*, and was rejected by
him in 1701.[135] In itself, Arnold's teaching on celibacy was not
in opposition to Lutheran doctrine, although it was repugnant
to Lutheran piety. He did not claim that celibacy was necessary for salvation, only that for the full experience of Christ's
love it was necessary in the believer. In this, he was radicalising earlier Pietist practice, which distinguished between weak
and mature Christians and expected fuller devotion and ascetic
practice from the latter.

Arnold's use of Quietist materials was similar to his use of Boehmist texts. His interest in Quietism was far more extensive than was his interest in Boehmism and went well beyond his publication of Guyon, Molinos, Petrucci, and authors, such a Gertrude More, who might be read within the background of this later spiritual development.[136] He was closely acquainted with the life of Antoinette Bourignon and the continuing work of Pierre Poiret who played a significant role in directing Arnold to late medieval mysticism. But in his attraction to Quietist texts Arnold was not alone. They were read by all Pietists—August Hermann Francke was deeply indebted to the spirit of Molinos,[137]—and many of the specific characteristics of Quietism are not present in Arnold's work. Arnold did borrow themes from the *Spiritual Guide*, but they did not reshape his thought; they were used as further explications of the path to the mystical marriage and the experience undergone on its consummation.[138]

Admitting that 'Quietism is a direction of the human mind and not a series of conclusions,'[139] and that Arnold's direction in the *Sophia* and his poetry before 1701 is similar to it,[140] it is important to add that there are equally great differences between Quietist thought and Arnold's theology. As has been pointed out, in Arnold there is not taught the same passivity in prayer as in the Quietists, although he has used their words to describe the peace and stillness in the experience of spiritual marriage. There is some discussion of a permanent act of contemplation, but this is in the context of virtue, which is to rise out of it. Nor are intellectual considerations and mental pictures in prayer rejected by Arnold, who intended the profuse imagery of his poetry and the *Sophia* to serve as meditative material. Finally, Arnold shows a much greater interest in affections; unlike the Quietists, one of his chief interests in experiencing the spiritual marriage is to gain thereby consolation and peace, with which to face the sufferings of life about him.

b.   Medieval Mysticism and the Rise of Mystical Spiritualism

Much more important than Quietism, or even Boehmism, for the study of Arnold's theology and of the role of late medieval texts in it is his reading of materials written within the Spiritualist wing of the Radical Reformation. Arnold has been associated with the Spiritualists,[141] and there are many aspects of his work which support this description of his theology, particularly his dualistic division of true mystical theology from false scholasticism, his emphasis on the inner word and direct inspiration, and his antagonism to sacramental practice and the use of symbolic books or credal statements as final directives in religious life. He was especially interested in the work of Caspar Schwenckfeld[142] (the relations between whose thought and Pietism have never been properly unravelled[143]), he edited a number of Schwenckfeld's works, some of which he had in manuscripts which are no longer extant,[144] and he published a work by the seventeenth-century Schwenkfeldian, Christian Hoburg (1607-1675).[145] All of these facts, not the least of which is Arnold's extensive revision of the Schwenkfelder Daniel Sudermann's poetry, make an analysis of his relationship to Schwenkfeldianism and its medieval roots necessary.[146]

It is not surprising that in the search for medieval mystical influence on non-Catholic Christian thought, Caspar Schwenckfeld's work should have come to the attention of many. Success in determining the exact nature of that influence has not, however, been in keeping with the number of attempts,[147] for despite the great interest in the Silesian nobleman's theology and the array of monographs treating aspects of his work, many important areas of his thought still remain to be critically analysed.[148]

Schwenckfeld's theology grew in the humanist environment of early sixteenth-century Silesia, under the influence of late medieval spirituality and the theology of the young Luther.[149] Thus, while Luther's works initiated a major change in Schwenckfeld's religious outlook sometime around 1518,[150] Schwenckfeld himself cannot be described as a Lutheran, despite his statements to the contrary.[151] His earliest works indicate that in him, Lutheranism was redirected by a practical ethical humanism. His position as a court diplomat, his concern with reform rather than revolt,[152] and his continuing loyalty to the humanist Roman Catholic bishop, John of Salza, necessitated his support of a reform qualitatively different from that in Saxony.

Unfortunately, few documents on his early period remain, but in his first major work, the *Ermanung des Missbrauchs* (1542),[153] he opposes Lutheranism directly on what are essentially ethical grounds, maintaining that Lutheran teaching on justification, the bondage of the will, the role of works, the law, and Christ's satisfaction result, although not so intended, in immoral libertarianism.

At this time, as well, one notes in his work the beginnings of his Spiritualism, of his distinction between nature and 'supernature,' between flesh and spirit, between the created and uncreated realms.[154] This distinction almost certainly grew out of Luther's differentiation between the outer and inner word of Scripture, and between the physical and spiritual church which are split apart in Schwenckfeld. As a result, Schwenckfeld could not accept the doctrine of the Lord's Supper as taught by Luther or by Roman Catholics.[155] His conclusions, with the help of his scholarly friend Valentine Crautwald, whose vision on the subject lay at the basis of Schwenckfeld's reinterpretation,[156] was that the words of institution are to be understood as saying, 'My body is this, namely, food.' Such food, he believed, was real food, really the glorified body of Christ, of which the believer becomes a spiritual partaker.

Schwenckfeld continued to develop his theology of the Supper up to 1530.[157] Prior to 1527, he encountered Anabaptism for the first time, and it is not surprising as a result, that the majority of his treatises up to that time deal with the question of baptism,[158] which is interpreted within a Spiritualist framework in the same way that the Supper is. The distinction between physical and spiritual was the controlling force, as well, in Schwenckfeld's approach to the Scriptures[159] and to his doctrine of the church,[160] as well as his views on religious toleration.[161]

It was his christology, however, which, influenced by early Fathers like Hilary of Poitiers[162] and Radical Reformers like Melchior Hofmann,[163] held a growing importance for him. At the centre of Schwenckfeld's mature theology was a concern with the glory of the risen Christ.[164] Christ's flesh, he taught, was not that of a creature, but rather, of heavenly origin, a celestial flesh, which was progessively divinised, reaching its completion in his glorification at the right hand of the Father.

On the basis of this christology, Schwenckfeld developed a deeply personal and practical Christianity. For him, faith not only declares that an individual is justified (Luther's insight) but, as knowledge, it unites the believer with that which is believed. In baptism, one is united with the glorified body of Christ; one feeds on it spiritually. Faith is a seed of the divine in the believer, God's very being in the old creature;[165] it works an actual, real change in the individual.[166] The carnal gives way to the spiritual in a series of ascents.[167] At one point, Schwenckfeld details the progression in ten points, from attraction to full imitation of Christ;[168] at another, in fifteen, from knowledge of sin to eternal praise.[169] At the root of his thought is his belief that the individual was created and is recreated to the image of God, i.e., the person of Christ,[170] in which image one will reach final perfection.[171]

Faith, according to Schwenckfeld, is the spirit which directs the Christian toward full knowledge of Christ (*Erkenntniss Christi*).[172] This knowledge is two-fold according to the two natures in Christ's person. It is knowledge of the life of Jesus of Nazareth, the humiliated Christ, and knowledge of the glorified Christ at the right hand of the Father.[173] It is not so much knowledge of, as knowledge with. Grace incites the actions of conscience[174] by which the believer learns, with the humiliated life of Christ within, the Master's obedience, suffering for others, love, and, with the glorified life of Christ, comes to know the depths of reality and thereby to gain spiritual discernment.[175]

Of all the medieval authors used by Schwenckfeld, Tauler stood first, but Schwenckfeld seldom quotes him—only some twenty times during his career—and, although he began reading the sermons in 1524,[176] it was only after 1531 that he studied them carefully.[177] After 1531, Tauler's term *Gelassenheit* appears with regularity in Schwenckfeld's writings,[178] but it is used in a significantly different context from that in which Tauler applied the term. For Tauler, it was a means by which an individual left behind those earthly things which were of concern to him, so as to prepare himself for full union with the divine.[179] Schwenckfeld—who if not influenced by the earlier

Radical Reformer Karlstadt in this regard, at least had much
in common with him[180]—counseled Christians to resignation,
as he counseled them to the other fruits of faith.[181] Growing
in love in a faith union with Christ, one is to resign oneself for
active suffering and loving. This is the end of Christian life for
the *viator*, not mystical fulfillment.

In all cases, Schwenckfeld chooses words from the medieval
mystics and reconstructs them within his own theological perspective. Two-thirds of all his Tauler quotations state that
there is no mediator between God and the individual other
than Christ and are quoted to support his sacramentology and
ecclesiology.[182] Likewise, in his defence of his christology[183]
and his teaching on the Eucharist,[184] the same reinterpretation of Tauler's text is evident. The Pseudo-Tauler piece on
the inner and outer word Schwenckfeld clearly edited to support his teaching on the Scriptures and his spiritualism in
general.[185] In all cases, medieval quotations are given a characteristic Schwenkfeldian twist,[186] and he often relates them to
Scripture, or slightly changes their wording, so as to make them
more applicable to a this worldly imitation of Christ, rather
than to the pursuit of mystical union, as Tauler intended.[187]

What was of greatest interest to Schwenckfeld in all the
medieval sources he used, was, in fact, the practical advice
they offered for the convert to the spiritual life.[188] Such advice
he found, for example, in the *Imitation of Christ*, a work which
he greatly appreciated,[189] for which he wrote annotations,[190]
and which he probably edited.[191]

Tauler and the *Imitation of Christ* were not alone, however, among the late medieval mystics Schwenckfeld used.[192]
The writings of St. Bernard may have shaped aspects of his theology on the love of God, and on the distinction between the
carnal and spiritual knowledge of Christ.[193] Some familiarity
with Bonaventure is also evident,[194] but little with Aquinas.[195]
Most of his knowledge of Gerson seems to have come through
the sermons of Geiler von Kaisersberg.[196] His knowledge of
Nicolas von der Flue is certain.[197] Only once, though in a long
quotation, does he mention Harphius.[198] It is not the speculative elements in Harphius' work which interest him, however, but the distinction the latter makes between mystical
and scholastic theology. Indeed, in Schwenckfeld one senses

an antipathy toward all speculation, the goal of which is the mystical experience. Perhaps this is why he never quotes Pseudo-Dionysius and why he reacted against the Platonist elements in the Taulerian corpus.

His attitude in general is perhaps best illustrated by his remarks concerning the *Theologia deutsch*. In a letter in April of 1545, he expresses his reservations.[199] The *Theologia* has much in it of value, he says. It makes significant mention of *Gelassenheit* and of the necessity of ridding oneself of the old Adam. But the depths and heights of its teaching are obscure, and he wishes it had mentioned Christ more often. The matter was still in his mind in July of the same year, when he wrote once more comparing the *Theologia deutsch* to the *Imitation of Christ* and Staupitz's *Von der Liebe Gottes*.[200] With such works, he says, the *Theologia* is unworthy of comparison. Perhaps in this he was influenced by his disputes with Sebastian Franck (1499-1542), who had made such great use of the *Theologia*.[201]

Among Schwenckfeld's contemporaries, the only figures of significance for our study are the Silesian, Michael Hiller (d.1559)[202] and his contemporary Theophilus Agricola. Agricola is alone among the early Schwenkfelders in making extensive use of Tauler to support Schwenckfeld's distinctive emphases; but, in so doing, he narrowed the mystic to one issue, that of the direct action of God in the soul, without means of sacrament, preaching, or Scripture.[203] In Hiller's sermons, one finds the same emphasis with respect to the union of the believer in Christ, although the emphasis shifts to a growing concern with one aspect of christology, namely soteriology.[204] With that shift, the mystical orientation of Schwenckfeld's system grows more marked and is developed later in the century, particularly by Daniel Friederich (d.1610)[205] and Daniel Sudermann (1550-c.1631).

Among the many Schwenkfelder students of late medieval spirituality who followed Schwenckfeld and his contemporaries, Daniel Sudermann was the most significant for his role in the transmission of that material within the Protestant tradition. It was through him and Christian Hoburg that Arnold contacted later Schwenkfeldianism in its most vital form, and it is through them as well that he gained insights into the medieval mystics.[206]

Sudermann's career as a student of the Middle Ages can be discussed conveniently in its three closely related manifestations: his collection of manuscripts, his study and publication of texts, and his poetic popularisation of medieval spiritual themes. As a manuscript collector, Sudermann's significance can hardly be underestimated.[207] Without him, there seems little doubt that many important vernacular manuscripts would have been lost.[208] Eighty-six medieval manuscripts were in his possession, only three of which contain secular material, and only two of which are in Latin.[209] Most of his collection seems to have come from the Strassburg convent, St. Nicholas in undis.[210] Sudermann had the collector's instinct, however, and in all likelihood procured manuscripts from other locations as well.[211] He continually supplemented his collection by personally copying treatises which he could not purchase.[212] In his work on Tauler he made more use of the Basel (1522) and Cologne (1543) editions than of the manuscripts, because he found the printed texts easier to read.[213]

A consideration of only the major late medieval mystics whose works he owned suggests something of the importance of the collection preserved by Sudermann. Eight authentic Eckhart sermons[214] and a fragment of his tract *Von Abgeschiedenheit*[215] were contained among his materials, and his manuscripts have been used by modern scholars to establish the texts and their authenticity.[216] Genuine Tauler sermons are well represented,[217] as are original Suso materials.[218] Recent scholarship has indicated the significant role played by Sudermann in the preservation of the German tradition of Ruusbroec texts.[219] The many lesser authors are too numerous to note in full,[220] as are the important anonymous texts contained in the collection.[221]

Despite his collector's instinct, Sudermann was no mere bibliophile. Central to his career was the publication of works which he felt were useful for the development of the Christian life. Next in importance to the writings of Schwenckfeld were medieval texts.[222] In the last fifteen years of his life, he published works by Tauler,[223] Suso,[224] Ruusbroec,[225] and others,[226] and the numerous marginal references in his manuscripts and printed editions indicate something of the depth with which he knew these authors. Thus, in his annotations to the Schwenckfeld *Epistolars*,[227] in addition to noting numerous sections which reminded him generally of Tauler,[228] he quotes from the mystic five times, using him in the same way that Schwenckfeld had, to support a spiritual interpretation of the Eucharist, and to insist on the direct action of God in the soul.[229]

Sudermann's scholarship had it shortcomings. His great love for Tauler led him, like many of his contemporaries, to ascribe writings to the German mystic which were not his, to accept the authenticity of the *Meisterbuch*, and to make false attributions, as he did in the case of Ruusbroec[230] and Bernard.[231] He knew more of Suso than did Schwenckfeld, but, perhaps because of his master's reluctance to use that particular authority, he seldom quotes him.[232] However, that he copied the letters[233] indicates that he did realise their author's spiritual quality. Like Schwenckfeld, he seems antagonistic to the *Theologia deutsch*, which is seldom mentioned. Although he makes greater use of Pseudo-Dionysius, he shows a marked reserve in quoting him, a reserve which may have increased in him, as in Schwenckfeld, by their reading of Luther[234] and Calvin[235] on the subject.

The poetical compositions of Sudermann have, unfortunately, not been treated at any length, despite their significance as literary monuments, and as texts which utilise the medieval mystical vocabulary, although not necessarily for the ends of the medieval mystics. As a poet, Sudermann was highly esteemed in his own day, and he may possibly have known Fischart, some reminiscences of whose work are evident in his poetry.[236] Over 2,000 of his poems were published in his life time, the greater majority of which were either totally or in part inspired by late medieval texts. Every page of his poetical commentary on the Song of Songs, the *Hohe Geistreiche Lehren* and of the five parts of his *Schöne Auszerlesene Figuren* is, on his own admission,[237] influenced by passages in Bernard, Tauler, Eckhart, or materials which he took to be by them. The manuscript poems follow the same pattern.[238]

The theological structure underlying Sudermann's work is best outlined in an unpublished poem 'Im Himmel, und auf Erden.'[239] The piece is based on several Taulerian sermons

and is broken into five sections. Entitled 'How the divine Word
speaks and reveals itself in the ground of the soul,' the first part
of the poem discusses God's eternal decree to create the soul
like to himself and work his will in it. To accomplish this he
united himself with the soul and bears his Son in it. Through
this power the soul is able to leave all things and look inward
to hear the divine counsel. As detachment (*Gelassenheit*) increases, God's voice may be better heard and eventually the
believer may live in full obedience to God. The *ordo* is similar
to the Lutheran one, but major differences are to be noted. As
in Schwenckfeld, justification involves an essential change on
the part of the believer. Faith participates in the very being of
Christ, establishing an essential union with his celestial flesh
which is to grow to perfection.

Again, in the Eckhart sermon, 'Honour Thy Father,' Sudermann read the following:

> To this end, my parents were not able to contribute much, but
> God made my body without any help, and created my soul like that
> which is supreme. Thus I came to possess life (*possedi me*). One
> seed grows to be rye. The nature of another causes it to grow into
> wheat and never to stop until its end has been achieved. But this
> grain has the capacity to turn into everything and so it submits,
> and goes to its death, in order to change into everything. And this
> metal, copper, can be changed into gold and it will never stop until
> its end has been attained.[240]

The preacher continues to explain how wood has stone in its
nature and how all things can be changed into fire, since they
have all come from one element in the beginning and return to
it in the end. The example can be applied to the human soul.

> And if it is like this with nature, what shall it be like with that
> nature which is so pure that it seeks neither this nor that, but only
> to outgrow all its forms and hurry on to its primitive purity?[241]

This conclusion is referred to the beginning, to the God who
created the soul without using physical means (*on mittel*). It
was likely the specific phrase *on mittel*, understood in a distinctly Schwenkfeldian manner, which attracted Sudermann to
the sermon in the first place. Depicting the mystic way in alchemical terms but ultimately concerned with the return of
the human soul to its creator, the passage recalled to his mind
another corroborating piece:

> Just as all creatures have no peace until they have reached their
> natural perfection, so the loving faithful soul has no peace in the
> whole world until it returns to God, its origin.[242]

The latter passage Sudermann placed at the foot of a poem in his *Fünffzig Schöner auszerlesener sinnreicher Figuren...* which was inspired by the selection from the Eckhart sermon. The first part of his poem merely reworked the image already noted in that sermon.

The envoy to the poem changed the emphasis of the original, however. Whereas both the passages from the sermon and that which he printed at the foot of the poem were intended to be understood as describing mystical progress through purgation to illumination and union, Sudermann, building on Schwenckfeld's christology. is ultimately concerned with the very practical affairs of the Christian life. For Sudermann, too, individuals are to purify themselves under the direction of the inner knowledge of Christ (*Erkenntniss Christi*), to live in imitation of Christ's earthly and perfect life and, thereby, to become like him. It is in this way, for him, that they return to their origin, both partially now and finally in resurrected bodies. His conclusion to the poem under discussion is to be understood within this theological framework.

> Consider this example; it is true and certain. Leave all things in this life so that you might come once again to God, your true beginning, eternity, and highest perfection. Follow Christ. He is the Way, the Truth, and the ladder of life. By living under the cross and suffering in this life, you will gain joy in the next.[243]

Similarly, a piece in his *Schöne Auszerlesene Figuren... Das II. Theil* is based on a section from a medieval sermon 'Vff Johannis Baptiste geburt.' For his readers Sudermann printed the section below the poem:

> A Godly person should close his or her eyes to all passing things, and lock the inner mind against all deadly fear. Such a person should turn all thoughts inward, be silent and hear what God says. One should lift oneself above oneself. One should be a mirror of the divine image, fill one's soul with the form of the divine and see the light in the divine light. Indeed, one should become the light in the light. One should have no more in this world than the body, should always have a new beginning, that is, always live in new knowledge. One should always have an experience of eternity.[244]

Sudermann has taken few major liberties with the text beyond the slight modernising necessary for the seventeenth-century reader. The poem based on the passage, however, makes specific his practical concerns which arise from this, and thereby significantly changes its direction.

> One who wishes to understand God's teaching correctly must leave oneself and step above all creatures for God works only in a pure

soul. One must gather oneself inwardly and lock oneself off from all the sorrows and concerns of this world. The person who wishes to hear God's word correctly, must climb quickly to the mountain top, as Christ did, and learn as he did in the wilderness. There one will know nothing but God alone and realise one's own poor creatureliness. What is high is near to God and distant from the sorrow and troubles of the world.[245]

The section from the sermon is intended by its author to be understood within the framework of mystical ascent. In it, as in the entire sermon from which it is taken, the emphasis falls on the progress *ad interiora* which continues until the soul becomes the light in the light after waiting in silence on the word of God. It is a progress to a purely personal experience of God which becomes itself a prelude to eternity. Sudermann's poem, on the other hand, teaches that it is for the Christian who wishes to understand the teaching of God. For such an understanding one must of necessity rise above one's own self-centredness, the seductions of earthly delight, and, having gathered one's inner life about one centre, shortly to be associated with the person of Christ, one must lay aside all vain fleshly concerns. Sudermann's concern, like that of the author of the sermon, is to hear the divine word, but their understandings of this word are quite different. One of the changes made by Sudermann from the text of the Basel edition in his quotation of it is noteworthy. The sermon advises 'Er sol schweygen vnnd hören was gott in im sprech.'[246] Sudermann has changed *sprech* (speaks) to *redt* (counsels), and in his poem he emphasises right hearing (*recht hören*). By 'hearing,' here, is implied obedience to God's directions in a given personal issue. To achieve such enlightenment one must imitate the life of Christ. Only by such an action can earthly obstacles to understanding be overcome and worldly temptation conquered. In this experience a person comes to a new comprehension of the relationship between oneself and God. God's divine purity will then be discerned as will paltry human creatureliness. The sermon which Sudermann in his quotation faithfully repeats, says that there will then happen, because of this progress to the light, an essential change in the human situation: the soul will, in the light, become the light (*er sol werden das liecht in dem liecht*). But this statement, with its possibly pantheistic implications, is hardly hinted at in the last lines of the poem.

That Sudermann notes in the marginalia that the poem is to be read with Book III of the *Imitation of Christ* in mind emphasises this point. Book III treats of internal consolation for a Christian contending with a love of self and of earthly joys. For the medieval author of the sermon, the ascetic life was only the beginning of the ascent to the mystical experience; but for Sudermann ascetic life was an end in itself, the means by which divine counsel was attainable, counsel which seems only to encourage one to live the ascetic life. Sudermann's thrust is particularly clear in a poem he placed at the beginning of one of his manuscript collections of poems:

> As soon as God himself in the Holy Spirit teaches the sinner and correctly gives direction, the sinner must leave all human teaching, spirit, and flesh, and not consider his own motives any longer. Thus such a person will be rejected on this earth by all, and will find Christ as one's holiness, not without a cross, throughout life.[247]

In Sudermann's work, then, as in Schwenckfeld's, late medieval mystical texts and imagery are most often used to describe the *unio mystica* between every believer and Christ, and the life of love in Christ, in much the same way as they are in Luther's writing. However, greater importance is placed on the moral implications of the *unio* in Schwenkfeldianism. For Schwenckfeld and Sudermann, the union is one which results from a renovation of the believer and is directed toward greater renovation. Justification, for them, is not forensic, as in Lutheranism, but essential, and the Christian life of love is therefore emphasised as necessary for salvation. The seed of faith, Christ's glorified flesh planted at conversion, is to grow to perfection.

Yet, Schwenckfeld did not suggest that full growth was possible for the *viator*, and even his more mystically inclined followers such as Sudermann are free of such teaching. There is no possibility of a complete union of essences or of wills between the believer and the divine until the judgement, resurrection, and glorification of all the elect. Nevertheless, Sudermann, unlike Schwenckfeld, expected that the *unio mystica* in faith would develop in love for God. As it did, the mature believer would come to know more clearly the will of God and would follow it; in this way, there was a union of wills. At the same time the believer might experience the working of grace more fully in a personal love for God and in the abnegation of earthly lusts; in this experience the believer might be transported in joy. This aspect of Sudermann's thought is most fully described in his *Hohe Geistreiche Lehren*, the poetic commentary on the Song of Songs which Arnold rewrote and partially edited in his *Poetische Lob- und Liebes Sprüche*.

The first poem of the *Hohe Geistreiche Lehren* reflects well Sudermann's technique throughout the work.[248] It was inspired, he points out, by Bernard's comments on the Song of Songs, 1:2. 'Let him kiss me with the kisses of his mouth.' The kiss, he notes, quoting a Taulerian passage, is that of the Holy Spirit.[249] The pure soul desires to receive this kiss inwardly.

> The pure soul speaks inwardly to its betrothed: 'Let him kiss me with his gracious divine mouth.' Do you wish to know what the kiss is? It comes from Christ alone.[250]

The kiss has three characteristics. First, the soul is enraptured to such an extent that it is able to see the order of reality, created and recreated.[251] Secondly, God speaks in the soul and counsels it in its silence.[252] Thirdly, the soul experiences great sweetness.

> In this the soul's intellect is so overwhelmed with grace, so completely filled by it and unified with it, that it believes it has been in God for a time.[253]

Such joy lasts for only a moment,[254] but a single experience of it will strengthen the soul to bear carnal temptations.[255] Once again, the emphasis is on joy in a union consummated earlier and now experienced more fully. This experience floods the intellect, is beyond words, and makes one feel as if one is in God. In it one finds direction for one's life. In a similar way, the soul will be drawn into eternity by its bridegroom.[256]

It is this experience which Sudermann is describing in the near-pantheistic imagery of his third poem on this verse from the Song of Songs:

> Hear! When the soul receives a kiss from the Divinity and the light of the Divinity, it stands in perfection and eternal holiness. A divine embrace of unity will hang firmly to it. Then God will share his being with the soul, out of which it will have life; it will not have life elsewhere. Where God is, there the soul will remain with its essence and life, and, where the soul is characteristically, there also is God who preserves it.[257]

The kiss is the perfected experience of the soul's divinisation for Sudermann; it is, he believes, the work of the Holy Spirit in a person. This Spirit—Sudermann's anthropology, like Arnold's, is tripartite, not dualistic, like Schwenckfeld's—works in the human spirit.[258] It is in the soul at the new birth and must be allowed room for growth by the purgation of impurities, if either salvation or the experience of salvation is to be attained.

> If the believing soul wishes Christ to be its bridegroom, it must firmly develop within itself these four virtues: In the first case, it must have pure thoughts at all times—this is, of course, God's gift.... Secondly, it must always have pure, upright, and true love.... Thirdly, it must destroy all vice.... Finally, it must clothe itself with virtue. The soul will then receive a ring ... with three stones.... The first stone is the new birth, allowing it to live correctly.... The second stone is a pure heart and conversation in spirit, soul, and flesh, so that it and God might be united completely in faithfullness and love.... The third stone is an upright conscience throughout life.[259]

In Sudermann's thought, as in Schwenckfeld's, two movements within the soul are always evident. Firstly, the grace of God directs the growth of the new person toward the image of the glorified Christ. Secondly, the believer is required to cast off the trappings of the old person, thereby allowing the seed of faith to grow to its fullness. At the same time, a demand is made that the new person direct thoughts inward, toward the reality of the union one has in Christ. By doing so, the believer may experience the joy of new life, and learn more fully God's will. This latter demand is emphasised by Sudermann in a much more positive way than it is by Schwenckfeld. In the writings of Christian Hoburg (1607-1675), it is developed more systematically than in either Sudermann's, or Schwenckfeld's, writings.

Like Sudermann, Christian Hoburg was influenced directly by Schwenckfeld's writings. Although he died in the year Spener published the *Pia Desideria*, and thus preceded the movement, he had much in common with the Pietists, many of whom found value in his work. Arnold had a close knowledge of his publications, and through these, as well as through Sudermann's poems, he must have contacted mystical ideas. Late in 1643, Hoburg edited and wrote a preface to a German translation of the Pseudo-Taulerian *Institutiones*, which were known in their German translation as the *Medulla Tauleri*. This work Arnold may have seen in its original edition, but certainly knew in its reprinted form in 'Spener's' Tauler edition. The *Medulla*'s call for penitence and a renewed life of virtue fitted well into Hoburg's system, a system described

most fully in his *Theologia Mystica*. A second influential work
by Hoburg, the *Postilla Mystica*, contains much corroborating
material.[260]

For Hoburg, justification is granted in faith and effects a
mystical union between the believer and Christ.[261] The believer
is to increase in knowledge of the reality of this union, and in
moral direction gained through it.[262] The life of repentance for
past sins (*Busse*) is equated with purgation by Hoburg in the
first part of his *Theologia Mystica*.[263] In the second section he
describes the illuminative way of the Christian's life. This way
leads to the new birth, and the union of the believer with the
bridegroom, Christ, and the church.[264] In spite of the traditional three-fold order, however, Johann Arndt's *ordo* is the
principal influence in shaping Hoburg's theology in these first
two parts, and it is present in an important way in his third
part, that on the unitive life. The unitive life for Hoburg, as
for Sudermann before him, and for Arndt, is the life of every believer, not of a select few.[265] In it, the believer turns
from falsehood and the multiplicity of life,[266] from impure crea-
turely lusts,[267] to know and love the Spirit's life within.[268] The
unitive life must be daily renewed.[269] On this the Fathers have
insisted.[270] Such a life is hindered by any sinful actions.[271] The
union spoken of is a union in Christ alone,[272] a union lived in
and by his power.[273] As the mind of the believer is directed
toward it, the believer learns more and more to live in accordance with God's directives, to be closely united with the will
of God, and to love his will.[274] In this way the believer more
fully experiences the union granted in faith.[275]

Hoburg and Arndt have much in common, and it is easily
seen how Pietists, with their love of the *Wahres Christentum*,
found Hoburg's work, as well, to their liking. With Arndt,
Hoburg places great emphasis on the role of grace; his work
is completely Christocentric, and he insists on the principle
of justification through faith. With Arndt, also, he emphasises
the need for repentance (*Busse*), the new birth (*Wiedergeburt*),
and a renovated life of love in the believer. Likewise, Hoburg
follows Arndt's *ordo salutis* closely, but he highlights experiential religion in a way Arndt does not. Like Arnold after him,
Hoburg builds on those passages in which Arndt discusses religious experience, suggesting that ecstatic love necessarily be

experienced in and by the believer, or that, at the least, a believer must attempt to achieve such an experience. There are other differences between Arndt and Hoburg, as well. Hoburg's Schwenkfeldian interests led him to neglect the doctrine of forensic justification, and, with Sudermann, to point to the moral directives available to the believer who looked inward. In this approach to morality he and Sudermann were followed closely by Arnold.

c. Sudermann, Arnold, and Medieval Sources

While he was composing the second half of the *Kirchen- und Ketzer-Historie*, Arnold became acquainted with Sudermann.[276] Whether he saw the complete Sudermann collection of medieval manuscripts is not certain, but they were close to him in Berlin.[277] Of all Sudermann's poetry, Arnold was best acquainted with the *Hohe Geistreiche Lehren*. The first sixty-three folios of that work, each commenting on a verse from the Song of Songs, contain some one hundred and fifty poems, as many lengthy prose passages selected from earlier medieval authors, and hundreds of Scripture references and minor citations to other works. Unfortunately, Sudermann never gave specific references, other than to note the name of the author cited—Augustine, Bernard, Eckhart, Tauler, or Suso. In most cases, he is satisfied to describe his source as 'an old teacher' or simply 'a teacher.' But whatever their source, these annotations and the poems they accompanied impressed Arnold for their value as aids in spiritual direction, and with this pastoral need in mind, he rewrote a majority of the poems, following the format of Sudermann's whole collection, and printed them together with a reprint of all the annotations in his *Poetische Lob- und Liebes-Sprüche*.[278]

Arnold followed his exemplar closely in its first forty-one poems, but thereafter, his reliance on the Sudermann text was slight.[279] In this latter half there is no indication that he went beyond Sudermann's poems themselves to their medieval exemplars, but there can be no doubt that the Schwenkfelder's work was a major factor in developing his interest in, and use of, medieval mystical texts.

Before investigating the implications of this for Arnold's poetry, the differences between Sudermann's theology and his own must be noted. In his poetic commentary on the Song of Songs 1:2 discussed above, for example, Sudermann did not take enough care to protect himself against the charge of Pelagianism or to reconsider vocabulary which, to his theological opponents, seemed pantheistic. Arnold was aware of these dangers in his exemplar and rewrote it accordingly. For him, the kiss is a sign of the new convenant made between God and the human person, rather than a gift necessarily sought, as Sudermann describes it.[280] For Arnold, it is more an assurance of salvation already gained than a greater degree of salvation itself.[281] By the experience of the kiss, according to Arnold, the soul discovers the life of God in itself and turns in greater love toward him.[282] Arnold describes this experience of union in language always reflecting the work of Christ in the believer.[283] Both Sudermann and Arnold consider the experience to be of short duration, but Arnold reworks Sudermann's portrayal of the joy continuing and growing after the moral insights have been given, by consoling the believer who cannot continually live in the full delight of assurance and finds himself or herself often in fear and pain;[284] in Arnold's poem, there is not the same expectation that if the believer turns aside from evil, he or she will gain the necessary directives to continue the ascetic life.[285] However, Sudermann's emphasis on the need for purity to obtain such an experience is similarly changed by Arnold, who highlights the work of grace in all acts of virtue and redirects the pantheistic implications in Sudermann's description of perfected unitive experience to serve as images of the way in which God's new life in the individual reflects his essence.

Parenthetically noting the role of grace in a believer's development, Sudermann had written that the unitive perfection to which one is called is rooted in the new birth, but that this birth is founded on pure thought, true love, progressive purgation, and the practice of virtue on the individual's part. It is expected, in addition, that a person born to new life will live in greater purity and develop a more upright conscience. Arnold, rewriting this poem, founds all achievement completely on the life of Christ within the believer.

> Jesus, adorn me for your wedding joy with a pure clean heart of sense and thought, with unmixed love no longer to turn from you, with freedom from sin, and with a cloak of innocence. After this you must give me the ring of betrothal which shines with three stones, and which is you, yourself.... I beg all of this from you Lord, and if

I achieve it soon, it is of faith....[286]

Sudermann's near pantheistic description of the believer's life in God is changed by Arnold, as follows, to describe the *unio mystica* of the believer in Christ:

> When the Divinity itself kisses the ground of my soul, I stand fully on the rung of perfection. God gives his being to me; for it I have hungered. He comes near with his incorruptibility to my inmost self. In short where God stands, there my life has footing, and where I am, the Divinity allows itself to be seen.[287]

In all these changes Arnold is defending himself against the charge of Spiritualism, for, although both he and Sudermann are interested in the practical moral results of the *unio*, and although both describe that union in medieval mystical terms, Arnold, as a Lutheran, insists on forensic justification and the role of grace in all good works, before and after the salvific act of faith.

How far the Baroque practice of poetically paraphrasing earlier authors and the example of Sudermann directly influenced Arnold to make use of medieval mystical texts in his poetry cannot be fully ascertained. Many conceits on which he built his poems appear in writings other than those of medieval authors as well as in them. Most of these conceits are commonplaces, however, were in general use in Arnold's day, and would, in all likelihood, have been brought to his attention by contemporary texts. In the *Neue Göttliche Liebes-Funcken*, for example, Arnold admits that over three-quarters of his poems were inspired by other authors,[288] but no direct relationship between any of them and late medieval writings has been established.

A closer dependency on medieval authors is more likely in the case of two groups of poems in the second half of the *Poetische Lob- und Liebes-Sprüche*, but it is unlikely that Arnold is the author of either. Both appear in a section which contains many pieces which are admittedly not by him, and both exhibit a style and vocabulary not his.[289] The first of these is entitled 'Vertrauliche Unterredung der Göttlichen Weiszheit';[290] it precedes a similar piece which Arnold says was inspired by a modern writer.[291] This suggests that the first poem was written at an earlier time. In its introduction and conclusion, as well as at several other points, the reader is reminded of passages in Suso's *Buchlein der Ewigen Wahrheit* and *Vita*. The author may have had these volumes at hand while he was working with the poem, but all parallels between the medieval and seventeenth century author are tenuous.[292] The relationships that can be documented between a second poem printed by Arnold, the 'Geheime Lauber-Hütten Fest,'[293] and Ruusbroec's *Van den Gheesteliken Tabernakel* are even more tenuous.[294]

But whether or not these latter pieces are directly influenced by medieval material, Arnold was attracted by such writing in the work of Sudermann. The *Poetische Lob- und Liebes-Sprüche* is the first indication of how seriously he was turning his attention to medieval spirituality, an action furthered significantly in his editorial work done during the same year as he was composing his most significant poetry.

Chapter Five:
Arnold's Editorial Use
of Late Medieval Texts

The speed with which Arnold's interest in late medieval texts developed after his first contacts with them is noteworthy. The weaknesses in the *Kirchen- und Ketzer-Historie*'s treatment of late medieval spirituality are obvious. Writers are discussed there in almost all cases not for their own value, but solely for their historiographic use as witnesses to the corruption of institutional Christianity. Omissions of important authors are many, and the mark of secondary sources is clear throughout the medieval section in particular. Nor are these shortcomings remedied by Arnold in his *Poetische Lob- und Liebes-Sprüche*, for which he had some texts from fourteenth-century German mystics directly available to him. Although his poetic interests indicate his contact with primary sources for the study of medieval spirituality, there is no clear indication that Arnold was fully open to their theology, and he continued to rewrite their thought for his own purposes. However, his purposes had broadened somewhat after the *Kirchen- und Ketzer-Historie*. Following its publication the pastoral value of medieval texts became rapidly evident to him, and in the same year as the *Poetische Lob- und Liebes-Sprüche* appeared, Arnold published an edition of the *Vitae Patrum* which contained a large amount of material edited from late medieval sources. His bulky *Leben der Gläubigen* of 1701 also contained medieval lives and treatises, and in the same year he published a German translation of Ruusbroec's works and was at work on a history and defence of mystical theology. The latter volume which appeared two years later contained an extensive discussion of the medieval period.

a. The Problem of Arnold's Separatism

Although Arnold's theological position was similar to that of his contemporary Lutheran Pietist brethren, his separatistic rhetoric prior to September of 1701 has been pointed to as proof of his total rejection of established religion at that time. This charge of separatism, however, must be examined in the full context of Arnold's life and thought.

Arnold's sharpest criticisms of the organised church were written between his resignation at Giessen in 1698 and his marriage in 1701. Many of his words and actions during this period were instigated within the framework of local Quedlinburg politics; they did not have broader theological significance for him. Political turmoil in the seventeenth century inevitably involved the religious institutions. In Quedlinburg Arnold and his colleagues supported the territorial demands of Brandenburg against those of the Saxon government. His refusal to attend regular religious services must be interpreted, then, not only as the act of an individual who rejected certain principles of organised church life but also as one who rejected the political and social interests represented by a local pastoral leadership which supported the Saxon claims to the town. It may not have been primarily initiated by theological premises, but intended as a condemnation of the quality of pastoral care in the community.

Any notion of a distinct separatistic period in Arnold's life must also be rejected. The year 1698 did not mark the beginning of Arnold's antagonisms to the religious authorities in Quedlinburg or of his attacks on them. He had been indicted as early as 1695, yet at that time he had been accepted as a loyal, orthodox Lutheran by Spener, Francke, and those who invited him to Giessen.[1] Even so fierce an antagonist as Coler considered Arnold's *Die Erste Liebe* orthodox.[2] There is nothing in that volume which indicates a conscious rejection of the established church. Its comments on Babel are directed to non-believers or hypocrites within Christendom, not against the Lutheran church as an institution.[3] Nor are his marriage and his acceptance of a pastorate a rejection of all that had gone before. Attacks on the evils of religious institutionalism continue after that time, as do his defences of earlier activity.

The clearest examples of Arnold's separatistic rhetoric are found in his short *Zeugen der Wahrheit* (1698), which was published again in 1700 under the title *Wahrnehmung jetziger Zeiten*.[4] The work is of special interest for present purposes because it offers not only a proper context for the interpretation of Arnold's separatistic statements, but presents as well a theological model influenced by mystical ideals, some of which he might have culled from medieval sources.

The fallen individual's physical eyes, Arnold writes, look outward to the world,[5] not within to God, the true good. As fallen, the individual turns from the one to the many.

> This occurs first through one's fall from one's only good, the Creator. In one's heart one goes out from the one to the many. One reaches after as many as a thousand creatures in one's desires, instead of God in whom one would have eternal fulfillment, and one cannot be satisfied. The eternal immortal being of the soul can never rest assured in the nothingness of the creature. It seeks ever further and wishes to obtain ever more possessions. It is like a fire which burns on without end. It does so because it is removed and far from its own true element and life, which is God himself.[6]

The soul is deceived by the creatures it reaches out to, and, as a result, it spends its time in useless endeavours.[7]

In the pastorally motivated passages which follow the description of fallen humanity, Arnold endeavours to encourage the erring sinner. God chooses and renews the soul through Christ, he points out.[8] The individual is made by God and is loved by him simply because of human nature.[9] Arnold is not negating the role of grace nor is he teaching pantheism. The individual is saved by faith alone. Faith comes from hearing the call of God in the Scriptures and the chancel.[10] It is against this background of an outer word that Arnold's major emphasis on the illumination of the inner word, and his insistence that every person, having experienced the wrath of God, turn toward the inner word, is built.[11] Arnold here again followed the normal pattern of the *ordo*. Having discussed election, vocation, illumination, and conversion, he proceeds, as expected, to regeneration,[12] and justification.[13] The *unio mystica*, too, grows from faith, and a new renovated person develops accordingly.

> Christ himself who earlier knocked at the door ... and made you humble, hereafter will enter in. He will not only dwell in you through faith, but will also root and ground himself firmly through love. In this union you will have communion with him and his Father and with all the living members of his blessed body.
>
> Then he will bring your new-born spirit close to himself and hold his supper with you internally.... The new being in you will receive a new mouth of faith with which one will be able to eat the flesh of the Son of Man and drink his blood.[14]

Renovation is the reclothing of the believer. Through it the old Adam is put off and the new person shines before God.[15] It is only necessary that one die to oneself and the world, begin in repentance, and continue therein. Freedom of the will is granted the Christian to give himself or herself to this task.[16] One may then progressively improve, and the evil within will continually die.[17] The new person experiences the marks of the Holy Spirit: love, peace, and joy. All things serve such a person; all lead him or her nearer to the grace of Jesus.[18] The outer eye tends to be used less, the inner is progressively renewed, and the Christian may experience ever more the grace which has been granted. 'Your inner sight will see in the Spirit, without end, the marks of grace and the promise of peace.'[19]

Striving to break down this divine work and to stall renovation, the Devil will bring persecution to bear.[20] He cannot be victorious. Against all odds, God will defend and prepare his people to serve the eternal Gospel.[21] He teaches by visions and deeper experience of the mystical union,[22] so that Christians may know the truth beyond the physical trappings of religious structures.

> Then the essence of divine goodness itself will come, when the shadows and images of ceremonies and human productions have held sway and souls have rested in eternal Levitical righteousness and have been satisfied with part. But they will possess Christ in his fullness as he is made in them by the Father.
>
> He will be their full wisdom so that no brother will be able to teach more to another. He will be for them their essential righteousness, the righteousness of God himself, since he is one with them. Thus, since they have put on Christ ... he will become their complete holiness so that no one need any longer seek it in imperfection and in hypocrisy. He will also be their perfection.... They shall not always remain children as earlier.... Christ will live in them with his essential fullness and will give his members infinite growth.[23]

It is following this discussion of the Christ living within and the experience of the mystical union beyond ceremony, sacrament, and work, that Arnold develops his criticism of the church of his day. Against such a goal of perfection, those who hold to the empty forms of religious life are hypocrites[24] and Judaisers.[25] They have made Christ's words heresy in their schools.[26] They have corrupted his Gospel with outward ceremonies. True Christians are to separate themselves from such activities. They must divide Christ from Beliel and turn to the

Christ within.[27] Only by being certain that he is within and alive, can one have peace.

Arnold's separatistic words were not those of the sectarians. He was not calling for a rejection of Lutheranism or its replacement by a purified community or brotherhood. For him, structures were to be transcended by inner life, the shape of which he described in terms owing much to the *Spiritual Guide* of Molinos, which he edited and published in 1699, and to the homilies of Macarius which he reprinted, with additional Patristic material, in the same year. Yet Arnold did not believe that these structures were to be frivolously cast aside. Nor were his words directed against those who upheld the value of such structures. They were intended rather to be warnings to those hypocrites who set the ceremonial, legal, and doctrinal aspects of Christian teaching above the practical activities of Christian life.

Other statements of Arnold on the same theme must be similarly interpreted. Thus, in his poem 'Babels Grablied,' which appeared in his first collection of poetry in 1698,[28] he lashed out against the evil of his day in terms which might lead one to believe he was calling for a rejection of all church forms. The poem may be read to prove Arnold's totally separatistic position, but it must be noted first and foremost that it is based on a concern with the inner Babel in each person, not the exterior Babel. It is founded on the subjective and not the objective aspect of the Babel theme. 'See to it,' he writes, 'that Babel is completely broken in yourself first; do not be hypocritical.'[29] The poem's detailed description of the contagious disease in the ecclesiastical body,[30] the loud call for the rejection of Babel,[31] and all of Arnold's other separatistic statements must be interpreted with this personal, individualistic, and not institutional emphasis in mind.

b. Medieval Admonitions on Solitude

Such individualism, governed Arnold's thought and life. The Pietist demand that each person cast off evil in the Christian community and in his or her own life was predominant in his work. It controlled his separatistic rhetoric and his use of late medieval texts with their emphasis on abnegation. Within his society, Arnold could use these texts to direct believers away

from sinful life, that is, for Arnold, away from scholastic theology and a religion which did not extend beyond empty ceremony. But the fullest and best use which could be made of
them was their application in pastoral care to admonish the
same believers to cast off personal sins.

The practical implications of Arnold's individualism are of
special interest. As a young graduate, he was faced with a
problematic vocational choice. Primarily concerned with pastoral care, he found himself unable to accept a clerical position because of the corruption he saw in the church of his day.
The work of a scholar-teacher might serve equally well, he believed, in improving the quality of Christian life. Scholarship
had its own temptations, however. At Giessen, where Arnold
had gone to carry out serious study for the reform of established Christianity in line with his pastoral concerns, he was
troubled with the implications of his choice of career. His resignation of the Giessen professorship was not a rejection of the
institutional Christian framework, but the reaction of a scrupulous Christian concerned with his own spiritual growth in the
face of scholarly pride, dismayed with contemporary religious
structures, and disillusioned in his belief that renewal might
come through academic endeavours. Under such pressures he
was attracted to a life of solitude. His departure from Giessen
and his harsh attacks on the church are indicative not of his
movement away from institutional Christianity, but of a flight
from the pursuit of worldly vanities.

In the *Auserlesene Send-Schreiben*, printed in 1700, as
in his earlier work, Arnold's central interest is in the early
Christian period, but medieval texts are well represented.
One-fifth of the Patristic letters edited in it are by Nilus.[32]
Other authors included are Ignatius,[33] Cyprian,[34] Anthony,[35]
Basil the Great,[36] Augustine,[37] Paulinus of Nola,[38] Synesius
of Cyrene,[39] and Ephraem of Syria;[40] some martyr acts are
also included.[41] Appended to the volume are approximately
sixty pages of seventeenth-century French, Dutch, and English
spiritual materials.[42]

Arnold's pastoral intentions in publishing the work are
made clear in his 'Erinnerung' to it. Its purpose is to make
people more fruitful.

> The purpose of these and all other spiritual writings can be none
> other than chiefly knowledge of the pure will of God concerning the

salvation of the individual and the simple obedience of faith arising
from it with all its salvific fruits and holiness, to the praise and
honour of the name of our God through Jesus in the Holy Ghost.[43]

The gifts of the Holy Spirit lead believers to praise. The letters are 'short histories of the inner lives of Christians'[44] and
thus serve as examples for believers. Christ is the only way
to full life, Arnold states. His directives in the texts printed,
will be evident to the enlightened reader.[45] In keeping with
Arnold's earlier work, the theme of martyrdom is also strongly
emphasised,[46] but it is the contention of the *Auserlesene Send-
Schreiben* that persecution and suffering are no longer the sole
marks of true Christians. True Christians are now seen as believers who live in solitude and total resignation.[47] All of the
Nilus letters are chosen to support this theme, as are those by
Basil, Augustine, and Paulinus of Nola. The theme also dic-
tated the selection of a majority of the Bernard letters,[48] many
more of which Arnold would have printed, he writes, had space
been available.[49]

To represent the late Middle Ages, Arnold chose letters by
Ruusbroec, Suso, and à Kempis. Of these Ruusbroec receives
the greatest attention. Arnold uses three pages of his introduction to discuss this author; to no other writer does he dedicate
so much space. His whole discussion is devoted to a defence of
the medieval mystic. Quotations from major Roman Catholic
and Protestant authors in support of his piety are added.[50]
With the exception of the second, all of Ruusbroec's letters
are accurately reprinted from G.J.C.'s German translation of
the Surius Latin edition, the translation which Arnold edited
the following year.[51] With Suso, Arnold is much more selective.
From the Surius' Latin edition, Arnold used German translations of only six letters of the mystic's work; from Thomas
à Kempis, three letters are printed.[52] On à Kempis himself,
Arnold adds little of interest.[53]

The large amount of space Arnold devoted to printing medieval texts is noteworthy. His interest in the life of solitude
again seems to have governed his selections from Ruusbroec,
Suso, and à Kempis, as it did his choice of earlier pieces. Solitude, for Arnold, meant inner solitude. For him the Christian
is called first of all to live inwardly, that is, to cast off the
evils of the old person and to focus attention on personal, spiritual growth. Ruusbroec's admonition to Margaret Meerbeck

as published by Arnold was in keeping with his Pietist purposes:

> If you wish now to strive after true life, you must give yourself over
> willingly in all difficulties and deny all disorderly desires. Then love
> itself will teach you all truth, and turn from, and drive off, through
> the power of the Lord, everything which stands against them. Love
> is the root and fruit of all virtue. The practice of love is founded
> on self-denial.[54]

Ruusbroec wrote these words to one who had chosen the contemplative, rather than the active life. Fully a Protestant,
Arnold understood such counsel as necessary for every believer in the same way as he understood mystical terminology as describing the union which each believer has with
Christ. The contemplative life, too, was democratised in
Protestantism; both counsels and precepts were to be followed
by all Christians.[55] All the texts printed by Arnold are to be interpreted accordingly. The demand, on Arnold's part, that all
Christians live a contemplative life lies at the basis of his ethical
rigorism. All believers are expected to develop toward relative
perfection if God has saved them even though such an endeavour never merits anything for them or changes their status
before a righteous God in any way. Those who do not so work
and pretend to be Christians, are hypocrites. A distinction is,
therefore, made between true Christians and false Christians
(*Die Erste Liebe*), true and false church (*Kirchen- und Ketzer-
Historie*), true Wisdom and false Wisdom (*Das Geheimnisz
der Göttlichen Sophia*), and true mystical theology and false
scholastic theology (*Historie und Beschreibung der Mystischen
Theologie*). Working within this dualism, Arnold had come
to classify Christian contemplatives of an earlier age with the
true Christians as witnesses to the evangelical truth. It is not
surprising that, faced with the decisions he had to make at
Giessen, he was drawn to these same Christian solitaries. Their
writings, printed in the *Auserlesene Send-Schreiben*, offered direction for his own life at the time as well as for the lives of
all his contemporary Christians. The *vitae* provided not only
examples, but defences, for his own withdrawal from active
institutions.

c. Medieval Descriptions of the Solitary Life

While Arnold was working on his *Auserlesene Send-Schreib-*

en, he was also completing an edition of the *Vitae Patrum* based on George Major's earlier edition, to which were appended a number of medieval lives.[56] Francke wrote the 'Zuschrift' to Arnold's edition, and in it, he reiterated themes common both to his own writings and to Arnold's.[57] Emphasis is placed on the practical effects of spiritual writing and on the need for spiritually-enlightened readers.[58] These points are developed further in Arnold's 'Anleitung,' but his major interest is in the life of solitude. Arnold's emphasis is Christocentric;[59] despite the fact that the *Sophia* was published the same year, no note of Boehmist influence can be traced in the *Vitae Patrum*. The volume is not for those who are pretending Christian life by practising empty formal rituals.[60] It is for those Christians who have either received the spirit of discretion or are still seeking it,[61] who in simple faith wait to fulfill the teaching of the Spirit.[62] The spirit alone will aid in distinguishing the true way from the false, self righteousness from Godliness, or, in Spener's terms, nature from grace.[63] In this Arnold differs not at all from the Pietism of his day, but the possibilities for a higher form of perfection in love, for a progressively developing restoration of the image of God in the individual,[64] are enunciated more clearly.

> [One must understand] the complete path of the restoration of our fallen nature as it is directed, sealed, applied, and made perfect *in faith according to the word of God by the Holy Spirit* in divine harmony.
>
> One may ask how this truth of the evangelical faith and assurance of it comes into reality. The answer is found in the words of Jesus and is briefly stated as follows: through prayer, striving, appropriation, and use. To this and by these means the Holy Spirit will grant the seeker enough light and strength to know and decide concerning what must be endured, done, and shunned at each moment of the day. If a person follows this divine guidance in his or her heart ever more earnestly and devotes himself or herself (forgetting all else) fully to the Lord Christ, to live and to die with Him in love, this Shepherd will give that person all that is needed. (italics mine)[65]

To such a seeker, the spirit of discretion is granted, and by it one can distinguish outward forms, be they of a hermitage or a Lutheran parish, from inner realities. But the Spirit speaks inwardly, and in that direction one is to look. To this end, not to the exterior forms of the contemplative life, the lives of the Christians in the *Vitae Patrum* direct the believer.[66]

All persons are to turn inward, but not all, Arnold insists, are called out from the struggles of active life to the life of a hermitage. Noting that for some the cloister is a hazard to righteous living,[67] Arnold adds that each person is called by God to one form of life or the other, that is, to a life lived actively in society, or one passed in solitude. To whichever of these two a believer is called, the believer must be contemplative; in whichever situation one finds oneself, one is to be continuously concerned with prayer and praise. The life in society and that in solitude are both opposed to the life of the hypocrites who pretend to grow in grace but who do not, in fact, do so.[68]

In all this Arnold follows Protestant principles. Where he differs from Protestant practice is in his defence of a Christian life of solitude. One feature which distinguishes Protestantism, until the advent of Pietism, from Catholicism is its rejection of contemplative institutions and its reduction of all contemplative ideals to the needs of the active life. This is best exemplified by Luther's use of an Augustinian monastary to house his family.[69] Even the Anabaptists, who seem to have looked to the forms of medieval contemplative institutions as models for their own religious communities, were antagonistic to the principles on which those medieval institutions operated.[70] Arnold's introduction to the *Vitae Patrum* is the first major attempt within continental Protestantism to seriously defend the monastic life.[71] Among true persons of faith, he therefore suggests, Christians of deeper spirituality will set themselves off from society. He is willing to admit that the dangers of pretence are as great among the solitaries as among Christians living in society,[72] but he insists, as well, on the importance of the life of solitude as equally great. It provides examples of strength for the weak, and the prayers of solitary Christians are offered for the good of all men.

> Enlightened minds ... do not seek Christianity in external form, yet they warn individuals not to disparage their [solitary] pattern of life, nor to cast aside the whole matter for any special reason.... They point out ... to the unpracticed and weak how in the true solitary life there is... an intensive work in continual striving and praying for all. It is the more blessed and certain, the farther it is from the view of humankind.
>
> And again it is written: 'We went to the desert as true warriors and workers of Christ, so that with our brothers we might learn to strive and fight against the evil powers, to strive boldly against inordinate desires.'[73]

Those who choose a life of retirement are not to be attacked. It is important that one first eradicate sin from oneself, before undertaking corporal works of mercy. In this respect, a life of solitude can serve a noble end.[74] It is spiritually healthy to leave the tumult of life and seek divine purity alone.[75]

The act of retirement will not be understood, Arnold believes, by hypocritical pharisaic Christians, although among such it is even more necessary.[76] It is, in fact, supported by Luther himself,[77] as well as by other Protestants, not to mention such medieval writers as Thomas à Kempis.[78]

For Arnold, as already noted, the ends of the life of solitude and that of the active life are the same: a return to the simplicity of love in Christ.[79] Although both lives have the same goal, the life of solitude is the better. It avoids the minor cares and distractions of the active life[80] and provides a physical example of the kind of detachment (*Gelassenheit*) necessary for spiritual well-being. Dying unto goods is a way of dying unto self-will.

The life of solitude begins to destroy evil in the individual,[81] but it does not leave aside works of love or concern for earthly life. In his exegesis of the Martha-Mary story, Arnold insists that both women are contemplative and active—both lead to a middle way.[82] Works of love are necessary even for the solitary;[83] the solitary life may be the better of the two forms of life, but it is not the only one, and one ought not to feel guilty if not called to it. Only external things which hinder spiritual conversion and growth are to be cast aside.[84] Nevertheless, one ought not to remain weak all one's life, but ought to practise piety and grow in it after the example of the solitary[85] and, fulfilling that example, find perfect discretion, which not only enables one to distinguish true and false in stories such as follow in the texts printed in the *Vitae Patrum*, but facilitates the discovery of the same truth or falsity in the religious life of one's contemporaries.[86] Above all, however, this discretion is to be used to distinguish the self-love and self-justification within the believer, and to give the believer the strength to reject it.[87]

While Arnold's defence of the life of solitude is immediately evident to the reader of his works, what he understood as comprising the form or content of that life is not. Certainly,

he expected a solitary to be celibate, but beyond this, it is
difficult to determine his conception. He seems to have made
no attempt to establish a Protestant monastic community as
did some of his contemporaries and followers, notably Johann
Conrad Beissel (1690-1766) who established in Pennsylvania
the first significant German Protestant monastic community,
the Ephrata Cloister.[88] Arnold's thought influenced Beissel
greatly. In Beissel one can perhaps best see the practical implications of Arnold's thought as reflected in the introduction to
the *Vitae Patrum*, for, like Arnold, Beissel was concerned that
the solitary not be completely cut off from more normal social intercourse with married believers. At the Sproegel home,
Arnold in all likelihood remained as much to himself as possible, devoting his time to private meditation and prayer, but he
was deeply involved in the turmoil which troubled the Sproegel
group. Lacking political acumen, he was not likely to organise
a contemplative institution, but in the midst of the difficulties
which faced him and his friends, he must have yearned many
times to enter such a retreat.[89]

Arnold opens his historical introduction to the *Vitae Patrum* emphasising once again the battle taking place between
true and pretended Christianity. Theologians of the Schools
will mock the stories in the *Vitae*, he states, but they are on
poor ground.[90] The lives in the volume are edifying for all true
believers, and their value for Christian life is witnessed to by
both Patristic[91] and Protestant scholars.[92] They are useful;[93]
they do not support novelties but are of the ancient truth.[94]
Arnold offers no detailed information regarding the provenance
of the work,[95] but is concerned that the best edition and most
scholarly translation be available so that the solitaries' lives
might be most clearly described.[96]

In his attempt to reestablish within Protestantism a distinctive role for the life of solitude and to justify his own search
at the time, Arnold called upon the examples of the great solitaries of history. Among the medievals he gives some attention
to Bernard of Clairvaux and Thomas Aquinas,[97] but the major
amount of space is devoted to fourteenth and fifteenth-century
German and Dutch mystics.

Had he had the time and space, Arnold writes, he would
have published notes on Richard Rolle[98] and Heinrich Suso,[99]

among others.   The first major figure he treats is Johann
Tauler, reprinting a German edition of the *Meisterbuch* published at Lüneburg in 1680 with some prefatory comments.[100]
The preface follows Arnold's normal pattern of apologetic.
Tauler, he notes, humbly suffered much through his life and
was visited by the divine.   He therefore deserves attention,
particularly since he was highly praised by great leaders of an
earlier period.

For information on Ruusbroec, Arnold refers readers of the
Vitae's introduction to his *Auserlesene Send-Schreiben*.[101] He
includes in his edition a translation of Pomerius' life, which was
made with the translation of G.J.C. at hand.[102] The final two-
thirds of the second part of the *Vitae*, the medieval section, are
accurate translations of the Thomas à Kempis' lives of Gerard
Groote, Florentius, and Arnold of Schoonhoven, and Francis
Tolensis' life of à Kempis.[103] The translation of Ruusbroec by
G.J.C. which Arnold had in his possession as early as 1700 was
published by him in 1701 with an introductory preface. Who
the translator was is not certain. The suggestion that the ini-
tials G.J.C. barely disguise the person of Gichtel, Johann Georg
is possible, particularly since Arnold came into possession of
the translation and printed it during the years in which he
was in continual association with the Boehmist teacher, but
it is more likely that it is the work of Georg Johann Conradi
as Kurt Aland has suggested.[104] Arnold's preface to the edition provides no new light either on Ruusbroec or on Arnold's
approach to medieval mysticism.[105] It reflects his approach to
medieval mystics during the period. He was drawn to them primarily out of pastoral concern. They are published as practical
guides to the spiritual life. The same spirit which inspired New
Testament and early Christianity inspired Ruusbroec, Arnold
believes, and this Spirit draws the enlightened reader to the
works of the Dutch spiritual master, so that the reader may
grow more fully in Christ. Indeed, only a reader enlightened by
the same Spirit can truly understand the directives in the text.
The worldly, scholastic hypocrites who approach it can never
gain such insights. Only after Arnold has made these points
does he attempt to justify Ruusbroec by quoting Protestant
and Roman Catholic recommendations of his work or by referring the reader to the medieval historical context.

d. The Broader Dimensions of Solitude

The *Leben der Gläubigen* of 1701 is much more than a simple, editorial sequel to the *Vitae Patrum*.[106] In its preface Arnold expands upon the theology he outlined in the introduction to his earlier work and displays in so doing the same personal concern with the texts under consideration. It is not surprising that he should let their message direct his life and thought. This was, after all, the demand he continually made of his readers.

At the close of his preface to the *Vitae*, he had already hinted at the direction his next work was to take and the necessary defence it would entail, for, in addition to the lives he added to the Patristic sources, which were acceptable to Lutheran readers, he included lives of medieval Catholics which were not acceptable.[107] Arnold defended their use according to the principles he had developed. The life of solitude is not always the best, he admitted; it can give way to pharisaism just as the active life can. What is to be defended is contemplation, and this is what the late medieval Catholics continued, despite the fall of their church.[108]

As he continued his study, he found late medieval mysticism giving birth to sixteenth-century Counter-Reformation mysticism in John of the Cross and Theresa of Avila. He was too knowledgeable a student of spirituality to be unaware that he was here in contact with masters of the spiritual life, and he could not, therefore, simply set them aside as deluded or not wise enough to convert from Catholicism. They did, after all, have a choice, whereas the medievals did not. In addition his own interests were at stake. He stood against the evil aspects of the church of his day as one of the solitary; he defended that position by association with the mystics of the past. He could not interpret them as disloyal members of the church of Rome, without accusing himself, in a parallel situation, of exactly the same disloyalty to Lutheranism. He avoided both problems by directing his attention to what he saw as the root of Christian life: The life of contemplation lived by all true members of Christ.

The bitterness against Rome one finds in Spener is not manifested in Arnold. God is no respecter of persons,[109] Arnold points out; the *Apology for the Augsburg Confession* as well

as Flacius Illyricus admit the continuation of Christian life in
the Catholic Church for the unseen spiritual church is present
in contemplative Christians among Roman Catholics as well as
among Protestants.[110] In his call to view the situation from the
point of view of the spiritual church, Arnold is obviously drawn
to the Spiritualists he had read so closely, but one must not
charge him with having entered their camp. His statement is
intended to be read within a Lutheran context. Luther himself
was the first to admit the primary importance of the spiritual church;[111] Arnold is building on this. He is not rejecting
Lutheranism in favour of a universal spiritual church, to which,
if a believer belongs, forms and doctrine make no difference. He
is convinced that Catholicism has its evils, and in his editing of
texts, according to his own testimony, he has deliberately ex-
punged some statements which support those evils.[112] The true
church of Christ exists in spite of these, but more important,
it leads beyond them.[113] It directs one to truth wherever truth
is manifested and in whatever church. Arnold is a Lutheran;
he accepts Protestant doctrine but is at the same time aware
of Protestant shortcomings. He too is willing to be led; it is
in this that his ecumenicity and, in fact, that of Pietism in
general, is to be understood. Christians are all concerned with
Christ's glory,[114] he insists throughout the rest of the preface;
all Christians are led by Christ's spirit[115] and must all strike
out against hypocrisy.[116]

The biographies in the *Leben der Gläubigen* were edited as
witnesses to the truth throughout the history of the Christian
church, and in Arnold, Spener's use of these as witnesses to
a particular type of truth within Lutheranism rather than to
Lutheran teaching against Catholicism is extended in a deeply
personal way. The lives of Christians in the past witness not
to the truth of a particular denominational standard but to
true, sincere contemplative Christian life set against Babel,
the hypocritical formal practices of established religious institutions. The words of the witnesses to the truth apply beyond
the boundaries of ecclesiastical structures; they are in the end
witnesses against the Babel within the believer's own life. This
is their primary purpose and Arnold, to support it, closes his
preface to the *Leben der Gläubigen* not unfittingly with a quotation from the *Theologia deutsch*:

> Therefore, although it be good and profitable that we should ask,
> and learn, and know what good and holy men have wrought and

suffered and how God hath dealt with them, yet it were a thousand
times better that we should in ourselves learn and understand who
we are, how and what our own life is, what God is and is doing
in us, what he will have from us, and to what ends he will or will
not make use of us.... Thus that proverb is still true, 'Going out
were never so good, but staying at home were much better,' [that
is, going into one's own heart and remaining there and learning to
know oneself and to test what is lacking. This is better than to look
to others and their examples.][117]

The quotation is not inconsistent with the publication of the
Leben der Gläubigen. The biographies in the volume are
printed so that readers might be stimulated to examine their
personal lives more closely. In the collection Arnold continued
his concern with the need for a revitalisation of the contemplative ideal and contemplative institutions by Protestants, but
his lengthy compilation of spiritual biographies contains only
two which treat medieval writers. A translation was printed of
the life of Angela of Foligno done from Poiret's reprint of the
Venice 1680 *Vitae Confessione maravigliosa della B. Angela
de Foligno*.[118] For some reason Arnold believed Angela was
a modern rather than a medieval writer. In the *Historie und
Beschreibung der Mystischen Theologie* as well, he included his
discussion of her among the sixteenth-century authors.[119]

Of greater interest for the present study is Arnold's in-
clusion of Nicolas von der Flue materials.   His principle
source for these was the edition of them by the Lutheran,
Johann Heinrich Ursinus, whose *Analectis Sacris* depended
on the earlier Neustadt anonymous text, *Vom Leben und
Lehr Puncten Bruder Nicolausen*.[120] Appended to this was
Eckhart's tract *Von Abgeschiedenheit* in a seventeenth-century
German revision,[121] which Arnold believed was written by
Nicolas and a brief life of Nicolas which centres interest
on the hermit's ascetic life, visions, and late entrance into
a hermitage.[122] Eckhart's comments on detachment suited
Arnold's thought at the time well. It contained themes which
had much in common with those of the Quietists and proto-
Quietists whose works he was editing at the time and offered
yet further inducement to support his position on the need for
a new approach to the contemplative life by Protestants.

Chapter Six:
The Culmination
of Arnold's Medieval Studies

What is immediately evident in a survey of Arnold's use of medieval spiritual texts is that once his attention had been directed to them by his research for the *Kirchen- und Ketzer-Historie* and his acquaintance with Quietist, Spiritualist, and Boehmist approaches to medieval mysticism, his interest in late medieval spirituality, quickened by his reading of Sudermann's poetry, blossomed in his editorial work of 1700-1701, and matured five years before his death in his final theological synthesis, the *Wahre Abbildung*. By 1708 it is no longer solely Patristic sources which are culled in search for authoritative proof-texts. By that year over half of these authorities are taken from medieval mystics. It is this developing use of medieval texts on the part of the later Arnold which the present chapter investigates.

a. The History and Defense of Mystical Theology

Arnold never worked toward the completion of one book at a time. Either he wrote two or more simultaneously, or he was arranging and augmenting material on the book with which he was involved for the composition of a second. Thus, *Die Erste Liebe* rose out of his work on the *Fratrum sororumque appelatio*, the *Kirchen- und Ketzer-Historie* out of *Die Erste Liebe*, and the *Historie und Beschreibung der Mystischen Theologie* out of the *Kirchen- und Ketzer-Historie*. In the *Historie und Beschreibung der Mystischen Theologie* premises were advanced essential to the *Wahre Abbildung der Ersten Christen* of 1709 in which his *Erste Liebe* is completely rewritten no longer on a basis of Patristic sources, but of late medieval mystical compositions.

Although the German edition of the *Historie und Beschreibung der Mystischen Theologie* was first published in 1703, Arnold was at work on the piece much earlier. A Latin version

appeared in 1702. The introduction to the German edition
is dated 1701 and ties the work closely to his earlier historical work.[1] The *Historie* is divided into twenty-three chapters,
the first seven of which describe the nature of mystical theology. A lengthy eighth chapter defends mystics against a
number of charges, and the remainder of the book outlines
Arnold's version of the history of mysticism from its beginnings to his own day. Two extensive bibliographies on sixteenth
and seventeenth-century mysticism are appended to the piece
which also includes a two hundred and seventy page defence of
mystics and their writings.

Arnold's dualism divided reborn, practising Christians from
Christians in name only.[2] Mystical theology is proper for the
first. They are taught by the Spirit and directed by it in their
life and thought.[3] Reason alone, on the other hand, is the principal force among those taught by the world (*Weltgelehrten*).[4]
Arnold's intent in treating his subject is practical. Mystical
theology is that of the early Christian church and is outlined
for the use of the enlightened reader who alone can understand
its depths.[5]

Theology, Arnold maintains, is teaching of and from God.[6]
True theology is, therefore, directly inspired by the power of
God himself.[7] Every Christian is necessarily[8] a theologian;[9]
grace is given to the believer in the act of faith.[10] Theosophy
is defined as wisdom of and from God, and religion is viewed
in a parallel way. Wisdom and true religion come to one
internally[11] in the enlightenment of the Holy Spirit.[12] Believers are taught by God (*theodidakti*);[13] the fruits they bear are
gifts of grace.[14] Here, as elsewhere in the volume, Arnold distinguishes true life in Christ from false religion,[15] simplicity from
complexity, wisdom from foolishness,[16] and seed from shell.[17]

In his treatment of theology, Arnold often modifies the term
with 'true'. Nearly synonymous with true theology is mystical
theology.[18] It is not heathen in its origins.[19] Opposed to the
theology of the schools, mystical theology treats of the secret
hidden or heavenly wisdom, has its source in God,[20] comes
through the Holy Spirit,[21] is based on Scripture,[22] and unites
God with the believer.[23] Mystical union may be understood in
two ways: in its narrowest sense it describes that general union
of every believer in Christ.[24]

In a wider sense, however, one is accustomed to describe everything as mystical which relates to the holy and spiritual internal life or true practical Christianity. Against these are set worldly, external, sensual matters. In particular, the term mystical theology is used to describe spiritual, allegorical, and deep exegeses and expositions of the Holy Scripture which are distinguished from the historical or literal sense. In addition the doctors have called those religious matters mystical which are unknown to catechumens and others unlearned or unholy, until they are among the number of the faithful.[25]

Arnold states that his interest in the *Historie und Beschreibung der Mystischen Theologie* is in the narrower sense of the word 'mystical,'[26] but that the wider sense is never rejected.

In this book not only the obvious material is understood as is found among the Catholics, but all secret truths which serve to the progression and goal of the inner life.[27]

The same theology is upheld in the *Historie und Beschreibung der Mystischen Theologie* as in *Die Erste Liebe*. All believers are reborn into this love and progress toward its fulfillment; none are excluded.[28] Opposed to a theology based on reason alone,[29] mystical theology endeavours to lead one in a growing experimental knowledge of the divine.[30] Beginning as a babe, the newborn believer progresses by a threefold path through spiritual youth and adulthood. A lengthy discussion based almost exclusively on Hugh of Balma's *Viae Syon* is devoted to this.[31] For any growth, purity of heart,[32] withdrawal and detachment (*stilles und gelassenses Leben*),[33] simplicity, purity,[34] obedient innocence,[35] humility,[36] and continual struggle are necessary.[37] Few arrive at the final goal.[38] All are led there by God, who alone works in them.[39]

Many mistake the purpose and thought of mystical writing because of the nature of its subject matter, Arnold believes. Mystical theology treats of an inner reality in its beginning and at its end.[40] A supernaturally endowed, experiential understanding of this reality,[41] is much beyond the human mind,[42] is expressible only in images or symbols,[43] and often appears to the inexperienced as foolishness. It is, in fact, divine foolishness.[44] For Arnold the mystical experience is not in any way an end in itself. Although not taking much space to discuss it, he follows the Lutheran *ordo salutis* at all times. After a discussion of the union itself, he describes the renovation which is to grow from it. One is united with God by God's love.[45] One's love, in turn, expresses itself in a renewed spiritual life,[46] holiness,[47] virtue,[48] and wisdom,[49] all of which are based on God's love. The virtues grow as one's understanding and experience of divine love grow. God's love is present at the beginning of the believer's life, strengthening[50] and directing[51] his or her activity.

On these principles Arnold defends the mystics. All their writings are reinterpreted according to his understanding of what constitutes the mystical life. His Lutheran interpretation of medieval authors is at its clearest when he handles the charge that they did not emphasise firmly enough the doctrine of the new birth. Making use of earlier mystical terminology, he applies it to the faith union and the conversion resulting from it:

> Some say that the mystics teach very little or almost nothing about the new birth, although it is almost the sum and the one thing necessary in Christianity. It is true that this word 'new birth' is not found at all times in their writings. Only the person who has spiritual eyes will be able to see the matter fully expressed and all that pertains to it, especially that concerning the purification of the soul, and its internal birth pangs, the revelation, transfiguration, spiritual birth, and growth of Jesus Christ in the soul, the soul's marriage and joy with Christ, etc. ... [The new birth] is not denied therefore by these writers.[52]

Nor is there, Arnold continues, any suggestion that mysticism emphasises works or omits reference to faith. The mystics teach nothing other than that 'the sum of the Gospel stands in the death of the old and the awakening of the new person.'[53]

> According to the witnesses of those who call themselves 'evangelicals,' it is clear how the mystics in all ways have built on the ground of the teaching of Christ.... If one reads the good and precious matters in Tauler regarding the necessary duties and activities of the soul for the desire of the divine promise, one must never interpret this aside from or outside of the only ground and mediator Jesus Christ or of the work and support of the good Spirit. [The words do not speak] of one's own works, personally-produced design, or seemingly good opinion. Rather, one must understand all such admonitions with the deepest knowledge of his own weakness and sink fully into the communion and gracious operation of God as such is placed before us and promised in Christ.[54]

These matters aside, other attacks on mysticism are easily met. Mystical freedom in the use of language is not heretical.[55] It is based on the Scriptures.[56] The mystics are not enthusiasts nor disruptive forces in society.[57] They were the witnesses to the truth of the Gospel throughout the ages,[58] and although many were Roman Catholics, 'one page of their writings contains more divine light, life, counsel, consolation, and peace for a soul eager for God than ten folios' of talk from the learned of this world.[59]

When an examination is made of Arnold's use of medieval citations in the first eight chapters of the *Historie und Beschreibung der Mystischen Theologie*, it is once again obvious that he went to earlier texts to support a position he had already formulated and that he was little influenced by them. In these chapters the medieval authors often quoted by Arnold are Bernard of Clairvaux, Denis the Carthusian, Hugh of Balma, and Jean Gerson.[60] Tauler is often referred to but seldom quoted.[61] The greatest number of citations reflect Arnold's insistence on the dichotomy he sees between mystical theology and scholasticism.[62] Associated with this theme is his demand for the practice of Christian virtue on the part of believers and their exhibition of the fruits of faith[63] in a simple life style.[64] The largest continuous unit of medieval quotations occurs in Arnold's discussion of the threefold path. Most of these are from Hugh of Balma's *Viae Syon*.[65] Perhaps to protect himself against the charge of precipitating enthusiasm, Arnold cites a number of instances in which the warning is made that the fullest mystical experience is available only to the mature and not to beginners.[66] The smallest block of citations refers to other aspects of the mystical life.[67] Very few describe mystical union in the narrow sense as Arnold defined it.[68]

The historical section of the *Historie und Beschreibung der Mystischen Theologie* (Chapters IX ff.) is a chronological catalogue of the major spiritual authors from the first to the seventeenth centuries. Following a treatment of Apostolic mystical theology,[69] there is a detailed discussion of the Pseudo-Dionysian corpus and its use,[70] as a survey to attitudes to mystical theology in general.[71] How much Arnold's interest has shifted from that of two years earlier can be noted in that two-thirds of the work is devoted to medieval authors, whereas discussions of both Patristic and early modern writers make up the remaining space.

Each of the articles on an author in the *Historie und*

Beschreibung der Mystischen Theologie follows the same pattern. Very brief biographical information is given, the author's works are listed, and in some cases earlier positive judgements on them are quoted. Almost no information is provided
on either spiritual or intellectual relationships between these
authors. Of twelfth century authors, Bernard of Clairvaux
receives the longest treatment, but that discussion does not
extend beyond a list of bibliographic information and earlier
judgements regarding his work.[72] Of Bernard's works, Arnold
lists the sermons on Sundays and Feast days, twenty miscel-
laneous sermons, and the eighty-six sermons on the first three
chapters of Canticles. The continuation of the Canticle sermons by Gilbert of Hoyland[73] was known to him through the
works of John Bona (1609-1674), an author whom he had read
closely.[74] Also noted are the five books to Pope Eugenius (*De
consideratione*), an admonition to the clergy (*De contemptu
mundi*), a book on the love of God to Haymeric, a treatise
on the interior house (ascribed by some to Hugh of St. Victor,
Arnold states),[75] a book on renovation of life (*De conversione*),
the well-known 'Jubilus,'[76] and four hundred and forty-four letters. Arnold had the Mabillon edition of the works available
to him.[77]

   Some attempt is made to indicate the existence of a Cistercian school by listing in order the major disciples of Bernard.
Arnold knew of William of St. Thierry's letter to the Brothers
of Monte Dei, three books on the love of God, a treatise on
the contemplation of God, the *Mirror of Faith*, the *Enigma
of Faith*, meditations, the treatise on the dignity and nature
of divine love, the commentary on Canticles, and a biography of Bernard.[78] No textual sources of these works or testimonies to their worth are noted. Arnold may have seen the
sermons of Guerric d'Igny, but his knowledge of them seems
to have come through Bona's work[79] as does his knowledge of
Arnold Carnotensis' (Arnold de Bonneval) books on the works
of Christ, on the six days of creation, on the last words of
Christ, his meditations,[80] and Aelred of Rievaulx's *Mirror of
Love*, *On Spiritual Friendship*, and his sermons.[81]

   Arnold's attempt to draw together the Cistercian authors
of the twelfth century into schools fails in that he uses the designation 'friend of Bernard,' by which he had characterised all

the Cistercians, to describe Hugh and Richard of St. Victor.[82] Numerous works by each are cited. No publication information is given for either man's compositions. From Hugh's writings the following are listed: a book on the security of the soul, five books on the ark of Noah, a book on the manner of prayer, a meditation, four books on the castle of the soul (which, Arnold notes, has been ascribed to Hugh of Fulieto[83]) on the love of bride and groom, an explication of Pseudo-Dionysius, allegorical interpretations of the Scriptures, explications of the ten commandments, a book on the healing of the soul, a book on spiritual and carnal marriage, four books on the vanity of the world, on the wisdom of the soul of Christ, on the power of the Word of God, one hundred sermons, and some letters.[84] Richard's books considered worthy of note by Arnold were: on the sacrifice of Abraham, on the tabernacle, on the temple of Solomon, expositions of Canticles and Daniel, on the preparation of the soul for contemplation, on contemplation, on the extermination of evil, three tracts on the interior state, on the training of the interior person, on the stages of love, on the four stages of powerful love, mystical annotations on the Psalms, the debate on certain apostles, and the commentary on the first seven chapters of Revelation.[85]

Anselm receives a careful treatment. Of his 'ascetic' works Arnold lists, with no indication of his source, the following: the *Soliloquies*, the ten books of meditations, the manual on the salvation of the soul, the meditation on the goodness of God, the meditation on the Passion of Christ, the heavenly homilies or sparks of holy desire for God, meditations and prayers, the admonition to despise the present world and to desire the eternal, the exhortation to the dying, the discussion on lapsed virginity, the book on happiness, the homilies on the Gospels, and the letters.[86] Hildegard of Bingen's works as published in Cologne, 1566, that is, three books of Revelations and thirty-eight letters were known to Arnold.[87] In addition several Greek writers of the century are noted[88] as are some lesser-known Latin authors.[89]

Arnold's chapter on the thirteenth century is the briefest, and most of it is devoted to Bonaventure, whose significance was clear to him.[90] How closely Arnold knew Bonaventure's works is difficult to say. His lengthy list of the great Fran-

ciscan's compositions[91] is taken from Maximillian Sandaeus'
(1578-1656) *Theologia Mystica*,[92] which Arnold consulted at
numerous places. Albert the Great, under whose works Arnold
lists the *De adhaerendo Deo*, the *Paradise of the Soul*, and
a commentary on Pseudo-Dionysius,[93] as well as Thomas
Aquinas,[94] both receive brief treatments, as do much lesser
authors of the century.[95] It is of special interest, however, to
note the attention that Aquinas receives. His relation to Albert is pointed out and a number of earlier positive statements
regarding his work are cited. The negative approach to him
taken in the *Kirchen- und Ketzer-Historie* is gone. Among
Aquinas' mystical works listed by Arnold are treatises on the
two laws of love, on the vanity of reason, on perfection of the
spiritual life, on the love of God and neighbour, on holiness,
on the virtues and vices, and a commentary on Canticles.[96]
Gertrude the Great[97] and Mechthild of Hackeborn[98] are mis-
takenly discussed under the fourteenth-century rubric, and
Angela of Foligno is listed as a sixteenth-century writer.[99]
As earlier pointed out, he knew Angela by way of Poiret's
translations,[100] and he was well aware of Arndt's use of her
work in his *Wahres Christentum*.[101] Suso is the first major
fourteenth-century author listed and praised.[102] Arnold knew
of his work through the Anselm Hoffman translation of Surius'
Latin translations, and believed as a result that the *Book of
the Nine Rocks* was by Suso.[103]

Arnold's knowledge of Eckhart was and remained scanty.
He knew only the scattered texts in the Tauler edition which
went under Eckhart's name and, therefore, spent little time discussing him.[104] Tauler and Ruusbroec receive fullest attention.
The Strassburg Dominican was known to Arnold in numerous editions; he lists Tauler's works as they appeared in the
1694 Frankfurt edition, but notes as well various Surius editions, Dutch, and other translations.[105] He accepted without
question the authenticity of the *Nachfolgung des armen Lebens
Christi*, the *Medulla Animae*, the meditations on the life and
passion of Christ, and the book on inner contemplation.[106] In
the list of judgements on Tauler, there is some attempt to step
beyond his normal process of quoting general praises for the
life and doctrine of a mystic,[107] but even in the case of Tauler
no comment is made on the writer's theology beyond a brief

statement that the Dominican taught that a believer should advance in the Christian life.[108]

With Ruusbroec the case is similar. The Dutch mystic's works are listed as they appear in the 1692 Cologne edition of Surius' translation: The treatise on the sum of the whole Christian life, a book on the mirror of eternal holiness, the commentary on the tabernacle of Moses, treatises on the chief virtues, on faith and judgement, on the four temptations, on preservation, on the eight steps of love, on the spiritual espousals, on the perfections of the children of God, on the kingdom of the lovers of God, and on true contemplation, seven letters, two hymns, Samuel, a 'deep' contemplation, and a short prayer.[109] Reference is made to the Pomerius' life as printed in the *Leben der Alt-Väter*, but, surprisingly, no indication of the 1701 translation is found. In describing Ruusbroec's theology, the only additional points made by Arnold, not earlier made concerning Tauler, are that Ruusbroec's teaching was directly inspired by God, that its depth and difficulty is not to be a cause of its rejection, that Ruusbroec spoke against the corruption of the clergy, loved meditation on the name of Jesus, as did Tauler, and taught the truth as understood by the Protestant tradition before the rise of Protestantism.[110] A short section is devoted to Gerhard Zutphen, whose books on spiritual ascent and on the reformation of the powers of the soul are noted.[111] A very short note is included on Gerhard Groote.[112] Fuller discussions are made of Catherine of Siena— her letters, sermons, the *Dialogue*, and revelations in Latin, Italian, and French versions are mentioned[113]—and of Bridget of Sweden.[114]

The articles on fifteenth-century authors are longer than others in the volume but this is in keeping with the extent of writing done by many of the writers of that period whom Arnold includes. Sixty works, for example, are ascribed to Gerson from the 1606 Paris edition of his works.[115] The *Imitation of Christ* is not his, Arnold adds; the spiritually-enlightened reader, it is his contention, will be aware that the style and spirit of the *Imitation* is very similar to that displayed in the works of Thomas à Kempis[116] which are listed in full as they appear in the 1680 Cologne edition.[117] Any discussion of the volume's authorship, however, Arnold adds, is empty con-

tention. It is best to remain clear of the problem. Past negative judgements on the work are easily revised, both because of
the popularity of the *Imitation*—it was translated into numerous languages[118]—and because of the love many Catholics and
Protestants have had for it.[119] Controversy has also centred on
the authorship and value of the *Theologia deutsch*,[120] Arnold
adds, but in this case, as well, the popularity of the work among
spiritually astute readers sets all questions regarding its value
at rest.[121]

Briefer studies are devoted to other fifteenth-century spiritual writers. Eighteen works are ascribed to Laurence Giustiniani, but no source is given; however, some brief comments
are made on his life.[122] The revelations of Catherine of Bologna
were known to Arnold through Sandaeus.[123] Of fifteen mystical
works cited by Denis the Carthusian, Arnold may have had
closer knowledge: the commentary on Pseudo-Dionysius, the
book on divine love, treatises on the narrow way, on light, on
the teaching and rule of Christian life, and on the four last
things, the dialogue on the judgement of the soul, the com-
mentaries on Cassian and Climacus, the mirror on conversion,
a book on the weight of sin, a meditation on counsel, the mirror
of holy life, five books on monastic progress, and revelations.[124]
John of Schoonhoven was perhaps better known to Arnold for
his defence of Ruusbroec, and his writings on solitude and
spiritual growth. Next to Tauler and the author of the *Theologia deutsch*, he is held by Arnold as the chief defender of
mystical theology against the scholastics of the late middle
ages.[125] Harphius receives equal praise but Arnold displays no
knowledge of an edition of his works.[126] He knows of a German
translation of Savonarola's work, and lists twenty-three titles,
but offers no further information.[127] For information on Nicolas of Flue, Arnold refers his reader to the *Leben der Alt-Väter*
[sic].[128]

Three defences of mystical theology (*Verthädigung*) are appended to the *Historie und Beschreibung der Mystischen Theologie*, in addition to a register of mystics taken from Pierre
Poiret[129] and Arnold's own register of German authors.[130]
The defences are Arnold's reworked translations of the French
Quietist's *Theologie reel*.[131] The appendices do not add much
to Arnold's earlier treatments, although they do indicate that it

may have been Poiret who shaped Arnold's defence of, or concern with defending, the mystics regarding charges of complexity and a questionable use of language.[132] The *Verthädigung's*
treatment of Tauler adds nothing to that of the *Historie*
other than the remark, inserted by Arnold, that Tauler died
in Strassburg in 1379.[133] The section on Ruusbroec, too,
is disappointing.[134] Harphius, Poiret believed, lived at the
same time as Tauler and held a doctrine similar to that of
John of the Cross. Arnold is seemingly in agreement with
both these ideas.[135] In keeping with the *Historie's* treatment,
too, are Poiret's discussion of Hildegard of Bingen, Elizabeth
of Schönau, Mechthild of Hackeborn, Briget of Sweden,[136]
Catherine of Siena,[137] Angela of Foligno,[138] and Heinrich
Suso.[139] The *Historie's* discussions go far beyond Poiret's, however. How closely, in fact, Arnold had studied the medieval
texts themselves is seen in his growing use of them in his
writings composed after the publication of the *Historie und
Beschreibung der Mystischen Theologie.*

b. Medieval Mysticism and Pastoral Care

In the preface to his expanded *Die Geistliche Gestalt*
printed in 1712, Arnold states his purpose in using earlier
sources to support his argument in a paragraph which also
reiterates his earlier practice:

> Many authors are quoted in this work, not for the sake of human
> authority, which does not apply in divine matters, but rather (1)
> because there are so many precious truths expressed in them for
> which we may thank God that in earlier times as well he allowed
> the open witness of much truth; (2) because I wish as much as
> possible to explain all my own ideas with the words of others so
> that one can see that there is nothing new or unusual here; (3)
> perhaps because by it, unchristian antagonism and contention of
> evil-minded persons may be protected against.[140]

The purpose of the *Geistliche Gestalt* was to prepare proper
pastoral leadership for the church and the work made use of
medieval sources to support its theme. Part One is introduced with a quotation from Gilbert of Tournai on the office of the priest,[141] and a Taulerian sermon is quoted on the
importance of the pastoral role.[142] Bernard and Taulerian sermons are thereafter each cited several times on the need for
humble, earnest, pure, moral priests[143] who show forth the

fruits of the Christian faith.[144] Bernard is called upon to support catechetics,[145] Bonaventure and Richard of St. Victor to point out that private confession was not a part of the primitive church's order.[146] The value of silence is applauded by Thomas à Kempis.[147]

A concern for pastoral practice is the overwhelming theme of *Die Geistliche Gestalt.* In a special way the pastor is chosen,[148] called,[149] and united[150] to Christ in the new birth.[151] He must grow in this union towards its perfection,[152] in wisdom,[153] holiness,[154] humility,[155] love,[156] and all the virtues.[157] Referring to Ruusbroec, Arnold makes the point that the person who has a spot or sin cannot receive the Holy Spirit, even if such a person is to be ordained as a priest.[158] Richard of St. Victor, too, according to Arnold, emphasises the need for a new birth and growth in it if spiritual discretion is to be available to the pastor.[159]

By 1708, Arnold's interest in medieval comments on the pastoral life which might be used as directives in it had become so great that he composed his large *Abwege oder Irrungen und Versuchungen gutwilliger und frommer Menschen* against the tendencies that he had been earlier accused of fostering. Divided into two books, the first treats temptations as they relate to the Christian's inner state, the second, as they relate to external matters. Over a thousand pages in length, the volume has a quotation from a medieval spiritual author on almost every page.

Many of the medieval sources with which Arnold had become acquainted were sermons, and it is necessary to ask how great the influence of these were on him.[160] The question is particularly important because of the significance of the role of the written sermon on the development of Protestant meditation generally. For Protestants, meditative handbooks and prayer collections were of secondary importance.[161] Of this Arnold was well aware, and he therefore included in his first major collection of sermons in 1703, *Die Verklärung Jesu Christi in der Seele*, directions to the reader for proper use of the work:

> Pray now assiduously to the Father of glory for his Holy Spirit, that he lead you in this [reading and learning] into all truth as his Son has so dearly promised. The Son out of his eternal faithfulness will not allow you to rest in knowledge alone or in brief devotion nor to find your joy in speculation or in grasping after divine matters .... For all [who desire Christ] this book is composed and written....

Accept this word, dear reader, quietly and willingly as an external witness of God's eternal will and purpose for you. Let yourself be led through it to the eternal, essential word of the Father and learn to turn to it eagerly as the bright morning star of your heart.... Anyone who wishes to read something valuable in this matter, should go to the well-known Tauler or similar authors until everything becomes spirit and life in the new birth. Then that person will read, eat, and enjoy the opened book. Every reader should take to heart the counsel of Tauler who notes the same concerning all books and sermons: ... Dear children, let go all things which I and all teachers have ever learned ... and look toward, consider, and learn only the One, that you might gain it. Then you will have worked well. The Lord says: Mary has chosen the better part. If you are able to achieve this One, you will have achieved not only a part (or knowledge as a piece) but the whole.[162]

It is for this 'mystical' purpose, Arnold writes in the preface to the 1709 *Evangelische Reden*, that he has written and published his sermons. Reading them and meditating upon them, one is to be led closer to understanding God's will for one's life, he points out.[163] Yet, in spite of the introduction's praise of Tauler, few of the sermons in *Die Verklärung Jesu Christi* show any signs of the influence of the pieces Arnold believed to be by him. Of the sixty-six sermons in the volume plus the additional twenty-one in the second edition of the work, only one gives any indication of direct Taulerian influence. In his first sermon for Christmas day based on John 1: 1-14, Arnold refers to a Tauler sermon on the same subject[164] and in it he often writes in language somewhat Taulerian but far more Boehmist in tone:

[We] note that ... the eternal Son of God, as the Word of the Father, was in the beginning, that is in the eternal beginning, when the loving will of the Father, in his eternal power and in a hidden manner, conceived himself in an unfathomable way and spoke his likeness in an eternal image and mirror, in which he saw himself and wished to love himself as in eternal wisdom and love for the Son. The eternal, essential word was then by God as the Father's infinite power and was in the beginning, since the free love and desire itself moved in God and came forth so that hereafter in the beginning of time out of such a conception and movement the Word would make all things.... Let us out of the divine ground through the Holy Spirit come to know the high and mighty Saviour we are able to have if we wish.... Therefore O Soul, you who desire him, turn your mind from things seen into the divine nature in which you must become a partaker according to your quality, and honour him as your Lord and God. Pray to the eternal Father for this his eternal Word, so

that he might speak it to reveal it to you that you might enjoy his
infinite power and divinity and see his glory as the only begotten
Son of the Father.[165]

Boehmist tone and citation of Tauler aside, it soon becomes
evident to the reader of Arnold's Christmas sermon that he is
not dealing with the themes which interested the seventeenth-
century visionary or the fourteenth-century German mystic
and that, although Arnold may well have read Tauler on the
topic, he reapplied that author's intent. Immediately following
the passage quoted, Arnold makes it clear that the experience
of the birth of Christ in the believer to which he is referring is
the experience of real life in a penitent believer who will turn
from worldly ways to live a virtuous life in the world.[166] His
conception of Christ's birth in the soul is not the experience of
a mystic ecstatically lifted into the divine presence but rather
of the result of an initial act of faith on the part of a new
believer.[167]

Two other sermons in the *Verklärung Jesu Christi* are written on the same themes as sermons believed by Arnold to be
by Tauler,[168] but in neither of these, nor in any of the sermons in the *Evangelische Postilla* of 1707 does one find distinct
Taulerian images or language. Such language is more frequent
in the *Evangelische Botschaft* of 1706, but in this work, as
well, and in spite of some citations and quotations from medieval authors,[169] any notion of direct influence on Arnold's
theology or style by medieval writers must be set aside. Often
when Arnold treats a pericope which can be read as emphasising a dichotomy between good and evil and is also discussed
in a Taulerian sermon, he turns the passage to a discussion of
his distinction between the true and false church, whereas the
medieval author quoted usually sees it in terms of the evil to
be purged within that individual.[170] Interestingly enough in
one case in which Arnold had Taulerian sources available to
him which did emphasise an ecclesiological dualism somewhat
similar to his own, he directed his attention to discussing the
differences between the old, carnal and the new, spirit-born
person.[171]

Nor is there any indication that medieval sermon style influenced Arnold's style. He divides his sermons into protheme
and body and subdivides the theme proper as does the me-

dieval scholastic *ars praedicandi*;[172] but all Arnold's Baroque contemporaries do the same, whereas the vernacular medieval pieces Arnold had at hand did not.[173] Even within the Baroque tradition he tends with his fellow Pietists to comment on a biblical passage or story, rather than to expand on a single biblical theme, and he displays remarkably less use of allegory than the medieval texts he read.

c. The Preface to the Writings of Thomas à Kempis

On December 24, 1711, Arnold completed the preface to a German edition of the works of Thomas à Kempis which was published in the following year. His preface includes an historical introduction and a discussion regarding the proper use of the volume's contents.[174] His last major consideration of late medieval mysticism, Arnold's discussion is of interest both because of its continuing pastoral concern in approaching medieval writers and because of its value as a summation of his earlier approaches to such authors as an historian, poet, and pastor.

It is not enough, Arnold points out, that a book be free of gross errors to be of value; it must also bring truth and spiritual blessings to the reader.[175] That such truth and blessings are available in Thomas à Kempis' works, among which he included the *Imitation of Christ*, Arnold has no doubt. The lengthy bibliographic list of editions and of earlier testimonies to the value of à Kempis' compositions, which he introduces in his historical introduction, is an obvious indication for him of the spiritual supremacy of the medieval author. The argument from popularity is well documented. Five fifteenth and sixteenth-century Latin editions of the *Imitation* and the *Opera* are noted, as are some later printings.[176] A bulky bibliographical guide is provided to translations of the *Imitation* in German,[177] Dutch, English, and French,[178] Swedish, Danish, and Hungarian,[179] Polish, Spanish, Italian, and Russian,[180] Latin verse and French verse, [181] Humanistic Latin,[182] Greek and Hebrew,[183] Turkish and Arabic.[184]

What is more, in a disunified religious world, all Christian traditions have acknowledged the worth of the *Imitation*.[185] On this Catholic, Magisterial Protestant, and seventeenth-century radical can all agree. With the works of Tauler and the *The-*

ologia deutsch, Lutherans from the Reformer himself onward
have praised it.[186] Likewise, Reformed Church Protestants,[187]
Roman Catholics,[188] and Socinians[189] have found the pages
stimulating.

Thomas à Kempis' life, too, bears testimony to his writing,
according to Arnold. He therefore reprinted the German translation of Tolensis' biography which he had earlier printed in the
Vitae Patrum.[190] In addition, he comments on Thomas' alleged
continual contemplation on, and uninterrupted enjoyment of,
divine things.[191] Although often called a doctor, Arnold takes
some time to point out, Thomas à Kempis was not a doctor of
the schools. Rather, like Tauler and Arndt, he may be called a
doctor in that he was taught by the Spirit and the Scriptures
and he, in turn, taught about these.[192]

Following the cataloguing of editions and various praises
of à Kempis' work, and before his full discussion of its use,
Arnold takes some time to defend Thomas against charges of
papalism and enthusiasm. In both instances the defence is carried out by extensively quoting from other writers who defend
Thomas from the respective charges.[193] One of the faults ascribed to Thomas by Protestants was his support of the monastic system.[194] As might be expected, Arnold defends Thomas
on this point, then defending the life of solitude by interpreting
solitude as interior solitude and—pressing à Kempis' admonition to monks beyond the clear meaning of his words—pointing
out that à Kempis stood opposed to the superstition of the *majority* of monks.[195]

Such deliberate tampering with the obvious meaning of the
text seemingly did not concern Arnold in the least. His historical introduction begins with an encomium of the spiritually-
enlightened reader, the new-born Christian, who can, it would
seem, do no wrong in his approach to dogmatic or devotional
materials and who remains the final court of appeal in any
question. Certainly, Arnold considers himself such a reader:

> Should all readers be united in their knowledge of the truth after
> the pattern of Jesus Christ, their common Saviour and Light of the
> world, it would not be necessary in a preface to discuss and outline
> the many judgements of the learned on their writings. However,
> since in our day so many have confused themselves with the all too
> frequent evil censures of this good gift of God, Christian love and
> truth necessitate at the very least a defence of this new German
> edition in so far as possible.[196]

Later in the introduction Arnold refers to the judgement of true Christians[197] and his approach to translation. Beginning his introduction to the use of the volume, he writes:

> A book, which offers so many characteristics of the true, simple, and divine—humble, soft, and at the same time earnest, mind and spirit of Christ,—if used by an enlightened and faithful reader, is blessed above all things by God, and thus in and by itself is not evil but useful.... One can be confident to call upon the knowledge of an upright reader, who has not been taken in and blinded by the spirit of the world.[198]

A reader such as this may make judgements on every aspect of the work before him or her. Such a reader does not pay attention to its questionable aspects—its papal overtones, for example,—but is intent on the practical directives for a living experiential knowledge of Christ contained in it. For this reason Arnold can support what from a scientific-historical point of view is a highly questionable editorial approach to his source:

> The translator ... sought in the first place to treat the most edifying material and since because of this the work would have become too large, he left the sermons for a future time. This was able to be done all the more since the sermons were somewhat rambling and did not all seem to be fully in the style and tone of Kempis.... In addition, there was much superstition in them with which one did not want to waste the reader's time.
>
> No understanding Christian will count it amiss that matters which are characteristic of papalism alone are left out.[199]

It may strike the reader that Arnold has distanced himself from his earlier position, particularly if one reads the quotation above in light of Arnold's demand for a scientific-historical approach to texts as described in the introduction to his *Die Erste Liebe* and in his *De corrupto historiarum studio*. Little in his actual approach has changed, however. There is less concern with visions and the miraculous, more concern with the effect of reading on the immature reader, a revision more closely along traditional Protestant lines of his understanding of the life of solitude and of his former stance against Catholicism and enthusiastic traditions. Yet there is no basic change in his interpretation of all theological and devotional texts within the context of his own Lutheran Pietism. In maintaining this position, he is not in the least embarassed. The text itself, he insists, supports this reading:

> With few exceptions the discourse [in Thomas] is throughout so earnest, loving, compressive, convincing, and rooted completely in divine manner, that a sincere mind will never leave it without

blessings.... [Thomas] at almost every point speaks out of and with
the writings of the apostles and prophets, fully recognises Christ always as the corner-stone, points to him alone, and directs one away
from human teachings and works. Everything which he set forth
to be done or to be left is always set out in an evangelical manner so that he always points to powerful reasons and advice and
makes the mind willing, without legal compulsion, to undertake the
counsel and to follow it.[200]

For the best spiritual guidance the reader of à Kempis is first
directed by Arnold to

consider yourself, and allow the Spirit of Truth to search you to see
whether your conversion is proper, that is if you have been truly
changed through grace from your earlier evil life and from the world,
the flesh, sin, and Satan, with your whole heart and mind, toward
God and the Saviour; or, at the least, if you now actually stand in
a changed manner of life so that you are in true earnest without
hypocrisy ... denying all else and following Christ according to his
word.[201]

For those who are not in this situation, the book will be of
no value unless they are already directed toward God. In this
latter case it will be a 'hoped for guide to the Scriptures and to
the path of repentance and faith.'[202] It is to such an individual that Arnold now directs his attention, leading him or her
through the various stages of the *ordo salutis*. In repentance
one is to ask for enlightenment.[203]

This gift of discretion you must pray for in reading all books, since
not everything serves everyone, but the state of the soul is manifold
and changes according to time, place, and questions so that one
person will use this, another that.[204]

Each individual must apply the text according to the spirit of
grace after the single image of Christ.[205]

The Christian life continues in this life and does not reach
perfection here. Because of this à Kempis is especially good
reading, since the deeper mysteries of faith are not openly discussed by him and thus the immature reader cannot easily be
led atray.[206] If, however, the reader discovers something which
seems dark or a mystery, he ought not to cast it aside as a
delusion but, rather, to 'knock on God's door for more light
in humility and innocent desire to learn more in the school
of Christ.'[207] In all these matters it is best to make use of
what can be used at the time, for the time will come, if one
is mature in grace, that all such things will be clear. In the

Scriptures themselves are deep mysteries not immediately to be understood.[208]

Above all, readers must protect themselves against idle curiosity:

> Let your mind become silent and empty of all other things. Turn earnestly to God in this holy light. Test yourself sharply concerning this clarity and truth. Strive against self-love, and do not be misdirected by yourself—until you see clearly that the Lord works in a thoughtful mind so that it might be faithful to him.[209]

Turning from things and self-love is turning toward an experience of the mystical union in the Lutheran sense, but regardless of the nature of the experience of hearing God's word, one must remain aware of one's spiritual poverty and human shortcomings. 'Whatever occurs regarding the overpowering love of God in Christ, it can and must stir up an insatiable hunger and thirst and drive you to follow after this treasure.'[210]

> Pray then for the pure evangelical spirit of Jesus Christ, *that it will open in you the fullness and gift of grace and open your mouth of faith* so that the knowledge and love of Christ will become complete. You need then fear no false papalism. The clarity of the Gospel, when it rises as the sun of righteousness, will scatter all clouds, and Christ will manifest himself in your heart so that his countenance will be revealed and in all things you will know what you are to do and hear from him. (italics mine)[211]

The devil will attempt to hinder this, but the persistent Christian will be victorious. In union with Christ the Christian will find the opportunity to develop in accordance with his admonitions, admonitions available in such books as those by Thomas à Kempis.

> You will then understand everything in the pure evangelical sense, be able to take it and use what you earlier treated as law. ... When you read as examples in this book the many good prescriptions and admonitions which pertain to piety, you will not understand these things in the pure legal sense but will learn to gain holy insight through the light of the Holy Spirit how God intends them.... It will be clear to you at the same time how your Saviour, who wishes to live in you, will bequeath in a pure manner all the power and grace necessary for you ... so that you will be able to do all things through him. This will make you joyous and willing to live faithfully in the will of God, to take his yoke upon yourself, and to follow him in cross and suffering.[212]

Following Christ means more than fulfilling the moral demands made on one by the texts read in the Spirit. It means, as well, growing in grace, in union with Christ[213] under the direction of the Spirit, so that it will 'flow out in your soul as a rich stream of water and direct you to eternal pleasure.'[214]

How closely Arnold's theological point of view matched that of the late medieval mystics is a topic to be discussed in the following section. There is no doubt, however, that Arnold believed that the author of the *Imitation* agreed with him in his approach to earlier spiritual writings, and, in the third edition of *Die Erste Liebe*, he appended a lengthy quotation from the work closely supporting a position he had outlined in the introduction to his edition of Thomas à Kempis. The quotation summed up his life's concern which had emphasised a dualism between true and false Christians, had attacked the false by contrasting them with the better examples of Christian life in the past, and had been directed to the inspiration and admonition of true believers by portraying for them the same examples:

> Consider the glowing examples of the holy Fathers, in whom shone true religion and perfection; compared with them, we do little or nothing. Alas, how can our life be compared with theirs! The Saints and friends of Christ served Our Lord in hunger and thirst, in cold and nakedness, in toil and weariness, in watching and fasting, in prayer and meditation, in persecutions and insults without number.
>
> How countless and constant were the trials endured by the apostles, martyrs, confessors, virgins, and all those others who strove to follow in the footsteps of Christ. These all hated their lives in this world, that they might keep them to life eternal. They were given for an example to all of us and they should encourage us to advance in holiness, rather than that the lukewarm should incline us to laxness.
>
> How deep was the fervour of all these thoughtful people in spiritual instruction! How great was their devotion in prayer, and their zeal for virtue! How strict was their observance of the Rule! What respect and obedience to the direction of the Superior flourished in those days!... But in these days, any who is not a breaker of rules, or who obeys with patience is accounted outstanding!
>
> Oh, the carelessness and coldness of this present time! Sloth and lukewarmness make life wearisome for us, and we soon lose our early fervour! May the longing to grow in grace not remain dormant in you, who have been priviliged to witness so many examples of the holy life.[215]

Part Three
Medieval Sources
and Arnold's Thought

Chapter Seven:
Pietist and Medievalist:
Arnold's Mature Theology

In 1709 Arnold published his *Wahre Abbildung des Inwendigen Christenthums*, the fullest outline of his mature theology. Its title was deliberately chosen to echo his first major work, *Die Erste Liebe, oder Wahre Abbildung der Ersten Christen*. What the later work immediately indicates is the shift in his intent. Whereas *Die Erste Liebe* was primarily historical in orientation and was concerned with the early church, the *Wahre Abbildung des Inwendigen Christenthums* is theological and makes extensive use of medieval mystics. Nevertheless, there is a spiritual dynamic in his later work which is one with that in his early writing. Earlier discussions by him of his intentions are expressed in differing contexts—for the most part, however, they were expressed against those who, Arnold felt, were upholding the necessity of believing in pure doctrine alone rather than fulfilling inner experiential religion—but the main emphases are the same as those outlined in the *Wahre Abbildung* and other works such as the *Theologia Experimentalis*.

In all his works Arnold stated in some way that he felt the need to explain the nature of his inner spiritual union with Christ and the way in which this union led him to direct others toward the fuller cleansing, illumination, edification, and spiritual purification possible to be experienced in the *unio*. In the preface to his *Kirchen- und Ketzer-Historie* of January 1, 1697, for example, Arnold noted that his study was the result of an attempt to explore the nature of his personal inner union with the truth, his need to follow truth's inner dictates rather than any external traditions devised by human ingenuity, and the need he felt to explain its operation for his own and others' practice and experience.[1] The same general pattern is outlined in his foreword to the *Wahre Abbildung*:

> It is now more than twenty years since divine grace began to offer me a taste for the ancient Christian truth in the writings of the first Christians. Through this, after much laborious research in ancient antiquity over external matters and ecclesiastical issues, I

was finally and most significantly led through the grace of the Holy
Spirit according to the guidance of the Holy Scriptures to interior
Christianity. I then studied the wisdom of the early Christians
and published *Die Erste Liebe*. Among these early Christians I
found such a rich treasury of the principal truths of the Gospel, and
especially of the truth which concerns the great mystery of Christ in
us that I continually collected their writings and with great desire
annotated them for my own edification. While I was aware in my
own heart of the value and significance of these witnesses, with many
friends I considered it unpardonable to hide such things from my
thirsty neighbours and to keep them for myself alone. The writings
were for the most part in foreign languages which hid them from
the unlearned. So soon as I had the time ... I sought to portray the
picture of the inner life of early Christians for myself and others as
I had earlier portrayed their exterior life. For this reason I began
some time ago to translate the words of the ancients which I had
gathered into our common speech and to connect them briefly.[2]

Arnold's spirituality is not, then, to be studied as that of an
historian, a poet, or a theologian, but primarily as that of a
believer seeking ever deeper understanding of the mystery of
the faith-union with Christ. Arnold wished to understand the
nature of the union and its operation fully. Understanding its
nature, he believed, would lead him to an ecstatic mystical
experience of love for the One who had wrought the union initially, and understanding its operation would lead him to know
God's will for himself and for the church. 'Understanding' for
him is *Erfahrung*—the whole of the *Theologia Experimentalis*
is written to elucidate this term. 'Erfahrung' is not simply experience; it is equated with 'Erkäntnüsz' and thereby takes on
the meaning of that term, namely 'experiential knowledge':

> What is, in fact, experience (*Erfahrung*) in spiritual things? In
> temporal matters one calls it experiential knowledge (*Erkäntnüsz*)
> which one reaches through use and practice.... In spiritual things,
> however, experience (*Erfahrung*) is to be completely distinguished
> from mere knowledge of a thing outside of us. It is rather a spiritual
> perception (*Empfindung*) or discovery (*Befindung*) in which a new
> born person knows (*erkennet*) spiritual things truly, possessing, en-
> joying, and uniting with them. By it one judges them according to
> the Word of God ... and thus comes to divine knowledge.... Expe-
> rience (*Erfahrung*) is a true experiential knowledge (*Erkäntnüsz*) of
> divine things in particular. One receives it through a spiritual mind
> or perception and through this one tastes and perceives through
> God's grace the truth and knowledge in oneself.[3]

The mystery which is to be understood, that is, experientially
known, is not for Arnold a religious truth which is not able to

be known, and thus simply to be believed in its verbal doctrinal dress. Rather it is a truth which is infinitely understandable. The dimensions of its truth will open to our understanding in an infinite number of ways:

> The teaching of Christ is a mystery in us (Col. 1:27), but the mystery of the Lord is only among those who fear him (Psalm 25:14).... The disciples of Jesus are granted the power to understand the mystery of the Kingdom of God (Mark 4:11).... It is not called a mystery because it cannot be understood even by the enlightened individual, but because unprepared hearts cannot learn of it in the common manner.... Luther writes in his Kirchen-Postilla I Th. f. 72... What are the *mysteria* of God? Nothing other than Christ himself, that is the faith and the Gospel from Christ.... The famous Englishman, H. More, writes in his Myst. Piet. Expl. Lib. l, cap. I: The Mystery is a part of divine knowledge (*Erkäntnüsz*) which is in one way hidden ... [but] brings with it a true and certain result, one also very necessary and powerful, so that the soul of the individual is prepared and returned to the earlier blessedness from which it had once fallen. Elsewhere More shows (Lib. II, cap. 9, 10) that the joy of divine life can be understood by no one except the person who has experienced it.[4]

It is thus the faith of the new person, not the reason of the old, which seeks to understand the primal mystery of the mystical union with Christ, the mystery of salvation. Since the mystery of this salvation union occurs in an instant or in a mathematical point, all its facets, that is, all the facets of the *ordo salutis* are to be understood together in the apprehension of this mystery:

> I wish to lead the discriminating reader into this matter so that he or she will consider the following with an earnest and unprejudiced mind in the sight of God and according to the precepts of true Christianity: Whether any discussion may be ... less polemical than this which, according to the Holy Scriptures and the witness of the earliest Christians, directs the immortal soul to the primal purity of the divine image, to the depth of its fall, to the pure redemption through Jesus Christ through faith, to the most certain mediator of it according to the Gospel, to the illumination, union, and communion of the Saviour, and also to the true new birth and to the holy fruits of this leading to the eternal union and love of God, the eternal Good? ... Let one look on all the truths which have been written here with faithful and understanding heart; let him seek by this to be faithfully obedient to the Holy Spirit.[5]

Understanding of this mystery is possible only for the person of faith. The enlightenment which comes in faith allows the believer to understand properly not only the truths of Scripture

but also the truths of history. On this Arnold insisted throughout his life. Moreover, enlightened faith is supported in its experiential knowledge of the union of the believer with Christ,
that is in its experiential knowledge of God's love and of his
will, by the truths of Scripture and those of history. Arnold's
argument here is circular to some extent, but one ought not
to suppose that it is so in a simplistic sense. Arnold did not
settle into a particular theological position and then force all
of Scripture and tradition into its mould. His hermeneutic was
dialectical; he set up a dialogue with Scripture and tradition,
finding at times support for his own experience in both and at
other times directives for it. His movement toward the ideal
of solitude and then away from it, and his interest in radical
spiritual themes and then orthodox Lutheran ones are in part
indicative of the reality of the dialogue. All examples of believers who experienced such a union in the past may be studied,
Arnold stated: The enlightened reader need have no fear of
papal teaching, for the Spirit will testify to the spirit of the
truth both understand. That so few have had the experience
is not proof of its falsity; it is in its fullness beyond the scope of
many.[6] Nor will the use of reason and scholastic terminology
destroy the dialogue; it may in some ways help it.[7] In addition many Protestants have testified to the use of such Roman
Catholic examples[8] as they have to the use of other writers.[9]
Numerous authors have praised the work of Hugh and Richard
of St. Victor, Bonaventure, Suso, Tauler, Ruusbroec, Gerhard Zutphen, John Gerson, Lawrence Giustiniani, Thomas
à Kempis, and the *Theologia deutsch*.[10] Scripture is the final
judge of all subsequent religious experience;[11] its judgement
alone allows earlier writers to serve as a mirror in which true
and false inner Christianity might be properly reflected.[12]

Necessary in the past as well as the present[13]—Tauler himself has witnessed to the fact[14]—the compilation of such a
mirror for the church has numerous uses, providing direction, inspiration, and admonitions.[15] Direction in the search
for understanding of this inner reality can lead all Christians
and Christianity with them[16] to practice love,[17] to renew
themselves,[18] to strengthen their spiritual senses[19] for spiritual discovery,[20] true knowledge of the law,[21] greater assurance in faith,[22] better knowledge of God in love and joy[23] of

the Scriptures,[24] and of the various topics (creation to the end
of time) in theology[25] which in itself is the study of the experience of the Cross,[26] developed according to the image of
Wisdom.[27]

a. The Spirituality of the Mature Arnold

The source out of which this movement to wisdom arises is, for
Arnold, the Trinity. In his treatise on this topic in the *Theologia Experimentalis*, for example, he writes in typical Augustinian manner:

> The eternal Father manifests himself in the soul for its salvation
> in a powerful way by a firm pull to the Son. He stirs up within
> us knowledge of our evil, convicts us of it, makes us humble, and
> reveals to us by the strength of his Spirit and Word our inability to
> deal with it.
>
> The eternal Son reveals then the love of the Father, his gracious
> virtue and free grace, for all who believe in it. He directs us to his
> perfect redemption in his blood and leads us in repentance as the
> emissary of the Father, so that we are able to experience his gospel
> freely and completely.
>
> The eternal Spirit expresses himself especially in the gracious-
> ness and influence of divine faith, light, and life. He encourages us
> at all times, warns, strengthens, and consoles us in our redemption.
> He gives the instigation and strength to weep and pray. He works
> faithfullness and obedience and all necessary graces and points to
> the proper distinction between true and false Christianity.[28]

This description of the threefold activity of the Trinity fits
Lutheran theology well. Law and Gospel are discussed in relation to the Father and the Son; the role of the Spirit is emphasised in place of human weakness. It is not surprising, as
a result, that when Arnold discusses this same topic in the
second book of the *Wahre Abbildung*, he refers immediately
to Luther.[29] Yet Arnold is equally aware of the significance
of this for medieval writers. As often as he refers to any of
the Fathers' words on the matter, he refers to the treatise on
each of the divine persons by Harphius in the third book of his
Theologia Mystica[30] and he could hardly have been unaware of
the same emphasis on the Trinity in Harphius' source, Arnold's
own beloved Ruusbroec. Thus, in his full treatment of the Trinity in the third book of the *Wahre Abbildung*, Arnold refers
extensively to Ruusbroec, quoting lengthy extracts from him

on experiencing the Holy Spirit,[31] on the revelation of the Father and the Son in the individual,[32] on the Holy Spirit as the love between the Father and Son,[33] and on the participation of the Trinity in the believer,[34] directing one in the new birth[35] to the full likeness of God's image.[36] Arnold is not unaware, however, of the significance of the Trinity in other medieval authors. Thus, he quotes passages from a Taulerian sermon and Bernard on the love relationship between the Father and Son,[37] the *Theologia deutsch* on the mystery of the Trinity in the human person,[38] the Taulerian *Medulla Animae* on the Trinity as the ground of human heart,[39] and Suso on the Trinity as the highest good.[40]

As the source and end of all spirituality the Trinity leads the individual to consider creation, primal state, and fall.[41] By meditation on the heights of his or her glorious origin, the believer comes to understand better the depth of the fall, the possibilities open in Christ, and the breadth of the divine mercy which makes these possibilities realities.[42] Like Bernard of Clairvaux and unlike those Gnesio-Lutherans such as Flacius Illyricus, Arnold endeavours in the opening chapter of the *Wahre Abbildung* to convince his reader of human dignity.[43] One's dignity is based on the nature of one's soul, the breath of God in the individual,[44] one's power and fruit.[45] Toward this breath one must turn; it is one's true image.[46] As source, the nearer one comes to it, the nearer one reaches perfection.[47]

Bernard of Clairvaux, Taulerian sermons, Suso, Ruusbroec, and Harphius all support this.[48] Each person's being depends on God's being, its first principle, and will find its perfection only to the extent that it remains so dependent. The writings of pre-Christian Greek authors, Platonists, Pythagoreans, and Stoics also support this teaching, Arnold contends,[49] but the pantheistic overtones of many of these authors are rejected. The soul is the breath of God, not a part of his being; it is mutable, whereas he is immutable.[50] Ruusbroec, in particular, is a help to Arnold in making this distinction as to how God must be distinguished from creatures:

> We all have a created being and an eternal life in God, who is our life-giving cause, who created us from nothing. But we are not God himself; we have not made ourselves nor have we flowed from God in a natural way. Because God knew us from all eternity, wished, and desired us in himself, he created us not from his nature or his own necessity but out of his free inclination.... [51] Because God lives in

all creatures and all creatures in him, they are not God nor is God a
creature, for the created and the uncreated remain two things at all
times and are eternally distinguished one from the other....[52] One
is indeed able to be purified, ennobled, and formed in the likeness
of God's image, but one will never lose one's creatureliness.[53]

It is in this context that Arnold discusses the spark of the soul
or *Füncklein*, a term he borrows directly from the medieval
mystics:

> Very thoughtfully they say that the rational soul has a ground or
> spark in it which God is not able to leave so that it can take anything
> else into itself or be filled with anything except God himself.... The
> high nobility of the soul stands in this relation with God which he
> has placed in the ground of the soul. This the learned call the spark
> of the soul, a primal base, an image of the Holy Trinity. This spark
> flies so high that darkness is not able to reach it, if it is properly
> used.[54]

The human person was created toward the image of God,[55]
that is, human beings were created with the purpose that they
develop toward the fulfillment of their Trinitarian ground or
spark.[56] In the original Edenic state the human person was,
Arnold believed, like the angels, and he calls Bernard, in particular, to his support.[57] As such, the individual was filled with
divine wisdom,[58] holiness,[59] freedom,[60] balance (of 'tempera-
tures'; Arnold is here making use of Boehmist imagery[61]), and
was lord of all,[62] but the memory, understanding, and will
turned from the divine to externals,[63] One cannot find any
peace until one turns back toward this life and lives once again
in it.[64]

In describing the paradisical life of Adam, Arnold makes
some use of Boehmist concepts. A whole chapter is devoted to
the topic in which various aspects of the original Paradise are
described and pagan, Jewish, and Christian sources quoted in
support of the description.[65] As in Boehme, the fall is associated with the sleep of Adam and divided sexuality thereafter,[66]
but the more orthodox teaching tying the eating of the fruit to
the fall is also noted.[67] In the chapters describing Paradise and
the fall, the only medieval text quoted is the *Theologia deutsch*
in its description of the eating of the forbidden fruit.[68] Somewhat greater use of medieval authors is made in the discussion
of the results of the fall. First among these is the loss of the
divine image.[69] Loss is not the best word in this case, Arnold

admits, although he is willing to use it. Better words would
be 'suppressed,' 'narrowed,' 'covered,' 'darkened,' for the spark
cannot be lost. It is, quoting a Taulerian sermon, so deeply impressed upon the soul that it can in no way be extinguished.[70]
God's likeness is the fullness of light toward which the spark is
directed, and it is this which is lost in the fall.[71] Other things
also result. In the fall one's nature is corrupted;[72] one runs
from God, and is cast from Paradise.[73] The tree of life is kept
from such a person,[74] the person suffers exile[75] and sin,[76] comes
under the power of the devil,[77] and is united to him.[78]

Arnold's discussion of the Edenic state and the fall from it
raises two problems which have caused major difficulty in the
interpretation of his work. One of these concerns the nature of
his anthropology. Does his emphasis on the spark of the divine
in the human person, matched with his call for radical moral
change, not suggest a more positive view of human possibility, out of keeping with the words of the Lutheran *Formula of
Concord* on this point?[79] Secondly, there is the closely related
problem of the relationship between grace and free will. Does
Arnold not at times support a synergism much like that of
some late medieval mystics, a synergism unacceptable within
the Lutheran framework?

Central to the consideration of either of these questions is
a review of Arnold's concept of the nature and method of theology. Neither question, that of anthropology or that of free
will, is treated by him outside of the context of the realm of
faith. In his view, true theology is faith in the guise of another
discipline, be that discipline history, literary criticism, or philosophy, Arnold had little tolerance, needless to say, for faith in
the guise of philosophy, that is, scholastic theology, but his implicit acceptance of many themes developed by that method,
particularly those associated with the *ordo salutis*, indicates
that his opposition was primarily rhetorical. All theological
discussion, in his opinion, is intended for the believer, the new-
born enlightened Christian whose faith searches for greater understanding of theological mysteries so as to embody itself in
the world both in a practical and speculative way. Thus, in
the opening chapters of the *Wahre Abbildung* Arnold discusses
the nature of his theologising:

> Instead of useless scrupulosity, however, our most important pur-
> pose here is to understand (*erkennen*) the first source, and emana-
> tion of our life from God— after whom we originated and in whose
> image we became his true children. In consideration of this, the

Holy Spirit works in us partly to bring about the submission and shame of our natural proud mind, and partly to raise up earnest desire for our lost glory and joy, and to lead us toward God, our eternal source, in the obedience of faith under Christ's cross and death to our final end. Such understanding (*Erkäntnüsz*) of the source and ground will be healing for the reader.... If one understands this in the spirit according to its true ground ... one will strive toward the goal and redemption and not rest until it is achieved. This vision may be reached with overwhelming blessings for those who wish to be obedient to the Gospel.[80]

All discussions of the original human state, then, are intended for the believer, the Christian who has experienced repentance for past sins and the new birth. The extensive treatment of the perfect Edenic state is to serve as a challenge, to inspire the believer to direct his or her steps toward the full perfection of that state in thankfullness and hope. The possibility of such a return is not simplistically considered. Total human corruption is emphasised in a typical Lutheran fashion, to avoid the sense of an overly easy solution and to increase the sense of gratitude for redemption.

Arnold's use of the concept of the spark of the soul is to be interpreted in a similar fashion. Not defined as a material part of the individual, the spark is understood by him rather as a mark of one's original perfection and as a continual reminder of one's proper direction. The passages referring to this spark in Arnold are not directed to questions of essence but of orientation. The *Theologia deutsch* with its emphasis on *Eigenheit* (non-attachment) in particular, is called upon to support this contention as are Bernard, Taulerian sermons, and Harphius.[81]

The fallen person is evil, turned from God in the reason which looks only to appearances,[82] will which is misdirected[83] and desire which turns from God.[84] Like Luther, Arnold insists that the will is bound,[85] and accordingly, as do his Lutheran contemporaries, he upholds the necessity of grace in Christ for human redemption and of the doctrine of predestination. One is unable to save oneself[86] and needs therefore the power of the Holy Spirit to be converted.[87] Bernard, in particular, is called upon to support the doctrine of the necessity of the Spirit for the new life of the believer.[88] Through the Spirit's work, a believer can know, Arnold insists, quoting Ruusbroec, that he or she is called to be a child of God.[89] Despite this emphasis on the bound will, however, Arnold does uphold, in a paradoxical manner, free will. The Spirit will work, he writes, quoting Ruusbroec and others, only in an obedient,[90] pure heart[91] which desires the Spirit's gift.[92] Only there, will it transmit its power,[93] and only there will be found the divine virtues.[94] As they stand, Arnold's words seem to be out of keeping with those of the *Formula of Concord* which discuss the free will.[95] It would be wrong, however, to read Arnold's words in light of the *Formula* alone. Arnold was fully aware of and accepted Luther's doctrine on the bondage of the will, and as a result in the *Wahre Abbildung* he insisted that redemption comes only through Christ's atoning reconciliation, effected on the Cross,[96] and that this is mediated to the believer through faith alone.[97] On the grace of salvation, in particular, he devotes a number of chapters in the *Theologia Experimentalis*, treating the election in Christ,[98] the harmony between divine mercy and justice,[99] atonement through Christ,[100] the grace of God for conversion,[101] and the Father's drawing of the believer to the Son.[102]

Arnold's numerous statements regarding free will and the necessity of human preparation for God's salvific work are not to be read outside of this context. Arnold was no Pelagian. Rather, when he comments on the free will—when he insists on the human role in salvation—he is writing with a purely pastoral purpose, in the same way as the *Formula of Concord* does in its discussion of God's election.

> However, that many are called and few chosen, Matt. 22, 14, does not mean that God is not willing to save everybody; but the reason is that they either do not at all hear God's Word, but willfully despise it, stop their ears, and harden their hearts, and in this manner foreclose the ordinary way to the Holy Ghost, so that he cannot perform his work in them, or, when they have heard it, make light of it again and do not heed it, for which [that they perish] not God or his election, but their wickedness, is responsible.[103]

Arnold does not intend to suggest that by purifying one's intentions, one may attain to salvation; he means to point out only that God is not unjust in his condemnation of the unrighteous.

It is all too easy to misinterpret Arnold's position on the doctrine of grace because of his near refusal to clarify terms. Often in his discussion of the topic, he moves very rapidly and with almost no transition from a comment on the initial role of grace in the salvation of a believer to one on the continuing life of grace in the believer leading to the fruits of faith. Arnold was certainly aware of the *Formula of Concord*'s distinction between the nature of free will in fallen individuals and that in regenerated persons,[104] but he takes it for granted in the *Wahre Abbildung*, rather than explaining it fully. Regenerated persons are expected, according to Lutheran Pietist doctrine, to use free will to grow in grace, to make use of the third use of the law.[105]

When discussing free will and grace in the redeemed individual, Arnold might be expected to place emphasis on the free will to a degree which, if he were discussing the same question in relation to the fallen individual, would be heretical. It is interesting to examine the seventh chapter of the *Wahre Abbildung* in light of this. In that chapter Arnold examines the role of the Holy Spirit in the conversion of the fallen person. As has already been noted, he insists at the beginning of the chapter on the necessity of the Spirit for redemption:

> Should an individual, so deeply fallen, wish to be torn out of the
> depths of natural wretchedness in a real and true way, the eternal
> powers and work of the divine are necessary.[106]

However, very soon after this statement and a lengthier section treating one's incapacity to bring anything of value to one's own conversion,[107] Arnold goes on to discuss the life of the Spirit in redeemed individuals and the Spirit's purifying activity.[108] All discussions of human preparation, the strength of free will, and the value of human activity occur after this section,[109] indicating that they are not to be understood in any way as causal factors in salvation.

God's election is made operative in his calling (*vocatio*) of the sinner through the words of Scripture and of the preacher.[110] The call makes effectual the sinner's knowledge of Law and Gospel. Knowledge of the Law[111] directs one to renew one's life in true repentance[112] and experience of the Gospel,[113] opens the possibility of new life, accepting and living according to the promises made in baptism.[114] What the redeemed sinner discovers, however, is the inevitable conflict between desire to live according to the new demands of Law and Gospel and attraction to the carnal ways of the flesh. The spiritual and physical trials accompanying this dual attraction are all characterised under the term *Anfechtungen*.[115] Tauler and Suso, Arnold points out, both insist on the rejection of those evil desires which bring such a spiritual battle about.[116] For direction in the battle, Arnold suggests the reader look to the *Imitation of Christ* and to Harphius.[117] The Taulerian writings in particular are called upon to describe the nature of *Anfechtungen*. These trials are allowed that faith might be strengthened;[118] despite their frightful power,[119] they are necessary. It is Tauler, as well, who describes the end of such trials. They are overcome through faith in Christ[120] and will be done away with at the end of time.[121] Numerous aids are available for the believer attempting to overcome these temptations: the grace of God,[122] Christ's support,[123] firmness,[124] watchfullness,[125] ready renewal,[126] prayer,[127] spiritual discretion,[128] self-understanding,[129] silence,[130] resignation (*Gelassenheit*),[131] and patience.[132]

References to medieval authors on guidance in spiritual trial are surprisingly few. Whereas Luther noted Gerson regularly on the topic, Arnold makes no reference to him whatever. He notes Bernard, Thomas à Kempis, and Harphius on spiritual discretion,[133] Tauler on self knowledge[134] and resignation,[135] and quotes lengthy passages from Ruusbroec on guarding patiently against the wiles of the devil.[136] In his treatment of *Anfechtungen*, Arnold exhibits none of the dire psychological or spiritual dread of these trials and temptations which one finds in Luther's treatment of the same subject. That Luther groups all of them together under a singular noun (*Anfechtung*) and associates with this the onslaughts of spiritual doubt, further helps to distinguish him from Arnold who saw the trials as obstacles slowly to be overcome throughout the believer's life. The Law, for Arnold, is not an indicator of God's wrath upon the sinner, as it is for Luther; it is, rather, a guide for the believer. The Gospel, for Arnold, is more an initiator of Christian life than a continual assurance of God's love and mercy. In this, however, Arnold was not radically different from other Lutherans at the time, all of whom in their acceptance and teaching of the doctrine of the *ordo salutis* had moved some distance from the spirituality of their founder.

God's election and call of the sinner to a holy life is continued in his illumination of the chosen soul through the Holy Spirit.[137] It is the Spirit which prays in such a soul and produces the fruit of that prayer. The prayer of the spirit is,

Arnold states, 'a faithful conversation and dialogue of our soul with God and a vision of unseen things.'[138] It is an ever present supernatural aspect of the Christian's life; on this à Kempis and Tauler agree.[139] This prayer is truly a prayer of faith.[140] It exists already at this stage in the *ordo* which occurs, as we have seen, in a point in time, reflective of the mystical union of the believer in Christ. Its direction is solely toward heaven,[141] helping the individual, according to Tauler, to overcome the evils of this world.[142] When a Christian turns inward and casts out the evil he or she discovers, Arnold writes, quoting Taulerian passages, the Christian does so by the power of this prayer,[143] through which he or she may remain obedient to God,[144] endure suffering in patience,[145] strength,[146] and resignation.[147] The Spirit is both the power and end of the prayer.[148] It is the spark, the third part of the believer (*Geist* as opposed to *Seele* and *Leib*), granted by grace through faith, by which the believer is united to the divine.

Regeneration follows upon illumination and is characterised by a denial of self[149] and the things of this world.[150] In regeneration one suffers and dies with Christ,[151] becoming nothing[152] and spiritually poor,[153] but in it also one rises with Christ in faith,[154] becoming united with one's Saviour in light, freedom, and purity.[155] Terms such as *Abgeschiedenheit* (detachment) and *Gelassenheit* (resignation) are common in Arnold's four chapters on regeneration. Nor is it surprising to discover that the vast majority of the citations of these terms are directly quoted from late medieval German sources. Taulerian materials account for most of the quotations, but Suso and Ruusbroec are also used.

b. The Mystical Union Proper

The regenerated individual rises by faith into a new life in Christ.[156] By faith one is justified (*justificatio*) before God.[157] Christ becomes the believer's life with whom, Arnold writes, citing Ruusbroec and Tauler, the believer shares a communion so close[158] that he or she dies[159] and experiences all things with the Lord.[160] It is necessary that Christ be so united with the believer, for:

> One must continually hold Christ in one's understanding, carry him in one's conscience, and honour him as ever present. He is truly with us and in us through faith until we see him in his person ... [161]

Christ's reception in the heart is the true Gospel;[162] It is secret, hidden from us, as Bernard and others write.[163] It is given in the same manner to all[164] and, according to Ruusbroec, may be directly experienced.[165] Christ is united with all creatures in a general way, writes Arnold, reminding one of the discussions on this topic by Quenstedt,[166] but in a special way he is present to the believer.[167] The believer is drawn by the Father to the Son through the fear of the Law and the joy of the Gospel and through the Son's stirring of the human heart. In his discussion of both these topics Arnold quotes from Harphius.[168] The believer is incited by this, according to Ruusbroec, to hunger and thirst for Jesus with a spiritual mouth[169] to seek him[170] and desire him,[171] and to turn with one's whole heart towards him.[172]

In this union Christ as the Morning Star[173] enlightens the believer according to the Holy Scriptures.[174] He is the Father's Word and Counsel[175] (according to Tauler, Ruusbroec, and others) both in the believer[176] and in the Scriptures.[177] Following this discussion, Arnold proceeds to describe more fully the nature of the faith union with Christ (*unio mystica*) and makes wide use of medieval sources to do so. The word of the Father revealed in the Scriptures is spoken directly in the heart[178] and can be heard if one turns toward it, writes Arnold.[179] Bernard, Ruusbroec, and à Kempis all agree, he notes, that this word can be known and trusted.[180]

How one can so receive Christ is unknown,[181] but it occurs in faith according to Ruusbroec and others.[182] Through the power and direction of this union, the believer is redirected to the Father,[183] learning through the pattern established by the incarnate Jesus.[184] At this point in his argument, Arnold sums up his concept of the birth of Christ in the soul in a chapter almost entirely composed of quotations from Bernard, Tauler, and Ruusbroec.[185] Arnold's treatment of the birth of Christ in the soul does not take up directly the initial faith union. The birth and the mystical union, rather, are often seen as generic terms which include all aspects of the *ordo* (*in instantu*). As has been pointed out above, the concept of union is already implied in the concept of illumination, although it is not discussed in a specific way until Arnold comes to describe the new birth and union in faith which occurs after regeneration, from a temporal point of view, and the concept of the *unio mystica* is implicit in the concepts of *renovatio, conservatio,* and *glorificatio.* Arnold used the notion of the birth of Christ in the soul in a parallel way. Christ is born in the soul with the election, born properly in faith, and born daily in every act of renovation by the believer.[186] This birth is brought about by God, not by one's own power, says Arnold, quoting Tauler.[187] Ruusbroec writes that it comes about through the Holy Spirit alone.[188]

In the rest of his treatment of the mystical union in itself, Arnold discusses the various images which best describe the nature of that union and which might serve the believer as guides in the Christian life. The first mark of this union is the reformation it brings about in the believer.[189] It makes out of a sinful person a true, practical, new creature, writes Tauler,[190] giving one correct understanding,[191] strength,[192] and victory in overcoming the world.[193] In this way the divine image is renewed,[194] and one is regenerated toward that image.[195] Thus, like Christ, the believer becomes humble[196] and patient,[197] overcomes evil, [198] and is renewed in virtue[199] and love.[200] Christ's union with the soul feeds it as spiritual bread—Arnold takes his image here from the medieval mystics, not Spiritualists such as Schwenckfeld or Sudermann.[201] In this union one puts on the new clothing of holiness.[202] The union is the pearl of great price, the hidden treasure for which a person will sell all.[203] The union makes a believer, like Christ, Priest,[204] Prophet,[205] and King.[206] As a priest one must offer oneself for others, as Christ himself did.[207] One must purify oneself,[208] and lay one's requests before God in the spirit of Christ and in faith.[209]

c. The Goal of the Mystical Union

Having described the nature of the mystical union, Arnold proceeds in the third book of his *Wahre Abbildung* to describe its results in the renovation, conservation, and glorification of the believer. Before he does so, however, he feels it necessary to outline once again the *unio*'s basic characteristics. Mystical union with Christ in faith is a great mystery, undescribable and unknown, according to Ruusbroec.[210] Such union is necessary,[211] God's life in the believer,[212] and his recreation of the individual,[213] developing by the grace of God, as Ruusbroec writes;[214] its progress in the believer can be hindered. On this latter point, Suso and Ruusbroec both agree.[215] With Tauler and Bernard, they insist that such progress is possible only by detachment from self and world[216] through simplicity of heart,[217] spiritual poverty,[218] a return to God,[219] and by a return inward.[220] One must commit oneself wholly to God,[221] seeking him avidly with the will[222] in prayer[223] and clinging solely to him.[224]

The first fruit of this union, according to Arnold, is the assurance[225] that one is united with God. In it the believer is hidden with him;[226] and, following the tradition of describing the mystical union established by Bernard and popularised by later writers, Arnold goes on to describe the relationship between God and the believer as fire and white hot iron, wine and water,[227] sun and air.[228] A distinction must be made between the two, he insists, following Gerson,[229] but at the highest point of progress in the Christian life, that is, in life lived in this union, the believer is completely lost in the divine.[230] Besides assurance, the union also gives the believer communion with God,[231] and reforms him or her after God's likeness.[232] By it one gains harmony with God,[233] and God himself becomes the believer's kingdom.[234]

Another way of describing the mystical union and its fruits is in terms of love and the fruits of love:

> The Son of God said in John 14:23 that he who loves him and keeps his word will love the Father and the two will come to him and make their dwelling with him. In this he convinces us that his divine indwelling will never occur without love, but that love is to be sought in the union and the union in love—indeed, that love brings pure unity and simplicity. The reason for this is clear, in that God himself is love (I John 4:26). God, however, in his being is pure and simple, of no division or compilation. For this reason it is necessary that love can be an undivided simple, unmixed, pure being which can give unity.[235]

Love comes from the Father and must of necessity return to him. This return, writes Tauler, comes out of faith.[236] Love is eternal,[237] but progresses by stages in the believer's life until it reaches its fulfillment. Arnold does not attempt to enumerate these states consistently—the possibilities for growth in love are, after all, infinite— but simply notes a number of them as they are described by medieval authors.[238] To understand this love, or word, of God, the believer must turn inwardly with the whole heart, soul, strength, and mind[239] so as to live the unitive life to the fullest, to experience its heat and fire when it is most completely in control.[240] As this union in love grows, it heals the believer and makes him or her holy,[241] obedient[242] and live a Godly life[243] in love toward neighbour,[244] humble,[245] patient,[246] and ever more renewed,[247] until, sunk in God,[248] the believer finds victory in all the trials of this life[249] and rejoices in the ecstatic sweetness of divine love.[250]

'There is no end in describing the holy and most precious matter, namely, divine love,' writes Arnold, introducing his chapter on the spiritual marriage between God and the soul.[251] His statement is important, for it makes clear his understanding of the term 'spiritual marriage.' This term is simply another way of describing that faith-union in Christ with every believer. It is not the end of the Christian's life, reached after arduous loving. It is not the consummation of love,[252] but a general description of the whole life of love. Arnold's attention is not on the journey to the marriage bed,[253] but rather on the spiritual offspring which result from the union.[254] Spiritual marriage brings satisfaction, spiritual quiet,[255] but this quiet is not that of an ecstatic mystical experience outside of space and time. It can be deepened and developed psychologically— indeed, it must be—by denial of the things of this world[256] until one rests in the depths of peace,[257] beyond mind and sense,[258] but even in such a state one must continually strive against sin.[259] In such peace one is able to contemplate the nature of God, to understand his mystery.[260]

United with Christ, the believer has assurance. Loving him, one enjoys the sweetness of love. Spiritually married, one consummates one's relationship, brings forth spiritual children, and finds peace of soul in which one may contemplate and understand the mystery of God. As a guide in this contemplation, the believer receives the gifts of the Holy Spirit. The Spirit is there at the beginning of the believer's life, directing one toward repentance and the new birth.[261] Thereafter it guides the believer in a new life in union with Christ, so that one can better understand how to overcome shortcomings and to practice love for one's fellow human beings and God.[262] The

indwelling of the Spirit is only another way of describing the
mystical union as, Arnold writes, Tauler and Ruusbroec make
clear.[263]

In the last section of the *Wahre Abbildung*, however, Arnold
begins to move beyond his earlier discussions which characterised the mystical union in itself and in its results. In all
cases he insists that the mystical union is the same for all believers. All are united by faith in love, all are married as brides
of Christ, all enjoy peace, and all receive the gifts of the Holy
Spirit. As he proceeds in his argument, however, Arnold takes
ever more interest in the relative perfection of the various aspects of the union. Thus, although all Christian believers rest
in the peace of the Spirit, Arnold places great emphasis on the
deeper rest possible for mature Christians.[264] In none of the
three books of the *Wahre Abbildung* does he suggest that there
is any qualitative difference in the union experienced by those
beginning the Christian life and those who have gained maturity, but he does suggest that there is a quantitative difference,
that is, that the union is more fully experienced by the mature,
than the babes in Christ. As a result, when he describes the
indwelling of the Holy Spirit in the believer and its operation
in such a person, Arnold places the greatest emphasis on the
gifts of experiential knowledge (*Erkäntnüsz*) and wisdom.[265]

In the mystical union the believer is renovated and preserved. The goal of that union is glorification. Yet glorification is not used by Arnold to mean human glorification in the
first place. In union with God and directed by the Holy Spirit
to understand the mystery of that union, the believer at the
height of maturity glorifies the Holy Trinity which, as has already been indicated, is the source of one's spiritual life.[266] As
the Father was the chief agent in calling the beginner in the
Christian life to the Son, and the Son was the chief agent in renewing the individual in conversion and union,[267] so the Spirit
directs the youth in Christ to develop maturely, to learn to 'experientially understand'[268] more fully the mysterious purpose
of the Trinity and thus to glorify the Triune God. One's glorification is dependent on participation in the glorification of
God. One glorifies God when one does the works of love which
God wishes one to do, both to one's fellow human beings and
in praise of the divine. One is able to do this completely only

to the degree that one directs one's attention to the divine will and word within.[269] To understand the mystery of the divine is to hear the Word of God united with the believer in faith and to know his will, but, to do so, one must turn from self and the attractions of the world and become renewed after the image of God.[270] Only in this way can one offer full praise to the eternal God[271] and be complete in Christ.[272] Arnold believes that relative perfection is possible for the believer,[273] although only by grace through faith[274] in Christ.[275] Such perfection is relative for the *viator* who must continually strive against sin while on earth,[276] and also because the *viator's* understanding of God is of a mystery which has no end. The *viator's* struggle is by grace; Arnold does not hold to the Pelagianism of the Boehmists,[277] nor is the believer's listening for the inner word a Spiritualist rejection of the outer words of Scripture.[278] Furthermore, the Quietist peace of Spirit is not, in Arnold's mind, fully possible.[279]

d. Tauler, Ruusbroec, and Arnold: A Comparative Survey

In the approximately five hundred pages of the *Wahre Abbildung*, Arnold quotes from medieval authors, in most cases with lengthy extracts, over six hundred and fifty times. Tauler accounts for two hundred and fourteen of these quotations; the *Medulla Animae*, quoted under his name, for an additional sixty-eight. One hundred and fifty-five are taken from Ruusbroec; one hundred and thirty-five from Bernard of Clairvaux. Harphius is cited forty-one times, Suso, twenty-eight, Richard of St. Victor, twenty-one, Bonaventure, fifteen, the *Theologia deutsch* and the *Nachfolgung des armen Lebens Christi*, thirteen times each, Thomas à Kempis, fifteen, and the *Imitation of Christ*, four. A number of passages are also quoted from Hugh of St. Victor, William of St. Thierry, Aelred of Rievaulx, Anselm, Gerhard Zutphen, Dionysius the Carthusian, Gerson, and others.

A study of the work of Tauler and Arnold immediately raises a major problem—that of Arnold's Tauler sources. Arnold accepted the *Nachfolgung des armen Lebens Christi*, and the *Medulla Animae* as by the Strassburg Dominican, and that the greater number of the sermons ascribed to him in the

1703 Frankfurt edition were his.[280] The question of Arnold's knowledge of authentic Tauler sermons is less problematic, however, than are the questions on the nature of the editions which he had at hand. Almost all the sermons now accepted as Tauler's were in the 1703 edition, but they were heavily edited. A parallel edition of the Frankfurt 1703 and Ferdinand Vetter editions of the sermon on the three births (see Addendum to this chapter) makes this immediately clear. That there is some question as to whether or not this is a Tauler or an Eckhart sermon need not delay us;[281] the question is how near the Frankfurt 1703 edition, the edition continually used by Arnold, comes to properly reflecting the intention of the authors of the individual sermons in it.

Almost from the first line of the 1703 edition's text of this sermon on the three births, a reader is aware of the 'Pietistic' tone. Whereas Tauler is describing a religious experience which takes the believer 'out of oneself' (*usser ime selber*) in love, the later edition makes no mention of this and describes the love experience rather as one of joyous triumph, and thankfulness.[282] It is the experience, according to the 1703 edition, of a 'soul rooted in proper faith' (*recht-gläubigen Seele*) rather than a 'good' soul.[283] The adjective 'true' is added to modify love, and 'heartfelt,' to modify experience, adding to the Pietistic dimension.[284] Likewise, the birth which Tauler says is found (*bevinden*) in the soul is described as experienced (*fühlen*) in the 1703 edition,[285] after one has turned to it in the new birth (*kehret und wendet*).[286] The 1703 edition, as well, insists on the necessity of faith for such an experience (*die gläubige Seele* is added, as is a description of the activity of the soul in God).[287] Rather than speaking about the new birth, the 1703 edition wishes to teach (*lehren*) concerning it, so that the parishioners (*Pfarrkinder*) listening to the sermon or meditating on it might be directed (*weisen*) to experimental knowledge of it (*erkennen*).[288]

The remainder of the parallels noted in the addendum below are self-explanatory. All indicate that, for a Pietist like Arnold approaching this Tauler text for the first time, there was ample reason to believe that the medieval mystic agreed fully with him. As a result, one may not charge Arnold with deliberately misinterpreting his text. The edition of Tauler which he had went a long way in predetermining his interpretation of that author, and the nuances of the 'modernisation' of the Tauler sermons suggested to Arnold that Tauler's theological system was the same as Arnold's own.

That Arnold was mistaken in his supposition is demonstrable. For both Arnold and Tauler, the source of all spirituality was God, but the ways in which they describe the divine are markedly different. There is much in Tauler's thought which finds its parallel in the German Dominican school of his immediate predecessors and contemporaries.[289] How well he knew Meister Eckhart's detailed discussions on God as intelligence and *esse*, or on the relationship to God of his creation,[290] cannot be said.[291] He did quote the Master,[292] but there are no careful defences of his thought, as there seem to be in the case of Heinrich Suso's *Buch der Wahrheit*, for example.[293] God, for Tauler, is always described over against his creatures. Against the manifold character of creation, God is absolutely simple;[294] although creation is imperfect, God is perfect;[295] it is transient, whereas he is eternal,[296] it is ignorant in light of his knowledge,[297] powerless in light of his power.[298] God is just[299] and merciful,[300] ever present,[301] and omniscient.[302] Tauler writes:

> Consider what a unified heart might think of. That you will find a thousandfold in him. If you wish for love or faithfulness or truth or consolation or constant presence, this is in him in every way without any matter or mode. If you desire beauty, he is the most beautiful; wealth, he is the wealthiest; power, he is the most powerful. Whatever the heart desires that will be found a thousand times over in him. Thus, you will find in the most simple, the Good above all goods which is God.[303]

And again:

> God alone is the being (*wesen*) of goodness, of love and of all things of which one is able to take being.... Let one look on the character of the single unity of being, for God is at the last, the end of simplicity, and in him all the manifold will be united and made simple in the one single being. His being is his working; his knowing, his giving, his love, his judgements are all one [as are] his mercy and his justice.[304]

Arnold, of course, ascribes to all the characteristics of God outlined by Tauler. For him, too, God is merciful and just, omnipresent and omniscient, eternal and perfect.[305] The emphasis on God's simplicity, on the unity of all the names one ascribes to him, is not of major importance for Arnold, however; he seems not even to have noticed this characteristic in

the texts he had before him. For Arnold simplicity is not so
much a characteristic of God, as of the redeemed person.[306]
True simplicity serves as a means of leading the individual
away from the many attractions of the world to desire God
alone, in unity and simplicity of desire. There is no suggestion
that this unity and simplicity of desire is rooted in the unity
and simplicity of God's being. For example, when Tauler treats
one's need for unity, he does so by describing humanity's pre-
existent state in God.[307] The individual has flowed from this
unity and must flow back to it.[308] Arnold chooses not to describe the pre-existence of the soul in this way. Rather, he
elects to discuss the unity of the relationship between the primal individual with God, a unity which is possible once again
in Christ:

> The ground of this first Adamic wisdom is clear, namely, Adam's
> close walk and communion with God, the eternal light.... [Compare
> Moses'] high wisdom and intelligence joined with his loving simplic-
> ity and his simple, childlike, harmonious, pure mind far from all
> digression, manifoldness, and dissipation.[309]

This emphasis on the unified relationship between a person and
God is paralleled in Arnold's work by a similar tendency in the
relationship within God, of the Trinity rather than the unity
of God. Tauler tends to maintain a dualism between body
and soul and, for both, the soul is the principle of the body's
life.[310] Arnold's use of these terms is not understood within
the same scholastic system as is Tauler's, nor is his division of
the powers of the soul into memory, understanding, and will.
Arnold makes no clear division between these higher powers
and the lower sensory, concupiscent, and irascible powers as
does Tauler.[311] Tauler retains this dualism of body and soul
throughout his work; he is consistent despite his discussion of a
threefold person in some of his sermons.[312] The trichotomous
division of Tauler is always a division of the soul—the internal
person, for Tauler—not the external. Thus, in his well-known
statement on the threefold aspect of the person Tauler writes:

> It is as if one were three and yet one. One is the external, animal,
> sensual; the second is the rational with rational powers, and the
> third is the mind (gemute), the highest part of the soul.[313]

That Tauler here speaks of an 'external, animal, sensual person' ought not to confuse his readers. The passage occurs in
the content of a discussion of the two eyes of the individual
and the will. One can look inward or outward. One can, and
may, follow either by an act of will. The three which are one
describe three orientations of the soul, not divisions of the individual, who may choose to use animal, rational, or 'mental'

(*gemute*) inclinations. Later, in the same sermon, Tauler goes on to parallel the inclination of the mind (*gemute*) with the power of love[314] and then to define it:

> That which encloses all other things is called the mind (*gemute*). It is named a measure since it measures everything. It gives them their form.... It is far higher and more inward than the powers since all the powers take their power from it;—they are in it and flow from it, and it is in all of them but without measure.[315]

This mind (*gemute*), parallel in many ways to the scholastic *mens*,[316] is also called spirit (*geist*):

> St. Paul writes 'You are to renew yourself in the spirit of your mind (*gemute*). The spirit of a person has many names .... At times it is called a soul, that is, insofar as it pours life into the body. Thus, it is in each member and gives movement and life. And when it is called a spirit, the soul has an eternal inclination and direction to return to the ground (*grunt*) of its origin. And because of the similarity of its spiritual nature, the spirit inclines and bends once again into its origin, into the similitude. This inclination is never extinguished, not even in the damned. This is called the mind (*gemute*).[317]

It is the power of the mind (*gemute*) which allows one to turn and cut oneself off from the things of this world:

> What is true detachment (*abgeschiedenheit*).... It is that one turn and detach oneself from all that is not purely and completely God, and that an individual with an intelligent mind (*gemute*), by the light of reason, in all one's work, see through word and deed, until by this one be in the ground (*grunt*).[318]

Tauler does not always distinguish as clearly between *gemute* and *grunt* as he does in the passages quoted above. At times he uses them synonymously.[319] This has led to many differences in interpreting him on this topic. In general, however, we can support the findings of Claire Champollion, who understands Tauler to mean by mind (*gemute*), 'the spiritual energy of that most intimate part of the soul, viz., the ground (*grunt*).'[320] The mind (*gemute*) gains its energy from the ground (*grunt*) and draws the soul back toward the ground (*grunt*).

Before analysing Tauler's concept of ground (*grunt*) and the journey of the mind (*gemute*) toward it, it is well to outline Arnold's anthropology and to compare it to Tauler's. Like Tauler, Arnold makes a sharp distinction between the exterior and the interior person:

> One finds in the Scriptures, in a literal manner clearly expressed, the characteristic distinction between the exterior and the interior

> person .... Paul distinguishes in himself his flesh from the inward
> person, and designates the flesh as his limbs; the inward person as
> his mind (*gemute*). The former has nothing good in it; the latter,
> however, rejoices in God's law.[321]

According to Arnold this is the distinction between the old and
the new person[322] and is supported by numerous passages of
Scripture[323] as well as by Patristic sources.[324] Working with a
comment of Luther's in his preface to Romans,[325] Arnold goes
on to define the mind (*gemute*) as the spirit (*geist*), given to the
new born believer as the act of faith[326] and, quoting Luther on
Romans 7:22, he writes, 'The internal person is here called the
spirit born out of grace, which here, in holy individuals, strives
against externality.'[327] The new person has as a result three
possible orientations, and in defence of his position, Arnold
not only refers his reader to *Die Erste Liebe*, but to the Tauler
passage we have already discussed on the three aspects in one.

> [The chief fruit of the new birth] is called by the Scriptures and
> all the learned 'spirit,' and those who have been granted this are
> alone rightfully called spiritual, as is precisely indicated in the *Die
> Erste Liebe*. See I, 5:9, II, 5:9-10. The threefold distinction made by
> the ancients is well-known. There is flesh, soul, and spirit... [Thus,
> Tauler writes:] Each person is as if three. The first is the external,
> animal, and sensual. The second is the interior, rational, and the
> third is the mind (*Gemüth*), the highest part of the soul.[328]

Arnold's quotation of Tauler is of special interest, for despite his statement that the *Gemüth* or spirit is 'the highest
part of the soul,' he effectively ignores this in many of his other
comments on the subject. The spirit is a third part of the new
person and has no relation to the other two.

> To this the Holy Scriptures testify clearly, that a person, according
> to nature, has body and soul; afterwards, in the new birth, one
> receives something new and different from God and the Spirit which
> is to be distinguished from body and soul. And this is the spirit
> (*geist*), or the image of God lost in the fall.[329]

A distinction is to be made between soul and spirit, he writes[330]
as one is to be made between the persons of the Trinity.[331]

That Arnold places so great an emphasis on the threefold
division of the individual in distinction to Tauler's twofold distinction ought not to be unduly emphasised, however. As in
Tauler, the three parts are related to orientations and are not
intended to be regarded as essential characteristics of either the
natural or redeemed person. But the significant difference between the two must not be overlooked. The spirit or *gemute* for

Tauler is part of every individual. For Arnold it is only granted to the new person in Christ. Secondly, Arnold's Lutheranism is evident in his rejection of any possibility for a natural path from the individual to God; Arnold relates the spirit to the spark of the soul[332] and to the image of God, whereas Tauler uses both these latter images to describe the ground (*grunt*) of the soul.

In his most fully developed passage on the ground (*grunt*) of the soul, Tauler writes:

> The powers of the soul are not able to come into this ground even within a thousand miles. The knowledge which manifests itself in this ground has neither image, nor form, nor manner. It has neither here nor there, since it is a groundless groundlessness (*abgrund*), suspended in itself without ground, just as water boils up and flows. At times it sinks into groundlessness (*abgrund*), and it seems as if there is no water; a short time later it wells forth as if it would drown everything. This occurs in a groundlessness (*abgrund*). In it God is in a real way living more than in heaven or in all creatures. The one who is able to attain him there will find God truly.... God will be present to such a person who will eternally find here knowing and tasting, for here is neither going nor coming.... This ground, for the one who considers it with dedication, will shine in the powers of the soul under it, and incline and incite both the superior and inferior powers back to their beginning and to their origin, if one attends to this in one's own image and is obedient to the loving call into the ground, into the wilderness....[333]

Often Tauler describes this ground in terms of a spark (*funkelin*) which both incites and attracts the soul to itself, although he uses the image of the spark primarily when he is referring to that operative aspect of the ground (*grunt*), that is, when he is more concerned with associating ground (*grunt*) with the mind (*gemute*).[334] In the ground (*grunt*) in itself one finds God—God dwells in it—and because reason may not enter there, Tauler may only speak of God discovered in the ground (*grunt*) in negative terms. God cannot be understood by reason; he is beyond it.[335] The most common of these negative terms for God, as we have seen reflected in the passage on the ground quoted above, are groundlessness (*abgrund*), and wilderness (*wuste*). At other points he will use such words as darkness (*finsternus*) and nothingness (*nichte*).[336]

Arnold does not distinguish between spirit (*geist= gemute*) and ground (*grunt*) the way Tauler does. The Lutheran Pietist, as we have already noted, relates all images of the spark of the soul to the spirit (*geist*), and his emphasis on a unity of simple love for God rather than on a search for simple unity in God, as well as his Lutheran concern with forensic justification, mitigated against the development on Arnold's part of a doctrine of the ground (*Grund*) of the soul as a part of the individual. For Tauler, mind (*gemute*) and ground (*grunt*) are different aspects of the same reality, but for Arnold there is no possibility for two such aspects. The reality (spirit [*Geist*]) which interests him is only evident in the life of every believer, not, as in Tauler, in every person. For Arnold this spirit is from the Holy Spirit—it is the Spirit's gift—but it is not in any way a piece of the divine in the individual; it is solely a new inclination toward God, who can be known and enjoyed only in glory. The spirit lives in the believer and the believer may turn with it in its (the spirit's) orientation toward a holy life. By directing the attention ever more fully toward this goal, a believer may experience and know the ecstatic joy of life in God and love for him, but such joy and love is always the believer's psychological joy and love resulting from one's own experienced knowledge that one is living ever more fully according to God's will. It is not the result of one's having attained experience or knowledge of the Spirit itself, that is, Christ's life in the individual, and certainly not of the divine unity.

It is helpful to compare Arnold with Tauler more closely on this matter of the spirit's (*geist* or *gemute*) activity in the individual. Both writers seem to treat reason in much the same way, but Arnold is more negative in his treatment of the topic, much more prone to distinguish reason from spirit, for Tauler's concept of reason is more closely tied to his scholastic background[337] than Arnold's is to his. For Tauler, reason has a positive role to play in the lower stages of one's journey toward spiritual perfection. To come to God one must learn to detach oneself from things (*Abgeschiedenheit*). The proper use of reason is the first step back to one's origin.[338] Arnold can accept no such position. Although he seems to suggest such a principle in the sections on self-knowledge in his *Abwege*,[339] he is insistent that natural reason after the fall is totally and irreparably false[340] and blind.[341] It is in opposition, he writes, to the Christian life[342] and must be denied with all the other evils of this world. Only in the redeemed person can reason have any vitality and then, Arnold suggests, one must be circumspect in one's use of it.[343] It is the spirit, not the power of reason, which directs one away from the things of this world and allows one to become detached[344] and resigned.[345] Both detachment and resignation are the work of grace.

This is not to suggest that Tauler underestimated the importance of grace in the path to perfection. His ascetic theology considered it closely,[346] and he did not in any way deny either the necessary mediatory role of the church,[347] or the sacraments,[348] in his work. Tauler is no more to be charged with semi-Pelagianism than is Arnold.[349] It is, for example, of interest to note that Arnold always quotes late medieval mystics' words on the necessity of human activity within the context of the Spirit's purifying work, and it would be unfair to suggest that Arnold always twisted their intention by so doing.

In the first place, to charge the great mystics of the late Middle Ages with semi-Pelagianism is improper because such an action misinterprets the central concern of these writers and fails to credit properly their implicit theological position. Thus Eckhart is sometimes read as under-valuing the importance of grace in the role of an individual's redemption,[350] whereas, in reality, he took that importance for granted and had no thought of neglecting it. In his sermon, 'Et cum factus esset,' for example, he insists, after reflecting on the speed of one's mind, that the grace of God is even more rapid. The speed of one's mind in acts of penitence is important, but the grace of God is prior.[351]

The same is true of Tauler, whose insistence on the bondage of fallen nature leaves no doubt as to his belief.[352] There is a similar pessimism with regard to human nature in Ruusbroec.[353] None of these medievals, however, were primarily concerned with discussing in detail causal factors in an individual's redemption. They were, in all likelihood, satisfied with accepting in a paradoxical manner the traditional Christian teaching regarding the question; that teaching upheld the mystery that salvation depended both on the predestining grace of God and the free act of the will of the believer.[354] The mystics' primary concern, however, was with the practicalities of spiritual direction. When they raise the question of grace and

free will it is often in this context and not in a purely theological one. Tauler and Eckhart, for example, were concerned
first of all with the spiritual development of the nuns to whom
they were preaching. Their emphasis on the role of grace was
for their listeners' assurance, and their emphasis on the need
for personal purification is directed against spiritual sloth.[355]
His audience each accepted as redeemed; the souls they ad-
dressed needed nourishment not begetting, and it was to the
completion of this nourishment, to the aiding of growth rather
than birth, that each directed his words. It is similar with
Ruusbroec. His lengthy descriptions of the gifts of the Holy
Spirit and their workings in the redeemed soul,[356] his outline
of the development of virtues in believers,[357] and his numerous
depictions of the ascent to perfection[358] all point to his central
interest in Christian growth.

There are similarities, then, between Arnold and the medieval mystics he used. Both he and they might be charged
with semi-Pelagianism, but the charge in all cases arises only
because their admonitions to spiritual growth are extended to
apply to the initial birth of saving grace in the believers. Both
Arnold and his medieval predecessors were pessimistic in regard to a fallen person's ability to save himself or herself, and
both were emphatic as to the necessity of divine grace.

It is, nevertheless, important to point out that there was for
Tauler, as for many medieval authors, what has been called a
'natural covenant'[359] between God and the believer, a covenant
which Arnold could in no way accept. There were other differences, as well, between the earlier writers and Arnold, for,
while all were interested in spiritual growth, for Arnold, in con-
trast to the medieval teaching on infused grace, such growth
was within the setting of forensic justification, and was the
proclamation of redemption to which the believer might grow
in thankfulness, love, and joy. The thankfulness of God's gra-
ciousness might be experienced in a more loving community,
more dedicated concern for others, and, finally, in ecstatic joy,
but it did not change in any way the relationship between the
individual and God. One was always the sinner in spite of
developed understanding or experiental knowledge of the nature of union one had with God in Christ. This was the im-
port of Arnold's personal motto 'als der Verführer und doch

Wahrhaftig.'[360] For Arnold there is no thought of a nature-grace continuum as there is for medieval authors. None of his quotations from Bernard of Clairvaux in the *Wahre Abbildung*, for example, give any indication whatsoever that Arnold understood the nuanced relationships in Bernard's work on the stages between 'carnal love' and the love of God.[361]

There has been much discussion as to how properly to describe Tauler's doctrine of the mystical union.[362] Strong arguments can be made in favour of describing Tauler's notion of the mystical union as a substantive (*wesentlich*) union rather than a union of wills, and three passages in Tauler in which the Dominican author distinguishes between a union by grace (*von gnaden*) and by nature (*von naturen*) bear reprinting.[363]

> Man is so completely deified that everything he is and does, God does and is in him. He is so completely lifted out of his natural way [of life] that he becomes *von gnaden* what God substantively is *von naturen*. Here he feels and experiences himself as lost; he neither knows, experiences nor feels himself anywhere. He knows nothing except one simple being.[364]
>
> The spirit loses itself in the abyss so deeply and in so groundless a way that it knows nothing of itself. It knows neither word nor way, neither taste nor feeling, neither perception nor love, for everything is one, pure, sheer, and simple God, one inexpressible abyss, one being, one spirit. *Von gnaden*, God gives the spirit what he is *von naturen*; there God has united His nameless, formless, mannerless being with the spirit.[365]
>
> Here the soul becomes completely God-colored, divine, and godly. It becomes everything *von gnaden* that God is *von naturen* in the union with God, in the absorption in God. It is held above itself in God. Thus, it becomes God-colored there. Should it then see itself, it would see itself completely as God. And whoever should see it would see it in the clothes, color, manner, and being of God *von gnaden*. And whoso sees would be blessed in his beholding for God and the soul are one in this union *von gnaden*, not *von naturen*.[366]

In his commentary on these passages Steven Ozment writes:

> ... the juxtaposition of 'by grace' and 'by nature' does not argue against a substantive union between God and man. 'By means of grace,' man becomes that which God substantively is 'by nature.' 'By means of grace,' God gives the created spirit what He is 'by nature.' 'By means of grace,' the soul becomes everything that God is 'by nature.'[367]

Ozment's decision to italicise the passages he has in this section is unfortunate for while it does lend credence to his argument,

there is no justification in Tauler's text for emphasising his
lines in such a way. The emphasis must surely have been intended by Tauler to fall on the juxtaposed phrases *von gnaden*
and *von naturen*, not on any other words, and if the emphasis
does not fall there, it is, one would expect on reviewing the full
context from which the selections are taken, that Tauler's intention in the juxtaposition was to highlight the gracious gift of
union to the individual who, although a creature, and remaining a creature,[368] has been graced with so boundless a gift.
To describe that union which is beyond rational description
as making one *von gnaden* what God is *von naturen* is simply
to describe it in yet another hyperbole designed to tease the
mind out of time into eternity, not to make apparent to reason
a relationship which cannot be even imagined.[369]

When the mystic breaks through[370] the barriers of reason
into the pure spirit (*geist* or *grunt*) itself, the mystic is, according to Tauler, one likeness with God. This experience is
one of faith, one in which the believer rests in the mind and
will of God, desiring nothing other than God's will and willing
nothing other than that will.[371] This willing, this sinking in
the wilderness of the divine, is achieved only by a few, according to Tauler, at the end of strenuous effort, and, in its purity,
only for a moment.[372] Arnold, too, is concerned with a union of
wills, but his point of view, as has been demonstrated above, is
quite different from Tauler's. Whereas Tauler, and particularly
Eckhart, describe the birth of God in the soul in terms of the
ecstatic mystical union,[373] for Arnold, it is always discussed
in terms of the new birth of the believer in Christ. Thus, in
the second book of the *Wahre Abbildung*, Arnold placed two
chapters describing the spiritual birth of Christ in the soul and
the manner by which this new birth takes place. This birth is
'nothing other than the Divine life and the real inward power of
the spirit of Jesus.'[374] All Christians must go to Bethlehem;[375]
the birth is possible for all persons.[376] It is to the Taulerian
corpus, however, to which Arnold turns most often to describe
this birth. It occurs in the ground of a pure, quiet heart[377] and
brings forth many fruits.[378] It is as if one sank into the wilderness of God and rejoiced in the peace and silent assurance of
salvation in Christ. It is a 'breakthrough' into freedom, experienced in faith, accepting the redemptive activity of Christ.[379]

The close association in Arnold's thought between the 'breakthrough' into salvation and the freedom which is associated with it may have taken over by him from Ruusbroec.[380] Such a borrowing is almost impossible to demonstrate, but Arnold's wide use of Ruusbroec makes it likely that he did borrow certain ideas from the Dutch mystic. Whatever he may have borrowed, however, did not exert any direct influence on his thought, as a comparison of Ruusbroec's thought with Arnold's makes clear.

Spirituality for both Arnold and Ruusbroec finds its source in the Trinity, but Arnold has none of the interest in the philosophical basis of a Trinitarian spirituality which, as Albin Ampe has so admirably demonstrated,[381] is held by Ruusbroec. One searches Arnold's works in vain for a discussion similar to Ruusbroec's on God as one and three, on one's relationship to these aspects of God, on God's essence as unity, his mode of existence, his nature as Trinity, and the external relationships between the persons in the Trinity. No aspect of the Neoplatonic model of emanation and return can be seen in the works of Arnold in the same way as in Ruusbroec or Tauler.

Arnold was, in all probability, unaware of the philosophic complexity of the Dutch mystic's work. When he turned to Ruusbroec, he was attracted, first, by the Dutch mystic's Christological emphasis. In *Van den Gheesteliken Tabernakel*, the Ruusbroec work Arnold quotes more than any other, the Lutheran Pietist would have been drawn immediately to such passages as that in which the Flemish mystic, describing the ark of Noah as Christ, writes:

> We must live and remain obedient each to the other eternally in
> Christ with love and joy. And because of this the tabernacle remains
> eternal: it fulfills the truth of all types.[382]

Christ, again, is Moses, the giver and writer of all law, the revelation of the will of the Father, the offering of Calvary like the calves offered by Moses on Sinai.[383] Like Moses who built the tabernacle, Christ can be seen as the builder of Holy Church.[384] The number of types fulfilled by Christ appear to have no end.[385]

Ruusbroec's Christology is not Arnold's, however. In the first place, his methodology is radically different from Arnold's. Arnold displays not the least interest in Ruusbroec's use of typology, allegory, or division and expansion of the text in the style of the medieval preaching manuals.[386] More important is

the concern of Ruusbroec to tie all discussions of Christ firmly
to a discussion of the church. Obedience to Christ is obedience
to the church. Loyalty and faithful obedience to the judgements of Holy Church is a demand made for all Christians by
Ruusbroec at various points in his writing, often at the beginning of a treatise, thereby emphasising that such obedience
is a necessary first act for the Christian.[387] This tie between
Christ and the church is also expressed in terms of Christ and
the sacraments.[388]

> There is yet another coming of Christ our Bridegroom, which takes
> place each day in multiplication of graces and in new gifts, that is
> when man receives one of the sacraments, with humble heart and
> with a proper disposition, he so receives new gifts and greater grace
> through humility and through the heavenly secret working of Christ
> in the sacrament. Lack of a proper disposition is to say lack of faith
> in baptism, of penitence in confession, to approach the sacrament
> of the altar in mortal sin or with evil will, and so forth with the
> other sacraments. Such as do so, receive no new grace, but rather
> sin the more. This is the second coming of Christ our Bridegroom,
> which now is present among us each day. And we should mark this
> with devout hearts till it come to pass in us. For there is need of
> it, if we are to persist or advance in the eternal life.[389]

For Arnold, of course, any such formalised relationship between Christ and the church and/or sacraments is not possible. He did not, as already noted, reject the role of the
church or sacraments in themselves, nor did he wish to disparage their importance for the life of the believer. In his
Pietist Lutheran setting, however, Arnold was concerned with
emphasising the testimony of the Spirit directly to the believer
in the word and sacraments and the nature of the hidden spiritual church so as to make Christians of his day more clearly
aware of the Lutheran distinction between the spiritual church
and the physical church, and between the inner testimony to
God's promise of salvation in word and sacrament and the eternal testimony. Fully a Pietist, Arnold could not accept any
compromise on these distinctions in theory or, his particular
concern, in practice. Ruusbroec's and Arnold's attacks on clerical shortcomings and sins are likewise to be differentiated, for
whereas Ruusbroec attacks unfit priests and religious because
they detract from the full glory and operation of Christ's body
in the world, Arnold, in addition to this concern, is much more
interested in pointing out the implication and suggestion made

by such persons that it is only the ritual forms and speculative theories in the established church which are of significance for Christian life. The dualism in Ruusbroec's work tends to be between adequate and inadequate forms of Christian life; for Arnold, such a dualism is rather between true and false, hypocritical forms.

If one sets aside, for the moment, this distinction between Ruusbroec and Arnold regarding their approaches to Christ and the church, some proximity between the two men can be found in their understanding of justification. For both Ruusbroec and Arnold the human person was created toward (*ad*) the image of God, with which he or she was to be united in a certain way. In the introduction to his *Gheestelike Brulocht*, next to the *Gheesteliken Tabernakel* the Ruusbroec treatise most often quoted by Arnold, the Dutch mystic describes the purpose of human creation as follows:

> 'See, the Bridegroom comes: go out to meet Him.' St. Matthew the Evangelist writes these words for us, and Christ spoke them to His disciples and to all men, as we may read in the parable of the virgins. This Bridegroom is Christ, and man's nature is the bride, whom God has made in the image and the likeness of Himself. And in the beginning He had set her in the highest place, and in the fairest, richest, and most splendid of dwellings, that was, in paradise. And to her He had subjected all creatures, and He had adorned her with graces, and to her He had given a commandment: and had she shown obedience, she would have deserved to live steadfast and secure in everlasting wedlock with her Bridegroom and never to fall into any distress or sin.[390]

But humanity fell and turned away from the image of its own desires. Having so fallen, however, Ruusbroec goes on to say, the individual can once again by the grace available in Christ's redemption turn toward the image.[391] Prevenient grace is available to all,[392] who, if they accept its promptings, are led to recognise their sinful state and to desire a better one.[393] There is a second occurrence, however, necessary before one may be justified. When one has done all that is in one, that is, under prevenient grace, God brings grace by which one merits justification; these two, human activity and God's grace, are both necessary

> When man has done all that he is able, and can do no more because of his own feebleness, then there is need of the immeasurable riches of God, that they may finish the work. So there comes from above the light of the grace of God, just as a ray from the sun, and it is sent suddenly into the soul, but not through any merit or desire.

> For in this light God gives to man His free riches and liberality, God
> Whom no creature may deserve before he possesses Him. And this
> is God's secret working in the soul, above time, and it moves the
> soul and all its powers. This is the end of preventive grace, and the
> beginning of the second, that is, the supernatural light. The light
> is the first point, and from it springs the second point, which is for
> the soul to do: that is, a free turning of the will, in a moment of
> time; and from this there springs charity in the uniting of God and
> the soul. These two points hang together, so that the one cannot
> be completed without the other. Where God and the soul meet
> together in the unity of love, there God gives the light of His grace
> above time; and the soul gives its free conversion, by means of the
> power of grace, in a brief instant of time; and there charity is born
> in the soul, of God and of the soul; for charity is the lover's bond
> between God and the loving soul.[394]

The grace which merits justification is, as Ampe succinctly describes it, 'the aid of God which efficaciously moves the soul so
that the soul consents connaturally with the freedom of grace
... and an infused habitual gift which elevates the soul that
through cooperating grace the soul is both united supernaturally with its Divine Image and operates supernaturally according to the "likeness" [of God].'[395] The activity of the soul
according to this likeness grows out of the union. As Ruusbroec
puts it:

> Out of these two proceeds a perfect love towards God, and out
> of love proceeds perfect contrition and cleansing of the conscience,
> and that takes place as man looks down upon the wrong-doing and
> the defilement of the soul. Because man loves well, there arises in
> him a dislike of himself and all his works. So it is ordained in the
> converted. From this there comes an anxious contrition and a per-
> fect sorrow that he ever did transgress, and a fervent desire never
> again to sin and evermore to serve God in devoted obedience; care-
> ful confession, free from concealment, ambiguity, and dissembling;
> perfect penance following the advice of a skilled priest; and then
> the beginning of a life of virtue and all good works.[396]

There is much in the passages quoted which reminds the reader
of Arnold. The union with God takes place at the beginning
of the believer's life in Christ, and yet it is a progressive union
which is to develop after the likeness of God. The union occurs in 'a moment of time'; it is a union of faith.[397] Interestingly enough, just as Ruusbroec in his *Brulocht* goes on to
describe the virtue of humility in Christ, immediately after this
discussion,[398] Arnold does the same in the second book of his
Wahre Abbildung.[399] It may well be that Arnold noted these
matters as he read Ruusbroec and interpreted them in light

of his own theology. The contemporary reader must, however, be aware of the significant differences. Arnold had studied under Quenstedt and wrote within the Lutheran tradition of the *unio mystica*. He would have supposed in all likelihood that Ruusbroec was simply interpreting the concept of union in the early part of the *Brulocht* in the same way as Arnold's Lutheran contemporaries would have understood it. In this Arnold was mistaken. Ruusbroec's complex notion of unity in which he outlines a supernatural unity of believers with God, as Edmund Colledge describes it, was

> in their lower powers, through the imitation of Christ and His saints in virtue and suffering; in their higher powers, in faith, hope and love, through God's grace and gifts; and in their personality, where they have a unity with God essential but beyond comprehension, and rest in God beyond all creation.[400]

These three aspects of the individual are not properly Arnold's body, soul, and spirit although he may have seen them as such. Union with God in the spirit (cf. Ruusbroec's 'personality') was for Arnold 'without comprehension' and 'without means' but in faith; faith, for Arnold, although not for Ruusbroec,[401] could not be considered a means;[402] it was for him, rather, the very union itself.

In Ruusbroec's *Brulocht* the threefold path to union, that of the active, yearning, and contemplative lives, is described in terms of his threefold nature of each person. The active life is concerned with the perfection of the lower powers, with the imitation of Christ's passion, and with the fostering of virtues. The yearning life is in the life of the higher powers, above all with the enlightenment of the believer's understanding and the believer's inner reflection on the life of God rather than on personal desires. The contemplative life is the final point in the ascent.[403] A similar threefold path is outlined in *Van den Gheesteliken Tabernakel*. The active life is the life that turns from sin to God;[404] the illuminative is directed to the ordering of understanding and will;[405] the unitive life rests in God alone.[406] There is no intention in Ruusbroec's work to suggest that one leaves the earlier lives behind as one progresses to the higher levels. All three lives are lived at the same time.[407] In general, Arnold's description of the threefold life has much in common with Ruusbroec's. Arnold, too, in the *Wahre Abbildung* outlines a purgative, illuminative, and unitive way and ties it to the active practice of virtues, the yearning for full understanding of God in love, and the contemplative union with him. In Arnold's chapter devoted to the question in the *Wahre Abbildung*, he quotes extensively from Taulerian and other medieval writings, but rather than describing the nature of the respective lives, he is much more concerned with allying them to levels of Christian maturity, that is, to children, youths, and mature persons in Christ.[408] The three lives for Arnold are lived simultaneously, as they are for Ruusbroec. When one reaches the higher stage, the activities of the lower lives are not given up. This too Arnold holds in common with Ruusbroec.

But the differences between the two men on this question continue. In the first place, Arnold's description of the spiritual life has none of the dynamism inherent in Ruusbroec's. The 'inflowing' of God into the individual and the 'outflowing' of the individual back to God so admirably described by Ruusbroec in the second book of his *Brulocht* is not even suggested in Arnold's work. Nor can one find in Arnold's writings anything of the overall unity between the three parts of the person and the three lives which one meets in Ruusbroec. Secondly, Arnold's decision to emphasise three types of spiritual growth, tends to formalise his spiritual doctrine and to deemphasise its dynamics. This is in keeping with his teaching as a whole, which is continually juxtaposing true Christians and false Christians; his major interest lies in describing the proper Christian life as he understood it, in chastising the false, and in demanding their reform, rather than in developing an integrated treatment of the dynamics involved in spiritual growth. One searches Arnold's writings in vain for as careful a treatment of the development of virtues, for example, as one finds in Ruusbroec. When Arnold treats humility, it is not as a necessary stage for obedience as it is in Ruusbroec,[409] but rather it is as the opposite of the pride among hypocritical, pharisaic Christians. The 'moment of time,' which Ruusbroec notes in the introduction to his discussion of the active life in the *Brulocht*, is the 'brief instant' in which God's grace and human free will meet and 'charity is born in the soul.'[410] From that initial moment proceed all the moments thereafter in which grace and free will cooperate in 'perfect contrition and cleansing of the conscience.'[411] The 'moment of time' in which Arnold understands faith as grasping God's promise of redemption is an instant in God's sight in which the believer is elected, justified, sanctified, and glorified. It includes all the virtues which, it is expected, will be manifested in the believer.

Ruusbroec's and Arnold's differing uses of the phrase 'in a moment of time' explain, as well, their respective positions on the mystical union and the renewal of the image of God in the believer. In Arnold, there is no suggestion, as there is in Ruusbroec, of a distinction (Ampe suggests a tension as there is a tension between God's unity and trinity) between an essential union by which God imprints in the believer his image, his very self, his essence, and an active union by which he gives the believer created grace, his nature, through which the soul can flow out to become like God.[412] For Arnold, there is only human faith, knowledge of God's acceptance, and the growing act of experienced love in the believer who continues throughout life to mature in both the assurance of salvation and loving thankfulness and joy in God for that salvation. At the supreme peaks of such love, one can gain experiences which are possible to be described in a manner similar to the way Ruusbroec described the 'delectable rest' and consuming love which is above rational explanation but the experiences described by Arnold are not those outlined in Ruusbroec's works. Arnold makes no distinction between image and likeness in the way Ruusbroec does. The image of God is reestablished in the believer with the act of gracious faith. It is not understood in association with an active agent by which it flows out and back to its origin. For Arnold, only the individual's own psychological love flows in such a way, and although one may be united by faith in Christ with God, although one may fulfill acts of love toward one's fellows, and practice virtue and purge sins under the illumination of a growing experiential knowledge of God's acceptance of oneself, although one may progressively bring the old person under control, overcome the flesh, and allow the new person to develop toward maturity, one remains as a *viator* at once always, albeit justified, a sinner, *simul justus et peccator, als der Verführer und doch wahrhaftig.*

Addendum: Parallel Texts of Tauler's Sermon 'On the Three Births' from the Frankfurt 1703 Tauler and Vetter Editions

[Important differences are italicised; significant omissions in either text are bracketed.]

Frankfurt 1703 Edition

Vetter Edition

[69] Heute begehet
man in der gantzen werthen
Christenheit dreyerley
Geburten/ in welcher ein
ieglicher Christen Mensch so
grosse Freud und Wonne *haben
solte/dasz er für hertz-
licher Liebe/ [für frölichem
Jauchzen/ für freudenreicher]*
Dancksagung/ ja für innig-
*licher Freude [seines
Hertzens hüpffen und]
springen solte.* Und warlich/
wer bey sich selbsten noch
seine Freude hieraus fühlet
und hat/ der mag sich [wohl
für Leid und Traurigkeit]
fürchten.

[7] Man beget húte drier leige
geburt in der heilgen cristen-
heit, in der ein ieglich
cristen mensche so grosse
weide und wunne *solte nemen
daz er rehte von wunnen solte
[usser ime selber] springen*
in iubilo und in minnen, in
dangnemekeit und inrelicher
frôude, und weler mensche des
nit in ime bevint, der mag
sich vôrhten.

Die erste und oberste
Geburt ist/ da der himml-
ische Vater gebieret seinen
eingebornen Sohn/ also dasz
er mit ihm ist ein einiger
gleich-wesentlicher ewiger
GOtt/ [und doch eine sonder-
bare] und von ihm unter-
schiedene Person. Die
andere Geburt ist/ da die
jungfräuliche Mutter einen
Sohn aus ihrem Leib gebieret/
in unverletzter Keuschheit/
ohn alle Sünde und Gebrech-
lichkeit. Die dritte Geburt
ist/ da Gott zwar warhafftig/
aber doch geistlicher weise
mit Lieb und Gnaden/ alle Tag
und Stunde geboren wird in
einer *rechtgläubigen* Seele.

Nu di erste und die úberste
geburt daz ist das der himelsche vatter gebirt seinen
eingebornen sun in gôtlicher
wesenlicheit, in persônlicher
underscheit. Die ander geburt
die man húte beget, das ist
die mûterliche behaftekeit
die geschach megdelicher
kúschikeit in rehter luterkeit.
Die dirte geburt ist daz Got
alle tage und alle stunde wurt
werlichen geistlichen geborn
in einre *gûten* sele mit gnoden
und mit minnen.

Die drey Geburten begehet man mit den drey Messen/ so an diesem hohen Fest gelesen werden. Denn die erste Messe singt man mitten in der finstern Nacht/ und fängt also an: Der HErr hat zu Mir gesprochen: Du bist mein Sohn heute/ [(das ist/ von Ewigkeit)] hab ich dich gezeuget: Und diese Messe bedeut die verborgene Geburt/ welch in der Finstern/ das ist/ in der verborgenen unbekandten Gottheit geschicht. Die andere Messe hebt also an: Das Licht scheinet heut über uns. Diese Messe bezeichnet den Glantz der vergötterten menschlichen Natur/ [das ist/ wie S. Paulus spricht/ dasz Gott in Fleisch offenbaret ist.] Diese Messe wird zum [70] theil in der Nacht/ zum Theil am Tage gesungen: weil die Geburt/ darvon sie handelt/ zum Theil bekandt/ zum Theil aber unbekandt gewesen ist. Die dritte Messe singt man am hellen Tage/ und fängt also an: Puer natus est nobis: Ein Kind ist uns geboren/ ein Sohn ist uns gegeben. Sie bedeut aber und zeigt an die holdselge liebliche Geburt/ die alle Tag und Stunden/ ja auch alle Augenblick geschehen soll/ und geschicht in einer jeglichen *rechtgläubigen* Seele/ wahn sie in [wahrer] Liebe und [hertzlichem] Auffmercken sich darzu kehret [und wendet.] Denn soll [die gläubige

Dise drie geburte beget man húte mit den drien messen. Die erste singet man in der vinster naht, und get an: dominus dixit ad me, filius meus es tu, ego [8] hodie genui te; und dise messe meinet die verborgene geburt die geschach in der vinsterre verborgenre unbekanter gotheit. Die ander messe get an: lux fulgebit hodie super nos, und die meinet den schin der gegôtteter menschlicher naturen, und die messe ist ein teil in vinsternisse und ein teil in

dem tage, su waz ein teil bekant und ein teil unbekant. Die dirte messe singet man in dem kloren tage, und die get an: puer natus est nobis et filius datus est nobis, und meinet die minnencliche geburt die alle tage und in allen ougenblicken sol geschehen und geschiht in einre ieglicher *gûten* heilgen selen, ob sú sich darzu kert mit warnemende und mit minnen, wan sol sú diser geburt in ir bevinden und gewar werden, daz mûs geschehen durch einen inker und widerker alle ir krefte, *und in diser geburt wurt ir Got also eigen und*

Seele] diese Geburt in ihr
fühlen und erkennen/so musz
sie alle ihre Kräffte [in
GOTT] richten und kehren.
Und wenn sie das thut/ *so*
schencket sich GOtt der
Seelen dermassen zu eigen in
und durch diese dritte
Geburt/ dasz sie nichts
eigeners haben kan/ als
eben ihren GOtt und Heyland
CHristum: wie denn die
göttliche Wort solches hell
und klar anzeigen/ als da es
heisset: Ein Kind ist uns
geboren/ uns ist ein Sohn
gegeben/ das ist/ disz
geborne Kind und Sohn ist
unser: es ist unser gantz
und gar eigen über alles:
Dann es wird ohn unterlasz/
zu allen Zeiten und Stunden
in uns geboren.
Nun von dieser
dritten und letzten Geburt/
[welche aber sehr lieblich
und freudenreich ist]/ habe
ich mir diszmal am ersten zu
lehren fürgenommen/ [und auch
meine liebe Pfarrkinder zu
weisen]/ wie wir können und
sollen dar zu gelangen.
[Damit wir aber etlicher
massen erkennen mögen]/ wie
diese Geburt gantz adelich
und fruchtbarlich geschehe/
so müssen wir *mit Fleisz*
bedencken die allererste und
oberste Geburt/ da GOtt der
Vater seinen eingebornen Sohn
in der Ewigkeit [zeuget und]
gebieret. Denn aus dem
unendlichen Uber[71]flusz des
überschwenglichen Reichthums
seiner Güte/ hat GOtt sich
nicht können enthalten/ er

git sich ir als eigen uber
alles daz ie oder ie
eigen wart. Daz wort daz
sprichet: ein kint ist uns
geborn und ein sun ist uns
gegeben; er ist unser und
zûmole unser eigen und úber
alle eigen, er wurt alle zit
geborn one underlos in uns.

Von diser minnenclichen
geburt, die dise leste messe
meinet, von der wellent wir
nu aller erste sprechen. Wie
wir herzû kummen súllent das
die edel geburt [in uns]
adellichen und fruhtberlichen
geschehe, daz súllent wir
leren an der eigenschaft der
ersten vetterlichen geburt,
do der vatter gebirt sinen
sun in der ewikeit, wan von
úberflússikeit

des úberwesenlichen richtûmes
in der gûte Gottes so enmôhte
er sich nút inne enthalten er

hat sich müssen ausgiessen/
und andern mittheilen. Denn
des guten Natur und Eigenschafft ist/ wie S. Augustinus zeuget/ dasz es sich
ausgiesse/ und andern
mittheile. So hat nun GOtt
der Vater sich ausgegossen/
indem er von Ewigkeit her
seinen Sohn also geboren hat/
dasz er zwar eines göttlichen
Wesens mit ihm/ und doch
gleichwol die andere Person
in der einigen und ewigen
Gottheit ist/ hernacher hat
GOtt sich auch ausgegossen in
alle Creaturen/ darum spricht
S. Augustinus abermal: Weil
GOtt gut ist/ so sind wir
auch gut: und alles guts/ so
die Creaturen in und an sich
haben/ kommt gantz und eigentlich her von der wesentlichen
Gütigkeit des Schöpffers.
Es möcht aber jemand
wol fragen: Ey/ welches ist
dann nun die Eigenschafft/ die
wir in der väterlichen Geburt
bedencken und lernen sollen?
Antw. Das ist also zu
verstehen: Der *himmlische*
Vater kehret sich mit seinem
göttlichen Verstand in der
Eigenschafft seiner Person in
sich selbst/ [und indem er
sich selbst anschauet]/ und
den wesentlichen Abgrund
seines ewigen Wesens mit
klarem Erkäntnüsz durchsiehet/
spricht er sich selbst/ aus
solchem seinem Verstand und
Erkäntnüsz gantz aus: solches
Aussprechen oder Wort ist
sein Sohn: und solches
Erkennen sein selbst ist das
Gebären seines Sohns in

mûste sich uzgiessen und
gemeinsamen, wan als [Boecius
und] sant Augustinus sprechent
daz Gottes nature und sin art
ist daz er sich uzgiesse, und
alsus hat der vatter sich
uzgegossen *an dem usgange der*
gôtlichen personen, und vor
hat er sich entgossen an die
creaturen. Darumb sprach sant
Augustinus: 'wan Got gût ist,
darumb sint wir, und als daz
alle creaturen gûtz hant, daz
ist alles von der wesenlichen
gûte Gcttes allein.'

Weles ist nu die eigenschaft
die wir an der vetterlichen
geburt *mercken* und leren
sullent? Der vatter *an siner*
Persônlicher eigenschaft so
kert er in sich selber mit
sime gotlichen verstentnisse
und durchsiht sich selber in
clorem verston den wesenlichen
abgrunde sins ewigen wesens,
und von dem [blossen] verstane
sin selbs so sprach er sich
alzûmole us, und daz wort ist
sin sun und daz bekennen sin
selbes daz ist daz geberen
sins sunes in der ewikeit; er
ist inne blibende in wesen
licher einikeit und ist uzgonde
an personlichem underscheide.
Alsus get er in sich und
bekennet sich selber, und er
get danne

Ewigkeit: So bleibet nun der
Vater in sich selbst in
wesentlicher Einigkeit/ und
geht gleichwol auch aus durch
persönlichen Unterscheid:
Denn indem der Vater [sich
selber anschauet/ und] in
sich selber gehet/ so
erkennet er sich selbst
[vollkömmlich:] und indem er
wiederum aus sich selbst
gehet/ bringet er[72]herfür
sein Ebenbild/ welches er in
sich selbsten erkannt/ und
verstanden hat [durch persönlichen Unterscheid:] und
gehet denn wiederum in sich
in vollkömmener Wolgefälligkeit sein selbst/ und diese
Wolgefälligkeit sein selbst
fliesset aus/ gleichwol in
sich selbst in ein unaus-
sprechliche Liebe/ und diese
Liebe ist der heilige Geist.
Also bleibet GOtt in sich
selbst und gehet doch aus/ und
gehet wieder in sich selbst.
*So ist es nun wahr/ was man
sagt: nemlich/ Dasz ein
jeder Ausgang geschicht an
des Eingangswillen.* Derohal-
ben/ gleich wie der Himmels-
Lauff der alleredleste und
vollkömmenste ist/ weil er
gantz eigentlich wieder gehet
in seinen Anfang/ daher er
entsprungen/ also ist auch
des Menschen [Bewegung oder]
Lauff gantz *edel und voll-
kommen*/ wenn derselbe gantz
ohne Mittel wiederum zu
seinem ersten Ursprung geht.

usser sich in geberenne sin
bilde, daz er do bekant und
verstanden het, und get denne
wider in sich in volkomene
behegenlicheit sin selbes;
die behegelicheit flússet us
in ein unsprechenliche minne,
daz do ist der heilge geist
[9] alsus blibet er inne und
get uz und get wider in.
*Darumbe sint alle uzgenge umb
die widergenge*, darumb ist
des himels louf alre edelste
und volkomenste, wan er alre
eigenlicheste wider [in sinen
ursprung] und in sinen begin
get, do er uzging; alsus ist
des menschen louf *alre edelste
und aller volkomenste*, wan er
aller eigenlichest wider in
sinen ursprung get. Nu die
eigenschaft die der himelsche
vatter hat an sime ingange
und an sime uzgange, die eigenschaft sol ouch der mensche
an ime haben der ein geistliche mûter wil werden diser
gôttelichen geburt, er sol
alzûmole in sich gon und denne
usser sich gon.

Appendix

a. Tauler

The medieval author best known to Arnold and his contemporaries was Johann Tauler, almost all of whose sermons were readily available to a seventeenth-century reader. Unfortunately these sermons were printed with others falsely ascribed to Tauler and with some authentic Eckhart sermons. For the purposes of this study I have accepted as authentic Tauler sermons only those printed in Ferdinand Vetter, hrsg., *Die Predigten Taulers* (Berlin, 1910; reprint, Dublin and Zurich: Weidman, 1968) with the exception of No. 79 which is obviously a translated selection of Ruusbroec's *Boec Van den vier becoringhen*. (See Christiane Pleuser, *Die Benennungen und der Begriff des Leides bei J. Tauler* [Berlin: Erich Schmidt Verlag, 1967], 14-15.) The occurrence of these sermons in the four most common editions of Tauler's sermons used by Arnold and the other writers discussed in this study are indicated in the chart below. The first column gives the sermon number in the Vetter edition. Since the sermons in *Sermones: des hoch geleerten in gnaden erleuchten doctoris Johannis Tauleri* ... ([colophon:] Gedruckt der kaiserlichnn stat Augspurg durch Maister Hannsen Otmar in Kostnn des fürsichtigen. weiszen herrnn Johann Rynnman von ougen Und vollendet in der wochnn rogat*ionem*. In dem .1508. Jahr) are generally referred to by number; these numbers are listed in the second column. The third, fourth, and fifth columns contain the respective folio and page numbers of the parallel sermons in *Johannis Tauleri des seligen lerers Predigt/ fast fruchtbar zu eim recht Christlichen leben. Deren Predigen gar nab hie in diesem Buch des halbtheyls meer sind denn in andern vorgetruckten bücheren die man sidhar mit der hilff gottes funden hat* ... (Gedruckt zu Basel Anno M.D. XXII), in *Postilla JOHANNIS TAULERI ... Item/ zwey Geistreiche Büchlein. Das erste/ die Deutsche Theologia ... Das ander/ die Nachfolgung Christi* ... Mit einer Vorrede Johannis Arndtes (Gerdruckt zu Hamburg/ durch Hans Moser, In Verlegung Michael Herings. ANNO MDC xxi), and in *Des hocherleuchteten und theuren Lehrers D. JOH. TAULERI Predigten Auff alle Sonn- und Feyertage* ... Nebst einer Vorrede Herrn D. Philipp Jacob Speners ... (Franckfurt am Mayn und Leipzig/ Verlegts Johann Friedrich Gleditsch/ Im Jahr Christi 1703).

Vetter No.	1508 No.	1522 F	1621 P	1703 P
1	1	i	1	68
2	3	v	11	139
3	4	vii	16	151
4	5	ix	19	159
5	7	xi	25	178
6	10	xvii	40	254
7	11	xix	43	267
8	12	ccii	50	—
9	13	cciiii	55	356
10	14	xxvi	An 16	380
11	15	xxxviii	65	202
12	16	xxx	70	393
13	17	xxxii	74	546
14	18	xxxiii	77	433
15	19	xxxiiii	80	530
16	20	xxxvi	83	569
17 (60a)	21	xxxvii	87	605
18 (60b)	22	xxxix	92	618
19	23	xli	96	633
20	24			
21	25			
22	26			
23	27	xlix	110	669
24	28	xlvii	114	681
25 (60c)	34			
26	30	lii	123	706
27	31	lv	128	749
28	32			
29 (60d)	33	lvii	132	757
30 (60e)	29	li	119	693
31 (60f)	35	lxiii	144	801
32	36	lxi	140	786
33	37			
34 (60g)	38	lxx	161	866
35 (60g)	39	lxxiix	164	874
36	40	lxxxv	173	901
37	41	lxxviii	179	921
38	42	lxxx	183	933
39	44	lxxxiii	194	962
40	69	cxxxvi	314	1490
41	45	lxxxix	205	994
42	48	xciiii	216	1085
43	47	xcii	210	1046

44	52	ci	231	1129
45	53	cii	234	1134
46	71	ccxci	325	1568
47	56	cviii	249	1182
48	72	cxliii	329	1578
49	73	cxlv	333	1406
50	74	cxlvi	341	—
51	76	cl	345	1588
52	75	cxlviii	336	1417
53	59	cxvi	267	1229
54	55	cvi	244	1158
55	79	clv	356	1612
56	61	cxix	274	1266
57	50	xcvii	223	1106
58	68 (Lieben)	clxii	—	—
59	68 (Nun)	clxiii	2171	1242
60	68 (Wie)	clxiiii	376	—
61	70	cxxxix	319	1502
62				
63	46			
64	54	ciiii	438	1146
65	77	cli	348	1594
66	57	cx	253	1194
67	58	cxiii	259	1210
68	80	clvii	360	1622
69	66	cxxxii	302	1710
70	60	cxviii	171	1242
71	83	clxi	369	
72	49	xcvi	219	1094
73	51	c	228	1121
74	62	cxxiii	282	1293
75	63	lxxv	287	1309
76	64	cxxvii	293	1324
77	65	cxxx	298	1558
78	67	cxxxiii	306	1715
79				
80	68 (Dilectus)	cxxxv	311	1400
81	81	cxxi	279	1284

[It is possible as well that the following may be authentic Tauler sermons. See Pleuser, 29-30 for details.]

9	xiv	32	186
78	ciii	352	1604
82	clviii	363	1634

On the text of the Vetter edition see Philipp Strauch's review 'F. Vetter, hrsg., *Die Predigten Taulers* ...,' *Deutsche Literaturzeitung*, 39

(1918), 183-188 and his 'Zu Taulers Predigten,' *Beiträge zur Geschichte der deutsche Sprache*, 44 (1919), 1-26. For details see Georg Hofmann, 'Literaturgeschichtliche Grundlagen zur Tauler-Forschung' in Ephrem Filthaut, hrsg., *Johannes Tauler: Ein deutsch Mystiker* (Essen: Hans Briewer Verlag, 1961), 436ff. Note also A.L. Corin, *Sermons de J. Tauler* (Liege et Paris: Imp. H. Vaillant- Carmanne et Edouard Champion, 1929) for details. On the text of the Franckfurt 1703 Tauler and its earlier editions see Filthaut, 476-477.

The ascription of much material to Tauler which was not by him was common until the studies of Henrich Suso Denifle in the nineteenth century. See Angelus M. Walz, 'Denifles Verdienst um die Taulerforschung' in Filthaut, 8-18 and H.S. Denifle, *Die deutschen Mystiker des 14. Jahrhunderts*, hrsg., Otwin Spiess (Freiburg in der Schweiz: Paulusverlag, 1951), IXff. The *Historia Tauler*, commonly called the *Meisterbuch* and printed with the early editions of the sermons, is not of Tauler. The work was translated into English by Suzanna Winkworth, *The History and Life of the Reverend Doctor John Tauler* (London: H.R. Allenson, 1905). On authorship see H.S. Denifle, *Taulers Bekehrung Kritisch Untersucht* (Strassburg and London: Karl J. Trübner and Trübner and Comp., 1879) in *Quellen und Forschung zur Sprach- und Culturgeschichte der Germanischen Völker*, Bd. XXXVI. and his 'Die Dichtungen Rulman Merswins,' *Zeitschrift für deutsches Altertum*, 24 (1880), 463-540 and A. Chiqot, *Histoire ou Legende? Jean Tauler et le 'Meisters/ Buoch'* (Strassburg et Paris: A. Vix et Cie et E. Champion, 1922). On the anonymity of *Das Buch von geistlicher Armut* regularly ascribed to Tauler under the title *Nachfolgung des armen Lebens Christi* see Denifle's edition (München, 1877). The *Medulla Tauleri* is the title given by later writers to reprints of the *Epistolen* as printed in *Des erleuchten D. Johannis Tauleri/ von eym waren Evangelischen leben/ Gotliche Predig/ Leren/ Epistolen/ Cantilenen/ Prophetien ...* (Gedruckt zu Cöllen im jar Vnsers Herren M. D. xliij den vierten tag Junij), cccxxj-cccxxxj. The letters were reprinted from the earlier edition by the Schwenckfelder Christian Hoburg (see above, Chapter Four) in the Franckfurt 1703 Tauler and by Gottfried Arnold in his *Güldene Send-Schreiben derer Alten Christen* (Büdingen/ Drucks und verlegts Joh. Fried. Regelein. 1723), 286-341. For Arnold and his contemporaries the contents in the Surius translation of Tauler which were not ascribed to another author were considered to be by the Strassburg Dominican. See *D. Ioannis Thavleri. Clarissimi ac illuminati theologi, sermones, de tempore & de Sanctis totius anni, plane piissimi: reliquaque ejus pietati ac devotioni maxime inservientia. Opera omnia.* a R.F. Lavrentio Surio Carthusiano in latinum sermone in translata, postremo recognita, & nunc. iterum diligentissime recusa. Quorum catalogum post praefationem in venies (Parisiis, Apud societatem Minimam. M. DCXXIII). The contents of the volume are as follows:

D.J.T. Conversionis vitaeque historia.
Conciones de tempore.

Conciones de sanctis.

Tractatus de veris virtutibus institutionibusque divinis

Epistolae complures, devotionem divinumque spirantes amorem.

Prophetiae de plagis nostri temporis.

Cantica quaedam spiritulia animae.

De IX rupibus sive gradibus Christianae perfectionis.

Speculum lucidissimum.

Convivium M. Eckarch.

Colloquium theologi.

Exhortatio, seu oratio fidelis, praeparatoria ad mortem.

Praeparationes IIII notabiles ad mortem felicem.

Alia notabilis ad mortem felicem preparatio.

Epistola divi Henrici Susonis ad quendam in mortis agone Constitutum.

De X Caecitatibus et XIII divium amoris radicibus libellus optimus.

T. de vitae ac passione Christi exercitia.

b. Eckhart

Although some authentic or possibly authentic Eckhart sermons were included in the sermons ascribed to Tauler in the editions described above, most were printed in a separate section to those editions. For present purposes only those sermons are considered to be authentic Eckhart sermons which appear in Josef Quint *et al.*, hrsg., *Meister Eckhart. Die deutschen und lateinischen Werke* (Stuttgart: W. Kohlhammer Verlag, 1958-) — hereafter: Eckhart, *Werke*, which cites earlier studies, but note continuing discussion in Max Pahnke, 'Neue textkritische Eckhart Studien,' *Zeitschrift für deutsche Philologie*, 80 (1961), 2-39 and Josef Quint, 'Zu Max Pahnkes neuen Editionsversuchen an Meister Eckhart,' *ibid.*, 80 (1961), 272-287. Note especially Josef Quint, *Die Uberlieferung der deutschen Predigten Meister Eckharts* (Bonn: Ludwig Rohrscheid Verlag, 1932) which treats in detail the text ascribed to Eckhart and printed in Franz Pfeiffer, hrsg., *Deutsche Mystiker des Vierzehnten Jahrunderts: Meister Eckhart* (Leipzig, 1857; reprint; Aalen: Scientia Verlag, 1962). Because of the common use of the sermon numbers as printed in Pfeiffer in citing Eckhart sermons, these have been printed in the first column below. The second column indicates the place of the sermon in Eckhart, *Werke*. The third column lists a sermon's appearance in Josef Quint, hrsg., *Meister Eckehart: Deutsche Predigten und Traktate* (München: Carl Hanser Verlag, [1963]) according to its number. The final three columns indicate the location of a sermon in the Basel 1522 Tauler, the Hamburg 1621 Tauler, and the Franckfurt 1703 Tauler respectively.

Pfeiffer	Deutsche *Werke*	Quint trans.	1522 Tauler	1621 Tauler	1703 Tauler
I		57	III	5	114
II		58	X	20	159

III					
IV		59	XII	28	186
V					
VI	I, 1, 3ff.	1	clxxxvi	426	433
VII		35			
VIII	I, 2, 21ff.	2	ccxcvi	Anh. 86	—
IX		28			
X	II, 25, 3ff.	38	ccl	Anh. 13	—
XI	II, 26, 19ff.	49	ccli	Anh. 15	—
XII	II, 27, 37ff.	50	cclxxxii	Anh. 65	—
XIII	I, 5b, 83ff.	6	cclxvi	Anh. 38	—
XIV	I, 16b, 261ff.	16	ccxcix	Anh. 91	—
XV		44			
XVI					
XVII			clxviii	386	81
XVIII			cclxxv	Anh. 47	—
XIX		37	ccxlii	Anh. 1	—
XX	II, 44, 331ff.		ccxlvii	Anh. 6	—
XXI	I, 17, 279ff.	17			
XXII	II, 53, 525ff.				
XXIII	II, 47, 389ff.		cclxiiii	Anh. 34	741
XXIV	I, 13a, 223ff.	15			
XXV	I, 3, 46ff.	3	cclxxxvi	Anh. 69	
XXVI					
XXVII	II, 34, 156ff.				
XXVIII					
XXIX	II, 38, 224ff.				
XXX	II, 45, 352ff.				
XXXI	II, 37, 205ff.	51			
XXXII	I, 20a, 322ff.	20			
XXXIII	II, 35, 170ff.				
XXXIV	II, 55, 572ff.				
XXXV	I, 19, 308ff.	19			
XXXVI	I, 18, 249ff.	18	cclxx	Anh. 45	
XXXVII					
XXXVIII	II, 36a, 184ff.				
XXXIX					
XL	I, 4, 58ff.	4	xxxvi	Anh. 27	
XLI		53	xxxvi	Anh. 25	
XLII		40	cclviii	Anh. 23	
XLIII	II, 41, 282ff.	46			
XLIV					
XLV		45	ccxci	Anh. 79	
XLVI	II, 54b, 562ff.				
XLVII	II, 46, 374ff.				
XLVIII	II, 31, 110ff.	47			

XCV	II, 50, 452ff.		
XCVI	I, 12, 190ff. 13	cccxii	Anh. 113
XCVII	55		
XCVIII	56	cccv	Anh. 101
XCIX	42		
C	I, 21, 353ff. 22		
CI			
CII	II, 51, 461ff. 24	cii	Anh. 10
CIII			
CIV			
CV			
CVI			
CVII			
CVIII			
CVIX			
CX			

c. Ruusbroec

The Ruusbroec editions available to Arnold throughout his career were the Latin translation by Surius (edition used for this study: *D. IOANNIS RVSBROCHII ... OPERA OMNIA: Nunc demum post annos ferme ducentos e Brabantiae Germanico idiomate reddita Latine per F. Laurentium Surium Carthusiae Colonien alumnum ...* (COLONIAE Ex Officina Haeredum Iohannis Quentel, mense Martio, M. D. LII.) and the German translation of this work by G.J.C. *D. JOHANNIS RUSBROCHII, Weiland Canonici Regularis Augustiner Ordens/ und Prioris des Klosters Grünthal/ DOCTOR ECSTATICUS, Bestehend ausz allen desselben sehr Gottseligen Schrifften/ Welche die höchsten geheimnüsse der Göttlichen Lebens lehren/ Eine wanderwürdige art allerhand tugenden ausz zu üben/ vorlegen und anzeigen. Und/ weil sie von dem geist Gottes eingegeben/ allenthalben/ voller Gottseligkeit/ gesunder sitten=lehre/ und nach eines jeden menschen zustand eingerüchtet seynd/ Vorahls von dem P. F. Laurentio Surio, einen Carthäuser zu Cölln ausz dem Holländischen ins Lateinische/ Nun aber zum gemeinen nutz: Alles ins Teutsche treulichst übersetzet/ von G.J.C. Und mit einer Vorrede heraus gegeben von Gottfried Arnold* (Offenback am Mayn/ Druckts Bonaventura de Haunog, Ysenburg und Büdingischer Hof=Buchdr. Im Jahr 1701-). On earlier translations see Wolfgang Eichler, *Jan van Ruusbroecs 'Brulocht' in oberdeutscher Uberlieferung* (München: C.H. Beck'sche Verlagsbuchhandlung, 1969).

Abbreviations

Arnold, Macarius

Arnold, Gottfried. *Des Heiligen Macarii Homilien*, 2. Aufl. Leipzig, 1702.

AS

Arnold, Gottfried. *Auserlesene Sendschreiben*. Franckfurt und Leipzig, 1700.

Augsburg 1508 Tauler

Tauler, Johann. *Sermones* . . . Augsburg, 1508.

Basel 1522 Tauler

Tauler, Johann. *Predigen* . . . Basel, 1522.

BSN

Arnold, Gottfried. 'Von dem Bruder- und Schwester-Namen' in Christian Thomas, *Historie der Weiszheit und Thorheit*. Halle, 1693.

CS

Schwenckfeld, Caspar. *Corpus Schwenckfeldianorum*, ed. Chester D. Hartranft. Leipzig, 1907-1961.

DS

Dictionnaire de spiritualité. Paris, 1937-

Ehmann

Arnold, Gottfried. *Sämmtliche Geistliche Lieder*, hrsg., K.C.E. Ehmann. Stuttgart, 1856.

EL

Arnold, Gottfried. *Die Erste Liebe*. o.O., 1696.

Franckfurt 1703 Tauler

Tauler, Johann. *Predigten* . . . Vorrede Herrn D. Philipp Jacob Speners . . . Franckfurt und Leipzig, 1703.

FSA

Arnold, Gottfried. *Fratrum sororumque appellatio.* Francofurti ad Manum, 1696.

GG

Arnold, Gottfried. *Die Geistliche Gestalt.* Halle, 1704; reprint, Franckfurt und Leipzig, 1723.

GLF

Arnold, Gottfried. *Gottliche Liebes Funcken.* Franckfurt am Mayn, 1701.

Hornung

Hornung, Hans. 'Die Handschriftensammler Daniel Sudermann' in *Zeitschrift fur die Geschichte des Oberrheins*, 107 (1959), 338-399.

KKH

Arnold, Gottfried. *Unparteyische Kirchen- und Ketzer-Historie* Franckfurt, 1699-1700; reprint, Franckfurt am Mayn, 1729.

LG

Arnold, Gottfried, hrsg. *Das Leben der Gläubigen.* Halle, 1701; reprint, Halle, 1732.

MT

Arnold, Gottfried. *Historie und Beschreibung der mystichen Theologie.* Franckfurt am Mayn, 1703.

NGLF

Arnold, Gottfried. *Neue Gottliche Liebes Spruche.* Franckfurt am Mayn, 1700.

OB

Arnold, Gottfried. *Offenherziges Bekänntnüsz.* o.O., 1699.

PL

Patrologia Cursus Completus: Series Latina, ed. J.P. Migne. Paris, 1878-1890.

PLLS

Arnold, Gottfried. *Poetische Lob- und Liebes-Sprüche.* Franckfurt am Mayn, 1700.

RRG3

Die Religion in Geschichte und Gegenwart, 3. Aufl. Tübingen, 1957-1965.

Ruusbroec, Beghinen

Ruusbroec, Jan van. *Vanden XIJ Beghinen* in his *Werken*, IV, 1ff. Tielt, 1948.

Ruusbroec, Brulocht

Ruusbroec, Jan van. *Die Gheestelike Brulocht* in his *Werken*, I, 103ff. Tielt, 1944.

Ruusbroec, Sloten

Ruusbroec, Jan van. *Vanden VII Sloten* in his *Werken*, III, 81ff. Tielt, 1947.

Ruusbroec, Spiegel

Ruusbroec, Jan van. *Een Spiegel der Euwigher Salicheit* in his *Werken*, III, 129ff. Tielt, 1947.

Ruusbroec, Tabernakel

Ruusbroec, Jan van. *Van den Gheesteliken Tabernakel* in his *Werken*, II. Tielt, 1946.

Ruusbroec, Trappen

Ruusbroec, Jan van. *Van VII Trappen* in his *Werken*, III, 223ff. Tielt, 1947.

Schaffhausen KKH

Arnold, Gottfried. *Unparteyische Kirchen- und Ketzer-Historie.* Schaffhausen, 1740-1742.

Seeberg

Seeberg, Erich. *Gottfried Arnold: Die Wissenschaft und die Mystik seiner Zeit.* Meerane i.S., 1923; reprint, Darmstadt, 1964.

Sophia

Arnold, Gottfried. *Das Geheimnisz der Göttlichen Sophia.* Leipzig, 1700.

Stoeffler, Pietism

Stoeffler, F. Ernest. *German Pietism During the Eighteenth Century.* Leiden, 1973.

Stoeffler, Rise
Stoeffler, F. Ernest. *The Rise of Evangelical Pietism*. Leiden, 1970.

TE
Arnold, Gottfried. *Theologia Experimentalis*. Frankfurt, 1715; reprint Franckfurt am Mayn, 1725.

VC
Arnold, Gottfried. *Die Verklärung Jesu Christi*. 1708; reprint, o.O., 1721.

Vetter
Tauler, Johann. *Predigten*, hrsg., Ferdinand Vetter. Berlin, 1910; reprint, Dublin and Zurich, 1968.

VP
Arnold, Gottfried, hrsg. *Vitae Patrum*. Halle, 1701.

WC
Johann Arndt, *Sechs Bücher von Wahres Christentum ... 6. Aufl.; Stuttgart, 1747*

WA
Luther, Martin. *Werke*. Weimar, 1883-.

WAIC
Arnold, Gottfried. *Wahre Abbildung des Inwendigen Christenthums*. Frankfurt, 1709; reprint, Leipzig, 1732.

Notes

Notes to Introduction

1 Emil Brunner, *The Philosophy of Religion from the Standpoint of Protestant Theology*, trans. by A.J.D. Farrar and Bertram Lee Woolf (London: James Clarke and Co. Ltd., 1958), 40. Cf. Karl Barth, *Die protestantische Theologie im 19. Jahrhundert* (3. Aufl.; Zurich: Evangelischer Verlag, 1952), 100.

2 See Kurt Aland, *Spener-Studien* (Berlin: Walter de Gruyter und Co., 1943), 40.

3 A good example of such reservations is expressed by Johann Heinrich Feustking, *Gynaecum Haeretico-Fanaticum, Oder Historie und Beschreibung der falschen Prophetinnen* (Franckfurt und Leipzig/ Bey Christiano Gerdesio, Anno 1704), 180ff., 204ff., 249ff., 251ff., 290ff., 308ff., 314ff., 351ff., 451ff., 536ff., 612ff.

4 Albrecht Ritschl, *Geschichte des Pietismus* (3 Bde.; Bonn: Adolph Marcus, 1880-1886).

5 The substance of Ritschl's argument is found in his *Geschichte*, I, 7-36. Cf. his earlier 'Prolegomena zu einer Geschichte des Pietismus,' *Zeitschrift für Kirchengeschichte* 2 (1878), 1-55 and note his 'Wiedertäufer und Franziskaner,' *Zeitschrift für Kirchengeschichte*, 3 (1883/4), 499-502. See also Albrecht Ritschl, *Three Essays*, trans. by Philip Hefner (Philadelphia, Pa.: Fortress Press, 1972), Introduction and 53ff. A criticism of Ritschl's attempt to link Franciscans and the Anabaptists is provided in Kenneth Ronald Davis, *Anabaptism and Asceticism* (Kitchener, Ont. and Scottdale, Pa.: Herald Press, 1974) which rightly points to Ritschl's heavy reliance on Heinrich Bullinger's polemical accounts of the Anabaptists. Note Ritschl's own qualifications concerning the relationship between Franciscans and Anabaptists (*Geschichte*, I, 30) and, to a lesser degree, those concerning the ties between Pietists and Anabaptists (*Geschichte*, I, 7). Ritschl's suggestions regarding the relationship between late medieval mysticism and the Anabaptists were, in all likelihood, the result of his use of H.W. Erbkam, *Geschichte der protestantischen Sekten im Zeitalter der Reformation* (Hamburg und Gotha: Friedrich und Andreas Perthes, 1848). See Gottfried Maron, *Individualismus und Gemeinschaft bei Caspar von Schwenckfeld* (Stuttgart: Evangelisches Verlagswerk, 1961), 23.

6 On a similar use of medieval mystics among English authors slightly later, see Henri Talon, ed., *Selections from the Journals and Papers of John Bryon, Poet - Diarist - Shorthand Writer, 1691-1763* (London: Rockliff, 1950), 156, 198, 222-223.

7 See, for example, Ernst Benz, *Die protestantische Thebais* (Mainz und Wiesbaden: Verlag der Wissenschaften und der Literatur, Steiner in Konn., 1959), 8f.; Walter Fellmann, '250 Jahre Gottfried Arnolds *Unparteiische Kirchen und Ketzer Historie*,' *Mennonitische Geschichtsblätter*, 8 NF 3 (1951), 1920; W. Hadorn, *Geschichte des Pietismus in der Schweitzerischen Reformierten Kirchen* (Konstanz und Emmishofen: Verlag von Karl Hirsch, 1901), 50, 70, 82, 473; Emanuel Hirsch, 'Schwenckfeld und Luther' in his *Lutherstudien* (Gütersloh: C. Bertelsmann, 1954), II, 67; Jean Leclercq, Francois Vanderbroucke, Louis Bouyer, *The Spirituality of the Middle Ages*, trans. by The Benedictines of Holme Eden Abbey, Carlisle (London: Burns and Oates, 1968), 388; J. Lortzing, 'Der Pietismus lutherischer Prägung als rückläufige Bewegung zum Mittelalter,' *Theologie und Glaube*, 34 (1942), 316-324; Friedrich Otto zur Linden, *Melchior Hofmann, Ein Prophet der Wiedertäufer* (Haarlem: De erven F. Bohn, 1885), 1; A.C. McGiffert, *Protestant Thought before Kant* (London, 1911; reprint, New York: Harper and Row, Publishers, 1961), 155-161; Werner Mahrholz, hrsg., *Der deutsche Pietismus* (Berlin: Furche-Verlag, 1921), 6. Of less value are the studies of Vernon Miller, 'Would St. Francis make a Good Dunker?' *Schwartzenau*, 3 (1942) 130-144, and Earl S. Mitchell, 'The Development of Practical Ethical Mysticism or the Roots of Pietism.' *Schwartzenau*, 1 (1939), 5-13. More critical reviews of the relationship are to be found in F. Ernest Stoeffler, *The Rise of Evangelical Pietism* (Leiden: E.J. Brill, 1965), 11-16 and Friedrich-Wilhelm Wentzlaff-Eggebert, *Deutsche Mystik zwischen Mittelalter und Neuzeit* (Tübingen: J.C.B. Mohr (Paul Siebeck), 1947), 222-226, 228.

8 Heinrich Heppe in his *Geschichte des Pietismus und der Mystik in der Reformierten Kirche, nämentlich der Niederlände* (Leiden, 1879), 7 sets Pietism against all Roman Catholic principles, but cf. 12-13 where he seemingly contradicts himself on the use of late medieval mystics among the theologians he is studying. Note, as well, Koppel S. Pinson, *Pietism as a Factor in the Rise of German Nationalism* (New York, 1934; reprint, New York: Octagon Books, 1968), 51.

9 See Paul Hazard, *The European Mind* (New York: Meridian, 1963). Numerous scholars have made mention of the impact of late medieval mysticism on Arnold, but none have discussed the question in detail. See, for example, Max Goebel, *Geschichte des christlichen Lebens in der rheinisch-westphälischen evangelischen Kirche* (Coblenz: Carl Badeker, 1852-1860), II, 703 n.1; Erich Seeberg, *Gottfried Arnold: Die Wissenschaft und die Mystik seiner Zeit* (Meerane i. S., 1923; reprint, Darmstadt: Wissenschaftliche Buchgesellschaft, 1964)— hereafter: Seeberg, 106-108; Erich Seeberg, hrsg., *Gottfried Arnold*

in Auswahl (München, 1934), 17; Traugott Stählin, *Gottfried Arnolds Geistliche Dichtung, Glaube und Mystik* (Göttingen: Vandenhoeck und Ruprecht, 1966), 18f., 39ff., 73. Note, in particular, William Freiherr von Schroeder, *Gottfried Arnold* (Heidelberg: Carl Winters Universitätsbuchhandlung, 1917), 8-9, 13, 80-88 and Ingeborg Degenhardt, *Studien zum Wandel des Eckhartbildes* (Leiden: E.J. Brill, 1967), 85-86.

10 See Seeberg, 535ff. for one aspect of Arnold's influence as historian. Cf. Peter Meinhold, *Goethe zur Geschichte des Christentums* (Freiburg/München: Verlag Karl Alber, 1958), 3-10. Arnold's extensive theological and literary influence has never been traced fully, but it extended throughout Lutheran and secretarian communities down to the mid-nineteenth century. See F. Ernest Stoeffler, *Mysticism in the German Devotional Literature of Colonial Pennsylvania* (Allentown, Pa.: Schlechters, 1950), 46-47; Donald E. Miller, 'The Influence of Gottfried Arnold upon the Church of the Brethren.' *Brethren Life and Thought*, 5 (1960), 39-50.

11 The last attempt at a complete biography was Franz Dibelius, *Gottfried Arnold: Sein Leben und seine Bedeutung für Kirche und Theologie* (Berlin: Verlag von Wilhelm Hertz, 1873).

12 Jürgen Büchsel, *Gottfried Arnold: Sein Verständnis von Kirche und Wiedergeburt* (Witten: Luther Verlag, 1970).

13 Cf. Harald Wagner, *Die eine Kirche und die vielen Kirchen: Ecclesiologie und Symbolik beim jungen Möhler* (München: Ferdinand Schöningh, 1977), 45-49, 160-161, 244, 292.

14 Above all, note the related correspondence in Staatsarchiv Magdeburg, A 12 Spez. Werben, 1, 48-54; A 22, 154, 50-70; 156, 1-163; Ms Berlin, Deutsche Staatsbibliothek, all. ms 1966.7; Archiv der Franckische Stiftung, Halle, Sign. 188a, F 10 (5 letters), Giessen Universitätsbibliothek MS Phil. K 8, 3 folios (Erinnerung Arnolds zum Professor der Geschichte, 1697), Hs 19a, IV, 46. In addition to the copperplates of Arnold in various printed editions, separate pieces exist in Giessen (622) and in the Hauptbibliothek der Franckische Stiftung (Ia, Ib, Ic).

15 On this topic see, above all, Willi Fleming, 'Die Auffassung des Menschen im 17. Jahrhundert,' *Deutsche Vierteljahrsschrift*, 6 (1928), 403-446, Hans. R.G. Günther, 'Psychologie des deutschen Pietismus,' *Deutsche Vierteljahrsschrift*, 4 (1926), 144-175. Cf. Will-Erich Peuckert, 'Die Zweite Mystik,' *Deutsche Vierteljahrsschrift*, 32 (1958), 286-304. Cf. Frank C. Roberts, *Gottfried Arnold as a Historian of Christianity* (unpublished Ph.D., Vanderbilt University, 1973) who in his third chapter reaches much the same conclusions on the Pietistic nature of Arnold's historiographic principles. In his moral and ecclesiological dualism, Arnold has much in common with earlier church historians, both Catholic and Protestant. Cf. Cyriac K. Pullapilly, *Caesar Baronius: Counter-Reformation Historian* (Notre Dame, Ind.: University of

Notre Dame Press, 1975), 174f.

16 See discussion in Otto Zöckler, *Askese und Mönchtum* (2. Aufl.; Franckfurt a.M.: Heyder und Zimmer, 1897), II, 558-582.

17 For a general introduction to the visionary experience with numerous citations of visionary contemporaries of Arnold, see Ernst Benz, *Die Vision: Erfahrungsformen und Bilderwelt* (Stuttgart: Ernst Klett Verlag, 1969). Note also Peter Dinzelbacher, *Vision und Visionsliteratur im Mittelalter* (Stuttgart: Anton Hiesemann, 1981).

18 For discussion, see Gottfried Fischer, *Geschichte der Entdeckung der deutschen Mystiker Eckhart, Tauler und Seuse im XIX. Jahrhundert* (Freiburg: Universitätsbuchhandlung Gebr. J. and F. Hess, 1931). Note also Wilhelm Preger, *Geschichte der deutschen Mystik im Mittelalter* (1874-1893; reprint, Aalen: Otto Zeller Verlagsbuchhandlung, 1962), I, 7ff. et al. for similarities to Arnold.

19 See below, Chapter One, note 63.

20 See Richard Hofstadter, *Anti-Intellectualism in American Life* (New York: Knopf, 1966).

Notes to Chapter One

1 On the designation 'magisterial', see George H. Williams, *The Radical Reformation* (Philadelphia, Pa.: The Westminster Press, 1962.)

2 For introductions to sixteenth-century Radical Protestantism see, above all, Williams. Cf. as well, Roland H. Bainton, 'The Left Wing of the Reformation,' *Journal of Religion*, 21 (1941), 124-134, and *The Mennonite Encyclopedia*, ed. by Harold S. Bender, et al. (Scottdale, Pa.: Herald Press, 1955-1959).

3 Above all, see Seeberg, *passim*. Note, as well, Heinrich Ritter von Srbik, *Geist und Geschichte vom deutschen Humanismus bis zur Gegenzeit* (München und Salzburg: Verlag F. Bruckmann und Otto Müller Verlag, 1950), I, 95f.; Eduard Fueter, *Geschichte der neueren Historiographie* (München und Berlin: Druck und Verlag von R. Oldenbourg, 1911), 267-269; Franz X. von Wegele, *Geschichte der deutschen Historiographie* (München und Leipzig: Druck und Verlag von R. Oldenbourg, 1885), 738-740.

4 Gottfried Arnold's *Unparteyische Kirchen- und Ketzer-Historie, Vom Anfang des Neuen Testaments Bisz auf das Jahr Christi 1688* was first published 1699-1700 by Thomas Fritsch in Franckfurt am Main. It was translated into Dutch in 1701 and published at Amsterdam under the title *Historie der kerken en ketteren van den beginne des Nieuwen Testaments tot aan het jaar onses Heeren 1688*. Of the later editions of the work, two deserve particular attention. In 1729 the Fritsch firm reprinted an accurate edition of the first edition including Arnold's *Supplementa...* of 1703. This edition, referred to hereafter as KKH, has been used throughout this study. It is cited by part, book, chapter and section. A variorum edition was printed at Schaffhausen by Emanuel

and Benedict Hurter, 1740-1742 which included reprints of a number of the attacks on the *Kirchen- und Ketzer-Historie* as well as Arnold's defences of his work. When this work is referred to, note is made of the fact by indicating the place of publication, volume and page number.

5 For an outline of these controversies, see F. Bente, *Historical Introduction to the Book of Concord*, in *Concordia Triglotta* (St. Louis, Mo.: 1921; reprint, St. Louis, Mo.: Concordia Publishing House, 1965), and *Die Bekenntnisschriften der evangelisch-lutherischen Kirche* (Berlin: Deutsches Evangelisches Kirchenbundesamt, 1930), I, xi-xliv.

6 On the history of scholastic orthodoxy within Protestantism, see Isaac A. Dorner, *History of Protestant Theology*, trans. by George Robson and Sophia Taylor (2 vols.; Edinburgh, 1871; reprint, New York: AMS Press, 1970); Otto Ritschl, *Dogmengeschichte des Protestantismus* (3 Bde.; Göttingen: J.C. Hinrich'sche Buchhandlung und Vandenhoeck und Ruprecht, 1908-1926); A. Tholuck, *Der Geist der lutherischen Theologen Wittenbergs im Verlaufe des 17. Jahrhunderts* (Hamburg und Gotha: Friedrich und Andreas Perthes, 1852); A. Tholuck, *Geschichte des Rationalismus, Erste Abtheilung: Geschichte des Pietismus und des ersten Stadiums der Aufklärung* (Berlin: Wiegandt und Grieben, 1965); A. Tholuck, *Vorgeschichte des Rationalismus* (Berlin: Wiegandt und Grieben, 1861); Hans Emil Weber, *Reformation, Orthodoxie und Rationalismus* (2 Bde.; Gütersloh: Gütersloher Verlagshaus Gerd Mohn, 1937-1951), and the relevant sections in Hans Leube, *Kalvinismus und Luthertum im Zeitalter der Orthodoxie* (Leipzig, 1928; reprint, Aalen: Scientia Verlag, 1966). On the introduction of the scholastic method into Protestant theology, see also Hans Emil Weber, *Der Einfluss der protestantischen Schulphilosophie auf die orthodox-lutherische Dogmatik* (Leipzig, 1908; reprint, Darmstadt: Wissenschaftliche Buchgesellschaft, 1959), and Robert P. Scharlemann, *Thomas Aquinas and John Gerhard* (New Haven and London: Yale University Press, 1964), 13-43. Note, as well, Paul Althaus, *Die Prinzipien der deutschen reformierten Dogmatik im Zeitalter der aristotelischen Scholastik* (Leipzig, 1914; reprint, Darmstadt: Wissenschaftliche Buchgesellschaft, 1967). A more recent though much narrower and less useful work despite its bulk, is that of Robert D. Preuss, *The Theology of Post-Reformation Lutheranism, A Study of Theological Prolegomena* (2 vols.; St. Louis, Mo.: Concordia Publishing House, 1970-).

Excellent compendiums of scholastic doctrine are available. See Heinrich Heppe, *Reformed Dogmatics*, trans. by G.T. Thomsen (London: George Allen and Unwin Ltd., 1950); Heinrich Schmid, *The Doctrinal Theology of the Evangelical Lutheran Church*, trans. by Charles A. Hay and Henry E. Jacobs (Philadelphia, Pa.: Lutheran Bookstore, 1876); Carl Heinz Ratschow, *Lutherische Dogmatik zwischen Reformation und Aufklärung* (2 Bde.; Gütersloh: Gütersloher Verlagshaus Gerd Mohn, 1964-). See also Winfried Zeller, hrsg., *Der Protestantismus des 17. Jahrhunderts* (Bremen: Carl Schünemann Verlag, 1962).

7 See Scharlemann, 5, 22-28.

8 Ibid., 13-22.

9 On Orthodoxy's interest in personal piety, see Hermann A. Preuss and
   Edmund Smits, eds., *The Doctrine of Man in Classical Lutheran Theology* (Minneapolis, Minn.: Augsburg Publishing House, 1962), xix-
   xxii, and cf. Heinrich Schmid, *Die Geschichte des Pietismus* (Berlin,
   1863), 1, and Martin Schmidt, *Wiedergeburt und Neuer Mensch* (Witten: Luther Verlag, 1969), 5-6. Above all, see Hans Leube, *Die Reformbestrebungen der deutschen lutherischen Kirche im Zeitalter der
   Orthodoxie* (Leipzig: Verlag von Dörffling und Franks, 1924), and Heinrich Bornkamm, *Mystik, Spiritualismus und die Anfänge des Pietismus
   im Luthertum* (Giessen: Verlag von Alfred Topelmann, 1926).

10 See R. Preuss, *Post Reformation Lutheranism*, I, 44-47.

11 See Goebel, Bd. II.

12 The fullest study of Arndt's life and thought, its background and influence is Wilhelm Koepp, *Johann Arndt: eine Untersuchung über die
   Mystik im Luthertum* (Berlin: Trowitzsch und Sohn, 1912). See also his
   *Johann Arndt und sein 'Wahres Christentum': Lutherisches Bekennt-
   nis und Oekumenie* (Berlin: Evangelische Verlagsanhalt, 1959). The
   medieval sources which influenced his work are extensively discussed
   in Edmund Weber, *Johann Arndt's Vier Bücher vom Wahren Christentum, als Beitrag zur protestantischen Irenik des 17. Jahrhunderts:
   Eine quellenkritische Untersuchung* (Marburg/ Lahn: N.G. Elwert Verlag, 1969), and F.J. Winter, 'Johann Arndt der Verfasser des *Wahres
   Christentums*' in *Schriften des Vereins für Reformationsgeschichte*, 28
   (1910), 30ff. For general introduction, see my *Johann Arndt: True
   Christianity* (New York: Paulist Press, 1979). Above all, see Christian
   Braw's excellent *Bücher im Staube: Die Theologie Johann Arndts in
   ihrem Verhältnis zur Mystik* (Leiden: E.J. Brill, 1986), the findings of
   which could not be fully critiqued and integrated for this study.

13 See Stoeffler, *Rise*, 202ff.

14 See Koepp, *Arndt*, 67-143 for details on the controversy. Its scope and
   duration is evidenced by a mid-seventeenth century Silesian manuscript,
   which charts the various treatises written for and against Arndt. (See
   Schwenkfelder Library, Pennsburg, Pa., SB33.)

15 See Koepp, *Arndt*, 43-66. On Weigel, see introductions to his *Sämtliche
   Schriften*, hrsg., Winfried Zeller und Will-Erich Peuckert (Stuttgart:
   Friedrich Fromann Verlag, 1962-).

16 For a general introduction to Boehme, see particularly Alexandre
   Koyré, *La philosophie de Jacob Boehme* (Paris: Libraire philosophique
   J. Vrin, 1929), and the biography by Will-Erich Peuckert, *Das Leben
   Jakob Boehmes* (Jena, 1924); reprint in *Jacob Böhme: Sämtliche
   Schriften*, hrsg., Will-Erich Peuckert (3. Aufl.; Stuttgart: Fr. Fro-
   mann Verlag, 1961), Bd. 10. Note, as well, John Joseph Stoudt, *Jacob
   Boehme: His Life and Thought* (New York: Seabury Press, 1968).

17 On the Boehmist tradition in Germany and its relationship to Pietism, see Nils Thune, *The Boehmenists and the Philadelphians: A Contribution to the Study of English Mysticism in the 17th and 18th Centuries* (Uppsala: Almqvist & Wiksells, Boktrykerei A B, 1948), 99-114, and Arlene A. Miller, *Jakob Boehme: From Orthodoxy to Enlightenment* (unpubl. Ph.D., Stanford, 1971).

18 On the structure of Calvin's *Institutes*, see especially Francois Wendel, *Calvin: The Origins and Development of His Religious Thought*, trans. by Philip Mairet (London: William Collins, Sons and Co. Ltd., 1963).

19 KKH, II, 17, 7.

20 See particularly the discussion in Heppe and Wilhelm Goeters, *Die Vorbereitung des Pietismus in der Reformierten Kirche der Niederlände* (Leipzig und Utrecht: J.C. Hinrichs' sche Buchhandlung und A. Oosthook, 1911).

21 Note the lengthy discussion in Stoeffler, *Rise*.

22 For biographical details, see Paul Grünberg, *Philipp Jakob Spener* (3 Bde.; Göttingen: Vandenhoeck und Ruprecht, 1893-1906). Of value too are the shorter popular works by Helmut Appel, *Philipp Jakob Spener: Vater des Pietismus* (Berlin: Evangelische Verlagsanstalt, 1964); Hans Bruns, *Philipp Jakob Spener: Ein Reformator nach der Reformation* (Giessen und Basel: Brunnen Verlag, 1955). For theological and other issues related to this study, see Dietrich Blaufuss, *Spener-Arbeiten* (2. Aufl.; Bern: Peter Lang, 1980).

23 Philipp Jakob Spener, *Pia Desideria*, hrsg. Kurt Aland (3. Aufl. (Berlin: Verlag Walter de Gruyter und Co., 1964). See also Allen C. Deeter, *An Historical and Theological Introduction to Philipp Jakob Spener's Pia Desideria: A Study in Early German Pietism* (unpubl. Ph.D., Princeton, 1963).

24 For bibliographical details on the early editions of the *Pia Desideria*, see Aland, *Spener-Studien*, 1-21.

25 On the effects of the war and their relationship to the development of Pietism, see Wedgewood, *Thirty Years War*, 510-526, and Eugene Sachsse, *Ursprung und Wesen des Pietismus* (Wiesbaden und Philadelphia: Julius Niedner Verlagshandlung und Schäffer und Koradi, 1884), 1-16.

26 See Grünberg, I, 165.

27 *Pia Desideria*, 9-43. Spener here continues the tradition of detailing corruptions of the three estates. See Ruth Mohl, *The Three Estates in Medieval and Renaissance Literature* (New York, 1933; reprint, New York: Frederich Ungar Publishing Co., 1962).

28 *Pia Desideria*, 53-54.

29 Cf. ibid., 54-55.

30 Ibid., 54-55. Translated by Theodore G. Tappert (Philadelphia, Pa.: Fortress Press, 1967), 89-90.

31 *Pia Desideria*, 58-60.

32 Philipp Jakob Spener, *Hauptschriften*, hrsg., Paul Grünberg (Gotha: Friedrich Andreas Perthes, 1889), 93. Translation by A.G. Voigt (Philadelphia, Pa.: The Lutheran Publication Society, 1917), 15.
33 *Pia Desideria*, 60.
34 Ibid., 60-62.
35 Ibid., 62-67.
36 Ibid., 67ff.
37 Ibid., 74-76. Translated by Tappert, 110-112.
38 On the genesis of the name, Spener's rejection of it, and its later positive connotations, see Dibelius, 53-54, n. 3.
39 F. Ernest Stoeffler, *German Pietism During the Eighteenth Century* (Leiden: E.J. Brill, 1973), ix.
40 For general histories of Pietism, see my *Pietists* (New York: Paulist Press, 1983) and the useful articles by Carl Mirbt in *The Schaff-Herzog Encyclopedia of Religious Knowledge* (IX, 53-67) and Martin Schmidt, *RGG3*, V, 370-383. The finest continuing bibliography and journal dedicated to the topic is *Pietismus und Neuzeit* (1974-). In addition, over twenty volumes treating individual aspects of Pietism have been published in the *Arbeiten zur Geschichte des Pietismus* (Witten: Luther Verlag). Note, as well, Martin Schmidt, *Pietismus* (Stuttgart: W. Kohlhammer, 1972), and Martin Greschart, hrsg., *Zur Neueren Pietismus Forschung* (Darmstadt: Wissenschaftliche Buchgesellschaft, 1977). The best detailed histories are Friedrich Wilhelm Barthold, *Die Erweckten im protestantischen Deutschland während des Ausgangs des 17. und der ersten Hälfte des 18. Jahrhunderts* (1852/ 1853; reprinted, Darmstadt: Wissenschaftliche Buchgesellleschaft, 1968); Ritschl, *Geschichte*; Stoeffler, *Rise*, and *German Pietism*; Horst Weigelt, *Pietismus-Studien, I. Teil: Der Spener-hallische Pietismus* (Stuttgart: Calwer Verlag, 1965); W. Hadorn, *Geschichte des Pietismus in der schweizerischen Reformierten Kirche* (Konstanz und Emmishofen: Verlag von Carl Hirsch, 1901). See also Marianne Beyer-Fröhlich, hrsg., *Pietismus und Rationalismus* (Leipzig: Reclam, 1933). On the character and influence of Pietism, see Pinson, *Pietism as a Factor in the Rise of German Nationalism*, which despite its questionable premises remains valuable, and August Langen, *Der Wortschatz des deutschen Pietismus* (Tübingen: Max Niemeyer Verlag, 1954). For the Reformed church see Heppe, and Goeters. The influence of English Puritanism on both the Reformed and Lutheran churches was strong during the period. See August Lang, *Puritanismus and Pietismus: Studien zu ihrer Entwicklung von M. Butzer bis zum Methodismus* (Neukirchen Kreis Moers: Buchhandlung des Erziehungvereins, 1941), and Auguste Sann, *Bunyan in Deutschland: Studien zur literarischen Wechselziehung zwischen England und der deutschen Pietismus* (Giessen: Wilhelm Schmitz Verlag, 1951). Note also Martin Schmidt, 'England und der deutschen Pietismus.' *Evangelische Theologie*, 13 (1953), 213-224. On the spirit of the movement, see

Martin Fischer and Max Fischer on the theme 'Die bleibende Bedeutung des Pietismus' in Oskar Söhngen, hrsg., *Die bleibende Bedeutung des Pietismus ... Zur 250-Jahrfeier* (Witten und Berlin: Cansteinisch Bibelanstalt, 1960), 76ff., 93ff. and the modern apologies of Theodor Steinman, 'Der Pietismus und sein Problem.' *Zeitschrift für Theologie und Kirche*, 26 (1916), 26-70, and Dale Brown, *Understanding Pietism* (Grand Rapids, Mich.: Eerdmans, 1978). The structure of Pietist conventicles is well outlined in Friedrich Baum, *Das schwäbische Gemeinschaftleben* (2. Aufl.; Stuttgart: Quellverlag der Ev. Gesellschaft, 1929). Note also F. Ernest Stoeffler, *Continental Pietism and Early American Christianity* (Grand Rapids, Mich.: Eerdmans, 1976) and Mary Fulbrook, *Piety and Politics: Religion and the Rise of Absolutism in England, Württemberg and Prussia* (Cambridge: Cambridge University Press, 1983).

41 See Kurt Dietrich Schmidt, 'Labadie und Spener,' *Zeitschrift für Kirchengeschichte* 46 (1928), 566-583, but note Aland, *Spener-Studien*, 41-62.

42 See Philipp Jakob Spener, *Theologische Bedencken* (Halle/ in Verlegung des Waysen-Hauses, 1700-1702), III, 595, 924, 944. Cf. I, 368, 369, 373, 377, II, 409 and his *Efördertes Theologisches Bedencken* (Ploen/ Gedruckt durch Tobias Schmidt, 1690), C3ff. and *Sieg der Wahrheit und der Unschult* (Cölln an der Spree/ In Verlegung Jeremiae Schrey und Heinrich Joh. Meyers Sel. Erben. Im Jahr 1693), [vi], 7, 13 et al. For a good introduction to the broader questions of Spener's relationship to radical thought, see Dietrich Blaufuss, hrsg., *Pietismus-Forschungen: Zu Philipp Jacob Spener und zum spiritualistisch-radikalpietistischen Umfeld* (Frankfurt: Peter Lang, 1986).

43 These controversies are well outlined by Stoeffler, *Pietism*, 57-71.

44 See Erich Beyreuther, *August Hermann Francke 1663-1727* (Hamburg: Herbert Reich Evangelisches Verlag, 1958).

45 On Halle, see Stoeffler, *Pietism*, 39-87.

46 On Francke's theology, see Ritschl, *Pietismus*, II, 249-294; Stoeffler, *Pietism*, 7-23; Weigelt, *Pietismus*, 46ff. Cf. Peter Baumgart, 'Leibnitz und der Pietismus: Universale Reformbestrebungen um 1700,' *Archiv für Kulturgeschichte*, 48 (1966), 364-386.

47 See Stoeffler, *Pietism*, 23-31.

48 See Ernst Benz, 'Pietist and Puritan Sources of Early Protestant World Missions,' *Church History*, 20 (1951), 28-55.

49 See Martin Schmidt, 'Der ökumenische Sinn des deutschen Pietismus und seine Auswirkungen in der Bibelverbreitung,' in Söhngen, 60-75.

50 Cf. Carl Hildebrand von Canstein, 'Ohnmaszgeblicher Vorschlag' in ibid., 109ff.

51 Kurt Deppermann, *Der hallische Pietismus und der preussische Stadt unter Friedrich III* (Göttingen: Vandenhoeck und Ruprecht, 1961).

52 See R. Dannenbaum, *Joachim Lange als Wortführer des hallischen Pietismus gegen die Orthodoxie* (unpublished diss., Göttingen, 1952).

53 See Weigelt, *Pietismus-Studien*, 46ff. Note, as well, Stoeffler, *Pietism*, 9, n. 4.

54 Cf. Seeberg, 498-515.

55 On Calixtus' theology of church history and ecclesiology, see J.L. Neve, *The Lutherans in the Movements for Church Union* (Philadelphia, Pa.: The Lutheran Publication House, 1921), 81-.

56 See Stoeffler, *Pietism*, 47.

57 Note Spener's edition *Christliches Ehren-Bedächtnüsz... Johann Caspar Schadens* (Daselbst gedruckt mit Salfeldischer Wittwe Schrifften, [O. J.]).

58 See Dibelius, 190.

59 On separatist Pietism, see David Ensign Chauncey, *Radical German Pietism (c.1675-c.1760)* (unpubl. Ph.D., Boston University School of Theology, 1955); and note, as well, Goebel, II, 681ff., III and Seeberg, *Auswahl*, 4-5.

60 See Goebel, II, 778-809. Note especially Donald F. Durnbaugh, 'Johann Adam Gruber: Pennsylvania Prophet and Poet.' *Pennsylvania Magazine of History and Biography*, 83 (1959), 382-408 and Walter Grossmann, 'Gruber on the Discernment of True and False Inspiration,' *Harvard Theological Review*, 81 (1988), 363-387.

61 See Goebel, II, 166-193.

62 See Goebel, II, 809-855, and Heinz Renkewitz, *Hochmann von Hochenau (1670-1721)* (Breslau, 1935; reprint, Witten: Luther-Verlag, 1969).

63 See Donald F. Durnbaugh, *European Origins of the Brethren* (Elgin, Ill.: The Brethren Press, 1958); Donald F. Durnbaugh, *The Brethren in Colonial America* (Elgin, Ill.: The Brethren Press, 1967) and Julius Friedrich Sachse, *The German Sectarians of Pennsylvania 1708-1800: A Critical and Legendary History of the Ephrata Cloister and the Dunkers* (2 vols.; Philadelphia: the Author, 1899-1900); F. Ernest Stoeffler, *Mysticism in German Devotional Literature*; Donald E. Miller, 'The Influence of Gottfried Arnold Upon the Church of the Brethren,' *Brethren Life and Thought*, V (1960), No. 3, 39-50, and Donald F. Durnbaugh, 'The Genesis of the Brethren,' *Brethren Life and Thought*, 4 (1959), 4-34.

64 Goebel, III, 71-125, and Martin Brecht, 'Die Berleberger Bibel' in *Pietismus und Neuzeit*, 8 (1983), 162-200.

65 See Goebel, III, 107-125.

66 See Goebel, 289-447; Emanuel Hirsch, *Geschichte der neuern Evangelischen Theologie* (Gütersloh: C. Bertelsmann Verlag, 1949-1954), II, 274-277 and my article 'Gerhard Tersteegen, Christopher Saur and Pennsylvania Sectarians,' *Brethren Life and Thought*, 20 (1975), 153-157 which includes a more detailed bibliography.

Notes to Chapter Two

1 The striking changes in Arnold's career have been of major concern to
all his biographers and students of his thought. His friends who composed his obituary and wrote a short spiritual biography (*Seel. Hn.
Gottfried Arnolds/ ... Gedoppelter Lebens-Lauff/ Wovon der eine von
Ihm selbst projectiret und aufgesetzt worden....* [Leipzig und Gardelegen, 1716] reprinted in *Gedächnisz-Rede, bey Beerdigung Des Hoch-
Ehrwürdigen und Hochgelährten Herrn, Herrn Gotfried Arnold ...* zum
Druck übergeben von Johanne Crusio, Perleberg und Gardelegen, Verlegt von Ernst Heinrich Campen, Anno, 1719) preferred to neglect facts
which indicated radicalism. But controversial literature of his day insisted on accenting the radical tendencies in his work. Johann Christoph
Coler's *Historia Gothofredi Arnold qva de vita scriptis actisqve illivs
... exponditur* (Vitembergae, apvd C.T. Lvdovicvm, 1718) began such
an approach although, despite its tone, Coler's piece does provide de-
pendable and much needed biographical data. At the same time separatists who admired the young Arnold and saw him as a Christian
who, at least during part of his career, held closely to their principles
emphasised what from their point of view were the positive aspects of
his radical period. See especially Johann Heinrich Reitz, *Historie de
Wiedergebohren. Oder Exempel gottseliger, so bekannt- und unbekannt-
Christen.* In parts II and III of the first edition (Offenbach am Mayn/
Druckts Bonaventura de Launsoy, der gesampt Hochgrafl. Ysenbergischen Hauserbestellter Hof- und Cantzley- Buchdrucker [1701]), Reitz
made extensive use of Arnold. Only two reasonably balanced studies ap-
peared in the decades immediately following Arnold's death. One, very
brief, was Johann Caspar Wentzel's *Hymnographia, oder Historische
Lebens-Beschreibung der berühmtesten Lieder-Dichter* (Herrnstadt, bey
Samuel Roth-Scholten, 1719-1728), I, 73-86. The other was in Johann
Georg Walch's *Historische und Theologische Einleitung in die Religion-
sstreitigkeiten der Evangelisch-Lutherischen Kirche* (Jena, bey Johann
Meyer's Wittwe, 1730-1739), II, 667-718; V, 973-998. Walch's use of
Arnold's work is also to be noted in his *Historische und Theologische
Einleitung in die Religions-streitigkeiten Welche sonderlich ausser der
Evangelisch-Lutherisch Kirche entstanden* (Jena, bey Johann Meyer's
Wittwe, 1733-1736), II, 68, 285, 335.

Major differences in interpretation have marked modern Arnold
studies as well. In 1842 Albert Knapp published an abridged edition of
Die Erste Liebe (Stuttgart, 1842; reprint, Stuttgart: Verlag von Becher
und Müller, 1845), and in 1845 a selection of Arnold's lyrics (*Gottfried
Arnold's sämmtliche geistliche Lieder* [Stuttgart und Cannstatt, 1845],
reprinted with the Knapp edition of *Die Erste Liebe* in the same year).
Unfortunately Knapp's edition was marred by extensive omissions and
Knapp took major liberties with the text of the poems. Knapp's tex-
tual tamperings can in some ways be explained by his interpretation of
Arnold's life as that of an orthodox Pietist. Ferdinand Christian Baur's

historiographical survey of church history published in 1852 emphasised
once again the opposition of the radical Arnold to the orthodoxy of his
day and centered its interest as a result on Arnold's greatest work, the
Unparteiische Kirchen- und Ketzer-Historie (1699-1700) rather than on
the more orthodox works which preceded and followed it. A similar interpretation was pursued by Ferdinand Christian Baur, *Die Epochen
der kirchlichen Geschichtsschreibung* (1852) in his *Ausgewählte Werke
in Einzelausgaben*, hrsg. von Klaus Scholder (Stuttgart-Bad Cannstatt:
Friedrich Fromann Verlag (Günther Holzboog), 1963-1970), II, 97-119,
and Albrecht Ritschl, *Pietismus* (1884), who accented the polarisation
between Arnold and his contemporary church, as well as the ascetic-
mystical tendencies in his thought.

The accentuation of the mystical tendency in Arnold's theology was
continued by numerous scholars throughout the nineteenth century.
On the approaches of Adolphe Riff, *Geoffroi Arnold: L'Historien de
l'Eglise* (Strasbourg, 1847); E. Steinmeyer, 'Gottfried Arnold,' *Evangelische Kirchen-Zeitung*, 77 (Berlin, 1865), 865-872; 879-884; 897-901,
and Friedrich Floring, *Gottfried Arnold als Kirchen-historiker: Beitrag
zur Culturgeschichte des 17. Jh.* (Darmstadt, 1883), see Büchsel, 14-
16. See also W. Roselmüller, *Gottfried Arnold als Kirchenhistoriker,
Mystiker und geistlicher Liederdichter: Ein Beitrag zur Würdigung G.
Arnolds* (Annaberg, 1884). The studies of greatest significance during
this period, the history by Max Goebel (1852) and the biography by
K.C.E. Ehmann (1856), follow to some degree the patterns established
by that tendency. See Goebel, II, 698-735 and K.C.E. Ehmann, hrsg.,
Gottfried Arnolds sämmtliche Geistliche Lieder (Stuttgart: Druck und
Verlag von J.F. Steinkopf, 1856), 1-43. When the biography of Franz Dibelius (1873) appeared, however, readers were presented with a picture
of Arnold which, while attempting to steer a middle course between emphasising the radical and orthodox periods, maintained Arnold's close
relationship to traditional theological forms.

The first serious attempt to deal with Arnold's sources was
by William Freiherr von Schroeder in the early twentieth century.
Schroeder centered his attention on the lyrics, noting their medieval
models, and discussed, as well, the influence of Philip Jakob Spener and
of Jacob Boehme. He emphasised, in particular, the role of Quietism.
While it is of permanent value, Schroeder's study presses the Quietist
influence far too strongly. A similar emphasis on the Quietist influence
is found in Max Weiser, *Der Sentimentale Mensch, Gesehen aus der
Welt holländischen und deutscher Mystiker im 18. Jahrhundert* (Gotha
und Stuttgart: Verlag Friedrich Andres Perthes A.-G., 1924), 111-123
and Max Weiser, *Peter Poiret* (München, 1934), passim. Cf. the ex-
plicit statements in this regard in Louis Bouyer, *Orthodox Spirituality
and Protestant and Anglican Spirituality*, trans. by Barbara Wall (London: Burns and Oates, 1969), 175.

A major breakthrough in understanding Arnold's development came in 1923 with the publication of Erich Seeberg's monumental study of the *Unparteiische Kirchen- und Ketzer-Historie.* Note Seeberg, Arnold, 1-64. Prior to the publication of this work Arnold scholarship took little regard to the dichotomies of his career, and focussed rather on one aspect of his life, at the same time reinterpreting the other aspects according to the one they had chosen. Seeberg insisted on the need to recognise the near incompatibility of segments of Arnold's life. For him, Arnold's career was broken in three places: at his conversion in 1689, his resignation from the Giessen lectureship in 1698, and his marriage in 1701. This three-fold break, Seeberg felt, could be explained by discussing the motivations for the changes. The conversion under Spener is relatively easy to understand as is the resignation, which, for Seeberg, resulted from the seriousness with which Arnold took the Pietist concept of the need for a pure church. The return of Arnold to the established church could be more readily accepted, Seeberg felt, if one viewed Arnold as eventually realising the full implications in his theology of dying unto oneself. These premises were further clarified and Arnold's place within the Pietist movement was succinctly described in the introduction to Seeberg's selected edition of Arnold's works, published some ten years later.

Seeberg's theory can be seriously questioned at several points. It does not seem proper, for example, to call the changes in Arnold's career breaks, nor must those motivations accepted by Seeberg as responsible for Arnold's changes be considered the only possible ones. His lengthy study will remain of value to all students of Arnold's historiography, but his emphasis on the radical Boehmist elements in Arnold's thought are misleading, although many studies after Seeberg's reaffirmed to various degrees the importance of the Boehmist period in Arnold's career. Most significant among these were Walter Nigg, *Die Kirchengeschichtsschreibung. Grundzüge ihrer historischen Entwicklung* (München: C.H. Beck, 1934); *Das Buch der Ketzer* (Zurich, 1949; trans. by Richard and Clara Winston as *The Heretics* [New York: Alfred A. Knopf, 1962]); *Heimliche Weisheit, Mystisches Leben in der evangelischen Christenheit* (Zurich/ Stuttgart: S. Hirzel Verlag, 1959); 'Einführung' to *Gottfried Arnold: Das Geheimnis der göttlichen Sophia* (Leipzig, 1700; reprint, Stuttgart-Bad Cannstatt: Friedrich Fromann Verlag (Günther Holzboog, 1963)); Hirsch, *Geschichte*, II, 260-273, and Roger Friedrich, *Studien zur Lyric Gottfried Arnolds* (Zurich: Juris Druck und Verlag, 1969), 62-116.

In 1963 Hermann Doerries (*Geist und Geschichte bei Gottfried Arnold* [Göttingen: Vandenhoeck und Ruprecht]) rejected Seeberg's assertion of the centrality of the *Unparteiische Kirchen- und Ketzer-Historie* in Arnold's career, reviewing his growth and directing attention to the importance of Macarius as a source for his development. Doerries has met with criticism. See E. Schering, 'Besprechung: Hermann Doerries, Geist und Geschichte bei Gottfried Arnold,' *Jahrbuch der hess.*

kirchen-geschichtlichen Vereinigung, 18 (1967), 266., Winfried Zeller, 'Rezension von Dörries: Geist und Geschichte bei Gottfried Arnold, (Göttingen, 1963),' *Zeitschrift für Religion in Geschichte und Gegenwart*, 18 (1966), 289f. Traugott Stählin also expressed reservations with Seeberg's approach to Arnold's biography. He saw Arnold primarily as a poet, whose dramatic turns are marks of his Baroque mentality which 'formed anew the same paradoxical life structure.' Stählin too opposed the suggestion that Boehmism was a major influence on Arnold by discussing various backgrounds to his thought, among which he included the late medieval mystics, Hohelied poetry, and Orthodox sources. One other modern study deserves mention. Jürgen Büchsel (1970) centered his interest on Arnold's concept of the church and rebirth, and freeing himself from the spell of Seeberg without neglecting important insights of that author's work, he provided students with a helpful, although at places inconsistent, study.

The following biography, in addition to its dependence on Arnold's numerous publications, is indebted to the work of Dibelius, Seeberg, and the eighteenth century biographies, as well as Arnold's *Offenhertziges Bekänntnüsz Welche Bey unlängst geschehener Verlassung Seines Academischen Ampts abgelegt worden...* (o.O., 1699)—hereafter: OB.

Numerous works of lesser importance have been consulted but are not of major significance for this study. See, for example, the semi-popular work of Hans Bruns, *Gottfried Arnold* (Gieszen und Basel: Brunnen Verlag, 1955), as well as Walter Delius, 'Gottfried Arnold in Perleberg,' *Jahrbuch für Berlin-Brandenburgische Kirchengeschichte*, 43 (1968), 155-160; Wilhelm Kähle, 'Gottfried Arnold Zur 250. Wiederkehr seines Todestages,' *Kirche in der Zeit*, 19 (1964), 205-209. Friedrich Wilhelm Kantzenbach, *Evangelium und Dogma: Die Bewaltigung des theologischen Problems der Dogmengeschichte im Protestantismus* (Stuttgart: Evangelisches Verlagswerk, 1959), 49-60; C. Friedrich Köhler, 'Gottfried Arnold, der Verfasser der Kirchen- und Ketzer-Historie,' *Zeitschrift für Historische Theologie*, 41 (1871), 3-35; Bernhard Willkomm, 'Gottfried Arnold als Professor historiarum in Giessen' *Mitteilungen des Oberhessischen Geschichtsvereins*, NF 9 (1900), 53-73; E. Haase, *Aus dem Leben des Gottfried Arnold ... in Perleberg von 1707-1714* (Perleberg: F. Grunick, 1912). For additional studies, see Dale R. Stoeffler, 'The Ecclesiology of Gottfried Arnold,' *Brethren Life and Thought*, 28 (1983), 91-100, 'The Life and Thought of Gottfried Arnold,' ibid., 26 (1981), 135-151, 'Gottfried Arnold's View of the Christian Life,' ibid., 26 (1981), 237-246, Frank C. Roberts, 'Gottfried Arnold on Historical Understanding,' *Fides*, 14 (1982), 50-59, Hans M. Barth, 'Theologia Experimentalis,' *Neue Zeitschrift für systematische Theologie*, 23 (1981), 120-136, Martin Schmidt, 'Die Interpretation der neuzeitlichen Kirchengeschichte,' *Zeitschrift für Theologie und Kirche*, 54 (1957), 174-212, Hans Schneider, 'Das Basler Konzil

in der deutschsprachigen Evangelischen Kirchengeschichtsschreibung,'
Theologische Zeitschrift, 38 (1982), 308-330, Wilhelm A. Schultze,
'Der Verlauf der Missionsgeschichte bei Gottfried Arnold,' *Zeitschrift
für Kirchengeschichte*, 64 (1952/ 53), 260-291, Erich Breyreuter, 'Die
Gestalt Mohammeds in Gottfried Arnolds Kirchen- und Ketzerhistorie,'
Theologische Literaturzeitung, 84 (1959), 255-263, Friedrich Wilhelm
Kantzenbach, 'Theologisch-soziologische Motive im Widerstand gegen
Gottfried Arnold,' *Jahrbuch der hessischen Kirchengeschichtlichen
Vereinigung*, 24 (1973), 33-51. Of special value for the present study is
the printed catalogue of Arnold's personal library (*CATALOGUS BIB-
LIOTHECAE B. GOTOFREDI ARNOLDI ... 1714*) preserved in the
Tübingen Universitätsbibliothek. See also Reinhard Breymeyer, 'Die
Bibliothek Gottfried Arnolds,' *Linguistica Biblica*, 39 (1976), 86-132.

2 See Dibelius, 20.

3 Arnold's development while at Wittenberg is difficult to define accurately because he reinterpreted the significance of the period several
times during his life. See Doerries, 49-53 for a succinct discussion of
the problem.

4 Arnold's teachers are known from a list in the *Gedoppelter Lebenslauf*,
2, 6-7.

5 *De lotione manuum* (defended March 27, 1689), *De Hermunduris* (defended April 3, 1689), *De locutione angelorum* (defended Dec. 14,
1687). The first two are printed in Dibelius, 195-201, 202-209. Although
much of the earlier literature indicates that *De locutione angelorum* is
lost, a copy does exist in the Nationale Forschungs- und Gedenkstätten
der klassischen Literatur in Weimar.

6 Doerries, 49-52.

7 On Spener's Wittenberg discussions with Arnold, see Doerries, 52, 54-
55. Note, as well, Büchsel, 26-27 and Ehmann, 2.

8 *Gedoppelter Lebenslauf*, 2, 9.

9 For details, see Dibelius, 41-46. Cf. Schroeder, 1-21.

10 Cf. OB 6.

11 M.G.A.A.M., that is Magister Gothofredus Arnoldus Annabergensis
Misnicus. See Seeberg, 16, 56-57.

12 Certe quoties nomen suum scripsit, diligenter ab ista se abstinuit hon-
oris ac dignitatis mentione (Coler, *Historia*, 16).

13 Cf. Büchsel, 24.

14 OB, 2-4.

15 On the earlier teaching within Protestantism concerning the role of
the prophet, see Ernst Benz, *Der Prophet Jacob Boehme* (Mainz and
Wiesbaden: Verlag der Wissenschaften und der Literatur, Steiner in
Komm., 1959).

16 On the political turmoil arising out of the territorial demands of Brandenburg relating to the city, see Dibelius, 55-58. The later issues over
religion were complicated by the fact that Sproegel, Arnold's future
father-in-law, and von Stammler, his employer, were on the side of

Brandenburg in the struggle, whereas the local pastors supported Saxon claims.

17 On Christian Scriver, see Martin Schmidt, 'Christian Scrivers "Seelenschatz",' in his *Wiedergeburt*, 112-118. Note, as well, the introduction by Johann Pritius in Christian Scriver, *Seelenschatz* ... (Schaffhausen/ Druckts und verlegts Emanuel Hurter, 1738).

18 See Goebel, II, 705. Cf. Dibelius, 58-59.

19 Cf. Dibelius, 55, 210, and Ritschl, II, 249 ff.

20 For details, see 'Des Qvedlinburgischen Ertz=Schwermers und qvaker= Propheten/ Heinrich Kratzensteins Geschichte ... ' in *Der alten und neven Schwärmer/ Wiedertäuffrischer Geister...* (Gedrucht im Jahr 1702).

21 Goebel, II, 705-707 suggests that Arnold wrote some of these.

22 On Arnold's praise of these radicals, see Dibelius, 61-62.

23 'Von dem Bruder- und Schwester-namen der ersten Christen' in Christian Thomas, ed., *Historie der Weiszheit und Thorheit... 1693 ...* (HALLE/ Gedruckt und verlegt von Christoph Salfelden ... IIIth, 114-202)—hereafter: BSN.

24 'Historia Christianorum damnatorum ad metalla' in Christian Thomas, ed., *Historia sapientiae et stultitio* (Oct. 1693). For details, see Seeberg, 56-57.

25 Thomas, Historie, III, 201.

26 See below, Chapter Two, n. 33.

27 Thomas, Historie, I, 1-60.

28 Thomas, Historie, I, 60-139. Cf. KKH II, 16 and 21.

29 Thomas, Historie, I, 140-205. Cf. KKH III, 3.

30 For Sproegel's statement, see Dibelius, 54-66. Note the role of his wife who had absented herself from the celebration of the Lord's Supper for too long a time according to the authorities. Sproegel's own orthodoxy was admitted although his role in the perpetuation of the movement was considered offensive. Ibid., 66-67.

31 See Seeberg, 56.

32 See Seeberg, 56. Note Doerries' appended chronological survey which includes a reference to Arnold's separate edition of the letters of Ignatius.

33 Arnold's foreword is printed in the Schaffhausen KKH II, 1556.

34 *FRATRUM SORORUMQUE APPELATIO Inter Christianos maxime & alios qvondam usitata, tum & COGNATIO SPIRITUALIS, ex Antiqvitate Monumentis Commentatione illustrata per GOTHOFREDUM ARNOLDUM Annaemontanum. Accessit CHRISTIANORUM AD METALLA DAMNATORUM HISTORIA* (Francofurti ad Manum Apud JOHANN-CHRISTOPH: Konig/ 1696)—hereafter: FSA. A second edition the following year appeared under the title *Historia cognitionis spiritualis*. See Seeberg, 56.

35 The *Christianorum ad metalla damnatorum historia* appeared in 1693. See Seeberg, 56-57. On the theology of this and other early works, and

its close relationship to Arnold's mature view of history, see Seeberg, 16-22.

36 Doerries, 148-150.

37 *Des Heiligen Macarii Homilien. Oder Geistlich Reden, Um das Jahr Christi CCCXL, gehalten, Anjetzo ihrer Vortrefflichkeit wegen zum ersten mahl Ins Teutsche übersetzt, Und Nebenst einer Errinerung Vom Brauch und Missbrauch böser Exempel, Angefertiget Von Gottfried Arnold* (Leipzig, 1696). An expanded second edition appeared in 1699 under the title *Ein Denckmahl des alten Christentums bestehend in des Heil. Marcarii und anderer hocherleuchteter Männer ... Schriften*, and a third edition with additions in 1702. (See Seeberg, 57). The second edition has been available for this study, is used throughout, and is cited as *Macarius*.

38 See Benz, Thebais, 11-25 and Doerries, 178ff.

39 Cf. Doerries, 151-178.

40 See Arnold, Macarius, 'Vorrede,' [ii].

41 *Die Erste Liebe Das ist: Wahre Abbildung Der Ersten Christen nach ihren Lebendigen Glauben und Heiligen Leben, Aus der ältesten und bewährtesten Kirchen-Scribenten eigenen Zeugnissen. Exempeln und Reden nach der Wahrheit der Ersten einigen Christlichen Religion, allen Liebhabern der Historischen Wahrheit, und sonderlich der Antiquität, als in einer nützlichen Kirchen-Historie, treulich und unparteyisch entworfen: Worinnen zugleich Des Hn. WILLIAM CAVE Erstes Christentum nach Nothdurft erläutert wird ....* (Zu finden in Gottlieb Friedeburgs Buchhandlung Jm Jahre 1696)—hereafter: EL with book, chapter and section number. Two later editions appeared during Arnold's life, the third with revised 'Vorrede' and 'Additamenta' in 1712. This was reprinted Leipzig, Bey Samuel Benjamin Walthern, 1732. In 1700 the work was translated into Dutch under the title *Waare afbeelding der eerste Christenen. Volgens hum leevendig geloof, en heylig leeven... Uyt het hoogduytsch vertaalad door W. Sewel.*

42 See Rupert Davies, *The Problem of Authority in the Continental Reformers: A Study in Luther, Zwingli, and Calvin* (London: Epworth Press, 1946).

43 On earlier discussion concerning this theme, see Karl F. Morrison, *Tradition and Authority in the Western Church, 300-1140* (Princeton, N.J.: Princeton University Press, 1969).

44 See, for example, Georges H. Tavard, *Holy Writ or Holy Church: The Crisis of the Protestant Reformation* (London: Burns and Oates, 1959), 22-26. Cf. Heiko A. Obermann, *The Harvest of Medieval Theology* (Cambridge, Mass.: Harvard University Press, 1963), 361ff., and his *Forerunners of the Reformation*, trans. by Paul L. Nyhus (New York: Holt, Rinehart and Winston, 1966), 51ff.

45 Preuss, *Post-Reformation Lutheranism*, I, 254ff.

46 Ibid.

47 Note particularly Williams, 815-832.

48 See Seeberg, 257-280.

49 See Seeberg, 431ff.

50 The first significant use of *Zeugen* within Protestantism begins with the Flacius circle of Lutherans. See Joachim Massner, *Kirchliche Uberlieferung und Autorität in Flaciuskreis* (Berlin und Hamburg: Lutherisches Verlagshaus, 1964), 36-56 in particular. Note also Heinz Scheible, *Die Entstehung der Magdeburger Zenturien* (Gütersloh: Gütersloher Verlagshaus Gerd Mohn, 1966).

51 Seeberg provides obvious examples. Note, as well, the introductory list of authors that Arnold claims to have studied in the *De corrupto historiarum studio*. See Dibelius, 211-225.

52 On Luther, see John M. Headly, *Luther's View of Church History* (New Haven, Conn. and London: Yale University Press, 1963), and Wolfgang Höhne, *Luthers Anschauungen über die Kontinuität der Kirche* (Berlin und Hamburg: Lutherisches Verlagshaus, 1963).

53 For introductions to these men, see above n. 47.

54 See Seeberg, 327-430.

55 The first edition was printed at London 'by J.M. for R. Chriswell' in 1673 and went through five more editions by 1702. Arnold would have had available to him the German translations *Erstes Christentum, oder Gottesdienst der alten Christen in der ersten Zeiten* published by J.T. Fritsch at Leipzig in 1694. A second German edition appeared in 1696.

56 For a discussion of Arnold's 'parteilichkeit', see Büchsel, 31-51. Cf. Seeberg, 228-233.

57 EL, 'Zuschrift,' [i].

58 Cf. Arnold, EL, 'Vorrede,' 3-6 and Macarius, 'Vorrede,' 1, and 'Erinnerung,' 1.

59 EL. 'Vorbericht,' 9-12.

60 EL, 'Vorrede,' IIX.

61 EL, I.

62 EL, II.

63 EL, III-V.

64 EL, VI, 1 and 6.

65 EL, VI, 2-5.

66 EL, VII.

67 EL, VIII.

68 EL, VIII, 9ff.

69 EL, VIII, 23, 8.

70 For Spener and Francke's comments, see EL (3. Aufl., Halle, 1712; reprint, Leipzig, 1732), 1082-1083.

71 On the upheaval in the university, see Dibelius, 77-80, and note the studies related to the background in *Die Universität Giessen*, hrsg. von der Universität Giessen (Giessen: Alfred Töpelmann, 1907), 48-81, 133-262. Note also Introduction, n. 14 and the dissertation over which Arnold presided (*Q.D.B.V. HISTORIAM GEORGI SAXONIAE*

DUCIS disquisitioni publicae submittit PRAESIDE GOTHOFREDO ARNOLDO, respondens JOHANNES HAUBOLDUS ab Einsiedel ... M DC XCVII [GISSAE HASSORUM, Typis Henningi Mulleri])

72 The complete text is printed in Dibelius, 211-225.

73 See OB, 9.

74 OB, A1.

75 See Dibelius, 96. Note, as well, 'Gottfried Arnolds Brief an den D. Spener/ die Niederlegung seiner Profession in Giessen betreffend,' *Hessische Heb-Opfer* (1740), 473-476.

76 EL, VIII, 23, 8. Cf. his earlier *Tabula historico-chronologica universalis* (1698) as noted by Seeberg, 57.

77 KKH, I, 'Vorrede,' 17.

78 This suggestion by Büchsel, 134, is much more likely than Doerries' conclusion that the date is an error for 1698. In any event, even a later date does not in any material way aid our understanding of his development 1696-1699.

79 This is particularly clear in the 'Allgemeine Anmerckungen' to the KKH, I. Cf. Hans-Walter Krumwiede, 'Zur Theologie von Gottfried Arnolds Kirchen- und Ketzerhistorie,' *Theologische Literaturzeitung*, 85 (1960), 224.

80 KKH, I, 'Allgemeine Anmerckungen,' Punct I and Beantwortung I.

81 KKH, I, 'Allgemeine Anmerckungen,' Punct II and Beantwortung II.

82 KKH, I, 'Allgemeine Anmerckungen,' Punct III and Beantwortung III.

83 KKH, I, 'Allgemeine Anmerckungen,' Punct III, 23 et al.

84 KKH, I, 'Allgemeine Anmerckungen,' Punct III, 37 et al.

85 KKH, I, 'Allgemeine Anmerckungen,' Punct IV and Beantwortung IV.

86 Cf. KKH, I, 1; V, 13-14.

87 KKH, I, 1, V; 2.

88 KKH, I, 1, V; 12.

89 KKH, I, 1, V; 13.

90 KKH, I, 1, V; 3.

91 Note, for example, his discussion of the controversies of the late sixteenth century (KKH, I, 1; XVI, 24-30). Cf., as well, the introduction to Cyprian's 1701 *Allgemeine Anmerckungen* (see below, n. 101) and Dibelius, 118, and, above all, Irmfried Martin, *Der Kampf um Gottfried Arnolds Unparteiische Kirchen und Ketzerhistorie* (unpubl. doct. diss., Heidelberg, 1973). On Arnold's later regrets concerning the controversy, see Friedrich Wilhelm Struder, hrsg., *Grundlage zu einer hessischen Gelehrten und Schriftsteller Geschichte* (Göttingen, in der Barmeierischen Buchdruckung, 1781), 153.

92 Especially to be noted are Arnold's sectarian treatment of the word and sacraments. For his discussions of this matter, see Seeberg, 181-198.

93 See Dibelius, 190.

94 See EL 3, 1082-1099.

95 OB, 22-31, et al.

96 The *Göttliche Liebes-Funcken/ Ausz dem Grossen Feuer Der Liebe Gottes in Christo JESU entsprungen* .... was first published in 1698. A second edition with a second part appeared in 1701 (Franckfurt am Mayn/ bey Johann David Zunnern/ 1701) and is referred to hereafter as GLF with part and page number. For 'Babels Grablied,', see GLF, I, 166-171.

97 Note his *VITAE PATRUM Oder: Das Leben Der Altväter und anderer Gottseliger Personen Auffs Neue erläutert und Vermehret* (HALLE/ In Verlegung des Waysen-Hauses/ 1700)—a Dutch translation appeared in 1702, *Erbauliche Sendschreiben der Alten*, 1700 (see Seeberg, 58), *Auserlesene Send-Schreiben Derer Alten/ Zum gemeinen Zug gesammelt und verteutscht* (Franckfurt und Leipzig/ In Verlegung Theod. Philippe Calvisio/ Buchhandl. Im Jahr Christi 1700). Cf. *Güldene Send-Schreiben derer Alten Christen/ Mit Sonderbaren Fleisz gesammelt und ins Teutsche gebracht von Gottfried Arnolden/ Past. Pr. und Inspectore zu Perleberg. Anitzo zum Erstenmahl Ihres fürtrefflichen und erbaulichen Innhalts wegen zum gemeinen Nutzen herausgegeben/ ...* (Büdingen/ Drucks und Verlegts Joh. Fried. Regelein. 1723), *Kurtzgefaszte Kirchenhistorie Des Alten und Neuen Testaments*, (Leipzig, 1700; reprint, Leipzig/ Bey Samuel Benjamin Walthern/ 1737), *Erbauliche theosophische Sendschreiben eines in Gott getreuen Mitgliedes aus der Gemeinschaft Jesu Christi*, 1700 (see Seeberg, 62). *Das Leben Der Gläubigen Oder: Beschreibung solcher Gottseligen Personen/ welche in denen Letzten 200. Jahren sonderlich bekandt worden ausgefertigt von Gottfried Arnold* (Halle, 1701; Andere Auflage ... HALLE, In Verlegung des Waysen-Hauses, 1732), and prefaces to a German edition of the works of Ruusbroec, Angelus Silesius' *Cherubinischer Wandersmann*, Johann Luyken's tract *Jesus und die Seele*, and selected writings by Madame Guyon, all in 1701 (See Seeberg, 60). *Auserlesene Send-Schreiben*, hereafter: AS; *Leben der Gläubigen*—hereafter: LG.

98 Gottfried Arnold, 'Antwortschreibung An einen Prediger in einer grossen Gemeine, von allerhand Scrupeln über seinem Amte,' in his *Die Geistliche Gestalt Eines Evangelischen Lehrers* (Halle, 1704; Dritte Auflage, LEIPZIG, Bey Samuel Benjamin Walter, 1737).

99 See KKH, II, 'Beschluss,' 15ff. Cf. Büchsel, 110-112.

100 *Das Geheimnisz der Göttlichen Sophia oder Weisheit* (Leipzig/ Bey Thomas Fritsch/ 1700). Printed and bound with this are Arnold's *Poetische Lob- und Liebes-Sprüche von der Ewigen Weiszheit* and his *Neue Göttliche Liebes-Funcken und Ausbrechende Liebes-Flammen*—hereafter: PLLS and NGLF. For general comments, see Ernst Benz, 'Gottfried Arnolds "Geheimnis der Göttlichen Sophia" und seine Stellung in der christlichen Sophialehre,' *Jahrbuch der hessischen Kirchengeschichtlichen Vereinigung*, 18 (1967), 51-83.

101 Ernst Salomon Cyprian, *Allgemeine Anmerckungen Uber Gottfried Arnolds Kirchen- und Ketzer-Historie* (Franckfurth und Leipzig/ bey Paul Günther Pfotenhauern/ Buchhandlern in Coburg Im Jahr 1701).

102 Ibid., 'Vorbericht,' 1.

103 Ibid.

104 Ibid., 'Vorbericht,' 6. Cf. the similar attack in Valentine Ernst Loescher, *PRAENOTIONES THEOLOGICAE Contra NATVRALISTARVM & FANATICORVM omne genus* (Vitenburgae, Impensis JO. LVDOVICI MEISELII, M. DCCXIII), Contra Indifferent., Praenotio, III, XVIII.

105 Cyprian, *Allgemeine Anmerckungen*, 'Vorbericht,' 7.

106 Ibid., 'Vorbericht,' 8.

107 Ibid., 'Vorbericht,' 9.

108 Ibid., 'Vorbericht,' 10.

109 Ibid., 'Vorbericht,' 11.

110 Ibid., 'Vorbericht,' 12.

111 Ibid., Cap. I.

112 Ibid., Cap. II.

113 Ibid., Cap. III.

114 Ibid., Cap. IV.

115 Ibid., Cap. V.

116 Ibid., Cap. VI-IX.

117 Gottfried Arnold, *Erklärung/ Von gemeinen Secten-wesen/ Kirchen- und Abendmahl-gehen* (Leipzig/ Bey Thomas Fritsch/ 1700).

118 Ibid., 'Vorbericht,' 1-5.

119 Ibid., 'Vorbericht,' 4.

120 Ibid., 'Vorbericht,' 14-20. See also ibid., Cap. IV, 1ff.

121 See Johannes Kühn, *Toleranz und Offenbarung* (Leipzig: Verlag von Felix Meiner, 1923), 427-452 for a discussion of Spener's position. See-berg's discussion (18ff.) on the question refers to later works for the most part, but rightly notes the significance of Pufendorf and Locke in Arnold's teaching.

122 *Erklärung*, Cap. I and IV.

123 Ibid., Cap. II.

124 Ibid., Cap. III and V.

125 Ibid., Cap. VI.

126 Ibid., Cap. II, 2-3.

127 Ibid., Cap. II, 5 and 16.

128 Ibid., Cap. VI, 14 and 38.

129 Ibid., Cap. I, 8-15.

130 Ibid., Cap. II, 2.

131 Ibid., Cap. IV, 8ff.

132 Ibid., Cap. IV, 5-8.

133 Ibid., Martin Luther, *Werke* (Weimar: Hermann Bohlau, 1883-), 7, 21—hereafter: WA with volume and page number.

134 See *Erklärung*, 'Anhang.'

135 *Eines Anonymi Erinnerung, die in Hrn. Arnolds Kirchen- und Ketzer-Historie Befindlichen special- und historischen fehler betreffend* (Schaff-hausen, KKH, III, A, 158-160).

136 For details, see Ehmann, 19-21, and Dibelius, 134-135.

137 For documents, see *Erläuterung*, V, 25, and Ehmann, 21.

138 *Der richtigste Weg durch Christum zu Gott: bey öffentlichen Versammlungen in dreyen Sermonen oder Predigten angewiesen ... Nebenst einer näheren Erklärung von seinem Sinn und Verhalten in Kirchen-Sachen* (Franckfurt, Bey Thomas Fritsch, 1700).

139 See Dibelius, 140-141.

140 Cf. Büchsel, 122.

141 The full text is printed in Schaffhausen, KKH, III, A, 1-30.

142 For Arnold's letters to Pfanner and Spener respectively, see ibid., 30-34, 35-36.

143 Elias Veiel, *Urtheil von G. Arnolds Kirchen- und Ketzer-Historie, aus der Vorrede des Zweyten Theils des Petrinischen Weg-Weisers* (Schaffhausen, KKH, III, A, 219).

144 Elias Veiel, *Theologisches Send-Schreiben, An Alle aufrichtige und Orthodoxe Theologoi, ihr vernünfftiges Gutachten von denen Arnoldischen und anderen dergleichen. Beginnen, offenhertzig zu eröffnen. Nebst einer Kurtzen Abfertigung einiger Pasquillanten und Tenebrionum* (Schaffhausen, KKH, III, A, 219-232).

145 H.G.W.E.M., *Augenscheinliche Erweisung, diesz Gottfr. Arnold das Valentinianische Ketzer-fragmentum Theodoti weder verständlich noch treulich übersetzet, und damit seine schlechte wissenschafft in der Griechischen sprache Selbst verrathen habe. Herausgegeben von D. Elias Veiel* (Schaffhausen, KKH, III, A, 232-248).

146 See Dibelius, 125. Spener's letter to Arnold is printed in Dibelius, 235-240.

147 Gebhardt Mayer, *Wahre Nothwendigkeit des Kirchen- u. Abendmal-Gehens, in Kurtzen ... Anmerckungen über einige Capital der sogenannten Erklärung Hrn. M. Gottfried Arnolds, vom Kirchen- und Abendmahl-Gehen* (Quedlinburg, 1701).

148 See article by E. Beyreuther RGG 3, VI, 380-381.

149 Gottfried Arnold, *Fernere Erläuterung seines sinnes und verhaltens beym Kirchen- und Abendmahl-gehen* (Franckfurt/ Bey Thomas Fritsch/ im jahr 1701).

150 For Pfanner's reply to the *Erläuterung*, see his *Gegen-Antwort* (Schaffhausen, KKH, 34-36). Note, as well, *Durch Herrn Gottfried Arnoldens DUPLIC An Hof-Rath Pfannern Fernerweit veränlaszte Erläuterung Seines unpartheyischen Bedenckens Uber die Arnoldische Kirchen- und Ketzer-Historie* (Schaffhausen, KKH, III, A, 360ff.).

151 Gottfried Arnold, *Endliche Vorstellung seiner Lehre und Bekäntnisz* (Franckfurt/ Bey Thomas Fritsch, 1701).

152 Note above, n. 97.

153 See Hirsch, *Geschichte*, I, 94, 110.

154 See A. Ritschl, *Pietismus*, II, 280-560.

155 Ibid., II, 225:249.

156 Johann Andreas Corvinus, *Gründliche Untersuchung der sogenannten unpartheyischen K. und K. Hist. und einiger anderer Schriften G. Arnolds* (Schaffhausen, KKH, III, A, 316-345).

157 Ernst Salomon Cyprians, *Fernere Anmerckungen von Arnolds Partheylichkeit und Verfälschung der Scribenten* (Schaffhausen, KKH, III, A, 95-103); Ernst Salomom Cyprian, *Urtheil von Arnolds Religion, woher, die Partheylichkeit nothwendig entspringen müssen* (Schaffhausen, KKH, A, 118-125); Ernst Salomon Cyprian, *Antwort Auf Arnolds sogenannte Erklärung vom gemeinen Seckten-wesen, Kirchen- und Abendmahl-gehen* (Schaffhausen, KKH, III, A, 125-158).

158 George Wächter, *Gründliche Gegen-Antwort auf die kurtze Beantwortung Herrn G. Arnolds betreffend die Dollmetschung des Valentinianischen Ketzer-Fragements beym Clemente Alex* (Schaffhausen, KKH, III, A, 308ff.). *Censuren Welche in denen unschuldigen Nachrichten hin und wieder über Gottfried Arnolds Kirchen- und Ketzer-Historie gefallet worden* (Schaffhausen, KKH, III, A, 61-66). *Eines ANONYMI der sich liebhaber der wahrheit nennet, aufrichtige Vorstellung vieler von Herrn. G. Arnold verübter fürsetzlichers Verfälschungen an alten und neuen Scribenten und ärgerlicher Vertheidigung der böszhafftigsten Ketzer und Atheisten* ... (Schaffhausen, KKH, III, A, 248-308).

159 See Dibelius, 148. For Arnold's correspondence with Gichtel, see Johann Georg Gichtel, *Theosophia Practica Halten und Kampfe ab dem H. Glauben bis ans Ende/ Durch die Drey Alter des Lebens JEsu Christi, Nach den Dreyen Principien Göttliches Wesens, mit derselben Ein- und Aus-Geburt Durch Sophiam in der Menschheit* ... (Dritte Edition, vermehret und verbessert. Gedruckt in Leyden, Anno 1722), 2451-2485, 1355-1360, (letters from 1699-1700), and Gichtel's post 1701 comments on Arnold in letters to others (409, 412, 425, 428, 572, 1406, 1416, 1419, 1426, 1430, 1435, 1440, 1448, 1458, 1474, 1512, 1519, 1591, 1750, 2022, 2190, 2194, 2430, 2446, 2692, 2700, 3057, 3078, 3415, 3423, 3429, 3435, 3610, 3617, 3639, 3647, 3655, 3698).

160 Dibelius, 149.

161 A second child was born three years later. Both, Sophia Gothofreda and Johann Gottfried died in 1709. See Ehmann, 40.

162 See Dibelius, 241ff. See also Werner de Boor, 'Das pietistische Anliegen und die luth. Bekenntnisschriften,' *Die Zeichen der Zeit*, 1 (1947), 89-93.

163 Ibid., 164.

164 *Das Eheliche und Unverehelichte Leben der ersten Christen/ nach ihren eigenen zeugnissen und exempeln* (Franckfurt/ Bey Thomas Fritschen/ 1702).

165 *Kurtze, Geistliche und Gottseelige Brieffe, Von Hrn. Petro Mattheo Petrucci, Weyland Bischoff zu Jesi und Cardinal geschrieben, Nunmehro aus der Italianischen in die Hochteutsche Sprache übersetzt* (1702; reprint Halle/ In Verlegung des Waysen-Hauses M DCCV).

166 Seeberg, 60.

167 Ibid.

168 *HISTORIA ET DESCRIPTIO THEOLOGIAE MYSTICAE, Seu*
THEOSOPHIAE ARCANAE ET RECONDITAE, item veterum &
Novorum MYSTICORVM (FRANCOFVRTI apvd Thomam Fritsch
Anno MDCII) with the supplement *Solida DEFENSIO THEOLOGIAE*
Mysticae; German translation: *Historie und beschreibung der mystis-*
chen Theologie/ oder geheimen Gottes Gelehrtheit/ wie auch derer alten
und neuen MYSTICORVM (Franckfurt bey Thomas Fritschen/ 1703)
with the supplement *Verthädigung der Mystischen Theologie*—hereafter
MT.

169 *Supplementa, Illustrationes, und Emendationes Zur Verbesserung Der*
Kirchen-Historie (Franckfurt, 1703; reprint, Franckfurt, KKH, III,
1205-1357). In the same year Arnold completed the 'Vorrede' for the
translation of Thomas White's *Villicationes* (*Betrachtung von dem Mit-*
tleren Zustand ... , [edition available for this study: N. pl.: N. publ.,
1725]).

170 *Neuer Kern wahrer Geistes-Gebete, bestehend in denen herrlichsten*
Morgen- und Abend-, Stand- und Beruffs-, Busz- und Kommunion-,
Creutz- und Anfechtung-, Sterbens- und Paszions-, wie auch Jesus-
Andachten; Ingleichen in allen andern Bitten, Gebeten, Fürbitten
und Dancksagungen, Dergleichen noch nie also aus denen ältesten
Lehrern beysammen gesehen worden; zusammt einen neuen Kern recht-
geistlicher lieblicher Lieder (Franckfurt/ bey Thomas Fritschen/ 1704).

171 *Die Geistliche Gestalt Eines Evangelischen Lehrers Nach dem Sinn*
und Exempel der Alten Ans Licht gestellet ... with *Anhang Eines*
Antwortschreibens An einen Prediger, Uber mancherley Angelegen-
heiten In deszen Amt und Beruff (Halle, 1704; Franckfurt und Leipzig,
Bey Johann Georg Böhmen, 1723)—hereafter: GG.

172 *Die Verklärung Jesu Christi in der Seele, aus denen gewöhnlichen Sonn-*
und Fest-Tags-Episteln, auf dem Fürstlichen Schlosze zur Allstedt
gezeiget (Gedruckt im Jahr 1721) was used for this study. A second
edition was published in 1708 —hereafter: VC.

173 First among these for the purposes of this study was the edition of
Thomas von Kempis Geistliche Scriften, So wol die vier Bücher Von
der Nachfolge Christi, als auch dessen anderer in vier und zwantzig
Büchern bestehende Betrachtunge.... Nebst einem historischen Vor-
bericht und Einleitung Gottfried Arnolds... (Leipzig und Stendal, 1712,
2 Aufl.; Leipzig, bey Samuel Benjamin Walthern, 1733). Among the
other forewords written were those to an edition of the Books of Wisdom and of Sirach (1705), Schroeder's sermons (1707), Peter Allixius'
work on the Trinity (1709), Luther's *Kirchenpostille* (1710), four tracts
of Johann Caspar Schade (1710), Christian Hoburg's *Teutscher Krieg*
(1710), Luther's *Catechism* (1712; [*D. Martin Luthers Kleine Cate-*
chismus ... (Altona: Joh. Friedrich Bähr, 1722)]), Albert Dranckmeister's tract on spiritual pride (1712), Schade's *Glaubens-Krafft* (1714),
and the Psalter (posthumous publication). Re-editions of the works

of Guyon (1707), the Pseudo-Clementine *Recognitions* (originally published in 1702) entitled *Historia von der Lehre Leben und Thaten ... Petri und Pauli* (1708) and Angelus Silesius (1713) also appeared. In 1712 a third edition of the Molinos' *Spiritual Guide* was printed, and in 1705 the bulky volume *Concilia und Responsa Theologica oder Gottsgelehrte Rathschläge und Antworten, über denen wichtigsten stücken und zuständen eines göttlichen wandels, nebenst neuen Geistlichen Gedichten, der weiszheit Garten-Gewächs genannt, gemein gemacht von Gottfried Arnold* (Franckfurt, bey Thomas Fritsch, 1705). On all these works, see Seeberg, 60-61.

174 *Die Evangelische Botschafft Der Herrlichkeit Gottes in Jesu Christo, nach denen ordentliche Sonn- und Fest-Tags Evangelien vorgetragen, Aus denen alten Kirchenlehrern erläutert, und nebenst einigen andern Geistlichen reden* (Franckfurt, 1706; reprint, Lemgo, in der Meyerischen Buchhandlung, 1759), *Evangelische Reden über die Sonn- und Fest-Tags-Evangelien zu einer bequemen Hauss- und Reise-Postill herausgegeben mit einer Vorrede von recht evangelischer Abhandlung der Sonntages-Episteln* (1709), *Epistolische Reden, oder kleine Postill über die Episteln nebst zwei vor der Preusz. Königin gehaltenen Predigten* (Franckfurt/ Bey Thomas Fritsch/ 1711), *Evangelische Hertzens-wecker ...* (1709), containing eight practical tracts (Stendal und Gardelegen: Ernst Heinr. Campen, 1724), *Ein rechter QVASIMODOGENITUS ... Bei volckreicher Beerdigung ... Herrn Laurentii Giessens* (Cölln an der Spree, druckts Ulrich Liebpert, [1709]), and second editions of *Die Verklärung Christi* (1708) and *Die geistiche Gestalt* (1713).

175 A second edition appeared in 1712, *Paradiesischer Lustgarten voller andächtigen Gebete, bei allen Zeiten, Personen und Zuständen...*, hrsg. von Karl Chr. Eberh. Ehmann ... (Reutlinger, Druck und Verlag von Rupp und Baur. 1852) has been used for the purposes of this study.

176 *Der Woleingerichtete Schul-Bau ...* (Leipzig und Stendal, Verlegt von Ernst Heinrich Campen, Im Jahre 1711).

177 *Theologia Experimentalis, Das ist: Geistliche Erfahrungs-Lehre, Oder Erkäntnisz und Erfahrung Von denen vornehmsten Stücken Des Lebendigen Christenthums, Von Anfang der Bekehrung bisz zur Vollendung: ...* (Franckfurt, 1715; reprint, Franckfurt am Mayn/ Bey Joh. Benjamin Andrea und Heinrich Hort. Anno M. DCC.XXV)—hereafter: TE.

178 *Historisch-Theologische Betrachtungen merckwürdiger Wahrheiten/ Auf Veranlassung derer biszherigen Einwürffe Gegen G. Arnolds Schrifften Von Einigen nach und nach bescheidentlich aufgesetzet/ Und nun Auf vieler Begehren zu nöthiger Verantwortung dargeleget* (Franckfurt/ zu Finden bey Thomas Fritschen/ 1709).

179 *Die Abwege, Oder Irrungen und Versuchungen gutwilliger und frommer Menschen, aus Beystimmung des gottseligen Alterthums angemercket* (Franckfurt, bey Thomas Fritschen, 1708). Note the apologetic *Nochmahlige Erinnerungen wegen einiger Puncten der Kirchen Historie* printed as a supplement with this work.

180 *Wahres Christentum des alten Testaments* (1707), *Der verursachte und
     gemässige Sündfluth, Bey der Am 14. und 15.* Februar 1709 Wasser-
     fluth nebst historischem Bericht von den Zeichen solcher Fluthen und
     grosser Kälte (Berlin. Joh. Michael Rüdiger/ 1709), and a *Historia von
     des beruffenen Erb-Kätzere, David Joris oder Görgi Lehr und Leben* ...
     (1713). See Seeberg, 57-59.

181 *Wahre Abbildung Des Inwendigen Christenthums, Nach desen An-
     fang und Grund, Fortgang oder Wachsthum und Ausgang oder Ziel
     in Lebendigen Glauben und Gottseligen Leben/ Aus den Zeugniszen
     und Exempeln der gottseligen Alten zur Fortsetzung und Erläuterung
     Der Abbildung der Ersten Christen dargestellet* (Franckfurt, 1709;
     reprint, Leipzig; Bey Benjamin Walthern, 1732)—hereafter: WAIC.
     Note, as well, Franz Banckmeister, 'Aus dem Briefwechsel Gottfried
     Arnolds,' *Mittel Verein Geschichte Annabergs*, 4 (1894), 1-15, Ferdi-
     nand Cohrs, 'Zwei vergessene Katechismen Gottfried Arnolds,' *Neue
     Kirchliche Zeitschrift*, 41 (1930), 602-641, and Arnold's *Das unz-
     ertrennliche Liebes-Band ... Marien Elizabeth ... Leichen Predigt ...*
     (Berlin [1714]).

Notes to Chapter Three

1 In particular, see Doerries.
2 On the present state of scholarship regarding the Macarian material,
   see Bethold Altaner und Alfred Stuiber, *Patrologie* (7. Aufl.; Freiburg
   i.B.: Herder, 1966), 264-265; Johannes Quasten, *Patrology* (Utrecht/
   Antwerp and Westminster, Md.: Spectrum Publishers and The Newman Press, 1950-1960), III, 161-168, and the comments of Hermann
   Doerries, 'Makarius,' RGG 3, 1V, 619. The climate of Macarian studies in which Arnold worked is briefly and accurately outlined by Benz
   in his Thebais. See especially Doerries, 148-193.
3 See BSN, 126 where Bernard is seemingly paraphrased on Christ the
   inner master who calls one from the things of this world, and BSN, 138,
   144, 185.
4 FSA, 35, 37, 69, 144, 161, 162, 229, 230, 244, 266, 293, 295.
5 FSA, 41, 142, 170, 244, 361.
6 FSA, 55.
7 FSA, 114, 119, 148, 197, 262.
8 See FSA, 119 on arrogant priests, FSA, 162 against superstition, FSA,
   69 on Christ as inner life.
9 FSA, 37, 55, 197, 262 and extensive list of citations on 266.
10 See, above all, Aelredi Rievallensis *Opera Omnia*, ed. by A. Hoste et
   C.H. Talbot (Turnholti: Typographi Brepols Editores Pontificii, MCM-
   LXXI), 287-350. For discussion of the theme, see Adele M. Fiske,
   Friends and Friendship in the Monastic Tradition (Cuernavaca, Mex.:
   Cidoc Cuaderno, 1970).

11 Cf. Bernard quotations at EL, I, 1:8, 16 (on conversion); I, 3:3, 6, 14, 19, 20 (on illumination); I, 5:7, 9 (on the gifts of the Spirit); I, 6:1, 16 (on Faith); I, 8:10, 12 (on Christ's example); I, 9:3, 9 (on obedience); I, 10:7 (on the Commandments); I, 11:11 (on the Commandments); I, 12:2, 7 (on perfection); I, 13:6, 9 (on love of God); I, 14:4 (on trust); I, 15:2, 15 (on hope); I, 16:8, 9, 16 (on humility); I, 17:10 (on praise of God); I, 18:11 (on the fruits of faith); I, 20:8, 13 (on union).

12 Cf. Bernard quotations at EL, II, 1:8, 9, 10, 13, 17, 20 (on prayer); II, 2:9, 12 (on song); II, 5:3 (on the laity); II, 8:2 (on the call of pastors); II, 9:9 13 (on the duties of pastors); II, 10:4, 16, 18 (on the duties of pastors); II, 11:1, 19, 20 (on the life of pastors); II, 12:5, 17, 25, 27; II, 14:2, 13, 17 (on baptism); III, 1:5, 17, 21 (on brotherly association); III, 2:2 (on brotherly love); III, 3:8, 19 (on submission to one another); III, 4:20 (on humility before others); III, 5:15 (on mutual aid); III, 6:5, 8, 11, 16 (on community); III, 7:5, 7, 14, 19, 21 (on admonition); III, 11:5 (on widows, orphans, etc.); IV, 1:18 (on denial of self); IV, 2:21 (on contempt for the world); IV, 4:7 (on fasting); V, 1 (on love for godless); V, 3:15 (on relations to the state); VI, 5:8, 9, 14, 25 (on death and burial); VIII, 2:4, 7 (on the decline of Christianity); VIII, 7:12 (on the decline of preaching); VIII, 8:18 (on the decline of clerical duties); VIII, 10:5, 15 (on hypocrisy); VIII, 12:18 (on clerics in war); VIII, 13:10, 22 (on clerics and pride, simony, etc.); VIII, 14:3 (on clerics and gluttony); VIII, 15:10 (on false clerics); VIII, 16:15 (on the tyranny of clerics); VIII, 21:21; VIII, 22:2 (on heresy).

13 EL, 'Vorbericht,' LXXXI.

14 On the development of the doctrine of the union in the seventeenth century, see W. Koepp, 'Würzeln und Ursprung der orthodoxen Lehre der unio mystica,' *Zeitschrift für Theologie und Kirche*, 29 (1921), 46ff., 134ff., which, despite its questionable thesis, traces the root of the doctrine to Arndt, is still a reliable guide. Note also Weber, *Schulphilosophie*, passim, and see W. Philipp, 'Unio Mystica,' RGG3, VI, 1335-1338. Cf. M. Schmidt, 'Prot. Mystik,' ibid., IV, 1252ff.

15 Bernd Moeller, 'Tauler und Luther,' *La mystique rhénane* (Paris: n. publ., 1965), 166. Note, as well, Henri Strohl, *Luther Jusqu'en 1521* (2e éd.; Paris: Press Universitaires de France, 1962), 193-199.

16 Cf. Theodosius Harnack, *Luthers Theologie* (München: Chr. Kaiser Verlag, 1927), I, 29; Gordon Rupp, *The Righteousness of God* (London: Hodder and Stoughton, 1953), 117, 193.

17 See Heiko A. Obermann, *The Harvest of Medieval Theology* (Cambridge, Mass.: Harvard University Press, 1963), 341-343, and cf. his *'Simul gemitus et raptus.* Luther und die Mystik' in Ivar Asheim, hrsg., *Kirche, Mystik, Heiligung und das Natürliche bei Luther* (Göttingen: Vandenhoeck und Ruprecht, 1967), 20-59. Note also Irwin Iserloh, 'Luther und die Mystik' in Asheim, 60-61 who outline the situation more accurately than does Moeller, 164.

18 See Obermann, 'Simul,' 34-35, 44-45 and Erich Vogelsang, 'Luther und

die Mystik,' *Luther Jahrbuch*, 19 (1937), 51-54.

19 Cf. WA, Tisch I:123, WA, Tisch I:46, 75, 557; Tisch II:35, 56, 435, et al.

20 See Strohl, 209ff.

21 The distinction is outlined in the Heidelberg Disputation. See WA, I:362. Cf. Paul Althaus, *The Theology of Martin Luther*, trans. by Robert C. Schultz (Philadelphia, Pa.: Fortress Press, 1966), 25-34 and Rupp, *Righteousness*, 229.

22 Cf. Anders Nygren, *Agape and Eros*, trans. by Philip S. Watson (London: S.P.C.K., 1953), 702-705; Obermann, 'Simul,' 44 and Philip S. Watson, *Let God be God* (Philadelphia, Pa.: Muhlenberg Press, 1948), 101, n.7. On this matter note the comments of R. Newton Flew, *The Idea of Perfection in Christian Theology* (Oxford: The Clarendon Press, 1934), 244ff., 275ff. Modern Protestant antagonism to mysticism is rooted in the thought of late nineteenth-century liberalism and the dialectical theologians of this century (see Bengt Hägglund, *The Background of Luther's Doctrine of Justification in Late Medieval Theology* [Philadelphia, Pa.: Fortress Press, 1971], 2-3). Among those who share this distaste are Gustav Aulen, *The Faith of the Church*, trans. by Eric H. Wahlstrom and G. Everett Arden (Philadelphia, Pa.: Muhlenberg Press, 1948), 50-53; Karl Barth, *Church Dogmatics*, trans. by G.W. Bromiley (Edinburgh: T. and T. Clark, 1962), IV/3/2, 539-540; Adolph Harnack, *History of Dogma*, trans. by Neil Buchanan (London, 1900; reprint, New York: Dover Publications Inc., 1961), VI, 97-108; Adolf Köberle, *The Quest for Holiness*, trans. by John C. Mattes (Minneapolis, Minn.: Augsburg Publishing House, 1938), 7-14; Anders Nygren, *Agape and Eros*, trans. by Philip S. Watson (London: SPCK, 1953), 228-29, 700-709, and Albert Ritschl, *The Christian Doctrine of Justification and Reconciliation*, trans. by H.R. Mackintosh, A.B. Macauley et al. (3rd ed., n. pl., 1888; reprint, Clifton, N.J.: Clifton Book Publishers, Inc., 1966), 112-114 etc., and cf. Friederich Kalb, *Theology of Worship in 17th-Century Lutheranism*, trans. by Henry P.A. Hamann (St. Louis, Mo.: Concordia Publishing House, 1965), 178-179. Note, however, the positive stance taken in this regard by Paul Tillich, *Systematic Theology* (Chicago, Ill.: University of Chicago Press, 1963), III, 241-243.

23 Obermann, 'Simul,' 35 notes his warnings in his explication of Psalms (WA 5:647-648).

24 Multi multa de theologia mystica ... moluntur et fabulantur, ingnorantes nec quid loquantur, nec de quibus affirment (WA 5:163).

25 WA 17,1:118. Cf. WA 40,1:769; 40,2:327; 45:518.

26 On the differences between Luther and the speculative mystics of the Middle Ages, see Bengt Hägglund, *Justification*, 4-16; Hägglund, 'Luther und die Mystik' in Asheim, 92:94; Karl Holl, *Gesammelte Aufsätze* (Tübingen: Verlag von J.C.B. Mohr (Paul Seibeck), 1948), 81, 477ff; Walter von Loewenich, 'Zum Verständniss Meister Eckhards,'

Jahrbuch des Martin Luther Bundes, 50 (1947), 68; Nygren, 689-709; Strohl, 111-115. For Luther there can be no final unitive experience in the same sense as that described by the late medieval mystics (see Hägglund, Luther, 89-90). All possibility of pantheism is ruled out in this thought (see Hägglund, Luther, 90-92; Holl, 36; Nygren, 706-707; Strohl, 207-209). Likewise any suggestion of an ascent to the divine is rejected, based as that is, Luther believed, on works, whether works of humility, prayer, or indifference to created things (see Nygren, 707-708 on the ascent in general; Holl, 132 on humility; Holl, 86 on prayer, and Holl, 90 on indifference to created things). Note, as well, Alois M. Haas, *Sermo Mysticus: Studien zu Theologie und Sprache der deutschen Mystik* (Freiburg/Schweiz: Universitätsverlag, 1979), 263.

27 WA, Tisch I:26.

28 WA, 3:111-112. Cf. WA 3:124.

29 See Bengt Hoffman, 'Luther and the Mystical,' *The Lutheran Quarterly*, 26 (1974), 321, 323.

30 Obermann, 'Simul,' 40-44.

31 Est etiam fides lux supra omnem captum nostrum. Quare hoc levare est aliud nihil quam lumen fidei, quod seipsum altissimum est, super nos effundire, quo ipsi elevemur. Undi et signatum dici potest, quia clausum et incomprehensibile nobis, comprehendens autem nos (WA 5:119).

32 See WA 5:176.

33 Rupp, Righteousness, 143-144.

34 Extasis illa Primo est sensus fidei, qui excedit sensum litere, in quo alii remanent increduli. Secundo est raptus mentis in claram cognitionem fidei, et ista est propre extasis. Tercio est alienatio seu pavor mentis in persecutione. Quarto est excessus iste, quem faciunt martyres, sicut luce 9 de excessi Christi Moses et Helias loquebantur (WA 4:265). Cf. WA 4:267; 9:97.

35 Iste est excessus, quando homo elevatur super se ... et illuminatus videt quam sit nihil, et quasi de supra respicit in seipsum in suas nebulas et tenebras, tanquam in monte positus infra respiciens (WA 4:519)

36 Note especially, Werner Elert, *The Structure of Lutheranism*, trans. by Walter A. Hanson (St. Louis, Mo.: Concordia Publishing House, 1962), 173-174, n. 26.

37 See Vogelsang, 48-50.

38 On Luther's use of *quasi*, see Elert, Structure, 168.

39 Tertia fidei gratia incomparabilis est hacc, Quod animam copulat cum Christo, sicut sponsam cum sponso. Quo sacramento (ut Apostolus docet) Christus et anima efficiuntur una caro (WA 7:54).

40 10,3:415-416.

41 Sihestu hie, dz er unsz geliebt und alle seyne werck getan. Darumb, das wir widderumb mit yhm (denn er darffs nicht), szondernn unszerm nehesten auch also thun sollen; das ist sey gepot, das ist unszer gehorsam, *also macht der glaub's* das Christus unser ist, und seine liebe macht das

wir seyn sind. Er liebt, szo gleuben wir, da wirt eyn kuch ausz. (WA
10,1:74; italics mine). For other images of union between the believer
and Christ, particularly the sacramental, see Iserloh, 75-83.

42 WA 10,1:74.

43 WA 20:229-31. Cf. Moeller, 163 and Strohl, 198-199.

44 On the young Luther's concern with progressive improvement in the
Christian life, see Jared Wicks, *Man Yearning for Grace: Luther's Early
Spiritual Teaching* (Washington and Cleveland: Corpus Books, 1968),
passim.

45 WA 10,3:157-158.

46 *Concordia Triglotta* (St. Louis, Mo.: Concordia, 1921), 940. The basic
pattern of the *ordo salutis* is already present in the *Formula of Concord* (ibid., 1069). In the *Formula* and the related writings, no medieval
mystics are quoted with the exception of Gerson, who is called upon consistently for proof texts to oppose the search for perfection within the
monastic life (ibid., 11860, 38786). The confessional writings insist that
sanctification follows upon justification, but that sanctification remains
imperfect in this life (ibid., 92018, 92121, 92328ff., 92734ff., 93148ff.)
(ibid., 92223, 92532, 9647, 96718, and 969). Perfection is not to be
achieved on earth (ibid., 214, 218, 282).

47 See Martin Chemnitz, *The Two Natures in Christ*, trans. by J.A.O.
Preuss (St. Louis, Mo.: Concordia Publishing House, 1971), 423ff.

48 See Elert, Structure, 160-166.

49 On Arndt, see above, Chapter One, n. 12.

50 See Koepp, Arndt, 131ff.

51 See Stählin, 48-51, 64.

52 Johann Arndt, *Sechs Bücher von Wahren Christenthum...* (6. Aufl.;
Stuttgart, bei den Gebrüdern Mantler, Buchdruckern, 1747) was available for this study—hereafter: WC, with book, chapter and section
number. The Braunschweig Andreas Dunckern edition of the first three
books 1606-1610 was checked in all cases as well.

53 WC, I, 1:1.

54 WC, I, 1:2.

55 WC, I, 1:3.

56 WC, I, 41:1-2.

57 WC, I, 2:10.

58 WC, I, 3:1..

59 WC, I, 4:1 and 10.

60 WC, II, 10-15.

61 WC, I, 5:2 and note his sermon on the subject in his *Predigten über die
alten Evangelien aller Sonn-Fest und Feiertage nebst einiger Passions-
Predigt*, hrsg. von S.C. Kopff (2. Aufl.; Stuttgart: Chr. Belser Buchhandlung, 1852), 611-622.

62 WC, I, 9. Cf. WC, II, 14.

63 WC, I, 12. Cf. WC, II, 17.

64 WC, I, 20.

65 WC, II, 15.

66 WC, II, 26.

67 Cf. WC, II, 28:4.

68 See WC, pp. 1178-1348 for edition of this book.

69 WC, V, Ver., 1:70-73.

70 WC, V, Ver., 3:79.

71 WC, V, Ver., 3:79-81.

72 WC, V, Ver., 4:81-82.

73 WC, V, Ver., 9:97-100. Cf. 11:103-105.

74 WC, V, Ver., 5:82-85.

75 WC, V, Ver., 6:85-88.

76 WC, V, Ver., 7:89-96.

77 WC, V, Ver., 12-106-100.

78 WC, V, Ver., 7:96-97. Cf. 13:110-112.

79 WC, V, Ver., 10:100-103.

80 WC, V, Ver., 14:112-114.

81 See WC, I, 34:8-9.

82 David Hollatz, *Examinem theologicum acroamaticum universam theologiam theoretico-polemicam complectens* (Rostochii et Lipsiae, Apud Joh. Ruswormium, M. DCC XVIII). The pagination for the entries following election (which is considered by Hollatz within the article on vocation) are 233, 251, 292, 318, 337, 383, 402, 420 and 430 respectively. For the respective pagination of the chapters in Arndt's treatise, see notes 55ff. above. Cf. the outline of similar *Stufe* in WC, 6, and David Hollatz, *Evangelische Gnaden-Ordnung* (edition available for this study was a reprint of the 1745 edition, Philadelphia, Pa.: Conrad Zentler, 1810).

83 WC, I, 24.

84 WC, II, 44ff.

85 WC, II, 40-43. Cf. WC,III, 14.

86 WC, IV, pt.II, 29.

87 WC, IV, pt.II, 30.

88 See WC, I, 41 for details.

89 WC, II, 34-38.

90 Weber, Arndt has documented all medieval mystical sources used by Arndt.

91 WC, IV, pt.II, 36.

92 See Weber, Arndt, 42-71, 77-108.

93 See above, Chapter One, n. 14.

94 Joh. Andreas Quenstedt, *Theologia Didactico-Polemica sive systema theologicum in duas sectionae didacticum et polemicum divisum ...* (Lipsiae, apud Thomam Fritsch, 1715).

95 Ibid., II,4, 646ff.

96 Ibid., II,5, 662ff.

97 Ibid., II,6, 684ff.

98 Ibid., II,7, 699ff.

99 Ibid., II,8, 736ff.

100 Ibid., II,9, 833ff.

101 Ibid., II,10, 886.: Unitio fidelium cum deo mystica est actus gratiae
Spiritus S. applicatricis, quo substantia hominum justificatorum atque
fidelium anima et corpore substantiae SS. Trinitatis et carnis Christi,
medianti fide, verbo imprimis Evangelii et Sacramentorum usu accensa,
vere, realiter, et arctissime, impermixtibiliter tamen, illocaliter et in-
circumscriptive conjungitur, ut facta Spirituali communicatione, Deus
familiariter et constanter praesens sancta operetur; Fideles autem Deo
et Redemptori suo ad gloriam Majestatis divina conjuncti, per mutuam immanentiam vivificae facultatis et omnium Christi beneficiorum
participes facti, de praesentissima gratia, amoreque paterno et subse-
cutura gloria certiores redditi in statu filiorum Dei atque unitate fidei
et charitatis, cum reliquis corporis mystici membris perseverent, aeter-
numque salventur. Nota, Ab aliis Unitio mystica non minus accuratae
et arctissima Substantiae SS. Trinitatis et Christi ... cum substantia
fidelium conjunctio, a Deo ipso per Verbum Evangelii, Sacramenta et
fidem facta, qua speciali essentiae approximatione et gratiosa opera-
tione in iisdem est, ita ut et fideles in eo sint, ut per mutuam and
reciprocam immanentiam vivificae facultatis et omnium beneficiorum e
jus participes facti, certi sint de gratia Dei et salute eterna, unitatemque
in fide et charitate cum reliquis corporis mystici membris servent.

102 Ibid., II,11, 913ff.

103 Cf. discussion in H. Schmid, *Doctrinal Theology*, 480f.

104 Ibid.

105 Quenstedt, Th. Did., II,10; I,16.

106 Ibid., II,10; I,1. Cf. ibid., II,10; I,19.

107 Ibid., II,10; I,2.

108 Ibid., II,10; I,3.

109 Ibid., II,10; I,5.

110 Cf. the attack on Schwenkfelders and Weigelians, ibid., II,10; II,5.

111 Ibid., II,10; I,8-10.

112 Ibid., II,10; I,11-12.

113 Ibid., II,10; I,11.

114 Ibid., II,10; I,16.

115 See H. Schmid, Doctrinal Theology, 480,481,483.

116 EL II,12.

117 EL I,1:1-2.

118 EL I,1:3.

119 EL I,1:6.

120 EL I,1:7.

121 EL I,1:9-11.

122 EL I,1:12.

123 EL I,1:13-14.

124 EL I,1:16. Cf. Arnold, Macarius, 'Vorrede,' 13.
125 EL I,1:17-22.
126 EL I,2.
127 EL I,2:9.
128 EL I,2:11 and 14.
129 EL I,3:19.
130 EL I,12:1; VI,3, 11 and 4,14.
131 EL I, 4:3-6.
132 EL I, 4:7-8.
133 EL I, 4:9.
134 Cf. Stählin, passim.
135 EL I, 1:5.
136 EL I, 4:6.
137 EL I, 4:12.
138 EL I, 5.
139 EL, I, 6.
140 EL I, 6:15.
141 EL I, 6:16.
142 EL I, 6:18. Cf. I, 4:13.
143 EL I, 7.
144 EL I, 8. Cf. his other brief discussion of *Nachfolge* (I, 19.3) and his only references to *Gelassenheit* in the *Erste Liebe* (EL IV, 8:3 and 20).
145 EL I, 9-10.
146 EL I, 11.
147 EL I, 12.
148 EL I, 13.
149 EL I, 14.
150 EL I, 15.
151 EL I, 16.
152 EL I, 17.
153 EL I, 18.
154 Note EL 1, 5, 1. Cf. Stählin, 84.
155 EL I, 13:2.
156 EL I, 13:11.
157 EL I, 13:10.
158 Cf. EL I, 14:7 and III, 5.1.
159 EL I, 20:2-3.
160 EL I, 20:7-11.
161 EL I, 20:6.
162 EL I, 20:13
163 See Paul Althaus d.A., *Forschungen zur Evangelischen Gebetsliteratur* (Gütersloh: Druck und Verlag von C. Bertelsmann, 1927).
164 See Koepp, 'Würtzeln.'
165 Elert, Structure, 166.

166 On Arnold and the young Luther, see, as well, Ernst Walter Zeeden, *The Legacy of Luther*, trans. by Ruth Mary Bethell (London: Hollis and Carter, 1954), 90ff. Cf. Stählin, 17, 93-95.

167 See above, n. 18.

168 Note WA 5:163. Cf. WA 39,1:390. See also Nygren, 705, 706 and Vogelsang, 33-37.

169 WA 7:647.

170 WA 6:562.

171 WA 13:604.

172 WA 40,3:543.

173 WA, Tisch, 2:654.

174 WA 8:65; 42:175

175 WA 7:647

176 WA 1:445 and 551.

177 WA 2:267.

178 WA 2:673; 5:187; 6:561-562.

179 See Rupp, Righteousness, 142-143 and Obermann, 'Simul,' 25-28.

180 Note WA, Tisch, I, 302-303; 391:389-399.

181 WA, Tisch, 3:564. Cf. Tisch, l:302; Tisch, 2:204.

182 WA, Tisch, 1:302.

183 WA, Tisch, 6:359.

184 WA, Tisch, 2:266. See also WA, Tisch, 2, 200 and Tisch, I:575.

185 WA, Tisch, 2:266.

186 WA, Tisch, I, 330.

187 WA, Tisch, I, 435. See also WA, Tisch, 3:295.

188 All Luther's references to Bridget are negative in opposition to her speculation. Cf. WA 9:134; 10,2:376; 30,2:296, 658; 34,1:383; 46:293.

189 WA 54:85.

190 WA 21:60.

191 WA 39,2:168.

192 WA 8:332.

193 WA Tisch, 5:24.

194 WA 43:581.

195 WA 50:519 (Cf. 50:525); Tisch, 1, 355; Tisch, 2:440.

196 WA, Tisch, I:272; Tisch, 4:222.

197 Among other citations, see WA 1:333; 2:602; 5:399; 8:641; 33:83; 36:205; 43:354; 47:598; Tisch, 4:39; Tisch, 5:683.

198 See Obermann, 'Simul,'31-32.

199 WA 14:667.

200 WA, Tisch, I:45, 219.

201 WA 47:597.

202 WA, Tisch, 3:587.

203 WA, Tisch, 3:607.

204 WA 8:617; 39,2:112.

205 WA 7:100.

206 WA, Tisch, 3:295. Cf. WA, Tisch, 1:272; Tisch, 4:480; Tisch, 5:154; Tisch, 6:357.
207 Iserloh, 61.
208 See Heinrich Boehmer, *Road to Reformation*, trans. by John W. Boberstein and Theodore G. Tappert (New York: Meridian Books, 1957), 89, 139 and Julius Köstlin, *Luthers Theologie in ihrer geschichtlichen Entwicklung* (Stuttgart: Druck und Verlag von J.F. Steinkopf, 1901), I, 25-26, 105.
209 Vogelsang, 39.
210 Obermann, 'Simul,' 29-30.
211 Vogelsang, 33.
212 See Vogelsang, 39-40.
213 Obermann, 'Simul,' 30.
214 Strohl, 67-69.
215 See WA 1:276. Luther knew Gerson's work at least two years before he read Tauler (Obermann, 'Simul,' 33) and therefore before 1515 (see Steven Ozment, *Homo Spiritualis. A Comparative Study of The Anthropology of Johannes Tauler, Jean Gerson and Martin Luther (1509-16) in The Context of Their Theological Thought* [Leiden: E.J. Brill, 1969], 1).
216 See WA 1:547.
217 WA 38:160.
218 See WA, Tisch, 1:128; Tisch, 5, 327.
219 WA 1:545, 656; 2:351, 355, 427; 42, 504; WA, Tisch, 1:303; Tisch, 5:213, 372.
220 Cf. WA, Tisch, 2:114 and WA 1:596.
221 Cf. WA, Tisch, 2, 516.
222 WA, Tisch, 1:40, 496; Tisch, 2, 64, 114, 468; Tisch, 4, 110; Tisch, 5, 440.
223 WA 1:596; 6:166; 25:232; 31,2:23; 34,2:202; 40,3:356.
224 See Rupp, Righteousness, 116 n.
225 Luther seldom expresses reserve with Tauler, for example, (Moeller, 159; but Cf. Köstlin, I, 112 and Vogelsang, 41-43), but he did change Tauler's intention to suit his own. See Hägglund, 'Luther,' 92-93, and Vogelsang, 32.
226 See WA, Tisch, 3:508; Tisch, 4:661.
227 WA 26:130-136.
228 Ibid., Intro.
229 See WA 56:313 and 102:329 respectively. Note also Elert, Structure, 169. No direct influence of Eckhart can be traced. See Richard Friedenthal, *Luther: Sein Leben und Zeit* (München: R. Pieper und Co. Verlag, 1967), 149 and Heinrich Bornkamm, *Eckhart und Luther* (Stuttgart: W. Kohlhammer Verlag, 1936).
230 WA 1:152-153: 9:375-359.
231 Heinrich Boehmer, *Luther im Lichte der Neueren Forschung* (2. Aufl.; Leipzig: Verlag von B.G. Tuebner, 1910), 57 suggests a relationship

between thesis 15 of the Ninety-Five Theses and Chapter 11 of the *Theologia deutsch.*

232 Köstlin, I, 107.

233 Wentzlaff-Eggebert, 169.

234 Cf. Obermann, 'Simul,' 39-40; Strohl, 194-196 and Steven E. Ozment, *Mysticism and Dissent. Religious Ideology and Social Protest in the Sixteenth Century* (New Haven, N.J. and London: Yale University Press, 1973), 17-25.

235 Cf. Wentzlaff-Eggebert, 169ff.

236 Joseph Lortz, *The Reformation in Germany*, trans. by Ronald Walls (2 vols.; London and New York: Darton, Longmans and Todd and Herder and Herder, 1968), I, 271.

237 See Uuras Saarnivaara, *Luther Discovers the Gospel* (St. Louis, Mo.: Concordia Publishing House, 1951). 92ff.

238 See Strohl, 193-194.

239 See Boehmer, Forschung, 57. Cf. Strohl, 197. For other early statements praising Tauler, see WA, Briefe, 1:30, 158, 79; WA 1:137, 557; 5:165; 102:329.

240 WA 56:378.

241 WA 56:377. CF. Holl, 67.

242 On Luther's concept of substance, see Gerhard Ebeling, *Luther: An Introduction to His Thought*, trans. by R.A. Wilson (Philadelphia, Pa.: Fortress Press, 1970), 87-88.

243 WA 56:391.

244 Augsburg, 1508, Tauler, No. 45. For details on sources, see Appendix below. Cf. Rupp, Righteousness, 146, 188f.; Strohl, 197-198; Ozment, Homo, 199-205.

245 WA 9: 95-104.

246 WA 9:99, 102.

247 WA 9, 102.

248 See Headley, 59-69.

249 See Seeberg, 431.

250 Ibid., 446-454.

251 See above, Chapter Two, n. 50.

252 Cf. Luther's exegetical practice as discussed in Gerhard Ebeling, 'The New Hermeneutics and the Early Luther,' *Theology Today*, 21 (1964), 34-46.

253 Winter, 20.

254 Ibid., 31.

255 *Postill Johannes Tauleri... zwey Geistreiche Büchlein, Das erste/ die Deutsche Theologia.... Das ander/ die Nachfolgung Christi ... Mit einer Vorrede Johannes Arndtes...* (Gedruckt zu Hamburg/ durch Hans Mosen. In Verlegung Michael Herings. Anno MD CXXI).

256 WC, 'Vorrede,' 8. Translation by Charles F. Schaeffer (Philadelphia, Pa.: General Council Publication House, 1917), xlii.

257 See Weber, Arndt, 53-63.

258 Ibid., 53-56, 62-63, suggests parallels for I, 2 and 31.

259 Ibid., 56-63, notes I, 11-12, 15, 16; II, 6, 22, 23.

260 *Zwey Uhralte vnd Geistreiche Büchlein. Das Erste/ Die Deutsche Theologia... Das Ander/ Die Nachfolgung Christi... deutlicher vnd verständiger an Tag gegeben Durch Iohannem Arndten* ... (Leipzig, In Verlegung Johann Francken [1605]), Avvi-A viir.

261 See Weber, Arndt, 45.

262 II, 20:1-8, translation by Schaeffer, 234-236.

263 The edition of Angela used by Arndt has been unavailable for reference for this study. The translation is that of Mary G. Sheegman, *The Book of Divine Consolation of the Blessed Angela of Foligno* (New York: Cooper Square Publishers, Inc., 1966), 98-101.

264 For a list of Arndt's use of Tauler quotations, see Weber, Arndt, 77-100.

265 WC, III, 1:3, translation by Schaeffer, 379.

266 WC, III, 2:1, translation by Schaeffer, 381.

267 See Weber, Arndt, 102ff.

268 WC, III, 2, 3, translation by Schaeffer, 382-383. For Arndt's source, see Basel 1522 Tauler, 313.

269 WC, III, 4, 1, translation by Schaeffer, 388.

270 Arndt's source was the Basel 1522 Tauler, f. LXXIX.r

271 WC, III, 4, 2, translation by Schaeffer, 388-389.

272 WC, VI, 1, 2. For Arndt's source, see Basel 1522 Tauler, f.CCXXr.

273 WC, III, 6, 3, translation by Schaeffer, 391.

274 Pia desideria, 76.

275 Ibid.

276 Ibid.

277 *Des Hocherleuchteten und theuren lehrers D. Joh. Tauleri Predigten ... Samt dessen übrigen geistreichen Schrifften... Sodann einiger anderer geistreicher Männer erbauliche Schrifften... Nebst Einer Vorrede Herrn D. Philipp Jacob Speners...* (Franckfurt an Mayn und Leipzig/ verlegts Johann Friedrich Gledilsch/ Im Jahr Christi 1703) is used throughout this study.

278 Ibid., [pt. II], 653.

279 See Spener, *Theologische Bedencken*, II, 536 regarding his role in publishing the Franckfurt 1703 Tauler.

280 Franckfurt 1703 Tauler, A2r.

281 Philipp Jacob Spener, *Natur und Gnade/ Oder der Unterschied der Wercke* ... (Franckfurt am Mayn/ Verlegt von Johann David Zunners Seeligen Erben/ 1705), C4v-C5r.

282 Ibid., 355-384.

283 Ibid., 355-360. Passages quoted from pp. 220, 198, 244 of the Franckfurt 1703 Tauler.

284 Ibid., 360-386. Passages quoted from III, XL of Franckfurt 1703 Tauler.

285 Ibid., 386-389. Passages quoted from chapters 23, 38-41 of *Theologia deutsch* (Arndt edition) as published in Franckfurt 1703 Tauler.

286 Ibid., 389. Passages quoted from *Imitation*, I, 3, 9, 16; II, 2, 3; III,
7, 12 (Arndt edition) as published in Franckfurt 1703 Tauler. A Latin
edition of Spener's *Natur und Gnade, De Natvra et Gratia...* (Praefationem praemisit Gottfridvs Olearivs ... Francofurti ad Moenvm ex officina zvnnero-Ivngiana Typis Antonii Heinscheidiis) appeared in 1715.
The medieval passages in that edition are from the Surius translation
of Tauler (see *De Natura et Gratia*, 334). Cf. D. Ioannis Thavleri
Clarissimi Ac Illvminati Theologi, *Sermones .... R.F. Lavrentio Svrio
Carthvsiano in Latinvm Sermonem translata ...* (Parisiis Apvd Societatem Minimam MDCXXIII); the *Theologia deutsch* quotation from
the Latin edition of that work published by Oporinus in Basel, 1557
(see Georg Bäring, *Bibliographie der Ausgaben der 'Theologia deutsch'*
[Baden-Baden: Verlag Heitz Gmbh., 1963], 32 and *De Natura et Gratia*, 345). The source of the *Imitatio* quotations (*De Natura et Gratia*,
355ff.) is not given, but cf. respective sections in Thomae Malleoli à
Kempis, *Opera Omnia*. Ad autographa eiusdem emendata, aucta, et in
tres tomos distributa opera ac studio R.P. Henrici Sommalii ... (Editio
tertia; Antverpiae, Apud Heredes Mart. Nvtii et Ioann. Mevrsivm,
1615).

287 Text printed in Philipp Jacob Spener, *Hauptschriften*, ed. by Paul
Grünberg (Gotha: Friedrich Andreas Perthes, 1889), 184-231.

288 Ibid., 219. Philipp Jacob Spener, *Gerechter Eifer wider das Antichristliche Pabsthum ... aus seinen Schrifften zusammen getragen, und
mit einer Vorrede herausgegeben von Jo. Georgio Pritio* (Franckfurth
am Mayn, In der Zunnerisch- und Jungischen Handlung, Gedruckt bey
Anton Heinscheit, MDCCXIV), 263.

289 Spener, Hauptschriften, 219, 220.

290 Ibid., 220. Cf. Spener, *Gerechter Eifer*, 209, 264.

291 Spener, Hauptschriften, 220-221.

292 Ibid., 221.

293 See Philipp Jacob Spener, *Gerechter Eifer*, passim; *Kleine Geistliche
Schriften* (Magdeburg und Leipzig: Verlegts seel. Christoph Seidels Witwe und Georg Ernst Scheidhauer. Gedruckt bey Christian
Leberecht Faber, 1741-1742), I, 417, 967; II, 255-258, 349, 381, 494ff.,
524ff., 816ff.; III, 164; IV, 502 et al., *Theologische Bedencken*, I,
354, 364; IV, 362-366 and *Der Evangelischen Kirchen Rettung von
falscher trenung und gemeinschaft mit alten Ketzereyen* (Franckfurt am
Mayn/ in verlegung Johann David Zunners im Jahr 1695); *Christliche
Aufmunterung zur Verständigkeit... wie auch Christlichen Unterricht
von selbiger Wiederkehr zu der evangelischen Wahrheit, Der zu dem
Pabsthum verführten* (Franckfurt am Mayn/ In Verlegung Johann
David Zunners seel. Erben, und Johann Adam Jungen, Jm Jahr 1718.
Gedruckt bey Anton Heinscheit).

294 Spener, Hauptschriften, 221-222.

295 Ibid., 223.

296 Spener, *Theologische Bedencken*, III, 274f., 302ff., et al., *Der hochwichtige Articul Von der Wiedergeburt* (Franckfurt am Mayn, Verlegt von Johann David Zunners seel. Erben und [... 1715], 431, 820, 877, *Lauterkeit Des Evangelischen Christenthums* ... (Halle/ in Verlegung des Waysen=hauses MDCCIX), I, 525; II, 188ff., 195ff., 1178-1180.

297 Ibid., II, 113. and Philipp Jacob Spener, *Erste Geistliche Schriften* (Franckfurt am Mayn/ In Verlegung Johann David Zunners/ Buchhandlers Anno MDCXCIX), 744ff.

298 Cf. Philipp Jacob Spener, *Kurtz Catechismus Predigten* (St. Louis, Mo.: Verlag von L. Volkening, 1867), 213-220; *Der hochwichtige Articul*, 862, 876-889. See particularly, *Theologische Bedencken*, I, 190-192.

299 See Philipp Jacob Spener, *Die Evangelische Lebens-Pflichten* ... (In Franckfurt am Mayn, verlegt Von Zunnerischen Erben/ und Joh. Adam Jungen, MDCCXV), 341ff., 363ff.

300 See, for example, August Hermann Francke, *Der Unterschied der Selbst-Rechtfertigung Und der Wahren Rechtfertigung* ... (HALLE, In Verlegung des Waysen hauses/ 1714), 1-3, *NICODEMUS Oder Tractätlein von der Menschen-Furcht* ... (5. Ed.; HALLE, gedr. im Waysen hause MDCCXXIX), 174ff., *Predigten über die Sonn- und Fest-Tags-Episteln* ... (Die dritte EDITION. HALLE, in Verlegung des Waysen-Hauses, MDCCXXXXI), 489, 818ff., 1022f., *Erklärung Der Psalmen Davids; Anderer Theil* ... (HALLE, in Verlegung des Waysen hauses MDCCXXXXV), 534, 575ff., 585, 654, 737f., 1086f., 1143f., 1261f., 1256., and *Busz-Predigten* ... (Fünfte Auflage; HALLE, in Verlegung des Waysenhauses, MDCCXLV), I, 34, 224f.

301 See Francke, *Predigten*, 46, 1023 and Spener, *Theologische Bedencken*, I, 43f., 213; III, 536, 712, 714, 752, 828, 889 for examples.

302 Cf. Philipp Jacob Spener, *Die Evangelische Lebens-Pflichts* ... (In Franckfurt am Mayn, verlegt Von Zunnerischen Erben/ und Joh. Adam Jungen, MDCCXV), b557-560. (Cf. ibid., b356-b370), *Bedencken*, II, 851ff.; IV, 442, 451 and Francke, *Erklärung*, 817, *Busz-Predigten*, II, 23ff., 113ff., 108ff.

303 See above.

304 KKH I, 13; II, 8-11.

305 KKH, I, 13; II, 13.

306 KKH I, 13; II, 12.

307 KKH I, 12; III, 3.

308 KKH I, 12; III, 4.

309 KKH I, 12; III, 8. Arnold refers the reader to Trithemius' works. Cf. the comments on Hildegard and Elizabeth in Trithemius *Catalogus illustrorum virorum* and *Chronicon Spanheimense* in Johann Trithemius, *Opera Historica*... (Francofvrti, typus Wechelianis apud Claudium Marnium et heredes Ioannis Aubrij. M.DCI), I, 137-138 and II, 254, respectively.

310 KKH IV, n. 33, 165.5.

311 KKH I, 13; II, 14-15.

312 KKH I, 13; V, 4.

313 KKH I, 13; II, 10-12 and III, 4.

314 KKH I, 14; III, 8.

315 KKH IV, n. 33, 163.1.

316 KKH I, 14; III, 10.

317 KKH I, 14; III, 10.

318 [Er] hat in seiner muttersprache geschrieben, eine summam des gantzen geistlichen lebens, ein buch von der hütte Mosis, einen spiegel des ewigen lebens, von viererley versuchungen, von sieben schlössern oder verwahrungen der geistlichen schule, 3 bücher von der geistlichen hochzeit, von dem stein oder der vollkommenheit der kinder Gottes, von dem Reich der liebhaber Gottes, von der wahren beschaulichkeit, item eines von der hohen beschaulichkeit, von den 7 stuffen der liebe, von glauben und gerichte, von den vornehmsten tugenden. (Ibid.)

319 See Arnold's introduction to Ruusbroec, 5-16.

320 Wie allen mysticis gegangen, dasz sie von wenigsten mit gedult gelesen, von noch wenigern verstanden, und von den allerwenigsten gebilliget werden, in dem ihre lehrart so gar der verderbten vernunfft und dem eigenen willen zuwider ist ... (KKH I, 14; III, 10).

321 KKH I, 14; III, 11.

322 See A. Chiquot, *Histoire ou Legende... ? Jean Tauler et le 'Meisters Buoch'* (Strasbourg et Paris: A. Vix et Cie et E. Champion, 1922) and, above all, Heinrich Seuse Denifle, *Taulers Bekehrung kritisch untersucht in Quellen und Forschung zur Sprach- und Culturegeschichte der Germanischen Volker*, Bd. XXXVI (Strassburg und London: Karl J. Trübner und Trübner und Comp., 1879) and his 'Die Dichtungen Rulman Merswins,' *Zeitschrift für deutsches Alterthum*, 24 (1880), 463-540.

323 See KKH I, 16; XX, 7 and 17; XVII, 7, respectively.

324 KKH I, 14; III, 12.

325 KKH I, 15; III, 4.

326 KKH I, 15; III, 6.

327 KKH I, 15; III, 7.

328 KKH I, 15; III, 6.

329 KKH I, 15; III, 7.

330 KKH I, 15; III, 3.

331 KKH I, 15; III, 4.

332 See R Haubst, 'Johannes von Franckfort als der mutmassliche Verfasser von 'Eyn deutsch Theologie',' *Scholastik*, 33 (1958), 385-398.

333 KKH I, 15; III, 7.

334 KKH I, 15; III, 5.

Notes to Chapter Four

1 For a brief but reliable guide to the characteristics of German Baroque literature, see Marian Szyrocki, *Die deutsche Literatur des Barok* (Reinbeck bei Hamburg: Rowohlt Taschenbuch Verlag, 1968), 1-57. Also

of value are Herbert Cysarz, hrsg., *Baroklyrik* (2. Aufl.; Hildesheim: Georg Olms Verlagsbuchhandlung, 1964), I, 1-88; A. Closs, *The Genius of the German Lyric* (London: The Cresset Press, 1962), 118-121, and Roy Daniells, *Milton, Mannerism and the Baroque* (Toronto: University of Toronto Press, 1963), 51-63. A good selection of texts from the period is found in Albrecht Schöne, hrsg., *Das Zeitalter des Barok* (München: C.H. Beck' sche Verlagsbuchhandlung, 1963). On Arnold and the Baroque, see Stählin, 29-30.

2 See Friedrich, 8. Cf. GLF I, 14-15, 33.

3 See GLF I, 38-39, 77.

4 Cf. GLF I, 46, 55-58, 68-69.

5 See Stählin, 82-83 and note GLF, passim. On the use of emblemata and a guide to emblem books, see Arthur Henkel und Albrecht Schöne, *Emblemata: Handbuch zur Sinnkunst des 16. und 17. Jahrhunderts* (Stuttgart: J.B. Metzler, 1967) and Albrecht Schöne, *Emblematik und Drama im Zeitalter des Barok* (München: C.H. Beck'sche Verlagsbuch handlung, 1968), 17-138. Note, as well, Peter M. Daly, *The European Emblem: Towards an Index Emblematicus* (Waterloo, Ont.: Wilfrid Laurier University Press, 1980)

6 Cf. GLF I, 75.

7 Cf. GLF I, 7, 12-13.

8 Cf. GLF I, 16-17, 32.

9 Cf. GLF I, 67, 72.

10 See Stählin, 19. Cf. GLF I, 10, 14-15, 41.

11 GLF I, 52-53, 82-83, 91-92.

12 GLF I, 16-17, 50, 75, 94, 114, 155, 162ff., 195.

13 GLF I, 30.

14 See Daniells, 53.

15 See his 'Liebste Braut' in George C. Schoolfield, *The German Lyric of the Baroque in English Translation* (New York: AMS Press, Inc., 1966), 58-59.

16 GLF, 'Zuschrift,' B3v. See discussion in Stählin, 73-76.

17 See Stählin, 75-76. Note the biographical study by Walter Dietze, *Quirinus Kuhlmann* (Berlin: Rutten und Loening, 1963) and Quirinus Kuhlmann, *Der Kühlpsalter*, hrsg., Robert L. Beare (Tübingen: Max Niemeyer Verlag, 1971) as well as Martin Lackner, *Geistesfrömmigkeit und Enderwartung* (Stuttgart: Evangelisches Verlagswerk, 1959). For a general guide to the German literature of the period under discussion, see Richard Newald, *Die deutsche Literatur Vom Späthumanismus zur Empfindsamkeit, 1570-1750* (München: C.H. Beck'sche Verlagsbuchhandlung, 1957). Note, as well, Rudolf Haller, *Geschichte der deutschen Lyrik von Ausgang des Mittelalters bis zu Goethes Tod* (Bern und München: Francke Verlag, 1967), Johannes Klein, *Geschichte der deutschen Lyrik von Luther Bis zum Ausgang des Zweiten Weltkrieges* (Wiesbaden: Franz Steiner Verlag, 1951), and Wolfgang Stammler, *Von*

der Mystik zum Barok, (2.Aufl.; Stuttgart: J.B. Metzlersche Verlags-buchhandlung, 1950).

18 See Stählin, 55-61. Silesius' works are edited in *Sämtliche Poetische Werke*, hrsg., Hans Ludwig Held (3 Bde.; München: Carl Hanser Verlag, 1949-1952). Note, in particular, Joachim H. Seyppel, 'Freedom and the Mystical Union in *Der Cherubinische Wandersmann*,' *The Germanic Review*, 32 (1957), 93-112. See also Mary Hilder Godecker, *Angelus Silesius' Personality through his 'Ecclesiologia'* (Washington, D.C.: The Catholic University of America Press, 1938). For a reliable background to the religious environment in Silesia at the time, see Gustav Hoffmane, *Die religiösen Bewegungen in der evangelischen Kirche Schlesiens während des siebzehnten Jahrhunderts* (Breslau: Eduard Trewendts Buchdruckerei, 1880).

19 See GLF, 'Zuschrift,' A8v, A12v.

20 GLF, 'Vorrede,' B3v-B4r. Cf. ibid., A11v, B4, B7r-B8v.

21 See Stählin, 66.

22 Cf. ibid., 18, 67-68.

23 See ibid., 61-65.

24 Cf. Friedrich, Studien, 76-77 for example.

25 KKH I, 17; V, 26 and KKH III, 19.

26 See Dietze, 335-336, n. 116.

27 Johann Angelus Silesius, *Cherubinischer Wanders-Mann Oder Geistreiche Sinn- und Schlusz- Reime, Zur Göttlichen Beschaulichkeit...* aufs neue mit Gottfried Arnolds Vorrede herausgegeben ... (Altona, Auf kosten guter Freunde, 1737), 'Vorrede,' 3r.

28 Ibid., 4r-4v.

29 Ibid., 4r, 5v.

30 Ibid., 4v-5r.

31 Ibid., 5v.

32 See Seyppel, 'Freedom,' 97, 100, 101 and note Charles Waldemar, hrsg., *Der Cherubinischer Wandersmann* (München: Wilhelm Goldmann Verlag, 1960), 5.

33 Cf. Newald, 263 and Fritz Usinger, 'Die mystische Lehre Angelus Silesius,' in his *Gesichter und Gesichte* (Darmstadt: Eduard Roether Verlag, 1965), 17-22.

34 Cf. Koyré, Boehme, 282, 306f., 361 and elsewhere.

35 Note particularly Hoffmane, 14ff.

36 See ibid., 30-38, 54-61.

37 See ibid., 24-30, 61-63.

38 In Hoffmane's bibliography, note especially I, 31, 33.

39 Note, as well, my 'Ein bisher unbekanntes quietistisch-boehmisches manuskript,' *Jahrbuch für Schlesische Kirchengeschichte* (1977), 127-129.

40 Arnold knew Sudermann's manuscripts for example. See Supplementa, XXV.

41 See above, n. 39.
42 KKH I, 17; XIX and KKH III, 9.
43 GLF, 'Zuschrift,' A5rff.
44 GLF, 'Vorrede,' B8vff.
45 GLF, 'Vorrede,' B10vff.
46 GLF, 'Vorrede,' B10r.
47 GLF, 'Vorrede,' B11r.
48 GLF, 'Vorrede,' B11v.
49 GLF I, 251.
50 GLF I, 253.
51 GLF I, 254.
52 GLF I, 254-255.
53 GLF I, 255-256.
54 GLF I, 259.
55 GLF I, 261.
56 GLF I, 263.
57 GLF I, 266.
58 GLF I, 269.
59 GLF I, 279.
60 GLF I, 280.
61 GLF I, 281.
62 GLF I, 283.
63 GLF I, 283-284.
64 GLF I, 284-285.
65 GLF I, 286.
66 GLF I, 287-288.
67 GLF I, 290.
68 Ibid.
69 GLF I, 291.
70 GLF I, 296.
71 GLF I, 297-298.
72 GLF I, 299.
73 GLF I, 298.
74 GLF I, 1-11, 124.
75 GLF I, 98.
76 Ibid.
77 GLF I, 75.
78 GLF I, 129.
79 GLF I, 105f.
80 GLF I, 25, 43, 95. 200. Cf. GLF, 'Zuschrift,' A11r.
81 GLF I, 32, 70f., 74f.
82 GLF I, 119, 182.
83 GLF I, 14, 15, 110.
84 GLF I, 17, 29.
85 GLF I, 125-126.

86 GLF I, 173.

87 GLF I, 37-39, 215.

88 GLF I, 171-172, 179. Cf. GLF, 'Zuschrift,' A9vf.

89 GLF I, 50, 83ff., 118, 131.

90 GLF I, 4-5.

91 GLF I, 28, 36, 39-41.

92 GLF I, 16, 18, 20, 155.

93 GLF I, 98, 120, 123, 132, 220. Cf. the mystical vocabulary at GLF I, 22-23, 50, 88, 121, 135ff., 155ff., 185ff., 190, 192, 195 and II, 7, 11-15, 25, 31, 39, 43, 46, 50, 57, 75.

94 GLF I, 85f.

95 GLF I, 61, 98, 206ff., 210, 223ff.

96 GLF, 'Zuschrift,' A6v.

97 GLF, 'Zuschrift,' A8r, A11r, A12r.

98 GLF, 'Zuschrift,' A11v.

99 GLF I, 314-327.

100 See *Endliche Vorstellung*, 493. Cf. Büchsel, 125-132 and Daniel P. Walker, *The Decline of Hell: Seventeenth Century Discussions of Eternal Torment* (Chicago: University of Chicago Press, 1964), 238.

101 GLF I, 79, 99-105.

102 See KKH I, 17; XVIII, 10, 23ff., 40ff.

103 The only medieval author quoted in the Sophia is Bernard (Sophia, XIII, 10 and XXIV, 12).

104 Sophia, 'Vorrede,' 21.

105 Ibid.

106 Sophia, I.

107 Sophia, III, VI, 19ff.

108 Sophia, V, 4.

109 Sophia, V, 7-8.

110 Cf. Augustine, *Ennarrationes in Psalmos*, LXXIV in PL 36, 952.

111 Sophia, VIII, 2.

112 Sophia, VIII, 7.

113 Sophia, VIII, 8ff.

114 Sophia, VIII, 22, 25.

115 Sophia, VIII, 23; IX, 4-7.

116 Sophia, XII, 6.

117 Sophia, XI, 6.

118 Sophia, XIII, 4-7.

119 Sophia, XV, 11-17.

120 Sophia, XV, 16.

121 Sophia, XV, 27.

122 Sophia, XVI, 7.

123 Cf. Sophia, IV, 6.

124 Cf. Sophia, XVIII, 7 and note Sophia, XVI, 12, 16.

125 On Osiander's doctrine, see Jörg Rainer Fligge, *Herzog Albrecht von Preussen und der Osiandrismus, 1522-1568* (Bonn: Rheinische Friedrich-Wilhelms-Universität, 1972), 16-116 and 526-586.

126 Sophia, XV, 11 and XVI, 2.

127 Cf., for example, Sophia, XV, 1-3.

128 Sophia, XVII, 13.

129 Sophia, XVII, 1, 8.

130 Sophia, XVII, 7.

131 Sophia, XVII, 28 and XVIIIff.

132 Sophia, XXIII, 8.

133 See Koyré, Boehme, 451ff.

134 On this topic, see Büchsel, 148-160. For background to the question, see Fritz Tanner, *Pietismus* (Zurich: Zwingli Verlag, 1952).

135 Cf. Büchsel, 153ff.

136 On Poiret's interest, see Weiser, Poiret, 209.

137 See Stoeffler, *German Pietism*, 5, 9.

138 See Stählin, 43ff.

139 Ronald A. Knox, *Enthusiasm* (New York: Oxford University Press, 1961), 260. The characteristics of Quietism which follow are based on Knox, 260-287.

140 Note Schroeder, 37-71.

141 See, for example, *Schvengfeldismvm in Pietismo Renatvm*, Praeside Val. Ernesto Loeschere ... D. XX. Octobr. Anno 1 1 VIII. Dispvtatione Pvblica Reiiciet Avtor Samvel Zelenka ... (Vitembergae, Literis Christiani Gerdesii), D1v, D2v.

142 KKH I, 16; XX, 1-27. For a full bibliography on Schwenckfeld see my *Schwenckfeld in His Reformation Setting* (Pennsburg, Pa.: Schwenkfelder Library, 1977) and the additional bibliographic material in *Schwenckfeld and Early Schwenkfeldianism*, ed. by Peter C. Erb (Pennsburg, Pa.: Schwenkfelder Library, 1985). For works of particular importance in this study note Otto Borngräber, *Das Erwachen der philosophischen Spekulation der Reformationszeit* (Schwarzenberg i. Sa.: Buchdruckerei von C.M. Gärtner, 1908); Karl Ecke, *Schwenckfeld, Luther und der Gedanke einer apostolischen Reformation* (Berlin: Verlag von Martin Warneck, 1911); Edward J. Furcha, *Schwenckfeld's Concept of the New Man* (Pennsburg, Pa.: Board of Publication of the Schwenkfelder Church, 1970); Ernest L. Lashlee, *The Via Regia: A Study of Caspar Schwenckfeld's Ideas of Personal Renewal and Church Reform* (unpubl. Ph.D., Harvard, 1969); Paul L. Maier, *Caspar Schwenckfeld on the Person and Work of Christ* (Assen: Van Gorcum Ltd., 1959); Maron, *Individualismus*; Reinhold Pietz, *Der Mensch ohne Christus: Untersuchung zur Anthropologie Caspar Schwenckfelds* (unpubl. diss., Tübingen, 1956); Selina G. Schultz, *Caspar Schwenckfeld von Ossig*, with an introduction by Peter C. Erb (4th ed.; Pennsburg, Pa.: Board of Publication of the Schwenkfelder Church, 1977). The writings of Schweckfeld have been published in Chester D. Hartranft

et al., eds., *Corpus Schwenckfeldianorum*, (19 Bde.; Leipzig: Breitkopf
und Härtel, 1907-1961)—hereafter: CS.

143 See above, n. 141 and n. 145 below.

144 See KKH I, 16; XX, 27 and Supplementa, XXIV-XXVI. Cf. CS V, 329.

145 On Hoburg, see my 'Christian Hoburg und schwenckfeldische Wurtzeln
des Pietismus,' *Jahrbuch für Schlesische Kirchengeschichte* (1977), 92-
125. Arnold published his *Teutscher Krieg*. (See Seeberg, 60).

146 Partial attempts have been made by Stählin and Friedrich.

147 For discussions on Schwenckfeld as a mystic, see Erbkam, 357-475;
Borngräber, 22-25; Maron, 154-159. Opposed to these are CS I, L-LI;
Schultz, 374-376; Ecke, 43-48.

148 In particular, his precise understanding of grace, his doctrine of predestination and free will, and his concept of spiritual regeneration must be
studied.

149 Cf. Horst Weigelt, *Spiritualistische Tradition im Protestantismus* (Berlin: Walter de Gruyter, 1973), 42-46. Weigelt's work appeared in English translation under the title *The Schwenkfelders in Silesia*, trans. by
Peter C. Erb (Pennsburg, Pa.: Schwenkfelder Library, 1985).

150 See Schultz, 6-7.

151 See CS XIII, 212.

152 See CS I, 128.

153 CS II, 1-105. On Schweckfeld's early view of the Lutheran doctrine of
justification, see Weigelt, 31-46.

154 See especially CS II, 583-599. On the possible relationship between
this and the 'two eyes' in Tauler and the *Theologia deutsch*, see Maron,
42-43.

155 On Schwenckfeld's early sacramentology, see Weigelt, 47-106.

156 CS II, 173-209. On Crautwald's teaching, see Weigelt, 53-65.

157 This chronological division is based on Pietz, 9-10.

158 For treatments of this theme in Schwenckfeld and his colleagues, see
Weigelt, 107-126.

159 Schwenckfeld's most extensive treatment of this question is found in CS
XII, 417-541.

160 For details, see Maron, passim, and Lashlee, 171-205.

161 On Schwenckfeld's view of religious freedom, see Kuhn, *Toleranz und
Offenbarung*, 140-161.

162 This has been established by research presently under way at the
Schwenkfelder Library.

163 On the doctrine of the celestial flesh, see Hans Joachim Schoeps, *Vom
himmlischen Fleisch Christi* (Tübingen: J.C.B. Mohr (Paul Siebeck),
1951); Williams, 325-335.

164 A full discussion of Schwenckfeld's Christology is lacking. It is most
nearly filled by Maier.

165 See CS XVII, 88.

166 CS XVII, 369.

167 On this theme, see Valentine Crautwald's tract *Novus Homo*, translated and published several times by Schwenckfeld (CS VIII, 35-79). My translation from the Latin is available through Schwenkfelder Library.

168 CS III, 571-575.

169 CS X, 775-833.

170 See CS IV, 642-653. Cf. CS XVIII, 607-608 and XV, 166-172.

171 CS IX, 102ff.

172 This is experiential knowledge but is not mystical in the way Maron, 79ff. suggests.

173 See Maron, 47-66 for citations.

174 CS IV, 894. On this topic, see my 'Schwenckfeld, the Anabaptists, and the Sixteenth-Century Crisis of Knowing,' in *Anabaptists and Dissidents* ed. by Jean Rott, (Baden-Baden: Koerner, 1987), 131-47.

175 Cf. CS IV, 56, 734; V, 53.

176 CS I, 252.

177 See CS XII, 141 nn. and 554.

178 Cf. Maier, 99, but note earlier uses as well (CS II, 31, 61, 63).

179 For a full discussion of Tauler, see below Chapter Seven.

180 For a discussion of Karlstadt on this theme, see Ronald J. Sider, *Andreas Bodenstein von Karlstadt* (Leiden: E.J. Brill, 1973), 101, 216, 223, 228.

181 Cf. CS II, 31, 61, 63, 69, 75, 505, 559; VI, Doc CCLV, XVIII, 167-169. Note Maron, 52.

182 Cf. CS VII, 445; VIII, 404; X, 307, etc. For a brief survey of Schwenckfeld's use of medieval mystics, see George R. Seltzer, *Aspects of the Thought of Caspar Schwenckfeld* (unpubl. Ph.D., Hartford Theological Seminary, 1934), 30ff.

183 CS X, 437.

184 CS VII, 445, 748; VIII, 404; XII, 500.

185 See CS IX, 349-357.

186 Note especially those used in the years 1556-1558, when Schwenckfeld with his colleague, Theophilus Agricola, was engaged in an elaborate defence of his thought. On the historical background, see Schultz, 345-347. For Schwenckfeld's use of Tauler during these years, see CS XV, 165; XVI, 154-155, 201, etc. Agricola too, made extensive use of Tauler. See CS XIV, 962; XV, 102ff., 296; XVI, 431, etc. Particular use is made of selections from the Basel 1522 Tauler, IIIb, IIII, IXb sq., XIIIb, CLXVIIIb sq., CCLVIIb sq., etc.

187 Cf. CS X, 438; XVII, 539, both of which quote from the Augsburg 1508 Tauler, f. XCIX and CS X, 437 which quotes from the same edition of Tauler, f. Ccviijb. Note the discussion of the passages in Joachim H. Seyppel, *Schwenckfeld: Knight of Faith* (Pennsburg, Pa.: Schweckfelder Library, 1961), 84-88.

188 See Schultz, 385-388.

189 See CS IV, 262-277.

190 CS IV, 413. The annotations are now lost.

191 CS IV, 278-413.

192 On other medieval mystics and their possible influence on Schwenckfeld, see Furcha, 31ff., 40-42, 70f.

193 See CS III, 806-09 (selections from Sermon 23 on the Song of Songs and from *De consideratione*), XII, 141-142; XVI, 340 (paraphrases of *De consideratione*). See also Furcha, 40-43.

194 See CS II, 431; XVI, 200-202. Furcha, 99 notes lines in Schwenckfeld with a Bonaventurian tone.

195 The only exception is a marginal note to II Quodlibet, Art. 4, Dist. 24, and Art. 8 (CS XI, 696).

196 See CS II, 422 for allusion to Geiler.

197 CS IV, 238.

198 CS XII, 554-556.

199 CS IX, 319-320.

200 CS IX, 361.

201 On Franck, his use of medieval mysticism and the role of medieval mysticism among other radical reformers, see my original thesis, 646-653.

202 On Hiller and his use of Tauler, see Weigelt, 194-199.

203 See CS XIV, 962, 970-971, 974, 9800; XV, 102, 131-134, 281, 289, 295-296, 306; XVI, 155, 159, 165, 197, 201, 256, 431, 447; XVII, 529, 539, 765.

204 This is especially to be noted in Erasmus Weichenhan. On Weichenhan, see Weigelt, 212-213. Weichenhan's use of Tauler may be noted in his *Christliche Betrachtungen über die Evangelischen Texte...* (Allentown, Penns.: Gedruckt bei V. und W. Blumer, 1842), 29, 115, 385, 505.

205 See Ernst Eylenstein, *Daniel Friedrich (+1610): Ein Beitrag zum mystischen Separatismus am Ende des 16. Jahrhunderts in Deutschland* (Langensalza: Druck von Julius Beltz, 1930).

206 On Sudermann, see Monica Pieper, *Daniel Sudermann (1550-ca. 1631): Als Vertreter des mystischen Spiritualismus* (Stuttgart: Franz Steiner, 1985). Note, as well, Hans Hornung, *Daniel Sudermann als Handschriftensammler* (unpubl. diss., Tübingen, 1957), Hornung, 'Der Handschriftensammler Daniel Sudermann und die Bibliothek des Strassburger Klosters St. Nikolaus in undis,' *Zeitschrift für die Geschichte des Oberrheins*, 107 (Der neuer Folge 68. Bd.) (1959), 338-399 (hereafter: Hornung), and Gottfried H. Schmidt, *Daniel Sudermann: Versuch einer wissenschaftlichen Monographie* (unpubl. diss., Leipzig, 1923).

207 See Ingeborg Degenhardt, *Studien zum Wandel des Eckhartbildes* (Leiden, 1967), 98-100, for his significance in Eckhart scholarship.

208 Hornung, 382.

209 Hornung, 359-360. For manuscript listing, see Hornung, diss., 17ff., and Schmidt, 181ff.

210 On that library and its relationships to Sudermann, see Hornung, 382-397.

211 See Allen A. Seipt, *Schwenkfelder Hymnology* (Philadelphia, Pa., 1909), 21-24.

212 The manuscripts involved are in the Staatsbibliothek der Stiftung Preussischer Kulturbesitz, formerly Preussische Staatsbibliothek, Berlin and designated MS germ. 40 336, MS germ. 40 338, MS germ. 40 340. Hereafter manuscripts from the Preussische Staatsbibliothek will be referred to by entry numbers alone. On Sudermann's previous ownership of these and other manuscripts listed below, see Hornung, diss., 17ff., and Schmidt, 181ff.

213 Cf. Hornung, 360.

214 Sermons 1, 2, 4, 5b, 16b, 25, 26, 44 in Meister Eckhart, *Die deutschen und lateinischen Werke, Die deutschen Werke*, I-II, ed. by Josef Quint (Stuttgart, 1958-71), see MS germ. 40 125, MS germ. 40 191 , MS germ. 80 12, MS germ. 80 841.

215 See Quint, *Deutsche Werke*, V, 377. The manuscript was MS germ. 40 191.

216 See Josef Quint, *Die Uberlieferung der deutschen Predigten Meister Eckeharts* (Bonn, 1932), 927-928. Among the most important manuscripts used are MS germ. 40 165, MS germ. 80 4, MS germ. 80 65 and those cited above in n. 214.

217 See Georg Hofmann, 'Literaturgeschichtliche Grundlagen zur Tauler Forschung,' in E. Filthaut, hrsg., *Johannes Tauler: Ein deutscher Mystiker* (Essen, 1961), 441-442, 452. The manuscripts which were once in Sudermann's possession are MS germ. 40 149, MS germ. 40 166, MS germ 40 841 and MS Leipzig Universitätsbibliothek Cod. Nr. 560.

218 See Karl Bihlmeyer, ed., *Heinrich Seuse: Deutsche Schriften* (Stuttgart, 1907), 3-28∗. Sudermann owned manuscripts containing copies of the Exemplar (MS germ. fol. 658, MS germ. 40 840), the *Vita* (MS germ. 80 69), the *Buch der ewigen Weisheit* (MS germ. 40 173, MS germ. 80 379, MS germ. 40 125, MS germ. 80 364, MS germ. 80 42, MS germ. 80 393, MS germ. 80 380, MS germ. 80 349, MS germ. 80 346, MS germ. 40 553, MS germ. 40 172), the *Buch der Wahrheit* (MS germ. fol. 76). the *Grosse Briefbuch* (MS germ. 80 69), and sermons (MS germ. 80 69, MS germ. 80 329). Schmidt notes in addition a copy of the *100 Betrachtungen* (Schmidt, 204) in MS germ. 80 66 and other pieces (Schmidt, 184).

219 See Wolfgang Eichler, ed., *Jan van Ruusbroecs 'Brulocht' in ober deutscher Uberlieferung: Untersuchungen und kritische Textausgabe* (München, 1969), 2, 24-28, 32 for specific note of Sudermann's role in the tradition. Note also Eichler's use of MS germ. 40 194.

220 Among others note Geiler von Kaiserberg (MS germ. 40 163, MS germ. 40 197, MS germ. 40 598, MS germ. 80 63), Nicolas von Strassburg (MS germ. 80 12), Otto von Passau (MS germ. 40 105), Johann Nider (MS germ. 80 30), Johann Kreutzer zu Gebweyler (MS germ. 40 158), Heinrich von Weissenberg (MS germ. 40 164), Elizabeth von Schönau (MS germ. 40 202).

221 The materials include many tracts on the Passion (MS germ. 80 53, MS germ. 80 35, etc), treatises on the Eucharist (MS germ. 40 125, MS germ. 80 25), prayer collections and anonymous sermons. Note also the German translations from the Gospels (MS germ. 40 167) and *Das Myrrhen Buchlein* (MS germ. 80 30, MS Wolfenbüttel Braunschweigische Landesbibliothek 83 Aug. oct.).

222 For a survey of Sudermann's publications, see Schmidt, 22-52, 64 74.

223 Joh. Tauler, *Predigten auf die Evangelien durch das ganze Jahr* (Franckfurt a. M., 1621) (cited in Schmidt, 70).

224 *Güldene Sendtbrieff/ vieler Gottseligen Kirchen-lehrer: als/ Johann Taulers,/ Heinrich Seussen, Johann Crätzers/ vnnd mehr Anderer ...* , o.O., 1622 (cited in Hornung, 374; Schmidt, 71).

225 *Ain alt vnd werdes Buchlein/ von der Gnade Gottes./ ... von Johan Rusebruch einem Hayligen/ Waldt Priester in Brabandt... geschrieben, ... ,* o.O., 1621 (cited in Hornung, 373; Schmidt, 69) contained the first two books of *The Spiritual Espousals.* Note also his edition of Ruusbroec's *De calculo* in German translation, ascribed to Tauler, *Ein Edles Buchlein/ ... Doctor Johann Taulers/ Wie der Mensch möge Ernsthafftig/ Jnnig/ Geistlich vnnd GOttschawende werden ... , o. O,* 1621 (cited in Hornung, 373; Schmidt, 68).

226 Sudermann published, in addition, several poems he believed to be by Tauler (Schmidt, 67-68), *The Book of the Poor in Spirit* (Schmidt, 69); Heinrich von Weissenburg's *Seven Steps to Divine Love*, as well as materials taken from writings ascribed to Eckhart and Tauler.

227 See *Epistolar... Caspar Schwenckfeldts von Ossig... Der ander Theil,...* o.O., 1570 (hereafter: Epistolar II, annotated by Sudermann, is presently in the Schwenkfelder Library).

228 Cf. Epistolar II, 364, etc.

229 Epistolar II, 372, 1005.

230 Hornung, 361-362.

231 Ibid., 367.

232 Exceptions are to be found in his *Hohe geistreiche Lehren vnd Erklärungen vber die fürnembsten Sprüche desz Hohen Lieds,...* o.O., 1622.

233 MS germ. 40 344, 95-121.

234 Martin Luther, *De captivitate babylonica...* in WA 6, 561f.

235 John Calvin, *Institutes of the Christian Religion*, trans. by Ford Lewis Battles. (2 vols.; Philadelphia, Pa.: The Westminster Press, 1960), I, 164-165 (Part I, ch. 14, sect. 4).

236 See Schneider annotations on 'Liederdichter', 11 in Schwenkfelder Library.

237 The title, making specific mention of the sources, reads in part: '... Ausz der alten Christlichen Kirchen-lehrern vnd jhren Nachfolgern Schrifften gezogen ... '

238 MS ger. f. 451, fasc. 7, f. 6.

239 MS germ. f. 431, fasc. 11, ff. 125b-126b.

240 Basel 1522 Tauler, f. CCXLIXb-CCLa.

241 Ibid., CCLa.
242 not identified.
243 *Fünffzig Schöner ... Figuren*, 14.
244 *Schöne ... Figuren* II, 2, quoted from Basel Tauler, f. CCLXXVIIIa.
245 *Schöne... Figuren* II, 2.
246 Basel 1522 Tauler, f. CCLXXVIIIa.
247 MS germ. 40 431, IIIa.
248 The poems follow in a parallel fashion in both authors, but note PLLS, 179-193 as well.
249 Ibid., Sudermann, prose to third poem.
250 Ibid., Sudermann, first poem, 11. 1-5.
251 Ibid., Sudermann, first poem, 11. 7-18.
252 Ibid., Sudermann, first poem, 11. 19-30.
253 Ibid., Sudermann, first poem, 11. 37-41.
254 Ibid., Sudermann, first poem 1. 51.
255 Cf. ibid., Sudermann, first poem, 11. 53-54.
256 Ibid., Sudermann, first poem, 11. 55ff.
257 Ibid., Sudermann, third poem.
258 Ibid., Sudermann, second poem, 1. 32.
259 Ibid., Sudermann, second poem.
260 For a full bibliography on Hoburg, see n. 145 above.
261 Hoburg, *Theologia Mystica*, I, 3.
262 Ibid., I, 8-12.
263 Ibid., I, 13.
264 Ibid., II, 1.
265 Ibid., III, 'Vorrede,' 2.
266 Ibid., III, 4.
267 Ibid., III, 5.
268 Ibid., III, 6.
269 Ibid., III, 9.
270 Ibid., III, 7.
271 Ibid., III, 15.
272 Ibid., III, 10.
273 Ibid., III, 11.
274 Ibid., III, 13.
275 Cf. ibid., III, 16.:2.
276 See above n. 144.
277 On the Sudermann collection and its fate after his death, see relevant sections in L.C. Bethmann, *Herzog August der Jüngere, der Gründer der Wolfenbüttler Bibliothek* (Wolfenbüttel, 1863); Otto von Heinemann, *Die Handschriften der herzoglichen Bibliothek zu Wolfenbüttel* (Wolfenbüttel, 1884-1913), Bd. 6, II. Abt. u. Bd. 7, and Friedrich Wilken, *Geschichte der Königlichen Bibliothek zu Berlin* (Berlin: Duniker und Humbolt, 1828).
278 See above, note 248.

279 See PLLS, 42ff.
280 See, in particular, PLLS, 1-2.
281 Cf. ibid., 1. 4.
282 Ibid., 11. 4-10.
283 Ibid., 11. 15-16, 20, 28.
284 Ibid., 11. 37-40.
285 Ibid., 11. 37-44.
286 Ibid., II.
287 Ibid., III.
288 NGLF, 257.
289 Note, in particular, the use of terms such as 'El Schaddai' and 'tingiret' (PLLS, 101) which are not used elsewhere by Arnold, and Arnold's admission that many of the poems in this section are not his.
290 PLLS, 100-108.
291 PLLS, 108.
292 Cf. PLLS, 100-101 with Seuse, 7-8 and 196-198 and PLLS, 108 with Seuse, 325. Cf. as well, Heinricus Suso, *Horologium Sapientiae*, ed. by Josephus Strange (Coloniae: J.M. Heberle [H. Lempertz], 1961), 15-17. On the relationship between the *Buch der Ewigen Weisheit* and its Latin original, *Horologium*, see Eric Colledge, 'The Buchlein der Ewigen Weiszheit and the Horologium Sapientiae,' *Dominican Studies*, 6 (1953), 77-89.
293 PLLS, 112-129.
294 For a discussion, see Schroeder, 84-86.

Notes to Chapter Five

1 EL, 1082-1084.
2 See Dibelius, 72.
3 EL 4, 2:17-18.
4 The text used in the following study is that reprinted in C.A. Roemeling, *Nachricht seiner von Gottgeschenen volligen Herausführung aus Babel* ... (Ephrata, gedruckt im Jahr 1792), 409ff.
5 Ibid., 411-412.
6 Ibid., 412.
7 Ibid.
8 Ibid., 414.
9 Ibid.
10 Ibid., 415.
11 Ibid., 416. His treatment of God's wrath appears on 417.
12 Ibid., 416.
13 Ibid., 418.
14 Ibid., 419.
15 Ibid., 420.
16 Ibid., sect. 38, 420.
17 Ibid., sect. 39-40, 420.

18 Ibid., sect. 40, 420.
19 Ibid., 421.
20 Ibid., 422.
21 Ibid., 424.
22 Ibid., 428.
23 Ibid., 430.
24 Ibid., 431.
25 Ibid., 444.
26 Ibid., 446.
27 Ibid., 449.
28 GLF, I, 167-171.
29 Ibid., 170.
30 AS, 167-168.
31 AS, 169-170.
32 AS, 422-508.
33 AS, 28-106.
34 AS, 145-184.
35 AS, 189-218.
36 AS, 219-270.
37 AS, 217-291.
38 AS, 292-362.
39 AS, 363-365.
40 AS, 366-421.
41 AS, 107-144, 183-188.
42 No authors are listed for any of these materials, almost all of which discuss prayer (AS, 'Anhang,' 16-42, 55ff.), one of which treats true Christianity (AS, 'Anhang,' 4-15), and another on marriage (AS, 'Anhang,' 43-54).
43 AS, 'Erinnerung,' [xxvi].
44 AS, 'Erinnerung,' [xxvii].
45 AS, 'Erinnerung,' [xxix].
46 AS, 'Erinnerung,' [xxxii].
47 Ibid.
48 Among the letters are the first to Robert (AS, 424-541), the twelfth to Guy (AS, 541-546), the eighteenth to Peter the Deacon (AS, 556-561), the one hundred and seventeenth to Thomas of Beverly (AS, 576-581), and the one hundred and fourteenth to a nun (AS, 581-585). The numbers follow the traditional ones used in the Benedictine edition and reprinted in PL, 184.
49 AS, 'Nachricht,' XVIII.
50 AS, 'Nachricht,' XIIX.
51 AS, 1-30.
52 For full edition and discussion, see original thesis, vol. 2, 535-576.
53 See AS, 'Nachricht,' XIX and XX for Arnold's brief comments on Suso and à Kempis respectively.

54 See note 52 above.

55 For a general discussion of the Protestant view of the contemplative life, see Francois Biot, *The Rise of Protestant Monasticism*, trans. by W.J. Kerrigan (Baltimore, Md. and Dublin: Helicon, 1963). For a detailed discussion on Luther's point of view, see Bernard Lohse, *Mönchtum und Reformation: Luthers Auseinandersetzung mit dem Mönchsideal des Mittelalters* (Göttingen: Vandenhoeck und Ruprecht, 1963).

56 Arnold's edition was based on *VITAE PATRUM Das ist: Das Leben der Altväter... Durch DOCT. GEORG: MAIOR ...* (Gedruckt in ... Lübeck/ Bey vnd in verlegung Laurenz Albrechts Buchhandlers dasselbst, Anno Christi 1604)— hereafter: VP.

57 VP, A2r-A4v.

58 VP, A3r and 'Anleitung,' 2.

59 VP, 'Anleitung,' 7, 35.

60 VP, 'Anleitung,' 1.

61 VP, 'Anleitung,' 2-3.

62 VP, 'Anleitung,' 3.

63 VP, 'Anleitung,' 4.

64 VP, 'Anleitung,' 5.

65 VP, 'Anleitung,' 5-6.

66 VP, 'Anleitung,' 7.

67 VP, 'Anleitung,' 8.

68 VP, 'Anleitung,' 9.

69 See Roland H. Bainton, *Here I Stand: A Life of Martin Luther* (New York: Abingdon-Cokesbury Press, 1950), 291.

70 On this theme, see particularly Davis, Anabaptism, passim.

71 See Biot, 65ff. for one earlier attempt. On the early development of monastic communities in England, see Peter F. Anson, *The Call of the Cloister* (London: SPCK, 1955), 1-219 in particular.

72 VP, 'Anleitung,' 9.

73 VP, 'Anleitung,' 10-11.

74 VP, 'Anleitung,' 12.

75 VP, 'Anleitung,' 13.

76 VP, 'Anleitung,' 16.

77 VP, 'Anleitung,' 17.

78 VP, 'Anleitung,' 18.

79 VP, 'Anleitung,' 19.

80 VP, 'Anleitung,' 21.

81 VP, 'Anleitung,' 22-23, 26.

82 VP, 'Anleitung,' 27.

83 VP, 'Anleitung,' 28.

84 VP, 'Anleitung,' 29.

85 VP, 'Anleitung,' 33.

86 VP, 'Anleitung,' 34, 41-42.

87 VP, 'Anleitung,' 44.

88 On this community, see introduction to my *The Spiritual Diary of Christopher Wiegner* (Pennsburg, Pa.: Schwenkfelder Library, 1977)

89 Arnold's understanding of the *ordo salutis* in the *Vitae Patrum* is described in an emblematic insert in his edition reprinted in my *Pietists*.

90 VP, 'Historischer Bericht,' 1-2.

91 VP, 'Historischer Bericht,' 3-7, 13-16.

92 VP, 'Historischer Bericht,' 8-9, 17-21.

93 VP, 'Historischer Bericht,' 10.

94 VP, 'Historischer Bericht,' 11.

95 VP, 'Historischer Bericht,' 12.

96 VP, 'Historischer Bericht,' 22-24.

97 Short lives of these men are edited at VP, 257 and 262.

98 VP, 'Historischer Bericht,' 33.

99 VP, 'Historischer Bericht,' 34.

100 VP, 'Historischer Bericht,' 46.

101 VP, 'Historischer Bericht,' 47.

102 See Appendix.

103 See VP, [2. Th.], 257-261, 262ff. respectively.

104 Seeberg, 60, and note, in particular, A. Ampe, *Ruusbroec: Traditie en Werkelijkheid* (Antwerp: Ruusbroec-Genootschap, 1975), 496.

105 See Arnold's introduction to Ruusbroec, 5-16.

106 See LG, 'Vorerinnerung,' 1.

107 Cf. LG, 'Vorerinnerung,' 2.

108 LG, 'Vorerinnerung,' 3.

109 LG, 'Vorerinnerung,' 3.

110 LG, 'Vorerinnerung,' 4.

111 See Althaus, Luther, 292-293 for discussion.

112 LG, 'Vorerinnerung,' 5.

113 LG, 'Vorerinnerung,' 5.

114 LG, 'Vorerinnerung,' 8,11.

115 LG, 'Vorerinnerung,' 7,9.

116 LG, 'Vorerinnerung,' 10.

117 LG, 'Vorerinnerung,' 16. Translation from Thomas S. Kepler edition, *Theologia Germanica* (Cleveland, Ohio: The New World Publishing Co., 1952), V, 54-55.

118 LG, 294-327.

119 MT, XXIII, sect. XXCVII.

120 LG, 13. The von Flue material is printed LG, 16ff.

121 See Eckhart, *Die deutschen Werke*, 5, 386-387.

122 LG, 14-15.

Notes to Chapter Six

1 MT, 'Vorrede,' A2r.
2 MT, 'Vorrede,' A2v.
3 MT, 'Vorrede,' A3v-A4v.
4 MT, 'Vorrede,' A2v.
5 MT, I, 2.
6 MT, I, 3.
7 MT, I, 6.
8 MT, I, 13.
9 MT, I, 7.
10 MT, I, 14.
11 MT, I, 25.
12 MT, I, 10-11.
13 MT, I, 12, 15-16.
14 MT, I, 17.
15 MT, I, 18-20; II, 9-13; VII, 12-13
16 MT, I, 21.
17 MT, I, 1; II, 2.
18 MT, II, 1.
19 The point is a major one for Arnold, See MT, II, 3; III, 9-12; IV, 36, Cf. MT, III, 7-8; VIII, 21-28.
20 MT, II, 17; III, 1, 3.
21 MT, III, 2.
22 MT, III, 5-6.
23 MT, II, 4.
24 MT, II, 5.
25 MT, II, 6.
26 MT, II, 7.
27 MT, II, 7
28 MT, IV, 1.
29 MT, II, 9.
30 MT, II, 8.
31 MT, VI. Arnold knew the *Viae Syon* under the title *Theologia Mystica* as in Abraham von Franckenburg's 1647 edition. For details on other editions, see Anselme Stoelen, 'Hugh de Balma' in Marcel Viller et al., edd., *Dictionnaire de Spiritualité Ascetique et Mystique, Doctrine et Histoire* (Paris: Gabriel Beauchesne et ses Fils Editeurs, 1937-) (hereafter: DS), 7, 859-860.
32 MT, IV, 3-11.
33 MT, IV, 9.
34 MT, IV, 12-13.
35 MT, IV, 14.
36 MT, IV, 15-18.
37 MT, IV, 19-22.
38 MT, IV, 27.

39 MT, V, 1-3.
40 MT, V, 6.
41 MT, V, 5.
42 MT, V. 8, 20.
43 MT, V, 11-16; II, 19.
44 MT, V, 23.
45 MT, VII, 2.
46 MT, VII, 4.
47 MT, VII, 5.
48 MT, VII, 6.
49 MT, VII, 7.
50 MT, VII, 11.
51 MT, VII, 12.
52 MT, VIII, 31.
53 MT, VIII, 32.
54 MT, VIII, 36.
55 MT, VIII, 6-7.
56 MT, VIII, 5.
57 MT, VIII, 11ff., 17ff., 29ff.
58 MT, VIII, 39-42.
59 MT, VIII, 38.
60 Bernard is quoted nine times, Denis eight, Hugh of Balma and Gerson sixteen times each. Harphius is cited three times.
61 Fleeting references to Tauler are made at MT, VIII, 17, 35, 38, 39; XII, 3, 15; to the *Theologia deutsch*, at MT, VIII, 33; XII, 8 and to Ruusbroec at MT, VIII, 17.
62 Cf. MT, II, 10; IV, 18, 20, 21, 22; V, 4; VII, 12. Cf. MT, III, 12; VIII, 24.
63 Cf. MT, IV, 19, 20; VII, 5, 7, 14, 15.
64 Cf. MT, IV, 12, 13, 14, 16.
65 Cf. MT, VI, 1, 3, 5, 7-11, 14, 19.
66 Cf. MT, IV, 24-27, 35.
67 On the reason for this hidden nature of the mystical experience, see MT, II, 4, 19; on the experience as one of love, see MT, II, 17-18. For the use of medieval authorities to define mystical union, see MT, II, 6; V, 1, 7, 23.
68 Cf. MT, VIII, 16-17.
69 MT, IX.
70 MT, X.
71 MT, XI. For details on this topic, see DS 3, 287-429.
72 MT, XIX, sect. XL.
73 See PL 184, 11-251 and note DS 2, 101-102 and 6, 372.
74 MT, XIX, sect. XL, 5. On Bona, see DS 1, 1762-1766. In his earlier chapters on the nature of mystical theology Arnold quotes regularly from Bona's theological writings. See Johannis Bona, *Opera Omnia* (Venetiis, Ex Typographia Balleoniana. MDCCLII).

75 PL 184, 507-552. See DS 1, 1501.
76 On the authorship, see F.J.E. Raby, *A History of Christian-Latin Poetry*
    (2nd ed.; Oxford: The Clarendon Press, 1953), 329f.
77 MT, XIX, sect. XL, 6. For works, see PL, 182-183.
78 MT, XIX, sect. XLI. For works, see PL, 180.
79 MT, XIX, sect. XLII. For works, see PL 185, 11-214, and note DS 6,
    1113-1121.
80 MT, XIX, sect. XLIII. For works, see PL 189, 1513ff., and note DS 1,
    888-890.
81 MT, XIX, sect. XLIV. For works note DS 1, 225-234.
82 MT, XIX, sect. LI, 1 and sect. LII, 1.
83 On the confusion between the two men in early editions, see DS 7,
    880-881.
84 MT, XIX, sect. LI, 3-4. For works, see PL, 175-177, and note DS 7,1,
    901-939.
85 MT, XIX, sect. LII, 2-3. For works, see PL 196.
86 MT, XIIX, sect. XXXIX. For works, see PL, 158-159 and note DS, I,
    690-696.
87 MT, XIX, sect. L. On Hildegard, see DS 7,1, 505-521.
88 See MT, XIX, sect. XLVII-XLIX.
89 See MT, XIX, sect. XLV-XLVI.
90 MT, XX, sect. LVI.
91 MT, XX, sect. LVI, 5.
92 On Sandaeus, see Joseph de Guibert, *The Jesuits: Their Spiritual Doc-
    trine and Practice*, trans. by William J. Young (St. Louis, Mo.: The
    Institute of Jesuit Studies, 1972), 331. For theological information on
    mysticism, Arnold consulted, as well, Sandaeus' *Pro Theologia Mystica
    Clavis* (Coloniae Agrippinae Ex Officina Gualteriana Anno Societatis
    Iesv Seculari, M. DC. XL.).
93 MT, XX, SECT. LVII. On the authorship of these works, see DS, I,
    270-271.
94 MT, XX, sect. LLIX.
95 See MT, XX, sect. LIII-LV for discussions of Nicetas Choniates, Gilbert
    of Tournai, and Humbert of Romans.
96 On these works by Aquinas, see I.T. Eschmann, 'A Catalogue of
    St. Thomas's Works' in Etienne Gilson, *The Christian Philosophy of
    St. Thomas Aquinas*, trans. by L.K. Shook (New York: Random House,
    1956), 425, 408, 389ff., and 395.
97 MT, XXI, sect. LXII. On Gertrude, her works, and editions available
    to Arnold, see DS 6, 331-339. He knew the 1657 and 1674 Cologne
    editions of her works.
98 MT, XXI, sect. LXIII. Arnold knew, in addition to the Latin version of
    1536 and an Italian translation, the German version of the revelations
    as published in Cologne in 1660.
99 MT, XXIII, sect. XXCVII.

100 See Chapter Four, notes 118 and 119.
101 MT, XXIII, sect. XXCVII, 4.
102 MT, XXI, sect. LXI.
103 MT, XXI, sect. LXI, 2.
104 MT, XXI, sect. LXVII.
105 MT, XXI, sect. LXVI, 2.
106 On the ascription of these works and others to Tauler, see Leclercq, Spirituality, 397f.
107 MT, XXI, sect. LXVI, 3-9.
108 MT, XXI, sect. LXVI, 10.
109 MT, XXI, sect. LXIIX, 1.
110 MT, XXI, sect. LXIIX, 10-11.
111 MT, XXI, sect. LXIX, 1-3. On Zutphen, see DS 6, 284-289.
112 MT, XXI, sect. LXIX, 4.
113 MT, XXI, sect. LXIV.
114 MT, XXI, sect. LXV.
115 MT, XXII, sect. LXX, 6.
116 MT, XXII, sect. LXXIII, 2.
117 MT, XXII, sect. LXXIII, 1.
118 MT, XXII, sect. LXXIII, 3.
119 MT, XXII, sect. LXXIII, 4-11.
120 MT, XXII, sect. LXXVI.
121 MT, XXII, sect. LXXVI, 4-14.
122 MT, XXII, sect. LXXI.
123 MT, XXII, sect. LXXII.
124 MT, XXII, sect. LXXIV. Cf. 3, 432-434.
125 MT, XXII, sect. LXXV. On his work, see DS 8, 725-730.
126 MT, XXII, sect. LXXVII. On Harphius, see DS 71, 346-366.
127 MT, XXII, sect. LXXIIX.
128 MT, XXIII, sect. LXXIX.
129 MT, XXIV.
130 MT, XXV.
131 See Weiser, Poiret, 98-99. Available for this study was the Latin edition, Petrus Poiret, 'Theologiae Mysticae ejusque Auctorum Idea generali' in his *De Eruditione Specialiora, Tribus Tractatibus* (Amstelaedemi, Ex Officina Wetsteniana. 1 1 VII), 459-602.
132 MT, 'Verthädigung,' [I], 14-15.
133 MT, 'Verthädigung,' [III], I, 4-7.
134 MT, 'Verthädigung,' [III], II, 8.
135 MT, 'Verthädigung,' [III], II, 9 and III, 10.
136 MT, 'Verthädigung,' [III], IX, 39.
137 MT, 'Verthädigung,' [III], IV, 23.
138 MT, 'Verthädigung,' [III], VI, 29-31.
139 MT, 'Verthädigung,' [III], VI, 34.
140 GG, 'Vorrede,' 7.

141 GG, 'Einleitung,' xii.
142 GG, I, 13, 14. Cf. Franckfurt 1703 Tauler, 1415. Note, as well, GG, I, 13, 18 and quotations from the *Theologia deutsch*, chapters 24 and 37 from Arndt edition in Franckfurt 1703 Tauler. Cf. GG, I, 6, 55; I, 7, 6 and 27; I, 14, 13-15.
143 GG, I, 15, 3 (Cf. Franckfurt 1703 Tauler, 1571); I, 17, 11 (Cf. Franckfurt 1703 Tauler, 661); II, 15, 14.
144 GG, I, 3, 21 (Cf. Franckfurt 1703 Tauler, 241).
145 GG, II, 13, 21.
146 GG, II, 14, 18.
147 GG, I, 1, 25 citing 'II Sermo ad Fratres fin.'
148 GG, I, 1.
149 GG, I, 2.
150 GG, I, 4.
151 GG, I, 4.
152 GG, I, 5.
153 GG, I, 5.
154 GG, I, 6.
155 GG, I, 7.
156 GG, I, 8.
157 GG, I, 9ff.
158 GG, I, 6, 17 and 28. Arnold here cites the translation of the *Gheestelike Tabernakel* in his 1701 edition, chapters LXX and LXXV.
159 GG, I, 1, 29; GG, I, 5, 21.
160 For a complete bibliography on medieval homiletics, see my *The Use of the Vernacular in the Sermons of MS University Library Cambridge Ii.III.8* (unpubl. licent. diss., Pontifical Institute of Mediaeval Studies, 1970), 209-262.
161 For a good discussion of this, see the introductory comments in Barbara K. Lewalski, *Donne's Anniversaries and the Poetry of Praise* (Princeton, N.J.: Princeton University Press, 1973).
162 VC, 'Vorerinnerung,' 3-7. The quotation is from the Franckfurt 1703 Tauler, 727.
163 Cf. *Evangelische Reden*, 'Vorrede,' 1-4, reprinted in *Verklärung Christi* (1721), B2rf.
164 VC, 35. Arnold's statement reads 'item Tauleri predigten über das heutige fest.'
165 VC, 32-33. Cf. Franckfurt 1703 Tauler, 81ff. and 86ff.
166 VC, 33.
167 VC, 33-34.
168 Cf. VC, 65ff. with Franckfurt 1703 Tauler, 178 and VC, 283ff. with Franckfurt 1703 Tauler, 693ff. and 703ff.
169 See *Evangelische Botschaft*, 109 (quotation from Franckfurt 1703 Tauler, and chapter 24 of the *Theologia deutsch* in that edition). Note, as well, ibid., 367, 399, 524, 590, 847, 912, 915, 1103.

170 Cf. ibid., 627 and 912.
171 Cf. ibid., 310 and Franckfurt 1703 Tauler, 356.
172 See my *Vernacular Material*, 219-221.
173 Note especially A. Korn, *Tauler als Prediger* (Münster: Aschendorffsch Verlagsbuchhandlung, 1928), 5-80.
174 Arnold, Kempis, Introductory section, 1-58 and 59-94 respectively.
175 Arnold, Kempis, 'Historischer Vorbericht,' 1-2.
176 Arnold, Kempis, 'Historischer Vorbericht,' 6-7.
177 Arnold, Kempis, 'Historischer Vorbericht,' 8.
178 Arnold, Kempis, 'Historischer Vorbericht,' 9.
179 Arnold, Kempis, 'Historischer Vorbericht,' 10.
180 Arnold, Kempis, 'Historischer Vorbericht,' 11.
181 Arnold, Kempis, 'Historischer Vorbericht,' 12.
182 Arnold, Kempis, 'Historischer Vorbericht,' 13.
183 Arnold, Kempis, 'Historischer Vorbericht,' 14.
184 Arnold, Kempis, 'Historischer Vorbericht,' 15.
185 Arnold, Kempis, 'Historischer Vorbericht,' 16-17.
186 Arnold, Kempis, 'Historischer Vorbericht,' 18-28.
187 Arnold, Kempis, 'Historischer Vorbericht,' 30-35.
188 Arnold, Kempis, 'Historischer Vorbericht,' 36-39.
189 Arnold, Kempis, 'Historischer Vorbericht,' 42.
190 Arnold, Kempis, 'Historischer Vorbericht,' appended pp. 47-58.
191 Arnold, Kempis, 'Historischer Vorbericht,' 46.
192 Arnold, Kempis, 'Anleitung,' 5.
193 Arnold, Kempis, 'Anleitung,' 1-20.
194 Arnold, Kempis, 'Anleitung,' 7-8.
195 Arnold, Kempis, 'Anleitung,' 9.
196 Arnold, Kempis, 'Historischer Vorbericht,' 1.
197 Arnold, Kempis, 'Historischer Vorbericht,' 4.
198 Arnold, Kempis, 'Anleitung,' 24-25.
199 Arnold, Kempis, 'Historischer Vorbericht,' 43-44. Arnold continues his discussion of the editorial procedures used by noting that they have been used earlier by other authors including Arndt. The fourth book of the *Imitation* is omitted, he points out, since it contains many 'papal' errors, but he adds that should any readers wish to have the full text, it will be made available in a second edition (Arnold, Kempis, 'Historischer Vorbericht,' 45). Arnold was never to, see a second edition of the work, but his suggestions were followed in the posthumus second edition which appeared in 1733. In that edition the whole of the *Imitation* was printed in a revised translation. (See note by editor of second edition, ibid.) The biographies by à Kempis have not been printed, Arnold adds, since they are not in keeping with the spirit of the man; they are filled with superstition and the best have already been printed in the *Leben der Altväter* (Arnold, Kempis, 'Historischer Vorbericht,' 46).

200 Arnold, Kempis, 'Anleitung,' 25-26.
201 Arnold, Kempis, 'Anleitung,' 27.
202 Ibid.
203 Arnold, Kempis, 'Anleitung,' 28.
204 Ibid.
205 Ibid.
206 Arnold, Kempis, 'Anleitung,' 29.
207 Arnold, Kempis, 'Anleitung,' 30.
208 Ibid.
209 Arnold, Kempis, 'Anleitung,' 31.
210 Arnold, Kempis, 'Anleitung,' 31.
211 Arnold, Kempis, 'Anleitung,' 32.
212 Arnold, Kempis, 'Anleitung,' 33.
213 Arnold, Kempis, 'Anleitung,' 36, 39.
214 Arnold, Kempis, 'Anleitung,' 38.
215 EL 3, 1101 quotes this passage from the Arndt edition of the *Imitatio*, I, 18. Translation adapted from that by Leo Sherley-Price (Harmondsworth: Penguin Books, 1952), 46-47.

Notes to Chapter Seven

1 KKH, 'Vorrede,' 8-9.
2 WAIC, 'Vorrede,' 2.
3 TE, 'Einleitung,' 11-12. On the relation between 'experience' and 'experiment' in seventeenth-century thought see Frederick Herbert Wagman, 'Magic and Natural Science in German Baroque Literature' in *Germanic Studies*, 13 (1942), 113-149.
4 WAIC, 'Vorrede,' 9.
5 WAIC, 'Vorrede,' 8.
6 WAIC, 'Vorrede,' 11.
7 WAIC, 'Vorrede,' 12.
8 WAIC, 'Vorrede,' 16-18.
9 WAIC, 'Vorrede,' 19-20.
10 WAIC, 'Nachricht,' B4v-C1v.
11 WAIC, 'Vorrede,' 13, 22 and TE, 'Einleitung,' 3.
12 WAIC, 'Vorrede,' 27.
13 WAIC, 'Vorrede,' 3.
14 WAIC, 'Vorrede,' 4.
15 WAIC, 'Vorrede,' 23 and TE, 'Einleitung,' 1.
16 TE, 'Einleitung,' 26.
17 TE, 'Einleitung,' 27.
18 TE, 'Einleitung,' 28.
19 TE, 'Einleitung,' 29
20 TE, 'Einleitung,' 30.
21 TE, 'Einleitung,' 31.
22 TE, 'Einleitung,' 33-34.

23 TE, 'Einleitung,' 35-39.

24 TE, 'Einleitung,' 40-47.

25 TE, 'Einleitung,' 51-86.

26 TE, 'Einleitung,' 51.

27 TE, 'Einleitung,' 52.

28 TE, 48:29-31.

29 WAIC, II, 3:9ff.

30 Cf. Henricum Harp, *Theologia Mystica* (Coloniae, ex officina Melchioris Nouesiani Anno M.D. XXXVII), clxxviiff.

31 WAIC, III, 13: 8 quotes from Ruusbroec, *Spiegel der eeuwigher Salicheit* (hereafter: *Spiegel*), 19. All references to Ruusbroec when quoted by Arnold are to the German translation of G.J.C. as published in 1701 and used by Arnold in his WAIC. The 1701 edition follows the Surius translation in its divisions of the Ruusbroec text. The respective Surius chapter numbers are indicated in the margins to Jan van Ruusbroec, *Werken*, ed. by J.B. Poukens et al. (Tielt: Drukkerij-Uitgeverij Lannoo, 1944-1948).

32 WAIC, III, 13:17 quotes from Ruusbroec, *Gheestelike Brulocht* (hereafter: *Brulocht*), III, 1.

33 WAIC, III, 13:21 quotes from Ruusbroec, *Vanden XIJ Beghinen* (hereafter *Beghinen*), 65. Cf. WAIC, III, 13:35 which quotes Harphius.

34 WAIC, III, 13:36 quotes from Ruusbroec, *Spiegel*, 8.

35 WAIC, III, 13:37 quotes from Ruusbroec, *Brulocht*, 4.

36 WAIC, III, 13:38 quotes from Ruusbroec, *Vanden VII Sloten* (hereafter: *Sloten*), 15.

37 WAIC, III, 13:6 quotes from the Franckfurt 1703 Tauler, 1340.

38 WAIC, III, 13:30 quotes from the *Theologia deutsch*, 53 (Arndt edition as printed in the Franckfurt 1703 Tauler).

39 Cf. WAIC, III, 13:31-34 quotes from the *Medulla* 29, 33, 38, 45, and 23 as printed in the Franckfurt 1703 Tauler.

40 WAIC, III, 13:34 quotes from the third sermon attributed to Suso. See Seuse, *Schriften* 518ff.

41 Cf. TE, I-II.

42 WAIC, I, 1:1.

43 On this topic, see Etienne Gilson, *The Mystical Theology of Bernard of Clairvaux*, trans. by A.H.C. Downes (London: Sheed and Ward, 1940), 34ff.

44 WAIC, I, 1:2.

45 WAIC, I, 1:3.

46 WAIC, I, 1:5.

47 WAIC, I, 1:6.

48 WAIC, I, 1:7-8 cites Bernard, *De diligendo deo* and Harphius, *Theologia Mystica*, and quotes from Ruusbroec's *Vanden Gheesteliken Tabernakel* (hereafter: *Tabernakel*), 19 and *Brulocht*, III, 4, the Franckfurt 1703 Tauler, 643, 1507 and Suso's *Buchlein der Ewigen Weisheit*, 9.

49 WAIC, I, 1:12-18.
50 WAIC, I, 1:4.
51 Arnold refers here to Ruusbroec, *Spiegel*, 17.
52 Arnold refers here to Ruusbroec, *Beghinen*, 21. Cf. Ruusbroec, *Beghinen*, 19 as well.
53 WAIC, I, 1:19.
54 WAIC, I, 1:20 quotes from the Franckfurt 1703 Tauler, 907 and 1148.
55 WAIC, I, 2:1-3.
56 WAIC, I, 2:4.
57 WAIC, I, 2:9.
58 WAIC, I, 2:10.
59 WAIC, I, 2:11.
60 WAIC, I, 2:13..
61 WAIC, I, 2:14.
62 WAIC, I, 2:15.
63 WAIC, I, 2:5.
64 WAIC, I, 2:16 quotes from the Franckfurt 1703 Tauler, 1176
65 WAIC, I, 3.
66 WAIC, I, 4:11.
67 WAIC, I, 4:14.
68 Ibid., quotes from the *Theologia deutsch*, 3.
69 WAIC, I, 5:1.
70 WAIC, I, 5:3 quotes from the Franckfurt 1703 Tauler, 1176.
71 WAIC, I, 5:5.
72 WAIC, I, 5:6.
73 WAIC, I, 5:7.
74 WAIC, I, 5:8.
75 WAIC, I, 5:9.
76 WAIC, I, 5:12.
77 WAIC, I, 5:16.
78 WAIC, I, 5:18.
79 *Formula of Concord*, I, 3 in *Concordia Triglotta*, 863.
80 WAIC, I, 1:22-23.
81 WAIC, I, 6:3, 6, 16-17 refers to the *Theologia deutsch*, 2, 3, 4, 6, 22 and 34, and quotes from the Franckfurt 1703 Tauler, 283, and the *Nachfolgung des armen Lebens Christi*, sections 30 and 125 as printed in the Franckfurt 1703 Tauler. Cf. as well, WAIC, I, 6:5 and 24.
82 WAIC, I, 6:9-13.
83 WAIC, I, 6:14-18.
84 WAIC, I, 6:19-20.
85 WAIC, I, 6:23-24.
86 WAIC, I, 7:4.
87 WAIC, I, 7:1-3.
88 WAIC, I, 7:11, 14 and 27.
89 WAIC, I, 7:15 quotes from Ruusbroec, *Tabernakel*, 48 and the Franckfurt 1703 Tauler, 707.

90 WAIC, I, 7:19.

91 WAIC. I, 7:20-21 quotes from Ruusbroec *Trappen* (hereafter: *Trappen*), 3 and from the Franckfurt 1703 Tauler, 435, 503.

92 WAIC, I, 7:24 quotes from Ruusbroec, *Trappen* 19 and the Franckfurt 1703 Tauler, 705, 708.

93 WAIC, I, 7:27.

94 WAIC, I, 7:28.

95 *Formula of Concord*, Epitome II, in *Concordia Triglotta*, 787.

96 WAIC, I, 8. Other than references to Bernard (I, 8:19-26) no medieval authors are cited.

97 WAIC, I, 9. Other than references to Bernard (I, 9:4, 6) no medieval authors are cited.

98 TE, 3.

99 TE, 4.

100 TE, 5-6.

101 TE, 7.

102 TE, 8.

103 *Formula of Concord*, Epitome XI in *Concordia Triglotta*, 835.

104 Ibid., 785.

105 *Formula of Concord*, VI in *Concordia Triglotta*, 9663.

106 WAIC, I, 7:1.

107 WAIC, I, 7:2ff.

108 WAIC, I, 7:8-9.

109 WAIC, I, 7:16-24.

110 TE, 12.

111 TE, 13.

112 TE, 16-17.

113 TE, 14.

114 TE, 15.

115 WAIC, I, 10:1.

116 WAIC, I, 10:17-18 quotes from the *Medulla*, 7 and Suso's first sermon. (Cf. Seuse, *Schriften*, 495ff.)

117 WAIC, I, 10:25 cites *Imitatio* I, 6 and III, 33 and Harphius, *Theologia Mystica*, I, 12 and II, 9.

118 WAIC, I, 11:2 quotes from the Franckfurt 1703 Tauler, 777 and the *Medulla*, 63. Cf. WAIC, I, 11:11.

119 WAIC, I, 11:5 quotes from the Franckfurt 1703 Tauler, 1129. Cf. references to Bernard, WAIC, I, 11:18-20.

120 WAIC, I, 11:24-26 quotes from the *Medulla*, 33 and the Franckfurt 1703 Tauler, 659.

121 WAIC, I, 11:31-33 quotes from the Franckfurt 1703 Tauler, 63, 234 and 717.

122 WAIC, I, 12:4-5.

123 WAIC, I, 12:6-13.

124 WAIC, I, 12:14-15.

125 WAIC, I, 12:16, 25-27, 38 quotes from the Franckfurt 1703 Tauler, 145.
126 WAIC, I, 12:17-20.
127 WAIC, I, 12:21-24
128 WAIC, I, 12:28-30.
129 WAIC, I, 12:31-32.
130 WAIC, I, 12:33 quotes from the Franckfurt 1703 Tauler, 1261.
131 WAIC, I, 12, 34-37 quotes from the Franckfurt 1703 Tauler, 686, 808, 1538, Ruusbroec, *Spiegel*, 2, and *Tabernakel*, 15.
132 WAIC, I, 12:38-39.
133 Cf. WAIC, I, 12:25.
134 WAIC, I, 12:33 quotes from the Franckfurt 1703 Tauler, 1261.
135 WAIC, I, 12, 34-37 quotes from the Franckfurt 1703 Tauler, 686, 808, 1538, Ruusbroec, *Spiegel*, 2 and *Tabernakel*, 15.
136 WAIC, I, 12, 34-37 quotes from the Franckfurt 1703 Tauler, 686, 808, 1538, Ruusbroec, *Spiegel*, 2 and *Tabernakel*, 15.
137 TE, 21.
138 WAIC, I, 13:2.
139 WAIC, I, 13:14, 17, 20 quotes from the Franckfurt 1703 Tauler, 584, 678, Thomas à Kempis, *In Hospitali Pauperum*, 17-18 and William of St. Thierry, *Ad fratres de monte dei*, 10.
140 WAIC, I, 13:29 quotes from Ruusbroec, *Sloten*, 4 and WAIC, I, 14:2. Cf. TE, 18-20.
141 WAIC, I, 14:3, 5 quotes from the Franckfurt 1703 Tauler, 937.
142 WAIC, I, 14:7 quotes from the Franckfurt 1703 Tauler, 585.
143 WAIC, I, 14:12-13, 16-17 quotes from the Franckfurt 1703 Tauler, 531, 1402.
144 WAIC, I, 14:19.
145 WAIC, I, 14:20.
146 WAIC, I, 14:21.
147 WAIC, I, 14:22-25 quotes from the Franckfurt 1703 Tauler, 1080, *Medulla*, 13 and Ruusbroec, *Het Rijck der Ghelieven*, 3.
148 WAIC, I, 14:29-30.
149 WAIC, I, 15 quotes extensively from the Franckfurt 1703 Tauler, 134, 187, 220, 284, 682, 1062, 1647, the *Medulla*, 7, 14, 16, 45, 64, the *Nachfolgung des armen Lebens Christi*, sections 58, 88, 115, 157, Ruusbroec, *Het Rijck der Ghelieven*, 3, 9 and others.
150 WAIC, I, 16 quotes extensively from the Franckfurt 1703 Tauler, 45, 88, 157, 632, 939, 1346, 1407, 1597, the *Medulla*, 29, 59, the *Nachfolgung des armen Lebens Christi*, 65, 104, 133, the *Theologia deutsch*, 5, Suso, *Buchlein der ewigen Weisheit*, 16 and Ruusbroec, *Spiegel*, 2.
151 WAIC, I, 17 quotes extensively from the Franckfurt 1703 Tauler, 226, 450, 473, 474, 477, 813, 897, 1089, 1428-1429, Suso, *Buchlein der ewigen Weishet*, Ruusbroec, *Spiegel*, 1, and Thomas à Kempis, *Liber de mortificatione sui*, 1.

152 WAIC, I, 18:1-12 quotes from the Franckfurt 1703 Tauler, 193, 413, 779, 1057, 1061, 1491, 1574, the *Theologia deutsch*, 48 and the *Imitatio Christi*, III, 9.

153 WAIC, I, 18:13-19 quotes from the Franckfurt 1703 Tauler, 94, 1653 and the *Medulla* 31, 58.

154 WAIC, I, 18:21-25 quotes from Ruusbroec, *Spiegel*, 3 and *Brulocht*, II, 67.

155 WAIC, I, 18:22-24, 26-27 quotes from the Franckfurt 1703 Tauler, 476, 1622.

156 WAIC, II, 1.

157 WAIC, II, 1:2, 19.

158 WAIC, II, 1:11 quotes from Ruusbroec, *Het Rijcke der Ghelieven*, 4.

159 WAIC, II, 1:12 quotes from the *Medulla*, 14.

160 WAIC, II, 1:13-14 quotes from the Franckfurt 1703 Tauler, 479, 1512.

161 WAIC, II, 2:19.

162 WAIC, II, 2:9.

163 WAIC, II, 2:22 quotes from Thomas à Kempis, *Sermo ad Novitios*, II, 4.

164 WAIC, II, 2:24-26 quotes from Ruusbroec, *Brulocht*, I, 2, 6 and others.

165 WAIC, II, 2:27 quotes from Ruusbroec, *Brulocht*, II, 6, 8ff.

166 WAIC, II, 3:1-7.

167 WAIC, II, 3:7-9.

168 WAIC, II, 3:11-12, 16 quotes from Harphius, *Theologica Mystica*, I, pt. II, 36, III, pt. III, 21.

169 WAIC, II, 3:19 quotes from Ruusbroec, *Tabernakel*, 120 and *Brulocht*, II, 55.

170 WAIC, II, 3:21 quotes from Ruusbroec, *Brulocht*, I, 26.

171 WAIC, II, 3:23 quotes from Ruusbroec, *Brulocht*, III, 4.

172 WAIC, II, 3:23 quotes from Ruusbroec, *Brulocht*, III, 4.

173 WAIC, II, 4:2 cites Richard of St. Victor, *De contemplatione*, 6 and Harphius, *Theologia mystica*, III, pt. V, 39.

174 WAIC, II, 4:1.

175 WAIC, II, 4:10.

176 WAIC, II, 4:11-12, 20-23, 30 quotes from the Franckfurt 1703 Tauler, 81, 125, 428, 1129, 1337, 1352, Ruusbroec, *Brulocht*, III, 1 and Suso, *Buchlein der ewigen Weisheit*, 7.

177 WAIC, II, 4:16.

178 WAIC, II, 5:6-7, 10-11, 13-14 quotes from the Franckfurt 1703 Tauler, 187, 429.

179 WAIC, II, 5:8.

180 WAIC, II, 5:20-21 quotes from Ruusbroec, *Spiegel*, 1.

181 WAIC, II, 6:15 quotes from the Franckfurt 1703 Tauler, 114.

182 WAIC, II, 7:6-8, 13 quotes from Ruusbroec, *Spiegel*, 18, *Brulocht*, III, 2-3, *Het Rijcke Der Ghelieven*, 15, the *Theologia deutsch*, 53, and the Franckfurt 1703 Tauler, 114.

183 WAIC, II, 7:16-17 quotes from Ruusbroec, *Spiegel*, 1, *Tabernakel*, 69 and *Trappen*, 5.

184 WAIC, II, 7:18-21 quotes from the Franckfurt 1703 Tauler, 390, 490, 500, 1342.

185 WAIC, II, 8-9.

186 WAIC, II, 88 quotes the Franckfurt 1703 Tauler, 69.

187 WAIC, II, 10:5 quotes from the Franckfurt 1703 Tauler, 97 and Ruusbroec, *Tabernakel*, 10.

188 WAIC, II, 10:21 quotes from Ruusbroec, *Trappen*, 14.

189 WAIC, II, 11:8.

190 WAIC, II, 11:22-23 quotes from the Franckfurt 1703 Tauler, 100 and Suso, *Buchlein der ewigen Weisheit*, 7.

191 WAIC, II, 11:29 quotes from the Franckfurt 1703 Tauler, 487.

192 WAIC, II, 13:7-10 quotes from the Franckfurt 1703 Tauler, 129, Ruusbroec, *Beghinen*, 79.

193 WAIC, II, 13:12-15, 25 quotes from Ruusbroec, *Beghinen*, 37, 68.

194 WAIC, II, 14:5, 9-11, 29 quotes from the Franckfurt 1703 Tauler, 772, 785, 930, 1339, Ruusbroec, *Beghinen*, 13 and Aelred of Rievaulx, *Speculum Charitatis*, I, 8.

195 WAIC, II, 15:6, 9-10, 18, 20 quotes from the Franckfurt 1703 Tauler, 13, 643 1607, Ruusbroec, *Spiegel*, 3, 8, the *Theologia deutsch*, 3, 16.

196 WAIC, II, 16 quotes extensively from the Franckfurt 1703 Tauler, 132, 457, 993, 1434, 1541, 1718, Ruusbroec, *Tabernakel*, 12, 20, 23, 43, *Brulocht*, I, 3, *Trappen*, 3, *Spiegel*, 12, *Medulla*, 2, 9, 21, 40, 63, and others.

197 WAIC, II, 17.

198 WAIC, IIII, 17:7, 10-11 quotes from the Ruusbroec, *Brulocht*, II, 34.

199 WAIC, II, 17:16-17.

200 Cf. WAIC, II, 17:19, 23. Note also WAIC, II, 17: 11-15 which quotes extensively from Ruusbroec, *Brulocht*, IIII, 34, *Beghinen*, 78, the Franckfurt 1703 Tauler, 1216, and Suso, *Buchlein der ewigen Weisheit*, 15.

201 WAIC, II, 20 quotes from the Franckfurt 1703 Tauler, 16, 212, 608, Ruusbroec, *Spiegel*, 7, 12, 16, *Tabernakel*, 92, 119, *Beghinen*, 9.

202 WAIC, II, 21 quotes from Ruusbroec, *Spiegel*, 1,8, *Tabernakel*, 121.

203 WAIC, II, 22.

204 WAIC, II, 23:1-29 quotes from Ruusbroec, *Tabernakel*, 34, 35, 69, 93.

205 WAIC, II, 23:30-40 quotes from the Franckfurt 1703 Tauler, 679.

206 WAIC, II, 23:40-45.

207 WAIC, II, 23:5-8.

208 WAIC, II, 23:22.

209 WAIC, II, 23:30-32.

210 WAIC, III, 1:2-3 quotes from Ruusbroec, *Spiegel*, 17.

211 WAIC, III, 1:4-12 quotes from the Franckfurt 1703 Tauler, 381, 661, Ruusbroec, *Tabernakel*, 20 Suso, *Buchlein der ewigen Weisheit*, 12. Cf. WAIC, III, 2:28 and 5:21, 23-25.

212 WAIC, III, 1:15-16.

213 WAIC, III, 1:17.

214 WAIC, III, 2:3, 6 quotes from Ruusbroec, *Trappen*, 12. Cf. WAIC, III, 7 which quotes extensively from the Franckfurt 1703 Tauler, 562, Ruusbroec, *Tabernakel*, 13, 14, 19, Sloten, 17, 18, *Brulocht*, II, 75.

215 WAIC, III, 2:5, 10, 13 quotes from Ruusbroec, *Brulocht*, 259, *Beghinen*, 64, Suso, third sermon. (Cf. Seuse, *Schriften*, 518ff.)

216 WAIC, III, 2:16-18, 20 quotes from Ruusbroec, *Brulocht*, II, 64, the Franckfurt 1703 Tauler, 22.

217 WAIC, III, 2:19, 21 quotes from Ruusbroec, *Brulocht*, II, 64.

218 WAIC, III, 2:22 quotes from the Franckfurt 1703 Tauler, 101, 1487, and cites Ruusbroec, *Spiegel*, 12, *Vanden Blinckenden Steen*, 2, 12.

219 WAIC, III, 2:23.

220 WAIC, III, 2:24.

221 WAIC, III, 2:30 quotes from the Franckfurt 1703 Tauler, 1247.

222 WAIC, III, 2:3-32 quotes from the *Theologia deutsch*, 51.

223 WAIC, III, 2:33 quotes from the Franckfurt 1703 Tauler, 588.

224 WAIC, III, 2:34, 36-37.

225 WAIC, III, 3:3-5 quotes from Ruusbroec, *Beghinen*, 16, 23, *Spiegel*, 17.

226 WAIC, III, 3:9.

227 WAIC, III, 3:10 quotes from Ruusbroec, *Tabernakel*, 19.

228 WAIC, III, 3:11 quotes from Ruusbroec, *Brulocht*, II, 59.

229 WAIC, III, 3:13.

230 WAIC, III, 3:15-21 quotes from the Franckfurt 1703 Tauler, 279, 470, 588, Ruusbroec, *Brulocht*, II, 53, 57.

231 WAIC, III, 4:5-6.

232 WAIC, III, 4:10, 14, 17 cites the Franckfurt 1703 Tauler, 482, 824, 907, 1248, Ruusbroec, *Brulocht*, I, 68, III, 4, *Beghinen*, 14, 51, 64.

233 WAIC, III, 4:22.

234 WAIC, III, 4:30 quotes from Franckfurt 1703 Tauler, 926.

235 WAIC, III, 5:1. Cf. III, 5:6-7.)

236 WAIC, III, 5:11, 14 quotes from the Franckfurt 1703 Tauler, 1513.

237 WAIC, III, 5:16 quotes from the Franckfurt 1703 Tauler, 464.

238 WAIC, III, 6:1-30 quotes from the Franckfurt 1703 Tauler, 463, 512, 525, 629, 732, 1016, Ruusbroec, *Beghinen*, 14, 25, *Spiegel*, 2, *Tabernakel*, 13, 158.

239 WAIC, III, 6:31-34 quotes from Ruusbroec, *Beghinen*, 24-27.

240 WAIC, III, 6:35-40.

241 WAIC, III, 8:3.

242 WAIC, III, 8:4 quotes from the Franckfurt 1703 Tauler, 189.

243 WAIC, III, 8:5-7 quotes from Ruusbroec, *Tabernakel*, 163, *Beghinen*, 77.

244 WAIC, III, 8:11.

245 WAIC, III, 8:12-14 quotes from the Franckfurt 1703 Tauler, 213, Ruusbroec, *Brulocht*, II, 20.

246 WAIC, III, 8:15.
247 WAIC, III, 1:16-17.
248 WAIC, III, 8:23-24 cites Ruusbroec, *Tabernakel*, 17, 156, Suso, *Buchlein der ewigen Weisheit*, 7, 20. Cf. WAIC, III, 8:19-20.
249 WAIC, III, 8:25-30 quotes from Ruusbroec, *Trappen*, 9, 12, Sloten, 13, the Franckfurt 1703 Tauler, 1170, *Imitatio Christi*, III, 5.
250 WAIC, III, 9 quotes from the Franckfurt 1703 Tauler, 206, 974, 1675, Ruusbroec, *Brulocht*, II, 5, 19, 20, 24, 25, and others.
251 WAIC, III, 10:1.
252 WAIC, III, 10:10, 11, 15-16.
253 WAIC, III, 10:33-34.
254 WAIC, III, 10:29-31.
255 WAIC, III, 11:1-2.
256 WAIC, III, 11:3-9.
257 WAIC, III, 11:10-11.
258 WAIC, III, 11:11-15, 20 quotes from the Franckfurt 1703 Tauler, 42.
259 WAIC, III, 11:16-17, 22-31 quotes from the Franckfurt 1703 Tauler, 88, 445, 943, 1016, 1226, 1303, 1585.
260 WAIC, III, 11:34-40 quotes from the Franckfurt 1703 Tauler, 456, Ruusbroec, *Beghinen*, 8.
261 WAIC, III, 12:1.
262 WAIC, III, 12:3.
263 WAIC, III, 12:8-16, 19, 23, 29 quotes from the Franckfurt 1703 Tauler, 683, Ruusbroec, *Tabernakel*, 18, *Beghinen*, 15, 16, *Brulocht*, 256.
264 WAIC, III, 11:35.
265 WAIC, III, 12:48-51.
266 WAIC, III, 13:5-6 quotes from the Franckfurt 1703 Tauler, 1340.
267 WAIC, III, 13:17, 21 quotes from Ruusbroec, *Brulocht*, II, 1, *Beghinen*, 65.
268 WAIC, III, 13:8 quotes from Ruusbroec, *Spiegel*, 19.
269 WAIC, III, 13:29-37 quotes from the *Medulla*, 23, 29, 33, 38, 45, Ruusbroec, *Spiegel*, 8, *Brulocht*, III, 4.
270 WAIC, III, 13:38 quotes from Ruusbroec, Sloten, 15.
271 WAIC, III, 14 quotes from the Franckfurt 1703 Tauler, 551, 1398, 1528, 789, 85, Suso, *Buchlein der ewigen Weisheit*, 24-25, Ruusbroec, *Brulocht*, II, 15, 16, *Trappen*, 5.
272 WAIC, III, 15.
273 WAIC, III, 15:1-2.
274 WAIC, III, 15:16, 20-21, 58, 74.
275 WAIC, III, 15:22, 75.
276 WAIC, III, 15:54-56.
277 Cf. WAIC, III, 15:80 et al.
278 Cf. WAIC, III, 15:23 et al.
279 Cf. WAIC, III, 15:81 et al.
280 On the subject of Tauler authorship, see Appendix.

281 For discussion, see Leopold Naumann, *Untersuchungen zu Johann Taulers Deutschen Predigten* (Halle a.S: Druck von Erhardt Karrass, 1911), 49. The sermon is that printed in Ferdinand Vetter, hrsg., *Die Predigten Taulers* (Berlin, 1910; reprint, Dublin and Zurich: Weidmann, 1968), 7-12.

282 See Addendum below

283 Ibid.

284 Ibid.

285 Ibid.

286 Ibid.

287 Ibid.

288 Ibid.

289 See Ephrem Filthaut, 'Johannes Tauler und die deutsche Dominikaner Scholastik des XIII./XIV. Jahrhunderts,' in his *Tauler*, 94-121. See also Günther Müller, 'Scholastikerzitate bei Tauler,' *Deutsche Vierteljahrsschrift*, (1921), 440-448 and note the biographical discussions by Herbert Christian Scheeben, 'Zur Biographie Johann Taulers' in Filthaut, 19-36 and his 'Der Konvent der Predigerbrüder in Strassburg—Die Religiöse Heimat Taulers' in Filthaut, 37-74. Also of value is the discussion by Gottlob Siedel, *Die Mystik Taulers* (Leipzig: J.C. Hinrich'sche Buchhandlung, 1911). Cf. Cl. Bäumker, 'Der Anteil des Elass an den geistigen Bewegungen des Mittelalters,' *Beiträge zur Geschichte der Philosophie und Theologie*, 25/1 (1927), 215-255. Note, as well, the introduction by Eric Colledge to John Tauler, *Spiritual Conferences*, trans. by Eric Colledge and Sister M. Jane (St. Louis, Mo. and London: B. Herder Book Co., 1961). On Tauler's influence, see Filthaut, 341-434 and cf. G.I. Lieftinck, *De Middelnederlandsche Tauler-Handschriften* (Groningen-Batavia: J.B. Wolter's Uitgevers-Maatschapij, 1936).

290 For the fullest discussion of this, see Vladimir Lossky, *Theologie negative et connaissance de dieu chez maitre Eckhart* (Paris: Libraire philosophique J. Vrin, 1960). Note as well, Bernard J. Muller-Thym, *The Establishment of the Universality of Being in the Doctrine of Meister Eckhart of Hochheim* (New York, N.Y.: Sheed and Ward, 1939). More general discussions are available in Jeanne Ancelet-Hustache, *Master Eckhart and the Rhineland Mystics*, trans. by Hilda Graef (New York, N.Y. and London: Harper and Brothers and Longmans, Green and Co. Ltd., 1957), James M. Clark, *Master Eckhart: An Introduction to the Study of his Works* (London: Thomas Nelson and Sons Ltd., 1957) and his *The Great German Mystics* (Oxford: Basil Blackwell, 1949). On Eckhart's life, see Josef Koch, 'Kritische Studien zum Leben Meister Eckharts,' *Archivum Fratrum Praedicatorum*, 29 (1959), 5-49; 30 (1960), 5-52. On his influence, see Josef Koch, 'Meister Eckhart's Weiterwirken in Deutsch-Niederländischer Raam im 14. und 15. Jahrhunderts' in *La mystique rhénane*, 133-156 and Maria Alberta Lucker, *Meister Eckhart und die Devotio Moderna* (Leiden: E.J. Brill, 1950).

291 See Dietrich M. Schlüter, 'Philosophische Grundlagen der Lehren Johannes Taulers' in Filthaut, 123 n. 6.
292 Cf. Vetter, 347.
293 Seuse, *Schriften*, 326-359. Cf. Herma Piesch, 'Seuses "Buchlein der Wahrheit" und Meister Eckhart' in Ephrem Albertus M. Filthaut, *Heinrich Seuse: Studien zum 600. Todestag* (Koln: Albertus Magnus Verlag, 1966), 91-133.
294 Cf. Vetter, 277-278. Because of God's simplicity he cannot be grasped by human understanding. Cf. Vetter, 20, 109, 114, 298, 299, 397.
295 Cf. Vetter, 425-426.
296 Cf. Vetter, 329.
297 Cf. Vetter, 215.
298 Cf. Vetter, 137.
299 Cf. Vetter, 10.
300 Cf. Vetter, 8, 137.
301 Cf. Vetter, 367.
302 Cf. Vetter, 215, 240.
303 Cf. Vetter, 425-426.
304 Cf. Vetter, 277.
305 Cf. WAIC, I, 1:18-19; II, 3:7-12; III, 8:18-19.
306 Cf. WAIC, I, 2:11; II, 19:13, 17, 21-22.
307 Vetter, 221-332.
308 Vetter, 8, 9, 81.
309 WAIC, I, 2:11.
310 For Tauler's position, see Schlüter in Filthaut, 124-125.
311 Schlüter, 125-126. See Vetter, 55-65, 330.
312 Vetter, sermons 64-70.
313 Vetter, 348.
314 Cf. Vetter, 349.
315 Vetter, 350.
316 On this, see Schlüter in Filthaut, 153.
317 Vetter, 261-262.
318 Vetter, 92.
319 Cf. Vetter, 155, 238.
320 Claire Champollion, 'Le vocabulaire de Tauler' in *La mystique rhénane*, 189.
321 WAIC, II, 12:1.
322 WAIC, II, 12:1-2.
323 WAIC, II, 12:2.
324 WAIC, II, 12:3-6.
325 WAIC, II, 12:7.
326 Ibid.
327 WAIC, II, 12:8.
328 WAIC, II, 12:12.
329 WAIC, II, 12:14.

330 WAIC, II, 12:13, 16.

331 WAIC, II, 12:19.

332 WAIC, I, 1:20; I, 6:25-26 and II, 12:14-15.

333 Vetter, 331.

334 Vetter, 80, 117, 137, 347. Cf. Vetter, 357.

335 Vetter, 20, 114, 199, 204, 239, 298, 368, 421.

336 Cf. Schlüter in Filthaut, 129-133 for discussion and numerous references in Tauler on the subject.

337 Cf. Schlüter in Filthaut, 135f.

338 Cf. Vetter, 97, 100, 158, 302, 323, 364-365.

339 In all, Arnold has some 40 citations.

340 WAIC, I, 6:9-10.

341 TE, 2:55 and 23:19.

342 TE, 59:17.

343 WAIC, I, 15:36-37.

344 WAIC, I, 14:9 and 15:5.

345 WAIC, I, 12:33-34; I, 14:23; I, 15:24-27; III, 11:23; 111, 12:5-7; TE, 59:32; 60:26, 29; 72:56; 82:24.

346 See Gangolf M. Scheiders, 'Die Askese als Weltentsagung und Vollkommenheitsstreben bei Tauler' in Filthaut, 178-207. Note, as well, Engrates Kihm, 'Die Drei-Wege-Lehre bei Tauler' in Filthaut, 268-300.

347 See Adolf Hoffman, 'Taulers Lehre von der Kirche' in Filthaut, 232-240, 'Maria in den Predigten Taulers' in Filthaut, 241-246, and 'Die Christesgestalt bei Tauler' in Filthaut, 208-231.

348 See Adolf Hoffman, 'Sakramentale Heilswerke bei Tauler' in Filthaut, 217-267.

349 Note Ozment, *Homo*, 46.

350 Cf. Gordon Leff, *Heresy in the Later Middle Ages* (New York, N.Y. and Manchester: Barnes and Noble, Inc. and Manchester University Press, 1967), II, 291-292.

351 Translation from Raymond Bernard Blakney, *Meister Eckhart: A Modern Translation* (New York: Harper and Row, Publishers, 1941), 121.

352 Cf. Vetter, 112.

353 Cf. Ruusbroec, *Werken*, I, 5-6.

354 On this topic, see especially the argument in Harry J. McSorley, *Luther: Right or Wrong* (New York, N.Y. and Minneapolis, Minn.: Newman Press and the Augsburg Publishing House, 1969).

355 One cannot extend Tauler's words directed to the ordained to every baptised person. Cf. Ozment's attempt to do so in his *Homo*, 33n. 1. On the purpose of the sermons, see Heinrich Suso Denifle, 'Uber die Anfänge der Predigtweise der deutschen Mystiker,' *Archiv für Literatur und Kirchen-Geschichte des des Mittelalters*, II, 641-652.

356 Ruusbroec, *Werken*, I, 26ff., 209ff.; II, 116ff.

357 Cf. ibid., I, 121ff.; III, 223ff.

358 Cf. ibid., I, 103; II, passim., et al.

359 See Ozment, *Homo*, 13ff.
360 See Dibelius, 3.
361 See Gilson, *Mystical Theology*, 37ff.
362 For discussion, see Ozment, *Homo*, 36n. 1.
363 The passages appear in Ozment, *Homo*, 42-43.
364 Vetter, 162.
365 Vetter, 109.
366 Vetter, 146.
367 Ozment, *Homo*, 43.
368 Note Vetter, 205 in particular.
369 Cf. Vetter, 30ff., 117.
370 Cf. Vetter, 167. For discussion, see Bernhard Dietsche, 'Uber den Durchbruch bei Tauler' in Filthaut, 301-320.
371 See Vetter, 157-158.
372 Cf. Vetter, 46, 56, 120.
373 For a succinct discussion of Eckhart's use of this concept see Karl G. Kertz, 'Meister Eckhart's Teaching on the Birth of the Divine Word in the Soul,' *Traditio*, 15 (1969), 327-363.
374 WAIC, II, 3:8.
375 WAIC, II, 8:4.
376 WAIC, II, 8:5.
377 WAIC, II, 8:7-14 quotes from the Franckfurt 1703 Tauler, 1500, 69, 775, 11, 84, 1451, 1483.
378 WAIC II, 8:15-16 quotes Ruusbroec, *Tabernakel*, 10, *Brulocht*, III, 3. Cf. WAIC, II, 9 which quotes from the Franckfurt 1703 Tauler, 85, 1223, 84, 87, 816, 986, Suso, *Buchlein der ewigen Weisheit*, 10.
379 Cf. Stählin, 106.
380 Ibid., 108.
381 Note particularly Albin Ampe, *De Grondlijnen van Ruusbroec's Drieen-heitsleer* (Tielt: Drukkerij-Uitgeverij Lannoo, 1950) and the continuing discussion in his *De Geestelijke Grondslagen van Zieleopgang naar de Leer van Ruusbroec. A. Scheppingen Christologie* (Tielt, 1951), *B. Genadeleer* (Tielt, 1952). Note, as well, Stephanus Axter, *Geschiedenis van de Vroomheid in de Nederlanden* (Antwerpen: DeSikkel, 1950-1953), II, 42ff. and A. Wautier d'Aygalliers, *Ruusbroec the Admirable*, trans. by Fred Rothwell (London and New York: J.M. Dent and Sons Ltd. and E.P. Dutton and Co., 1925).
382 Ruusbroec, *Werken*, II, 3.
383 Ibid., II, 6.
384 Ibid., II, 29.
385 Ibid., II, 110; IV, 46.
386 Ibid., II, 3. Cf. however, the models available in the Tauler and Eckhart sermons. See Eberhard Winkler, *Exegetische Methoden bei Meister Eckhart* (Tübingen: J.C.B. Mohr (Paul Siebeck), 1965) and Korn for discussion.

387 Ibid., III, 65-67, 297-298. Cf. III, 223-224.

388 Cf. Ibid., I, 5, 110-117; III, 129-220; IV, 170, 236-247.

389 Ibid., I, 117-118, translation by Eric Colledge, *The Spiritual Espousals* (New York: Harper and Row, Publishers, 1953), 59.

390 Ruusbroec, *Werken*, I, 103, translation by Colledge, 43.

391 Ruusbroec, *Werken*, I, 106.

392 Ibid., I, 107.

393 Ibid., I, 108.

394 Ruusbroec, *Werken*, I, 108, translation by Colledge, 50.

395 Ampe, *Grondslagen B.*, 206.

396 Ruusbroec, *Werken*, I, 109-110, translation by Colledge, 50-51.

397 Ampe, *Grondslagen B.*, 206.

398 Ruusbroec, *Werken*, I, 110.

399 WAIC, II, 16.

400 Colledge, 19.

401 Ibid., 20.

402 For Arnold's doctrine of the three parts of man, particularly union in spirit, see WAIC, II, 12 which quotes from the Franckfurt 1703 Tauler, 500-501, 1151, 1601.

403 Ruusbroec, *Werken*, I, 239, translation by Colledge, 179.

404 Ibid., II, 2-9.

405 Ibid., II, 9-352.

406 Ibid., II, 353-366.

407 Cf. Edmund Colledge, 'John Ruysbroeck,' in James Walsh, ed., *Spirituality Through the Centuries* (London: Burns and Oates, n.d.), 206-207.

408 WAIC, II, 19 quotes from the Franckfurt 1703 Tauler, 148, 201, 269, 736. Cf. WAIC, II, 18.

409 Ruusbroec, *Werken*, I, 122f.

410 Ruusbroec, *Brulocht*, I, 108, translation by Colledge, Espousals, 50.

411 Ruusbroec, *Brulocht*, I, 109, translation by Colledge, Espousals, 51.

412 Ampe, *Grondslagen A.*, 283 and *Grondlijnen*, passim.

Bibliography

Manuscripts.

MS Archiv der Franckische Stiftung, Halle, Sign. 188a, F 10.

MS Berlin, Deutsche Staatsbibliothek, all. ms 1966.71.

MS Berlin, Preussische Staatsbibliothek f. 431 (copy in Schwenkfelder Library, Pennsburg, Pa.).

MS Berlin, Preussische Staatsbibliothek f. 451 (copy in Schwenkfelder Library, Pennsburg, Pa.).

MS Pennsburg, Pa., Schwenkfelder Library. SB33.

MS Pennsburg, Pa., Schwenkfelder Library. VA 2-2.

MS Pennsburg, Pa., Schwenkfelder Library. VA 3-5.

MS Pennsburg, Pa., Schwenkfelder Library. VA 3-14.

MS Pennsburg, Pa., Schwenkfelder Library. VC 1-8.

MS Pennsburg, Pa., Schwenkfelder Library. VC 5-1.

MS Pennsburg, Pa., Schwenkfelder Library. VC 5-2.

MS Pennsburg, Pa., Schwenkfelder Library. VC 5-3.

MS Pennsburg, Pa., Schwenkfelder Library. VR 11-9.

MS Pennsburg, Pa., Schwenkfelder Library. VS 2-3,1.

MS Staatsarchiv, Magdeburg, A 12 Spez. Werben, 1, 48-54.

MS Staatsarchiv, Magdeburg, A 22 Spez. Werben, 154, 50-70.

MS Staatsarchiv, Magdeburg, A 22 Spez. Werben, 156, 1-63.

MS Universitätsbibliothek, Giessen, Phil. K 8.

MS Universitätsbibliothek, Giessen, 19a, IV, 46.

Arnold Publications. (Volumes indicated by date alone have not been consulted unless otherwise noted.)

Arnold, Gottfried. *Q.B.D.V. LOCUTIONEM ANGELORUM ERUDITIS contemplandam sistit PRAESES M. GODOFREDUS ARNOLDI, Annaebergâ-Misn. ... ad d. XIV. Decemb. Anno 1687 ....* WITTENBERGAE, Typis CHRISTIANI FINCELII.

Arnold, Gottfried. *De lotione manuum.* Defended March 27, 1689. See Dibelius, 195-201.

Arnold, Gottfried. *De hermunduris.* Defended April 3, 1689. See Dibelius, 202-225.

Arnold, Gottfried. *Historia Christianorum ad metalla damnatorum historia*, in Christian Thomasius, *Historia sapientiae et stultitiae.* October, 1693. See *Fratrum sororumque.* 1696.

Arnold, Gottfried. 'Von dem Bruder- und Schwester-namen der ersten Christen,' in Christian Thomas, ed. *Historie der Weiszheit und Thorheit... 1693 ....* HALLE/ Gedruckt und verlegt von Christoph Salfelden ... IIIth, 114-202.

Arnold, Gottfried. *Zwey Send-Schreiben Aus der ersten Apostolischen Kirchen: Deren das eine ist Des heiligen Jüngers und Paulinischen Gefehrten BARNABAE, Das andere/ Des heiligen Märtyrers und Aufsehers zu Rom CLEMENTIS, ...* Verlegts Joh. Georg Lipper 1695.

Arnold, Gottfried. *M.G.A.A.M. Erstes Martyrthum/ oder Merckwürdigste Geschichte der ersten Märtyrer ....* Bound with his *Zwey Send-Schreiben.* 1695.

Arnold, Gottfried. Edition of Ignatius of Antioch. 1695. Cited in Doerries.

Arnold, Gottfried. *FRATRUM SORORUMQUE APPELATIO Inter Christianos maxime & alios qvondam usitata, tum & COGNATIO SPIRITUALIS, ex Antiqvitate Monumentis Commentatione illustrata per GOTHOFREDUM ARNOLDUM Annaemontanum. Accessit CHRISTIANORUM AD METALLA DAMNATORUM HISTORIA.* Francofurti ad Manum Apud JOHANN-CHRISTOPH: Konig/ 1696.

Arnold, Gottfried. *Des Heiligen MACARII Homilien/ Oder Geistliche Reden Um das Jahr Christi CCCXL gehalten. Anjetzo ihrer Vortreflichkeitwegen zum ersten mahl Ins Teutsche übersetzt Un nebenst einer Erinnerung von Brauch und Missbrauch Böser Exempel ....* Leipzig. Bey Johann Christoph Königen, Buchhändler in Goszlar. 1696.

Arnold, Gottfried. *Die Erste Liebe, Das ist: Wahre Abbildung Der Ersten Christen nach ihren Lebendigen Glauben und Heiligen Leben, Aus der ältesten und bewährtesten Kirchen-Scribenten eigenen Zeugnissen, Exempeln und Reden nach der Wahrheit der Ersten einigen Christlichen Religion, allen Liebhabern der Historischen Wahrheit, und sonderlich der Antiquität, als in einer nützlichen Kirchen-Historie, treulich und unparteyisch entworfen: Worinnen zugleich Des Hn. WILLIAM CAVE Erstes Christentum nach Nothdurft erläutert wird* ..... Zu finden in Gottleib Friedeburgs Buchhandlung Jm Jahre 1696.

Arnold, Gottfried. Sebastian Châteillon [Castellio], *[De calumnia] Von Verlästerungen und Verläumbdungen der bösen wider die Frommen*. 1696. Preface in Schaffhausen *Unparteiische Kirchen- und Ketzer-Historie*, 2: 1556-1557.

Arnold, Gottfried. *Q.D.B.V. HISTORIAM GEORGI SAXONIAE DUCIS disquisitioni publicae submittit PRAESIDE GOTHOFREDO ARNOLDO, respondens JOHANNES HAUBOLDUS ab Einsiedel* ... *M DC XCVII*. GISSAE HASSORUM, Typis Henningi Mulleri.

Arnold, Gottfried. *Christophori Irenaei Paranaesis seu Commonefactio Necessaria Ad D. Johann Fredericum Mayerum, Ob Ejus De Pietistis Ecclesiae Veteris Commentum, Accessit Friderici Spanheimii De Zelopseudo theologico Judicium*. Magdeburgi Anno M.DC.XCVII.

Arnold, Gottfried. *Kurtzgefasste Kirchengeschichte des Alten und Neuen Testaments*. 1697.

Arnold, Gottfried. *Historia cognationis spiritualis*. 1697. Second edition of *Fratrum sororumque*.

Arnold, Gottfried. *Commentatio de corrupto historiarum studio* .... Francofurti, sumptibus Joannis Davidis Zunneri, 1697.

Arnold, Gottfried. *Zeichen dieser Zeit bey der Anfang der instehenden Trübsalen*. 1698. See *Wahrnehmung jetziger Zeiten*. 1700.

Arnold, Gottfried. *Tabula Chronologica Imperatorvm, Regvm [sic] Dynastarvm, Paparvm, Rervm, Virorvmque Illustrivm, in Ecclesia et Repvblica, a Christo Nato, Ad Annvm M DC XCII*. Lipsiae apud Thomas Fritsch, Bibliop. & Typis Christophori Flesheri Anno MDCXCVIII.

Arnold, Gottfried. *Göttliche Liebes-Funcken/ Ausz dem Grossen Feuer Der Liebe Gottes in Christo JESU entsprungen* .... Franckfurt am Mayn/ bey Johann David Zunnern/ 1698. Part One of 1701 edition.

Arnold, Gottfried. *Die Geistliche Wegeweiser* .... *Michael Molinos* .... Franckfurth/ bey Johann Christoph Koenig. Anno 1699.

Arnold, Gottfried. *Ein Denckmahl des alten Christentums bestehend in des Heil. Marcarii und anderer hocherleuchteter Männer* ... *Schriften*. Gosslar: J. C. Koenig, 1699.

Arnold, Gottfried. *Unparteyische Kirchen- und Ketzer-Historie, Vom Anfang des Neuen Testaments Bisz auf das Jahr Christi 1688*. 2 Bde.; Franckfurt am Main: Thomas Fritsch, 1699-1700.

Arnold, Gottfried. *Offenhertziges Bekäntnüsz Welche Bey unlängst geschehener Verlassung Seines Academischen Ampts abgelegt worden*.... Gedruckt im Jahr Christi 1699.

Arnold, Gottfried. 'Gottfried Arnolds Brief an den D. Spener/ die Nieder-legung seiner Profession in Giessen betreffend' [1699]. *Hessische Heb-Opfer* (1740), 473-476.

Arnold, Gottfried. *Wohlgegründete Remonstration An all Hohe und Niedere Obrigkeiten/ Wie auch An alle andere bescheidene und vernünfftige Leser/ In puncto Des Gewissens-Zwanges in dem Kirchen Wesen.* Publiciret Im Jahr 1700.

Arnold, Gottfried. *Offenhertzige Bekänntnisz ....* Franckfurt und Leipzig/ bey Samuel Müllern/ 1700.

Arnold, Gottfried. *Wahrnehmung jetziger Zeiten.* 1700; reprint of *Ze-ichen der Zeit* in C.A. Roemeling, *Nachricht seiner von GOTT geschehenen völligen Herausführung aus Babel ... Deme angehangt ... G. Arnolds Heil-same Wahrnehmung jetziger Zeiten ....* Ephrata, gedruckt im Jahr 1792.

Arnold, Gottfried. *Poetische Lob- und Liebes-Sprüche.* Leipzig/ Bey Thomas Fritsch/ 1700.

Arnold, Gottfried. *Kurtzgefaszte Kirchenhistorie Des Alten und Neuen Tes-taments.* Leipzig, bey Thomas Fritsch, 1700; reprint, Leipzig/ Bey Samuel Benjamin Walthern/ 1737.

Arnold, Gottfried. *VITAE PATRUM Oder: Das Leben Der Altväter und anderer Gottseliger Personen Auffs Neue erläutert und Vermehret.* HALLE/ In Verlegung des Waysen-Hauses/ 1700.

Arnold, Gottfried. *Erbauliche Sendschreiben der Alten.* 1700. See Seeberg, 58.

Arnold, Gottfried. *Auserlesene Send-Schreiben Derer Alten/ Zum gemeinen Zug gesammelt und verteutscht.* Franckfurt und Leipzig/ In Ver-legung Theod. Philippe Calvisio/ Buchhandl. Im Jahr Christi 1700.

Arnold, Gottfried. *Erbauliche theosophische Sendschreiben eines in Gott getreuen Mitgliedes aus der Gemeinschaft Jesu Christi ....* Gedruckt zu Heliopolis im Jahr 1700.

Arnold, Gottfried. *Das Geheimnisz der Göttlichen Sophia oder Weisheit.* Leipzig/ Bey Thomas Fritsch/ 1700.

Arnold, Gottfried. *Erklärung/ Von gemeinen Secten-wesen/ Kirchen- und Abendmahl-gehen.* Leipzig/ Bey Thomas Fritsch/ 1700.

Arnold, Gottfried. *Der richtigste Weg durch Christum zu Gott: bey öffentlichen Versamlungen in dreyen Sermonen oder Predigten angewiesen ... Nebenst einer näheren Erklärung von seinem Sinn und Verhalten in Kirchen-Sachen.* Franckfurt, Bey Thomas Fritsch, 1700.

Arnold, Gottfried. *[Johann Luyken] Jesus und die Seele Ein Geistlicher Spiegel vor das Gemüth/ Bestehende Ausz viertzig anmuthigen Sinn-Bildern ....* Franckfurt am Mayn/ In Verlegung Joh. David Zunners. 1701.

Arnold, Gottfried. *Johannis Angeli Silesii Cherubinischer Wanders-Mann Oder Geistliche Sinn- und Schlusz-Reime ....* 1701; reprint, Altona, Auf Kosten guter Freunde, 1737.

Arnold, Gottfried. *Etliche vortreffliche Tractätlein aus der Gehaimen GOttes-Gelehrtheit: Nehmlich I. Der Madame Guion ... II. Des berühmten Laurentii de la Resurrection ....* Franckfurt und Leipzig/ Verlegts Joh. Christoph König/ 1701.

Arnold, Gottfried. *Waare afbeelding der eerste Christenen. Uyt het Hoogd. door W. Sewel..* Amsterdam, by Jac. van Hardenberg, Bar. Visscher en Jac. van Nieuweveen, 1701.

Arnold, Gottfried. *D. JOHANNIS RUSBROCHII, Weiland Canonici Regularis Augustiner Ordens/ und Prioris des Klosters Grünthal/ DOCTOR ECSTATICUS, Bestehend ausz allen desselben sehr Gottseligen Schrifften/ Welche die höchsten geheimnüsse der Göttlichen Lebens lehren/ Eine wanderwürdige art allerhand tugenden ausz zu üben/ vorlegen und anzeigen. Und/ weil sie von dem geist Gottes eingegeben/ allenthalben/ voller Gottseligkeit/ gesunder sitten=lehre/ und nach eines jeden menschen zustand eingerüchtet seynd/ Vorahls von dem P. F. Laurentio Surio, einen Carthäuser zu Cölln ausz dem Holländischen ins Lateinische/ Nun aber zum gemeinen nutz: Alles ins Teutsche treulichst übersetzet/ von G.J.C. ....* Offenback am Mayn/ Druckts Bonaventura de Haunog, Ysenburg und Büdingischer Hof=Buchdr. Im Jahr 1701-.

Arnold, Gottfried. *Göttliche Liebes-Funcken/ Ausz dem Grossen Feuer Der Liebe Gottes in Christo JESU entsprungen .....* Franckfurt am Mayn/ bey Johann David Zunnern/ 1701.

Arnold, Gottfried. *Das Leben Der Gläubigen Oder: Beschreibung solcher Gottseligen Personen/ welche in denen Letzten 200. Jahren sonderlich bekandt worden ....* Halle, 1701; Andere Auflage ... HALLE, In Verlegung des Waysen-Hauses, 1732.

Arnold, Gottfried. *Fernere Erläuterung seines sinnes und verhaltens beym Kirchen- und Abendmahl-gehen ....* Franckfurt/ Bey Thomas Fritsch/ im jahr 1701.

Arnold, Gottfried. *Endliche Vorstellung seiner Lehre und Bekäntnisz ....* Franckfurt/ Bey Thomas Fritsch/ 1701.

Arnold, Gottfried. *Anmuthige Sinn-Bilder nach Johann Arnds Wahren Christenthum Eingerichtet und Erläutert.* Franckfurt/ Verlegts Johann David Zunner/ Anno 1701. Bound with *Göttliche Liebes-Funcken.*

Arnold, Gottfried. Preface to Gertrude More, *Confessio Amantis.* 1702. Cited in Preussische Staatsbibliothek Catalogue but unavailable in East or West Berlin collection.

Arnold, Gottfried. *Des Heiligen Clementis von Rom Recognitiones oder Historie/ Von denen Reisen und Reden des Apostels Petri ....* Berlin, Verlegts Johann Michael Rüdiger, 1702.

Arnold, Gottfried. *Brieffe Petrucci* .... 1702.

Arnold, Gottfried. *Ein Denckmahl des Alten Christentums/ Bestehend in des Heiligen Marcarii Und anderer hocherleuchteter Männer ... Schriften.* Goszlar: Verlegts Joh. Christoph König/ Buchhandl. Anno 1702.

Arnold, Gottfried. *Das Eheliche und Unverehelichte Leben der ersten Christen/ nach ihren eigenen zeugnissen und exempeln.* Franckfurt/ Bey Thomas Fritschen/ 1702.

Arnold, Gottfried. *HISTORIA ET DESCRIPTIO THEOLOGIAE MYS-TICAE, Seu THEOSOPHIAE ARCANAE ET RECONDITAE, item veterum & Novorum MYSTICORVM.* FRANCOFVRTI apvd Thomam Fritsch Anno MDCII.

Arnold, Gottfried. *Historie und beschreibung der mystischen Theologie/ oder geheimen Gottes Gelehrtheit/ wie auch derer alten und neuen MYS-TICORVM.* Franckfurt bey Thomas Fritschen/ 1703.

Arnold, Gottfried. *Supplementa, Illustrationes, und Emendationes Zur Verbesserung Der Kirchen-Historie.* Franckfurt, bey Thomas Fritschen, 1703.

Arnold, Gottfried. *Historia cognationis spiritualis.* 1703. Second edition.

Arnold, Gottfried. *Neuer Kern wahrer Geistes-Gebete, bestehend in denen herrlichsten Morgen- und Abend-, Stand- und Beruffs-, Busz- und Kommunion-, Creutz- und Anfechtung-, Sterbens- und Paszions-, wie auch Jesus-Andachten; Ingleichen in allen andern Bitten, Gebeten, Fürbitten und Dancksagungen, Dergleichen noch nie also aus denen ältesten Lehrern beysammen gesehen worden; zusammt einen neuen Kern recht-geistlicher lieblicher Lieder.* Franckfurt/ bey Thomas Fritschen/ 1704.

Arnold, Gottfried. *Die Geistliche Gestalt Eines Evangelischen Lehrers Nach dem Sinn und Exempel der Alten Ans Licht gestellet ... mit ... Anhang Eines Antwortschreibens An einen Prediger, Uber mancherley Angelegenheiten In deszen Amt und Beruff.* Halle, 1704; Franckfurt und Leipzig, Bey Johann Georg Böhmen, 1723.

Arnold, Gottfried. *Die Verklärung Jesu Christi in der Seele, aus denen gewöhnlichen Sonn- und Fest-Tags-Episteln, auf dem Fürstlichen Schlosze zur Allstedt gezeiget.* Franckfurt, bey Thomas Fritschen, 1704.

Arnold, Gottfried. *Confessio Amantis, Oder Heilige Liebes- Bekäntnisse/ in Englischer Sprache aus dem überflusz des hertzens geschrieben von Gertraut More* .... Franckfurt/ Bey Thomas Fritschen, 1704.

Arnold, Gottfried. *Die Geistliche Wegeweiser* .... *Michael Molinos* .... Franckfurth/ bey Johann Christoph Koenig. Anno 1704.

Arnold, Gottfried. *Das Buch der Weisheit Salomonis aud dem Grund-Text auffs neue übersetzet ... Durch Einige Liebhaber der Heiligen Schrifft.* Halle/ in Verlegung des Waysenhauses/ ANNO M DCCV.

Arnold, Gottfried. *Concilia und Responsa Theologica oder Gotts-gelehrte Rathschläge und Antworten, über denen wichtigsten stücken und zuständen eines göttlichen wandels, nebenst neuen Geistlichen Gedichten, der weiszheit Garten-Gewächs genannt* .... Franckfurt, bey Thomas Fritsch, 1705. Reprint, Leipzig, Bey Benjamin Waltern, 1736.

Arnold, Gottfried. *Kurtze, Geistliche und Gottseelige Brieffe, Von Hrn.* Petro Mattheo Petrucci, Weyland Bischoff zu Jesi und Cardinal geschrieben, Nunmehro aus der Italianischen in die Hochteutsche Sprache übersetzt.* Halle/ In Verlegung des Waysen-Hauses M DCCV.

Arnold, Gottfried. *Die Evangelische Botschafft Der Herrlichkeit Gottes in Jesu Christo, nach denen ordentliche Sonn- und Fest-Tags Evangelien vorgetragen, Aus denen alten Kirchenlehrern erläutert, und nebenst eini-gen andern Geistlichen reden.* Franckfurt, 1706; reprint, Lemgo, in der Meyerischen Buchhandlung, 1759.

Arnold, Gottfried. *PETRI ALLIX Eines Theologi der Kirchen in Engeland Ausspruch der alten Jüdischen Kirchen wider die UNITARIOS ....* Nebst einer Vorrede Hn. Gottfried Arnolds ... Von dem Gebrauch der Lehre der H. Dreyeinigkeit zur Gottseligkeit.* Berlin/ verlegts Johann Michael Rüdiger/ 1707.

Arnold, Gottfried. Second edition of Guyon edition. 1707.

Arnold, Gottfried. *Geistreichen Predigten M. Schroeder.* 1707.

Arnold, Gottfried. *Das wahre Christenthum Altes Testaments, im heil-samen Gebrauch der vornehmsten Sprüche aus dem ersten Buch Mosis ....* Franckfurth, Thomas Fritsch, 1707.

Arnold, Gottfried. *Die Abwege, Oder Irrungen und Versuchungen gutwilliger und frommer Menschen, aus Beystimmung des gottseligen Al-terthums angemercket.* Franckfurt, bey Thomas Fritschen, 1708.

Arnold, Gottfried. *Des Heiligen Clementis von Rom Recognitiones oder Historie/ Von denen Reisen und Reden des Apostels Petri ....* 1708.

Arnold, Gottfried. *Predigten.* No title page. Prefaced for three edi-tions, 1705, 1707, 1708. Copy at Mt. Airy Lutheran Theological Library, Philadelphia.

Arnold, Gottfried. *Die Verklärung Jesu Christi in der Seele, aus denen gewöhnlichen Sonn- und Fest-Tags-Episteln, auf dem Fürstlichen Schlosze zur Allstedt gezeiget.* Franckfurt, bey Thomas Fritschen, 1708.

Arnold, Gottfried. *Der verursachte und gemässige Sündfluth, Bey der Am 14. und 15. Februar 1709 Wasserfluth nebst historischem Bericht von den Zeichen solcher Fluthen und grosser Kälte.* Berlin. Joh. Michael Rüdiger/ 1709.

Arnold, Gottfried. *Wahre Abbildung Des Inwendigen Christenthums, Nach desen Anfang und Grund, Fortgang oder Wachsthum und Ausgang oder Ziel in Lebendigen Glauben und Gottseligen Leben/ Aus den Zeugniszen und Exempeln der gottseligen Alten zur Fortsetzung und Erläuterung Der Abbildung der Ersten Christen dargestellet.* Franckfurt, 1709; reprint, Leipzig; Bey Benjamin Walthern, 1732.

Arnold, Gottfried. *Historisch-Theologische Betrachtungen merckwürdiger Wahrheiten/ Auf Veranlassung derer biszherigen Einwürffe Gegen G. Arnolds Schrifften Von Einigen nach und nach bescheidentlich aufgesetzet/ Und nun Auf vieler Begehren zu nöthiger Verantwortung dargeleget.* Franckfurt/ zu Finden bey Thomas Fritschen/ 1709.

Arnold, Gottfried. *Evangelische Reden über die Sonn- und Fest-Tags-Evangelien zu einer bequemen Hauss- und Reise-Postill heraus gegeben mit einer Vorrede von recht evangelischer Abhandlung der Sonntages-Episteln.* 1709.

Arnold, Gottfried. *Evangelische Hertzens-wecker* .... 1709; reprint, Stendal und Gardelegen: Ernst Heinr. Campen, 1724.

Arnold, Gottfried. *Ein rechter QVASIMODOGENITUS... Bei volckreicher Beerdigung ... Herrn Laurentii Giessens.* Cölln an der Spree, druckts Ulrich Liebpert, [1709].

Arnold, Gottfried. *Paradiesischer Lust-Garten/ voller andächtiger Gebete und Gesänge, Bey allen Zeiten/ Personen und Zuständen* ..... Leipzig und Stendea/ In Verlegung Ernst Heinrich Kampen/ Buchhändlers. 1709.

Arnold, Gottfried. *Heutige/ langwieriger/ verwirreter Teutscher Krieg ... Christian Hoburg.* 1710.

Arnold, Gottfried. *D. Martini Lutheri Kirchenpostille* .... Leipzig, 1710.

Arnold, Gottfried. *Der Woleingerichtete Schul-Bau* .... Leipzig und Stendal, Verlegt von Ernst Heinrich Campen, Im Jahre 1711.

Arnold, Gottfried. *Epistolische Reden, oder kleine Postill über die Episteln nebst zwei vor der Preusz. Königin gehaltenen Predigten.* Franckfurt/ Bey Thomas Fritsch/ 1711.

Arnold, Gottfried. *Thomas von Kempis Geistliche Scriften, So wol die vier Bücher Von der Nachfolge Christi, als auch dessen anderer in vier und zwantzig Büchern bestehende Betrachtunge.... Nebst einem historischen Vorbericht und Einleitung Gottfried Arnolds....* Leipzig und Stendal, 1712, 2 Aufl.; Leipzig, bey Samuel Benjamin Walthern, 1733.

Arnold, Gottfried. *MICHAEL DE MOLINOS ... Geistliche Weg-Weiser* .... Frankfurt am Mayn, 1712.

Arnold, Gottfried. *Ein edles Büchlein/ Von der innerlichen Geistlichen Hoffart ... Durch Albertum Dranckmeisterum* .... 1712.

Arnold, Gottfried. *Offentliche Zeugniss, das die Giessische Theologi ihm zu seiner Kirchen und Ketzer-Historie keinen Vorschub getan* .... Perleberg, 1712.

Arnold, Gottfried. *D. Martin Luthers Kleine Catechismus* .... 1712; reprint, Altona, Zu finden bey Johann Friedrich Bähr, 1722.

Arnold, Gottfried. *Die Erste Liebe, Das ist: Wahre Abbildung Der Ersten Christen* ..... Franckfurt am Mayn, C. Bensch, 1712.

Arnold, Gottfried. *Paradiesischer Lust-Gartin, Erfüllet mit Andächtigen Gebehtern Bey allen Zeiten, Personen, Lebens-Arten und Umständen* .... 1712.

Arnold, Gottfried. *Die Geistliche Gestalt Eines Evangelischen Lehrers Nach dem Sinn und Exempel der Alten Ans Licht gestellet* ... 1713.

Arnold, Gottfried. *Historia von des beruffenen Ertz-Kätzers David Joris oder Georgi* .... 1713.

Arnold, Gottfried. *Geheime und Innige Betrachtungen über die Psalmen Davids* .... Ober-Neustadt Cassel/ druckts Justus Hampe MDCCXIII.

Arnold, Gottfried. *Angelus Silesius. Cherubinischer Wandersmann.* 1713

Arnold, Gottfried. *Das unzertrennliche Liebes-Band* ... *Marien Elizabeth* ... *Leichen Predigt* .... Berlin [1714].

Arnold, Gottfried. *Theologia Experimentalis, Das ist: Geistliche Erfahrungs-Lehre, Oder Erkäntnisz und Erfahrung Von denen vornehmsten Stücken Des Lebendigen Christenthums, Von Anfang der Bekehrung bisz zur Vollendung:* .... Franckfurt, 1715; reprint, Franckfurt am Mayn/ Bey Joh. Benjamin Andrea und Heinrich Hort. Anno M. DCC.XXV.

Arnold, Gottfried. *Seel. Hn. Gottfried Arnolds/* ... *Gedoppelter Lebens-Lauff/ Wovon der eine von Ihm selbst projectiret und aufgesetzt worden.* ... Leipzig und Gardelegen, 1716, in *Gedächnisz-Rede, bey Beerdigung Des Hoch-Ehrwürdigen und Hochgelährten Herrn, Herrn Gotfried Arnold* ... zum Druck übergeben von Johanne Crusio, Perleberg und Gardelegen, Verlegt von Ernst Heinrich Campen, Anno, 1719.

Arnold, Gottfried. *Betrachtung von dem Mittleren Zustand* .... o.O., 1725. Translation of Thomas White, *Villicationes.*

Arnold, Gottfried. *Die Verklärung Jesu Christi in der Seele, aus denen gewöhnlichen Sonn- und Fest-Tags-Episteln, auf dem Fürstlichen Schlosze zur Allstedt gezeiget.* Gedruckt im Jahr 1721.

Arnold, Gottfried. *Brunstige Geistes-Gebete, Bestehend in denen Kräftigsten Gebätern* ... *zusammt Einigen Briefen und Reden/ über wichtige Materien.* Augsburg, 1718.

Arnold, Gottfried. *Güldene Send-Schreiben derer Alten Christen/ Mit Sonderbaren Fleisz gesammelt und ins Teutsche gebracht von Gottfried Arnolden/ Past. Pr. und Inspectore zu Perleberg. Anitzo zum Erstenmahl Ihres fürtrefflichen und erbaulichen Innhalts wegen zum gemeinen Nutzen herausgegeben/* .... Büdingen/ Drucks und Verlegts Joh. Fried. Regelein. 1723.

Arnold, Gottfried. *Paradiesischer Lust-Gartin, Erfüllet mit Andächtigen Gebehtern Bey allen Zeiten, Personen, Lebens-Arten und Umständen ....* Leipzig und Gardelegen, In Verlegung Ernst Heinrich Campen, priviligierten Buchhändler. 1724.

Arnold, Gottfried. *Unparteyische Kirchen- und Ketzer-Historie, Vom Anfang des Neuen Testaments Bisz auf das Jahr Christi 1688.* 2 Bde.; Franckfurt am Main: Thomas Fritsch, 1729.

Arnold, Gottfried. *Anhang der Erfahrungs-Lehre, Hrrn Gottfried Arnolds, ... Zehen Betrachtungen über die Epistel Pauli an die Colosser ....* Franckfurt am Mayn/ Bey Johann Benjamin Andreä und Heinrich Hort. Anno M. DCC XXXV.

Arnold, Gottfried. *Cherubinischer Wanders-Mann Oder Geistreiche Sinn- und Schlusz- Reime, Zur Göttlichen Beschaulichkeit...* aufs neue mit Gottfried Arnolds Vorrede herausgegeben .... Altona, Auf kosten guter Freunde, 1737.

Arnold, Gottfried. *Unparteyische Kirchen- und Ketzer-Historie, Vom Anfang des Neuen Testaments Bisz auf das Jahr Christi 1688.* 3 Bde.; Schaffhausen: Emanuel and Benedict Hurter, 1740-1742.

Arnold, Gottfried. *Paradiesischer Lustgarten voller andächtigen Gebete, bei allen Zeiten, Personen und Zuständen ....* Hrsg. von Karl Chr. Eberh. Ehmann ... Reutlingen, Druck und Verlag von Rupp und Baur. 1852.

Arnold, Gottfried. *Geistliche Erfahrungs-Lehre, Oder Erkenntniss und Erfahrung Von denen vornehmsten Stücken Des Lebendigen Christenthums, Von Anfang der Bekehrung bisz zur Vollendung: ....* Milford, Bucks County, Pa., Gedruckt und herausgegeben von John B. Oberholtzer, 1855.

CATALOGUS BIBLIOTHECAE B. GOTOFREDI ARNOLDI ... 1714. Copy in Túbingen Universitätsbibliothek.

Works by Other Authors.

Aelredi Rievallensis. *Opera Omnia.* Eds., A. Hoste et C.H. Talbot. Turnholti: Typographi Brepols Editores Pontificii, MCMLXXI.

Aland, Kurt. *Spener-Studien.* Berlin: Walter de Gruyter, 1943.

Altaner Berthold und Alfred Stuiber. *Patrologie.* 7. Aufl.; Freiburg i.B.: Herder, 1966.

Althaus, Paul. *Forschungen zur Evangelischen Gebetsliteratur.* Gütersloh: Druck und Verlag von C. Bertelsmann, 1927.

Althaus, Paul. *The Theology of Martin Luther.* Trans. by Robert C. Schultz. Philadelphia, Pa.: Fortress Press, 1966.

Althaus, Paul. *Die Prinzipien der deutschen reformierten Dogmatik im Zeitalter der aristotelischen Scholastik.* Leipzig, 1914; reprint, Darmstadt: Wissenschaftliche Buchgesellschaft, 1967.

Ampe, Albin. *De Grondlijnen van Ruusbroec's Drieenheitsleer.* Tielt: Drukkerij-Uitgeverij Lannoo, 1950.

Ampe, Albin. *Geestelijke Grondslagen van Zieleopgang naar de Leer van Ruusbroec.* 2 vols.; Tielt: Lannoo, 1951-1952.

Ampe, Albin. *Ruusbroec: Traditie en Werkelijkheid.* Antwerp: Ruusbroec-Genootschap, 1975.

Ancelet-Hustache, Jeanne. *Master Eckhart and the Rhineland Mystics.* Trans. by Hilda Graef. New York and London: Harper and Brothers and Longmans, Green and Co. Ltd., 1957.

Angela of Foligno. *The Book of Divine Consolation of the Blessed Angela of Foligno.* Trans. by Mary G. Sheegman. New York: Cooper Square Publishers, Inc., 1966.

Arnkiel, Friedrich. *Rettung Des Ersten Nordischen Christenthums, Wider Herrn Gottfried Arnolds vielfältige Verstell- und Verdrehungen ....* Glückstadt und Leipzig/ bey Gotthilff Lehmann/ Königl. privil. Buchhändler. 1712.

Anson, Peter F. *The Call of the Cloister.* London: SPCK, 1955.

Appel, Helmut. *Philipp Jakob Spener: Vater des Pietismus.* Berlin: Evangelische Verlagsanstalt, 1964.

Arndt, Johann. *Zwey Uhralte vnd Geistreiche Büchlein. Das Erste/ Die Deutsche Theologia... Das Ander/ Die Nachfolgung Christi... deutlicher vnd verständiger an Tag gegeben Durch Iohannem Arndten ....* Leipzig, In Verlegung Johann Francken [1605].

Arndt, Johann. *Sechs Bücher von Wahren Christenthum....* 6. Aufl.; Stuttgart, bei den Gebrüdern Mantler, Buchdruckern, 1747.

Arndt, Johannes. *Predigten über die alten Evangelien aller Sonn-Fest und Feiertage nebst einiger Passions-Predigt.* Hrsg. von S.C. Kopff. 2. Aufl.; Stuggart: Chr. Belser Buchhandlung, 1852.

Arndt, Johann. *True Christianity.* Trans. by Charles F. Schaeffer. Philadelphia, Pa.: General Council Publication House, 1917.

Asheim, Ivar, hrsg. *Kirche, Mystik, Heiligung und das Natürliche bei Luther.* Göttingen: Vandenhoeck und Ruprecht, 1967.

Aulen, Gustav. *The Faith of the Church.* Trans. by Eric H. Wahlstrom and G. Everett Arden. Philadelphia, Pa.: Muhlenberg Press, 1948.

Axter, Stephanus. *Geschiedenis van de Vroomheid in de Nederlanden.* Antwerpen: DeSikkel, 1950-1953.

Bäring, Georg. *Bibliographie der Ausgaben der 'Theologia deutsch'.* Baden-Baden: Verlag Heitz Gmbh., 1963.

Bäumker, Cl. 'Der Anteil des Elass an den geistigen Bewegungen des Mittelalters,' *Beiträge zur Geschichte der Philosophie und Theologie*, 25 (1927), 215-255.

Büchsel, Jürgen. *Gottfried Arnold: Sein Verständnis von Kirche und Wiedergeburt*. Witten: Luther Verlag, 1970.

Bainton, Roland H. *Here I Stand: A Life of Martin Luther*. New York: Abingdon-Cokesbury Press, 1950.

Bainton, Roland H. 'The Left Wing of the Reformation,' *Journal of Religion*, 21 (1941), 124-134.

Banckmeister, Franz. 'Aus dem Briefwechsel Gottfried Arnolds,' *Mittel Verein Geschichte Annabergs*, 4 (1894), 1-15.

Barth, Hans M. 'Theologia Experimentalis,' *Neue Zeitschrift für systematische Theologie*, 23 (1981), 120-136.

Barth, Karl. *Die protestantische Theologie im 19. Jahrhundert*. 3. Aufl.; Zurich: Evangelischer Verlag, 1952.

Barth, Karl. *Church Dogmatics*. Trans. by G.W. Bromiley. Edinburgh: T. and T. Clark, 1962.

Barthold, Friedrich Wilhelm. *Die Erweckten im protestantischen Deutschland während des Ausgangs des 17. und der ersten Hälfte des 18. Jahrhunderts*. 1852/ 1853; reprint, Darmstadt: Wissenschaftliche Buchgeselleschaft, 1968.

Baum, Friedrich. *Das schwäbische Gemeinschaftleben*. 2. Aufl.; Stuttgart: Quellverlag der Ev. Gesellschaft, 1929.

Baumgart, Peter. 'Leibnitz und der Pietismus: Universale Reformbestrebungen um 1700,' *Archiv für Kulturgeschichte*, 48 (1966), 364-386.

Baur, Ferdinand Christian. *Die Epochen der kirchlichen Geschichtsschreibung* (1852) in his *Ausgewählte Werke in Einzelausgaben*. Hrsg. von Klaus Scholder. Stuttgart-Bad Cannstatt: Friedrich Fromann Verlag (Günther Holzboog), 1963-1970.

Die Bekenntnisschriften der evangelisch-lutherischen Kirche. Berlin: Deutsches Evangelisches Kirchenbundesamt, 1930.

Benz, Ernst. 'Gottfried Arnolds "Geheimnis der Göttlichen Sophia" und seine Stellung in der christlichen Sophialehre,' *Jahrbuch der hessischen Kirchengeschichtlichen Vereinigung*, 18 (1967), 51-83.

Benz, Ernst. 'Pietist and Puritan Sources of Early Protestant World Missions,' *Church History*, 20 (1951), 28-55.

Benz, Ernst. *Der Prophet Jacob Boehme*. Mainz and Wiesbaden: Verlag der Wissenschaften und der Literatur, Steiner in Komm., 1959.

Benz, Ernst. *Die protestantische Thebais*. Mainz und Wiesbaden: Verlag der Wissenschaften und der Literatur, Steiner in Konn., 1959.

Benz, Ernst. *Die Vision: Erfahrungsformen und Bilderwelt.* Stuttgart: Ernst Klett Verlag, 1969.

Bethmann, L.C. *Herzog August der Jüngere, der Gründer der Wolfenbüttler Bibliothek.* Wolfenbüttel, 1863.

Beyer-Fröhlich, Marianne, hrsg. *Pietismus und Rationalismus.* Leipzig: Reclam, 1933.

Beyreuther, Erich. *August Hermann Francke 1663-1727.* Hamburg: Herbert Reich Evangelisches Verlag, 1958.

Bihlmeyer Karl, ed. *Heinrich Seuse: Deutsche Schriften.* Stuttgart, 1907.

Biot, Francois. *The Rise of Protestant Monasticism.* Trans. by W.J. Kerrigan. Baltimore, Md. and Dublin: Helicon, 1963.

Blakney, Raymond Bernard, trans. *Meister Eckhart: A Modern Translation.* New York: Harper and Row, Publishers, 1941.

Blaufuss, Dietrich, hrsg. *Pietismus-Forschungen: Zu Philipp Jacob Spener und zum spiritualistisch-radikalpietistischen Umfeld.* Frankfurt: Peter Lang, 1986.

Blaufuss, Dietrich. *Spener-Arbeiten.* 2. Aufl.; Bern: Peter Lang, 1980.

Boehmer, Heinrich. *Road to Reformation.* Trans. by John W. Boberstein and Theodore G. Tappert. New York: Meridian Books, 1957.

Boehmer, Heinrich. *Luther im Lichte der Neueren Forschung.* 2. Aufl.; Leipzig: Verlag von B.G. Tuebner, 1910.

Bona, Johannis. *Opera Omnia.* Venetiis, Ex Typographia Balleoniana. MDCCLII.

Borngräber, Otto. *Das Erwachen der philosophischen Spekulation der Reformationszeit.* Schwarzenberg i. Sa.: Buchdruckerei von C.M. Gärtner, 1908.

Bornkamm, Heinrich. *Mystik, Spiritualismus und die Anfänge des Pietismus im Luthertum.* Giessen: Verlag von Alfred Topelmann, 1926.

Bornkamm, Heinrich. *Eckhart und Luther.* Stuttgart: W. Kohlhammer Verlag, 1936.

Bouyer, Louis. *Orthodox Spirituality and Protestant and Anglican Spirituality.* Trans. by Barbara Wall. London: Burns and Oates, 1969.

Braw, Christian. *Bücher im Staube: Die Theologie Johann Arndts in ihrem Verhältnis zur Mystik.* Leiden: E.J. Brill, 1986.

Brecht, Martin. 'Die Berleberger Bibel,' *Pietismus und Neuzeit*, 8 (1983), 162-200.

Breymeyer, Reinhard. 'Die Bibliothek Gottfried Arnolds,' *Linguistica Biblica*, 39 (1976), 86-132.

Breyreuter, Erich. 'Die Gestalt Mohammeds in Gottfried Arnolds Kirchen-
und Ketzerhistorie,' *Theologische Literaturzeitung*, 84 (1959), 255-263.

Brown, Dale. *Understanding Pietism*. Grand Rapids, Mich.: Eerdmans,
1978.

Brunner, Emil. *The Philosophy of Religion from the Standpoint of Protestant Theology*. Trans. by A.J.D. Farrar and Bertram Lee Woolf. London:
James Clarke and Co. Ltd., 1958.

Bruns, Hans. *Gottfried Arnold*. Giessen und Basel: Brunnen Verlag, 1955.

Bruns, Hans. *Philipp Jakob Spener: Ein Reformator nach der Reformation*.
Giessen und Basel: Brunnen Verlag, 1955.

Calvin, John. *Institutes of the Christian Religion*, Trans. by Ford Lewis
Battles. 2 vols.; Philadelphia, Pa.: The Westminster Press, 1960.

Cave. William. *Erstes Christentum, oder Gottesdienst der alten Christen
in der ersten Zeiten*. Leipzig: J. T. Fritsch, 1694.

Chauncey, David Ensign. *Radical German Pietism (c.1675-c.1760)*. Unpubl. Ph.D., Boston University School of Theology, 1955.

Chemnitz, Martin. *The Two Natures in Christ*. Trans. by J.A.O. Preuss.
St. Louis, Mo.: Concordia Publishing House, 1971.

Chiquot, A. *Histoire ou Legende... ? Jean Tauler et le 'Meisters Buoch'*.
Strasbourg et Paris: A. Vix et Cie et E. Champion, 1922.

Clark, James M. *The Great German Mystics*. Oxford: Basil Blackwell,
1949.

Clark, James M. *Master Eckhart: An Introduction to the Study of his
Works*. London: Thomas Nelson and Sons Ltd., 1957.

Closs, A. *The Genius of the German Lyric*. London: The Cresset Press,
1962.

Cohrs, Ferdinand. 'Zwei vergessene Katechismen Gottfried Arnolds,' *Neue
Kirchliche Zeitschrift*, 41 (1930), 602-641.

Coler, Johann Christoph. *Historia Gothofredi Arnold qva de vita scriptis
actisqve illivs ... exponditur*. Vitembergae, apvd C.T. Lvdovicvm, 1718.

Colledge, Edmund. 'John Ruysbroeck,' in James Walsh, ed. *Spirituality
Through the Centuries*. London: Burns and Oates, n.d., 206-207.

Colledge, Eric. 'The Buchlein der Ewigen Weiszheit and the Horologium
Sapientiae,' *Dominican Studies*, 6 (1953), 77-89.

Concordia Triglotta. St. Louis, Mo.: Concordia, 1921.

Corin, A.L. *Sermons de J. Tauler*. Liege et Paris: Imp. H. Vaillant-
Carmanne et Edouard Champion, 1929.

Cyprian, Ernst Salomon. *Allgemeine Anmerckungen Uber Gottfried Arnolds Kirchen- und Ketzer-Historie.* Franckfurth und Leipzig/ bey Paul Günther Pfotenhauern/ Buchhändlern in Coburg Im Jahr 1701.

Cysarz, Herbert, hrsg. *Baroklyrik.* 2. Aufl.; Hildesheim: Georg Olms Verlagsbuchhandlung, 1964.

'Des Qvedlinburgischen Ertz=Schwermers und qvaker= Propheten/ Heinrich Kratzensteins Geschichte ... ' in *Der alten und neven Schwärmer/ Wiedertäuffrischer Geister....* Gedruckt im Jahr 1702.

d'Aygalliers, A. Wautier. *Ruusbroec the Admirable,* Trans. by Fred Rothwell. London and New York: J.M. Dent and Sons Ltd. and E.P. Dutton and Co., 1925.

de Boor, Werner. 'Das pietistische Anliegen und die luth. Bekenntnisschriften,' *Die Zeichen der Zeit,* 1 (1947), 89-93.

de Guibert, Joseph. *The Jesuits: Their Spiritual Doctrine and Practice.* Trans. by William J. Young. St. Louis, Mo.: The Institute of Jesuit Studies, 1972.

Daly, Peter M. *The European Emblem: Towards an Index Emblematicus.* Waterloo, Ont.: Wilfrid Laurier University Press, 1980.

Daniells, Roy. *Milton, Mannerism and the Baroque.* Toronto: University of Toronto Press, 1963.

Dannenbaum, R. *Joachim Lange als Wortführer des hallischen Pietismus gegen die Orthodoxie.* Unpubl. diss., Göttingen, 1952.

Davies, Rupert. *The Problem of Authority in the Continental Reformers: A Study in Luther, Zwingli, and Calvin.* London: Epworth Press, 1946.

Davis, Kenneth Ronald. *Anabaptism and Asceticism.* Kitchener, Ont. and Scottdale, Pa.: Herald Press, 1974.

Deeter, Allen C. *An Historical and Theological Introduction to Philipp Jakob Spener's Pia Desideria: A Study in Early German Pietism.* Unpubl. Ph.D., Princeton, 1963.

Degenhardt, Ingeborg. *Studien zum Wandel des Eckhartbildes.* Leiden: E.J. Brill, 1967.

Delius, Walter. 'Gottfried Arnold in Perleberg,' *Jahrbuch für Berlin-Brandenburgische Kirchengeschichte,* 43 (1968), 155-160.

Denifle, Heinrich Seuse. *Die deutschen Mystiker des 14. Jahrhunderts,* Hrsg. von Otwin Spiess. Freiburg in der Schweiz: Paulusverlag, 1951.

Denifle, Heinrich Seuse. *Taulers Bekehrung Kritisch Untersucht.* Strassburg and London: Karl J. Trübner and Trübner and Comp., 1879.

Denifle, Heinrich Seuse. 'Die Dichtungen Rulman Merswins,' *Zeitschrift für deutsches Altertum,* 24 (1880), 463-540.

Denifle, Heinrich Seuse. 'Uber die Anfänge der Predigtweise der deutschen Mystiker,' *Archiv für Literatur und Kirchen-Geschichte des des Mittelalters*, II, 641-652.

Deppermann, Kurt. *Der hallische Pietismus und der preussische Stadt unter Friedrich III*. Göttingen: Vandenhoeck und Ruprecht, 1961.

Dibelius, Franz. *Gottfried Arnold: Sein Leben und seine Bedeutung für Kirche und Theologie*. Berlin: Verlag von Wilhelm Hertz, 1873.

Dietze, Walter. *Quirinus Kuhlmann*. Berlin: Rutten und Loening, 1963.

Dinzelbacher, Peter. *Vision und Visionsliteratur im Mittelalter*. Stuttgart: Anton Hiesemann, 1981.

Doerries, Hermann. *Geist und Geschichte bei Gottfried Arnold*. Göttingen: Vandenhoeck und Ruprecht, 1963.

Dorner, Isaac A. *History of Protestant Theology*. Trans. by George Robson and Sophia Taylor. 2 vols.; Edinburgh, 1871; reprint, New York: AMS Press, 1970.

Dranckmeister, Albert. *Ein edles Büchlein/ Von der innerlichen Geistlichen Hoffart/ und von der tieffen unerkannten und verborgenen Böszheit ... Durch Albertum Dranckmeisterum ... samt einen Bericht Johann Michael Dilherrns ....* Nürnberg/ In Verlegung Johann Andrea Endters Sel. Sohn und Erben. Anno M DCC IV.

Durnbaugh, Donald F. *European Origins of the Brethren*. Elgin, Ill.: The Brethren Press, 1958.

Durnbaugh, Donald F. 'Johann Adam Gruber: Pennsylvania Prophet and Poet.' *Pennsylvania Magazine of History and Biography*, 83 (1959), 382-408

Durnbaugh, Donald F. *The Brethren in Colonial America*. Elgin, Ill.: The Brethren Press, 1967.

Durnbaugh, Donald F. 'The Genesis of the Brethren,' *Brethren Life and Thought*, 4 (1959), 4-34.

Ebeling, Gerhard. 'The New Hermeneutics and the Early Luther,' *Theology Today*, 21 (1964), 34-46.

Ebeling, Gerhard. *Luther: An Introduction to His Thought*. Trans. by R.A. Wilson. Philadelphia, Pa.: Fortress Press, 1970.

Ecke, Karl. *Schwenckfeld, Luther und der Gedanke einer apostolischen Reformation*. Berlin: Verlag von Martin Warneck, 1911.

Eckhart, Meister. *Die deutschen und lateinischen Werke, Die deutschen Werke*, I-II. Ed. by Josef Quint. Stuttgart, 1958-71.

Ehmann, K.C.E., hrsg. *Gottfried Arnolds sämmtliche Geistliche Lieder*. Stuttgart: Druck und Verlag von J.F. Steinkopf, 1856.

Eichler, Wolfgang. *Jan van Ruusbroecs 'Brulocht' in oberdeutscher Uberlieferung*. München: C.H. Beck'sche Verlagsbuchhandlung, 1969.

Elder, E. Rozanne, ed. *The Roots of the Modern Christian Tradition*. Kalamazoo, Mich.: Cistercian Publications, 1984.

Elert, Werner. *The Structure of Lutheranism*. Trans. by Walter A. Hanson. St. Louis, Mo.: Concordia Publishing House, 1962.

Erb, Peter C. 'Gerhard Tersteegen, Christopher Saur and Pennsylvania Sectarians,' *Brethren Life and Thought*, 20 (1975), 153-157.

Erb, Peter C. 'Christian Hoburg und schwenckfeldische Wurtzeln des Pietismus,' *Jahrbuch für Schlesische Kirchengeschichte*, 1977), 92-125.

Erb, Peter C. 'Ein bisher unbekanntes quietistisch-boehmisches manuskript,' *Jahrbuch für Schlesische Kirchengeschichte*, (1977), 127-129.

Erb, Peter C. 'Schwenckfeld, the Anabaptists, and the Sixteenth-Century Crisis of Knowing,' in *Anabaptists and Dissidents*. Ed. by Jean Rott. Baden-Baden: Koerner, 1987, 131-47.

Erb, Peter C. *Jacob Boehme: The Way to Christ*. New York: Paulist Press, 1978.

Erb, Peter C. *Johann Arndt: True Christianity*. New York: Paulist Press, 1979.

Erb, Peter C. *Pietists*. New York: Paulist Press, 1983.

Erb, Peter C., ed. *Schwenckfeld and Early Schwenkfeldianism*. Pennsburg, Pa.: Schwenkfelder Library, 1985.

Erb, Peter C. *Schwenckfeld in His Reformation Setting*. Pennsburg, Pa.: Schwenckfelder Library, 1977.

Erb, Peter C. *The Spiritual Diary of Christopher Wiegner*. Pennsburg, Pa.: Schwenkfelder Library, 1977.

Erb, Peter C. *The Use of the Vernacular in the Sermons of MS University Library Cambridge Ii.III.8*. Unpubl. licent. diss., Pontifical Institute of Mediaeval Studies, 1970.

Erbkam, H.W. *Geschichte der protestantischen Sekten im Zeitalter der Reformation*. Hamburg und Gotha: Friedrich und Andreas Perthes, 1848.

Eylenstein, Ernst. *Daniel Friedrich (+1610): Ein Beitrag zum mystischen Separatismus am Ende des 16. Jahrhunderts in Deutschland*. Langensalza: Druck von Julius Beltz, 1930.

Fellmann, Walter. '250 Jahre Gottfried Arnolds *Unparteiische Kirchen und Ketzer Historie*,' *Mennonitische Geschichtsblätter*, 8 NF 3 (1951), 19-20.

Feustking, Johann Heinrich. *Gynaecum Haeretico-Fanaticum, Oder Historie und Beschreibung der falschen Prophetinnen*. Franckfurt und Leipzig/ Bey Christiano Gerdesio, Anno 1704.

Filthaut, Ephrem, hrsg. *Heinrich Seuse: Studien zum 600. Todestag.* Köln: Albertus Magnus Verlag, 1966.

Filthaut, Ephrem, hrsg. *Johannes Tauler: Ein deutscher Mystiker.* Essen: Hans Driewer Verlag, 1961.

Fischer Martin und Max Fischer. 'Die bleibende Bedeutung des Pietismus' in Oskar Söhngen, hrsg. *Die bleibende Bedeutung des Pietismus ... Zur 250-Jahrfeier.* Witten und Berlin: Cansteinisch Bibelanstalt, 1960.

Fischer, Gottfried. *Geschichte der Entdeckung der deutschen Mystiker Eckhart, Tauler und Seuse im XIX. Jahrhundert.* Freiburg: Universitätsbuchhandlung Gebr. J. and F. Hess, 1931.

Fiske, Adele M. *Friends and Friendship in the Monastic Tradition.* Cuernavaca, Mex.: Cidoc Cuaderno, 1970.

Fleming, Willi. 'Die Auffassung des Menschen im 17. Jahrhundert,' *Deutsche Vierteljahrsschrift*, 6 (1928), 403-446.

Flew, R. Newton. *The Idea of Perfection in Christian Theology.* Oxford: The Clarendon Press, 1934.

Fligge, Jörg Rainer. *Herzog Albrecht von Preussen und der Osiandrismus, 1522-1568.* Bonn: Rheinische Friedrich-Wilhelms-Universität, 1972.

Francke, August Hermann. *Der Unterschied der Selbst-Rechtfertigung Und der Wahren Rechtfertigung ... .* HALLE, In Verlegung des Waysen hauses/ 1714.

Francke, August Hermann. *NICODEMUS Oder Tractätlein von der Menschen-Furcht ....* 5. Ed.; HALLE, gedr. im Waysen hause MDC-CXXIX.

Francke, August Hermann. *Predigten über die Sonn- und Fest-Tags-Episteln ....* Die dritte EDITION. HALLE, in Verlegung des Waysen-Hauses, MDCCXXXXI.

Francke, August Hermann. *Erklärung Der Psalmen Davids; Anderer Theil ....* HALLE, in Verlegung des Waysen hauses MDCCXXXXV.

Francke, August Hermann. *Busz-Predigten ....* Fünfte Auflage; HALLE, in Verlegung des Waysenhauses, MDCCXLV.

Freiherr von Schroeder, William. *Gottfried Arnold.* Heidelberg: Carl Winters Universitätsbuchhandlung, 1917.

Friedenthal, Richard. *Luther: Sein Leben und Zeit.* München: R. Pieper und Co. Verlag, 1967.

Friedrich, Roger. *Studien zur Lyric Gottfried Arnolds.* Zurich: Juris Druck und Verlag, 1969).

Fueter, Eduard. *Geschichte der neueren Historiographie.* München und Berlin: Druck und Verlag von R. Oldenbourg, 1911.

Fulbrook, Mary. *Piety and Politics: Religion and the Rise of Absolutism in England, Württemberg and Prussia.* Cambridge: Cambridge University Press, 1983.

Furcha, Edward J. *Schwenckfeld's Concept of the New Man.* Pennsburg, Pa.: Board of Publication of the Schwenkfelder Church, 1970.

Günther, Hans. R.G. 'Psychologie des deutschen Pietismus,' *Deutsche Vierteljahrsschrift*, 4 (1926), 144-175.

Gichtel, Johann Georg. *Theosophia Practica Halten und Kampfe ab dem H. Glauben bis ans Ende/ Durch die Drey Alter des Lebens JEsu Christi, Nach den Dreyen Principien Göttliches Wesens, mit derselben Ein- und Aus-Gebuhrt Durch Sophiam in der Menschheit ....* Dritte Edition, vermehret und verbessert. Gedruckt in Leyden, Anno 1722.

Gilson, Etienne. *The Christian Philosophy of St. Thomas Aquinas.* Trans. by L.K. Shook. New York: Random House, 1956.

Gilson, Etienne. *The Mystical Theology of Bernard of Clairvaux.* Trans. by A.H.C. Downes. London: Sheed and Ward, 1940.

Godecker, Mary Hilder. *Angelus Silesius' Personality through his 'Ecclesiologia'.* Washington, D.C.: The Catholic University of America Press, 1938.

Goebel, Max. *Geschichte des christlichen Lebens in der rheinischwestphälischen evangelischen Kirche.* Coblenz: Carl Badeker, 1852-1860.

Goeters, Wilhelm. *Die Vorbereitung des Pietismus in der Reformierten Kirche der Niederlände.* Leipzig und Utrecht: J.C. Hinrichs' sche Buchhandlung und A. Oosthook, 1911.

Grünberg, Paul. *Philipp Jakob Spener.* 3 Bde.; Göttingen: Vandenhoeck und Ruprecht, 1893-1906.

Greschart, Martin, hrsg. *Zur Neueren Pietismus Forschung.* Darmstadt: Wissenschaftliche Buchgesellschaft, 1977.

Grossmann, Walter. 'Gruber on the Discernment of True and False Inspiration,' *Harvard Theological Review*, 81 (1988), 363-387.

Hägglund, Bengt. *The Background of Luther's Doctrine of Justification in Late Medieval Theology.* Philadelphia, Pa.: Fortress Press, 1971.

Höhne, Wolfgang. *Luthers Anschauungen über die Kontinuität der Kirche.* Berlin und Hamburg: Lutherisches Verlagshaus, 1963.

Haase, E. *Aus dem Leben des Gottfried Arnold ... in Perleberg von 1707-1714.* Perleberg: F. Grunick, 1912.

Hadorn, W. *Geschichte des Pietismus in der Schweitzerischen Reformierten Kirchen.* Konstanz und Emmishoffen: Verlag von Karl Hirsch, 1901.

Haller, Rudolf. *Geschichte der deutschen Lyrik von Ausgang des Mittelalters bis zu Goethes Tod.* Bern und München: Francke Verlag, 1967.

Harnack, Adolph. *History of Dogma*. Trans. by Neil Buchanan. London, 1900; reprint, New York: Dover Publications Inc., 1961.

Harnack, Theodosius. *Luthers Theologie*. München: Chr. Kaiser Verlag, 1927.

Harp, Henricum. *Theologia Mystica*. Coloniae, ex officina Melchioris Nouesiani Anno M.D. XXXVII.

Hartranft Chester D. et al., eds. *Corpus Schwenckfeldianorum*. 19 Bde.; Leipzig: Breitkopf und Härtel, 1907-1961.

Haubst, R 'Johannes von Franckfort als der mutmassliche Verfasser von "Eyn deutsch Theologie",' *Scholastik*, 33 (1958), 385-398.

Hazard, Paul. *The European Mind*. New York: Meridian, 1963.

Headly, John M. *Luther's View of Church History*. New Haven, Conn. and London: Yale University Press, 1963.

Heppe, Heinrich. *Geschichte des Pietismus und der Mystik in der Reformierten Kirche, nämentlich der Niederlände*. Leiden, 1879.

Heppe, Heinrich. *Reformed Dogmatics*. Trans. by G.T. Thomsen. London: George Allen and Unwin Ltd., 1950.

Hirsch, Emanuel. *Geschichte der neuern Evangelischen Theologie*. Gütersloh: C. Bertelsmann Verlag, 1949-1954.

Hirsch, Emanuel. 'Schwenckfeld und Luther,' in his *Lutherstudien*. Gütersloh: C. Bertelsmann, 1954.

Hoffman, Bengt. 'Luther and the Mystical,' *The Lutheran Quarterly*, 26 (1974), 321ff.

Hoffmane, Gustav. *Die religiösen Bewegungen in der evangelischen Kirche Schlesiens während des siebzehnten Jahrhunderts*. Breslau: Eduard Trewendts Buchdruckerei, 1880.

Hofstadter, Richard. *Anti-Intellectualism in American Life*. New York: Knopf, 1966.

Holl, Karl. *Gesammelte Aufsätze*. Tübingen: Verlag von J.C.B. Mohr (Paul Seibeck), 1948.

Hollatz, David. *Examinem theologicum acroamaticum universam theologiam theoretico-polemicam complectens*. Rostochii et Lipsiae, Apud Joh. Ruswormium, M. DCC XVIII.

Hollatz, David. *Evangelische Gnaden-Ordnung*. 1745; reprint, Philadelphia, Pa.: Conrad Zentler, 1810.

Hornung, Hans. *Daniel Sudermann als Handschriftensammler*. Unpubl. diss., Tübingen, 1957.

Hornung, Hans. 'Der Handschriftensammler Daniel Sudermann und die Bibliothek des Strassburger Klosters St. Nikolaus in undis,' *Zeitschrift für die Geschichte des Oberrheins*, 107 (Der neuer Folge 68. Bd.) (1959), 338-399.

Kähle, Wilhelm. 'Gottfried Arnold Zur 250. Wiederkehr seines Todestages,' *Kirche in der Zeit*, 19 (1964), 205-209.

Köberle, Adolf. *The Quest for Holiness*. Trans. by John C. Mattes. Minneapolis, Minn.: Augsburg Publishing House, 1938.

Köhler, C. Friedrich. 'Gottfried Arnold, der Verfasser der Kirchen- und Ketzer-Historie,' *Zeitschrift für Historische Theologie*, 41 (1871), 3-35.

Köstlin, Julius. *Luthers Theologie in ihrer geschichtlichen Entwicklung*. Stuttgart: Druck und Verlag von J.F. Steinkopf, 1901.

Kühn, Johannes. *Toleranz und Offenbarung*. Leipzig: Verlag von Felix Meiner, 1923.

Kalb, Friederich. *Theology of Worship in 17th-Century Lutheranism*. Trans. by Henry P.A. Hamann. St. Louis, Mo.: Concordia Publishing House, 1965.

Kantzenbach, Friedrich Wilhelm. *Evangelium und Dogma: Die Bewaltigung des theologischen Problems der Dogmengeschichte im Protestantismus*. Stuttgart: Evangelisches Verlagswerk, 1959.

Kantzenbach, Friedrich Wilhelm. 'Theologisch-soziologische Motive im Widerstand gegen Gottfried Arnold,' *Jahrbuch der hessischen Kirchengeschichtlichen Vereinigung*, 24 (1973), 33-51.

Kempis, Thomas à. Thomae Malleoli à Kempis, *Opera Omnia*. Ad autographa eiusdem emendata, aucta, et in tres tomos distributa opera ac studio R.P. Henrici Sommalii .... Editio tertia; Antverpiae, Apud Heredes Mart. Nvtii et Ioann. Mevrsivm, 1615.

Kempis, Thomas à. *Imitation of Christ*. Trans. by Leo Sherley-Price. Harmondsworth: Penguin Books, 1952.

Kertz, Karl G. 'Meister Eckhart's Teaching on the Birth of the Divine Word in the Soul,' *Traditio*, 15 (1969), 327-363.

Klein, Johannes. *Geschichte der deutschen Lyrik von Luther Bis zum Ausgang des Zweiten Weltkrieges*. Wiesbaden: Franz Steiner Verlag, 1951.

Knapp, A., hrsg. *Gottfried Arnold: Die Erste Liebe*. Stuggart, 1842; reprint, Stuttgart: Verlag von Becher und Müller, 1845.

Knapp, A., hrsg. *Gottfried Arnold's sämmtliche geistliche Lieder*. Stuttgart und Cannstatt, 1845.

Knox, Ronald A. *Enthusiasm*. New York: Oxford University Press, 1961.

Koch, Josef. 'Kritische Studien zum Leben Meister Eckharts,' *Archivum Fratrum Praedicatorum*, 29 (1959), 5-49; 30 (1960), 5-52.

Koepp, W. 'Wurzeln und Ursprung der orthodoxen Lehre der unio mystica,' *Zeitschrift für Theologie und Kirche*, 29 (1921), 46ff., 134ff.

Koepp, Wilhelm. *Johann Arndt: eine Untersuchung über die Mystik im Luthertum*. Berlin: Trowitzsch und Sohn, 1912.

Koepp, Wilhelm. *Johann Arndt und sein 'Wahres Christentum': Lutherisches Bekenntnis und Oekumenie*. Berlin: Evangelische Verlagsanhalt, 1959.

Korn, A. *Tauler als Prediger*. Münster: Aschendorffsch Verlagsbuchhandlung, 1928.

Koyré, Alexandre. *La philosophie de Jacob Boehme*. Paris: Libraire philosophique J. Vrin, 1929.

Krumwiede, Hans-Walter. 'Zur Theologie von Gottfried Arnolds Kirchen- und Ketzerhistorie,' *Theologische Literaturzeitung*, 85 (1960), 224.

Kuhlmann, Quirinus. *Der Kühlpsalter*, hrsg., Robert L. Beare. Tübingen: Max Niemeyer Verlag, 1971.

Lackner, Martin. *Geistesfrömmigkeit und Enderwartung*. Stuttgart: Evangelisches Verlagswerk, 1959.

Lang, August. *Puritanismus and Pietismus: Studien zu ihrer Entwicklung von M. Butzer bis zum Methodismus*. Neukirchen Kreis Moers: Buchhandlung des Erziehungvereins, 1941.

Langen, August. *Der Wortschatz des deutschen Pietismus*. Tübingen: Max Niemeyer Verlag, 1954.

Lashlee, Ernest L. *The Via Regia: A Study of Caspar Schwenckfeld's Ideas of Personal Renewal and Church Reform*. Unpubl. Ph.D., Harvard, 1969.

Leclercq, Jean, et al. *The Spirituality of the Middle Ages*. Trans. by The Benedictines of Holme Eden Abbey, Carlisle. London: Burns and Oates, 1968.

Leff, Gordon. *Heresy in the Later Middle Ages*. New York and Manchester: Barnes and Noble, Inc. and Manchester University Press, 1967.

Leube, Hans. *Die Reformbestrebungen der deutschen lutherischen Kirche im Zeitalter der Orthodoxie*. Leipzig: Verlag von Dörffling und Franks, 1924.

Leube, Hans. *Kalvinismus und Luthertum im Zeitalter der Orthodoxie*. Leipzig, 1928; reprint, Aalen: Scientia Verlag, 1966.

Lewalski, Barbara K. *Donne's Anniversaries and the Poetry of Praise*. Princeton, N.J.: Princeton University Press, 1973.

Lieftinck, G.I. *De Middelnederlandsche Tauler-Handschriften*. Groningen-Batavia: J.B. Wolter's Uitgevers-Maatschapij, 1936.

Loescher, Valentine Ernst. *Schvengfeldismvm in Pietismo Renatvm*, Praeside Val. Ernesto Loeschere ... D. XX. Octobr. Anno 1 1 VIII. Dispvtatione Pvblica Reiiciet Avtor Samvel Zelenka ... Vitembergae, Literis Christiani Gerdesii.

Loescher, Valentine Ernst. *PRAENOTIONES THEOLOGICAE Contra NATVRALISTARVM & FANATICORVM omne genus*. Vitenburgae, Impensis JO. LVDOVICI MEISELII, M. DCCXIII.

Lohse, Bernard. *Mönchtum und Reformation: Luthers Auseinandersetzung mit dem Mönchsideal des Mittelalters*. Göttingen: Vandenhoeck und Ruprecht, 1963.

Lortz, Joseph. *The Reformation in Germany*. Trans. by Ronald Walls. 2 vols.; London and New York: Darton, Longman and Todd and Herder and Herder, 1968.

Lortzing, J. 'Der Pietismus lutherischer Prägung als rückläufige Bewegung zum Mittelalter,' *Theologie und Glaube*, 34 (1942), 316-324.

Lossky, Vladimir. *Theologie negative et connaissance de dieu chez maitre Eckhart*. Paris: Libraire philosophique J. Vrin, 1960.

Lucker, Maria Alberta. *Meister Eckhart und die Devotio Moderna*. Leiden: E.J. Brill, 1950.

Luther, Martin. *Werke*. Weimar: Hermann Bohlau, 1883-.

Müller, Günther. 'Scholastikerzitate bei Tauler,' *Deutsche Vierteljahrschrift*, 1 (1921), 440-448.

Mahrholz, Werner, hrsg. *Der deutsche Pietismus*. Berlin: Furche-Verlag, 1921.

Maier, Paul L. *Caspar Schwenckfeld on the Person and Work of Christ*. Assen: Van Gorcum Ltd., 1959.

Maior, George. *VITAE PATRUM Das ist: Das Leben der Altväter... Durch DOCT. GEORG: MAIOR ....* Gedruckt in ... Lübeck/ Bey vnd in verlegung Laurenz Albrechts Buchhändlers dasselbst, Anno Christi 1604.

Maron, Gottfried. *Individualismus und Gemeinschaft bei Caspar von Schwenckfeld*. Stuttgart: Evangelisches Verlagswerk, 1961.

Martin, Irmfried. *Der Kampf um Gottfried Arnolds Unparteiische Kirchen und Ketzerhistorie*. Unpubl. doct. diss., Heidelberg, 1973.

Massner, Joachim. *Kirchliche Uberlieferung und Autorität in Flaciuskreis*. Berlin und Hamburg: Lutherisches Verlagshaus, 1964.

McGiffert, A.C. *Protestant Thought before Kant*. London, 1911; reprint, New York: Harper and Row, Publishers, 1961.

McSorley, Harry J. *Luther: Right or Wrong*. New York and Minneapolis, Minn.: Newman Press and Augsburg Publishing House, 1969.

Meinhold, Peter. *Goethe zur Geschichte des Christentums*. Freiberg/ München: Verlag Karl Alber, 1958.

The Mennonite Encyclopedia. Ed. by Harold S. Bender, et al. Scottdale, Pa.: Herald Press, 1955-1959.

Miller, Arlene A. *Jakob Boehme: From Orthodoxy to Enlightenment*. Unpubl. Ph.D., Stanford, 1971.

Miller, Donald E. 'The Influence of Gottfried Arnold upon the Church of the Brethren.' *Brethren Life and Thought*, 5 (1960), 39-50.

Miller, Vernon. 'Would St. Francis make a Good Dunker?' *Schwartzenau*, 3 (1942) 130-144.

Mitchell, Earl S. 'The Development of Practical Ethical Mysticism or the Roots of Pietism.' *Schwartzenau*, 1 (1939), 5-13.

Mohl, Ruth. *The Three Estates in Medieval and Renaissance Literature*. New York, 1933; reprint, New York: Frederich Ungar Publishing Co., 1962.

Mommaers, P. and N. de Paepe, eds. *Jan van Ruusbroec: The sources, content and sequels of his mysticism*. Leuven: Leuven University Press, 1984.

Morrison, Karl F. *Tradition and Authority in the Western Church, 300-1140*. Princeton, N.J.: Princeton University Press, 1969.

Muller-Thym, Bernard J. *The Establishment of the Universality of Being in the Doctrine of Meister Eckhart of Hochheim*. New York: Sheed and Ward, 1939.

Naumann, Leopold. *Untersuchungen zu Johann Taulers Deutschen Predigten*. Halle a.S: Druck von Erhardt Karrass, 1911.

Neve, J.L. *The Lutherans in the Movements for Church Union*. Philadelphia, Pa.: The Lutheran Publication House, 1921.

Newald, Richard. *Die deutsche Literatur Vom Späthumanismus zur Empfindsamkeit, 1570-1750*. München: C.H. Beck'sche Verlagsbuchhandlung, 1957.

Nigg, Walter. *Die Kirchengeschichtsschreibung. Grundzüge ihrer historischen Entwicklung*. München: C.H. Beck, 1934.

Nigg, Walter. *The Heretics*, Trans. by Richard and Clara Winston. New York: Alfred A. Knopf, 1962.

Nygren, Anders. *Agape and Eros*. Trans. by Philip S. Watson. London: S.P.C.K., 1953.

Obermann, Heiko A. *The Harvest of Medieval Theology*. Cambridge, Mass.: Harvard University Press, 1963.

Obermann, Heiko A. *Forerunners of the Reformation*, Trans. by Paul L. Nyhus. New York: Holt, Rinehart and Winston, 1966.

Otto zur Linden, Friedrich. *Melchior Hofmann, Ein Prophet der Wiedertäufer.* Haarlem: De erven F. Bohn, 1885.

Ozment, Steven. *Homo Spiritualis. A Comparative Study of The Anthropology of Johannes Tauler, Jean Gerson and Martin Luther (1509-16) in The Context of Their Theological Thought.* Leiden: E.J. Brill, 1969.

Ozment, Steven E. *Mysticism and Dissent. Religious Ideology and Social Protest in the Sixteenth Century.* New Haven, N.J. and London: Yale University Press, 1973.

Pahnke, Max. 'Neue textkritische Eckhart Studien,' *Zeitschrift für deutsche Philologie*, 80 (1961), 2-39

Peuckert, Will-Erich. 'Die Zweite Mystik,' *Deutsche Vierteljahrsschrift*, 32 (1958), 286-304.

Peuckert, Will-Erich. *Das Leben Jakob Boehmes.* Jena, 1924; reprint in *Jacob Böhme: Sämtliche Schriften*, hrsg., Will-Erich Peuckert. 3. Aufl.; Stuttgart: Fr. Fromann Verlag, 1961, Bd. 10.

Pfeiffer, Franz, hrsg. *Deutsche Mystiker des Vierzehnten Jahrunderts: Meister Eckhart.* Leipzig, 1857; reprint; Aalen: Scientia Verlag, 1962.

Philipp. Strauch. 'Zu Taulers Predigten,' *Beiträge zur Geschichte der deutsche Sprache*, 44 (1919), 1-26.

Pieper, Monica. *Daniel Sudermann (1550-ca. 1631): Als Vertreter des mystischen Spiritualismus.* Stuttgart: Franz Steiner, 1985.

Pietz, Reinhold. *Der Mensch ohne Christus: Untersuchung zur Anthropologie Caspar Schwenckfelds.* Unpubl. diss., Tübingen, 1956.

Pinson, Koppel S. *Pietism as a Factor in the Rise of German Nationalism.* New York, 1934; reprint, New York: Octagon Books, 1968.

Pleuser, Christine. *Die Benennungen und der Begriff des Leides bei J. Tauler.* Berlin: Erich Schmidt Verlag, 1967.

Poiret, Petrus. *De Eruditione Specialiora, Tribus Tractatibus.* Amstelaedemi, Ex Officina Wetsteniana. 1 1 VII.

Preger, Wilhelm. *Geschichte der deutschen Mystik im Mittelalter.* 1874-1893; reprint, Aalen: Otto Zeller Verlagsbuchhandlung, 1962.

Preuss Hermann A. and Edmund Smits, eds., *The Doctrine of Man in Classical Lutheran Theology.* Minneapolis, Minn.: Augsburg Publishing House, 1962.

Preuss, Robert D. *The Theology of Post-Reformation Lutheranism, A Study of Theological Prolegomena.* 2 vols.; St. Louis, Mo.: Concordia Publishing House, 1970-.

Pullapilly, Cyriac K. *Caesar Baronius: Counter-Reformation Historian.* Notre Dame, Ind.: University of Notre Dame Press, 1975.

Quasten, Johannes. *Patrology*. Utrecht/ Antwerp and Westminster, Md.: Spectrum Publishers and The Newman Press, 1950-1960.

Quenstedt, Joh. Andreas. *Theologia Didactico-Polemica sive systema theologicum in duas sectionae didacticum et polemicum divisum* .... Lipsiae, apud Thoman Fritsch, 1715.

Quint Josef et al., hrsg. *Meister Eckhart. Die deutschen und lateinischen Werke*. Stuttgart: W. Kohlhammer Verlag, 1958- .

Quint, Josef. 'Zu Max Pahnkes neuen Editionsversuchen an Meister Eckhart,' *Zeitschrift für deutsche Philologie.*, 80 (1961), 272-287.

Quint, Josef. *Die Uberlieferung der deutschen Predigten Meister Eckharts*. Bonn: Ludwig Rohrscheid Verlag, 1932.

Quint, Josef, hrsg. *Meister Eckehart: Deutsche Predigten und Traktate*. München: Carl Hanser Verlag, [1963].

Raby, F.J.E. *A History of Christian-Latin Poetry*. 2nd ed.; Oxford: The Clarendon Press, 1953.

Ratschow, Carl Heinz. *Lutherische Dogmatik zwischen Reformation und Aufklärung*. 2 Bde.; Gütersloh: Gütersloher Verlagshaus Gerd Mohn, 1964.

Reitz, Johann Heinrich. *Historie de Wiedergebohren. Oder Exempel gottseliger, so bekannt- und unbekannt-Christen*. Offenbach am Mayn/ Druckts Bonaventura de Launsoy, der gesampt Hochgrafl. Ysenbergischen Hauserbestellter Hof- und Cantzley- Buchdrucker [1701].

Renkewitz, Heinz. *Hochmann von Hochenau (1670-1721)*. Breslau, 1935; reprint, Witten: Luther-Verlag, 1969.

Riff, Adolphe. *Geoffroi Arnold: L'Historien de l'Eglise*. Strasbourg, 1847.

Ritschl, Albrecht. 'Prolegomena zu einer Geschichte des Pietismus,' *Zeitschrift für Kirchengeschichte*, 2 (1878), 1-55.

Ritschl, Albrecht. 'Wiedertäufer und Franziskaner,' *Zeitschrift für Kirchengeschichte*, 3 (1883/4), 499-502.

Ritschl, Albrecht. *Geschichte des Pietismus*. 3 Bde.; Bonn: Adolph Marcus, 1880-1886.

Ritschl, Albert. *The Christian Doctrine of Justification and Reconciliation*. Trans. by H.R. Mackintosh, A.B. Macauley, et al. 3rd ed., 1888; reprint, Clifton, N.J.: Clifton Book Publishers, 1966.

Ritschl, Albrecht. *Three Essays*. Trans. by Philip Hefner. Philadelphia, Pa.: Fortress Press, 1972.

Ritschl, Otto. *Dogmengeschichte des Protestantismus*. 3 Bde.; Göttingen: J.C. Hinrich'sche Buchhandlung und Vandenhoeck und Ruprecht, 1908-1926.

Ritter von Srbik, Heinrich. *Geist und Geschichte vom deutschen Humanismus bis zur Gegenzeit*. München und Salzburg: Verlag F. Bruckmann und Otto Müller Verlag, 1950.

Roberts, Frank C. 'Gottfried Arnold on Historical Understanding,' *Fides*, 14 (1982), 50-59.

Roberts, Frank C. *Gottfried Arnold as a Historian of Christianity*. Unpubl. Ph.D., Vanderbilt University, 1973.

Roemeling, C.A. *Nachricht seiner von Gottgeschehenen volligen Herausführung aus Babel ....* Ephrata, gedruckt im Jahr 1792.

Rupp, Gordon. *The Righteousness of God*. London: Hodder and Stoughton, 1953.

Ruusbroec, Jan van. *Werken*. Ed. by J.B. Poukens, et al. Tielt: Drukkerij-Uitgeverij Lannoo, 1944-1948.

Ruusbroec, Jan van. *D. IOANNIS RVSBROCHII ... OPERA OMNIA: Nunc demum post annos ferme ducentos e Brabantiae Germanico idiomate reddita Latine per F. Laurentium Surium Carthusiae Colonien alumnum ....* COLONIAE Ex Officina Haeredum Iohannis Quentel, mense Martio, M. D. LII.

Ruysbroeck, John. *The Spiritual Espousals*. Trans. by Eric Colledge. New York: Harper and Row, Publishers, 1953.

Saarnivaara, Uuras. *Luther Discovers the Gospel*. St. Louis, Mo.: Concordia Publishing House, 1951.

Sachse, Julius Friedrich. *The German Sectarians of Pennsylvania 1708-1800: A Critical and Legendary History of the Ephrata Cloister and the Dunkers*. 2 vols.; Philadelphia: the Author, 1899-1900.

Sachsse, Eugene. *Ursprung und Wesen des Pietismus*. Wiesbaden und Philadelphia: Julius Niedner Verlagshandlung und Schäffer und Koradi, 1884.

Sandaeus, Maximilian. *Pro Theologia Mystica Clavis*. Coloniae Agrippinae Ex Officina Gualteriana Anno Societatis Iesv Seculari, M. DC. XL.

Sann, Auguste. *Bunyan in Deutschland: Studien zur literarischen Wechselziehung zwischen England und der deutschen Pietismus*. Giessen: Wilhelm Schmitz Verlag, 1951.

Schöne, Albrecht. *Emblemata: Handbuch zur Sinnkunst des 16. und 17. Jahrhunderts*. Stuttgart: J.B. Metzler, 1967.

Schöne, Albrecht. *Embematik und Drama im Zeitalter des Barok*. München: C.H. Beck'sche Verlagsbuchhandlung, 1968.

Schöne, Albrecht, hrsg. *Das Zeitalter des Barok*. München: C.H. Beck' sche Verlagsbuchhandlung, 1963.

Scharlemann, Robert P. *Thomas Aquinas and John Gerhard.* New Haven and London: Yale University Press, 1964.

Scheible, Heinz. *Die Entstehung der Magdeburger Zenturien.* Gütersloh: Gütersloher Verlagshaus Gerd Mohn, 1966.

Schering, E. 'Besprechung: Hermann Doerries, Geist und Geschichte bei Gottfried Arnold,' *Jahrbuch der hess. kirchengeschichtlichen Vereinigung*, 18 (1967), 266.

Schmid, Heinrich. *The Doctrinal Theology of the Evangelical Lutheran Church.* Trans. by Charles A. Hay and Henry E. Jacobs. Philadelphia, Pa.: Lutheran Bookstore, 1876.

Schmid, Heinrich. *Die Geschichte des Pietismus.* Berlin, 1863.

Schmidt, Gottfried H. *Daniel Sudermann: Versuch einer wissenschaftlichen Monographie.* Unpubl. diss., Leipzig, 1923.

Schmidt, Kurt Dietrich. 'Labadie und Spener,' *Zeitschrift für Kirchengeschichte*, 46 (1928), 566-583.

Schmidt, Martin. 'England und der deutschen Pietismus.' *Evangelische Theologie*, 13 (1953), 213-224.

Schmidt, Martin. 'Die Interpretation der neuzeitlichen Kirchengeschichte,' *Zeitschrift für Theologie und Kirche*, 54 (1957), 174-212.

Schmidt, Martin. *Wiedergeburt und Neuer Mensch.* Witten: Luther Verlag, 1969.

Schmidt, Martin. *Pietismus.* Stuttgart: W. Kohlhammer, 1972.

Schneider, Hans. 'Das Basler Konzil in der deutschsprachigen Evangelischen Kirchengeschichtsschreibung,' *Theologische Zeitschrift*, 38 (1982), 308-330.

Schoeps, Hans Joachim. *Vom himmlischen Fleisch Christi.* Tübingen: J.C.B. Mohr (Paul Siebeck), 1951.

Schoolfield, George C. *The German Lyric of the Baroque in English Translation.* New York: AMS Press, Inc., 1966.

Schultz, Selina G. *Caspar Schwenckfeld von Ossig*, with an introduction by Peter C. Erb. 4th ed.; Pennsburg, Pa.: Board of Publication of the Schwenkfelder Church, 1977.

Schultze, Wilhelm A. 'Der Verlauf der Missionsgeschichte bei Gottfried Arnold,' *Zeitschrift für Kirchengeschichte*, 64 (1952/ 53), 260-291.

Schwenckfeld, Caspar. *Epistolar... Caspar Schwenckfeldts von Ossig... Der ander Theil,....* o.O., 1570.

Scriver, Christian. *Seelenschatz ....* Schaffhausen/ Druckts und verlegts Emanuel Hurter, 1738.

Seeberg, Erich, hrsg. *Gottfried Arnold in Auswahl.* München, 1934.

Seeberg, Erich. *Gottfried Arnold: Die Wissenschaft und die Mystik seiner Zeit.* Meerane i. S., 1923; reprint, Darmstadt: Wissenschaftliche Buchgesellschaft, 1964.

Seipt, Allen A. *Schwenkfelder Hymnology.* Philadelphia, Pa., 1909.

Seltzer, George R. *Aspects of the Thought of Caspar Schwenckfeld.* Unpubl. Ph.D., Hartford Theological Seminary, 1934.

Seyppel, Joachim H. 'Freedom and the Mystical Union in *Der Cherubinische Wandersmann,*' *The Germanic Review,* 32 (1957), 93-112.

Seyppel, Joachim H. *Schwenckfeld: Knight of Faith.* Pennsburg, Pa.: Schweckfelder Library, 1961.

Siedel, Gottlob. *Die Mystik Taulers.* Leipzig: J.C. Hinrich'sche Buchhandlung, 1911.

Silesius, Angelus. *Sämtliche Poetische Werke,* hrsg., Hans Ludwig Held. 3 Bde.; München: Carl Hanser Verlag, 1949-1952.

Spener, Philipp Jakob. *Christliches Ehren-Bedächtnüsz... Johann Caspar Schadens.* Daselbst gedruckt mit Salfeldischer Wittwe Schrifften, [O. J.].

Spener, Philipp Jakob. *Der Evangelischen Kirchen Rettung von falscher trenung und gemeinschaft mit alten Ketzereyen.* Franckfurt am Mayn/ in verlegung Johann David Zunners im Jahr 1695.

Spener, Philipp Jakob. *Efördertes Theologisches Bedencken.* Ploen/ Gedruckt durch Tobias Schmidt, 1690.

Spener, Philipp Jakob. *Sieg der Wahrheit und der Unschult.* Cölln an der Spree/ In Verlegung Jeremiae Schrey und Heinrich Joh. Meyers Sel. Erben. Im Jahr 1693.

Spener, Philipp Jakob, *Theologische Bedencken.* Halle/ in Verlegung des Waysen-Hauses, 1700-1702.

Spener, Philipp Jakob. *Lauterkeit Des Evangelischen Christenthums ....* Halle/ in Verlegung des Waysen=hauses MDCCIX.

Spener, Philipp Jakob. *Erste Geistliche Schriften.* Franckfurt am Mayn/ In Verlegung Johann David Zunners/ Buchhändlers Anno MDCXCIX.

Spener, Philipp Jakob. *Natur und Gnade/ Oder der Unterschied der Wercke ....* Franckfurt am Mayn/ Verlegt von Johann David Zunners Seeligen Erben/ 1705.

Spener, Philipp Jakob. *Gerechter Eifer wider das Antichristliche Pabsthum ... aus seinen Schrifften zusammen getragen, und mit einer Vorrede herausgegeben von Jo. Georgio Pritio.* Franckfurth am Mayn, In der Zunnerisch- und Jungischen Handlung, Gedruckt bey Anton Heinscheit, MDCCXIV.

Spener, Philipp Jakob. *Der hochwichtige Articul Von der Wiedergeburt*. Franckfurt am Mayn, Verlegt von Johann David Zunners seel. Erben und .... [1715].

Spener, Philipp Jakob. *Die Evangelische Lebens-Pflichts* .... In Franckfurt am Mayn, verlegt Von Zunnerischen Erben/ und Joh. Adam Jungen, MDCCXV.

Spener, Philipp Jakob. *Christliche Aufmunterung zur Verständigkeit... wie auch Christlichen Unterricht von selbiger Wiederkehr zu der evangelischen Wahrheit, Der zu dem Pabsthum verführten*. Franckfurt am Mayn/ In Verlegung Johann David Zunners seel. Erben, und Johann Adam Jungen, Jm Jahr 1718. Gedruckt bey Anton Heinscheit.

Spener, Philipp Jakob. *Kleine Geistliche Schriften*. Magdeburg und Leipzig: Verlegts seel. Christoph Seidels Witwe und Georg Ernst Scheidhauer. Gedruckt bey Christian Leberecht Faber, 1741-1742.

Spener, Philipp Jakob. *Kurtz Catechismus Predigten*. St. Louis, Mo.: Verlag von L. Volkening, 1867.

Spener, Philipp Jakob. *Hauptschriften*. Ed. by Paul Grünberg. Gotha: Friedrich Andreas Perthes, 1889.

Spener, Philipp Jakob. *The Spiritual Priesthood*. Trans. by A.G. Voigt. Philadelphia, Pa.: The Lutheran Publication Society, 1917.

Spener, Philipp Jakob. *Hauptschriften*, hrsg., Paul Grünberg. Gotha: Friedrich Andreas Perthes, 1889.

Spener, Philipp Jakob. *Pia Desideria*, hrsg. Kurt Aland. 3. Aufl.; Berlin: Verlag Walter de Gruyter und Co., 1964.

Spener, Philipp Jakob. *Pia desideria*. Trans. by Theodore G. Tappert. Philadelphia, Pa.: Fortress Press, 1967.

Stählin, Traugott. *Gottfried Arnolds Geistliche Dichtung, Glaube und Mystik*. Göttingen: Vandenhoeck und Ruprecht, 1966.

Stammler, Wolfgang. *Von der Mystik zum Barok*. 2.Aufl.; Stuttgart: J.B. Metzlersche Verlagsbuchhandlung, 1950.

Steinman, Theodor. 'Der Pietismus und sein Problem.' *Zeitschrift für Theologie und Kirche*, 26 (1916), 26-70.

Steinmeyer, E. 'Gottfried Arnold,' *Evangelische Kirchen-Zeitung*, 77 (1865), 865-872; 879-884; 897-901.

Stoeffler, Dale R. 'The Life and Thought of Gottfried Arnold,' *Brethren Life and Thought*, 26 (1981), 135-151.

Stoeffler, Dale R. 'Gottfried Arnold's View of the Christian Life,' *Brethren Life and Thought*, 26 (1981), 237-246.

Stoeffler, Dale R. 'The Ecclesiology of Gottfried Arnold,' *Brethren Life and Thought*, 28 (1983), 91-100. Stoeffler, F. Ernest. *Mysticism in the German Devotional Literature of Colonial Pennsylvania*. Allentown, Pa.: Schlechters, 1950.

Stoeffler, F. Ernest. *The Rise of Evangelical Pietism*. Leiden: E.J. Brill, 1965.

Stoeffler, F. Ernest. *German Pietism During the Eighteenth Century*. Leiden: E.J. Brill, 1973.

Stoeffler, F. Ernest. *Continental Pietism and Early American Christianity*. Grand Rapids, Mich.: Eerdmans, 1976.

Stoudt, John Joseph. *Jacob Boehme: His Life and Thought*. New York: Seabury Press, 1968.

Strauch Philipp. 'F. Vetter, hrsg., *Die Predigten Taulers*. ... ,' *Deutsche Literaturzeitung*, 39 (1918), 183-188.

Strohl, Henri. *Luther Jusqu'en 1521*. 2e éd.; Paris: Press Universitaires de France, 1962.

Struder, Friedrich Wilhelm. hrsg. *Grundlage zu einer hessischen Gelehrten und Schriftsteller Geschichte*. Göttingen, in der Barmeierischen Buchdruckung, 1781.

Sudermann, Daniel. *Güldene Sendtbrieff/ vieler Gottseligen Kirchen-lehrer: als/ Johann Taulers,/ Heinrich Seussen, Johann Crätzers/ vnnd mehr Anderer* .... o.O., 1622

Sudermann, Daniel. *Ain alt vnd werdes Buchlein/ von der Gnade Gottes./ ... von Johan Rusebruch einem Hayligen/ Waldt Priester in Brabandt... geschrieben,* .... o.O., 1621

Sudermann, Daniel. *Ein Edles Buchlein/ ... Doctor Johann Taulers/ Wie der Mensch möge Ernsthafftig/ Jnnig/ Geistlich vnnd GOttschawende werden* .... o. O, 1621

Sudermann, Daniel. *Hohe geistreiche Lehren vnd Erklärungen vber die fürnembsten Sprüche desz Hohen Lieds* .... o.O., 1622.

Suso, Heinricus. *Horologium Sapientiae*. Hrsg. von Josephus Strange. Coloniae: J.M. Heberle (H. Lempertz), 1961.

Szyrocki, Marian. *Die deutsche Literatur des Barok*. Reinbeck bei Hamburg: Rowohlt Taschenbuch Verlag, 1968.

Talon, Henri, ed. *Selections from the Journals and Papers of John Bryon, Poet - Diarist - Shorthand Writer, 1691-1763*. London: Rockliff, 1950.

Tanner, Fritz. *Pietismus*. Zurich: Zwingli Verlag, 1952.

Tauler, Johann. *Des erleuchten D. Johannis Tauleri/ von eym waren Evangelischen leben/ Gotliche Predig/ Leren/ Epistolen/ Cantilenen/*

Prophetien .... Gedruckt zu Cöllen im jar Vnsers Herren M. D. xliij den vierten tag Junij.

Tauler, Johann. *Sermones: des hoch geleerten in gnaden erleuchten doctoris Johannis Tauleri* .... [colophon:] Gedruckt der kaiserlichnn stat Augspurg durch Maister Hannsen Otmar in Kostnn des fürsichtigen. weiszen herrnn Johann Rynnman von ougen Und vollendet in der wochnn rogat*i*onem. In dem.1508. Jahr.

Tauler, Johann. *Johannis Tauleri des seligen lerers Predigt/ fast fruchtbar zu eim recht Christlichen leben. Deren Predigen garnab hie in diesem Buch des halbtheyls meer sind denn in andern vorgetruckten bücheren die man sidhar mit der hilff gottes funden hat* .... Gedruckt zu Basel Anno M.D. XXII.

Tauler, Johann. *Postilla JOHANNIS TAULERI ... Item/ zwey Geistreiche Büchlein. Das erste/ die Deutsche Theologia ... Das ander/ die Nachfolgung Christi* ... Mit einer Vorrede Johannis Arndtes. Gedruckt zu Hamburg/ durch Hans Moser, In Verlegung Michal Herings. ANNO MDC xxi.

Tauler, Johann. *D. Ioannis Thavleri. Clarissimi ac illuminati theologi, sermones, de tempore & de Sanctis totius anni, plane piissimi: reliquaque ejus pietati ac devotioni maxime inservientia. Opera omnia.* a R.F. Lavrentio Surio Carthusiano in latinum sermone in translata, postremo recognita, & nunc. iterum diligentissime recusa. Quorum catalogum post praefationem in venies. Parisiis, Apud societatem Minimam. M. DCXXIII.

Tauler, Johann. *Des hocherleuchteten und theuren Lehrers D. JOH. TAULERI Predigten Auff alle Sonn- und Feyertage* .... Nebst einer Vorrede Herrn D. Phillipp Jacob Speners ... Franckfurt am Mayn und Leipzig/ Verlegts Johann Friedrich Gleditsch/ Im Jahr Christi 1703.

Tauler, John. *Spiritual Conferences.* Trans. by Eric Colledge and Sister M. Jane. St. Louis, Mo. and London: B. Herder Book Co., 1961.

Tavard, Georges H. *Holy Writ or Holy Church: The Crisis of the Protestant Reformation.* London: Burns and Oates, 1959.

Tholuck, A. *Der Geist der lutherischen Theologen Wittenbergs im Verlaufe des 17. Jahrhunderts.* Hamburg und Gotha: Friedrich und Andreas Perthes, 1852.

Tholuck, A. *Vorgeschichte des Rationalismus.* Berlin: Wiegandt und Grieben, 1861.

Tholuck, A. *Geschichte des Rationalismus, Erste Abtheilung: Geschichte des Pietismus und des ersten Stadiums der Aufklärung.* Berlin: Wiegandt und Grieben, 1965.

Thomas S. Kepler, ed. and trans. *Theologia Germanica.* Cleveland, Ohio: The New World Publishing Co., 1952.

Thune, Nils. *The Boehmenists and the Philadelphians: A Contribution to the Study of English Mysticism in the 17th and 18th Centuries.* Uppsala: Almqvist & Wiksells, Boktrykerei A B, 1948.

Tillich, Paul. *Systematic Theology.* Chicago, Ill.: University of Chicago Press, 1963.

Trithemius, Johann. *Opera Historica....* Francofvrti, typus Wechelianis apud Claudium Marnium et heredes Ioannis Aubrij. M.DCI.

Usinger, Fritz. 'Die mystische Lehre Angelus Silesius,' in his *Gesichter und Gesichte.* Darmstadt: Eduard Roether Verlag, 1965.

Vetter, Ferdinand, hrsg. *Die Predigten Taulers.* Berlin, 1910; reprint, Dublin and Zurich: Weidmann, 1968.

Vogelsang, Erich. 'Luther und die Mystik,' *Luther Jahrbuch,* 19 (1937), 51-54.

Wagman, Frederick Herbert. 'Magic and Natural Science in German Baroque Literature' in *Germanic Studies,* 13 (1942), 113-149.

Wagner, Harald. *Die eine Kirche und die vielen Kirchen: Ecclesiologie und Symbolik beim jungen Möhler.* München: Ferdinand Schöningh, 1977.

Walch, Johann Georg. *Historische und Theologische Einleitung in die Religionsstreitigkeiten der Evangelisch-Lutherischen Kirche.* Jena, bey Johann Meyer's Wittwe, 1730-1739.

Walch, Johann Georg. *Historische und Theologische Einleitung in die Religions-streitigkeiten Welche sonderlich ausser der Evangelisch-Lutherisch Kirche entstanden.* Jena, bey Johann Meyer's Wittwe, 1733-1736.

Waldemar, Charles, hrsg. *Der Cherubinische Wandersmann.* München: Wilhelm Goldmann Verlag, 1960.

Walker, Daniel P. *The Decline of Hell: Seventeenth Century Discussions of Eternal Torment.* Chicago: University of Chicago Press, 1964.

Watson, Philip. *Let God be God.* Philadelphia, Pa.: Muhlenberg Press, 1948.

Weber, Edmund. *Johann Arndt's Vier Bücher vom Wahren Christentum, als Beitrag zur protestantischen Irenik des 17. Jahrhunderts: Eine quellenkritische Untersuchung.* Marburg/ Lahn: N.G. Elwert Verlag, 1969.

Weber, Hans Emil. *Reformation, Orthodoxie und Rationalismus.* 2 Bde.; Gütersloh: Gütersloher Verlagshaus Gerd Mohn, 1937-1951.

Weber, Hans Emil. *Der Einfluss der protestantischen Schulphilosophie auf die orthodox-lutherische Dogmatik.* Leipzig, 1908; reprint, Darmstadt: Wissenschaftliche Buchgesellschaft, 1959.

Weichenhan, Erasmus. *Christliche Betrachtungen über die Evangelischen Texte....* Allentown, Penna.: Gedruckt bei V. und W. Blumer, 1842.

Weigel, Valentin. *Sämtliche Schriften*. Hrsg. von Winfried Zeller und Will-Erich Peuckert. Stuttgart: Friedrich Fromann Verlag, 1962-.

Weigelt, Horst. *Pietismus-Studien, I. Teil: Der Spener-hallische Pietismus*. Stuttgart: Calwer Verlag, 1965.

Weigelt, Horst. *Spiritualistische Tradition im Protestantismus*. Berlin: Walter de Gruyter, 1973.

Weigelt, Horst. *The Schwenkfelders in Silesia*. Trans. by Peter C. Erb. Pennsburg, Pa.: Schwenkfelder Library, 1985.

Weiser, Max. *Der Sentimentale Mensch, Gesehen aus der Welt holländ-ischen und deutscher Mystiker im 18. Jahrhundert*. Gotha und Stuttgart: Verlag Friedrich Andres Perthes A.-G., 1924.

Weiser, Max. *Peter Poiret*. München, 1934.

Wendel, Francois. *Calvin: The Origins and Development of His Religious Thought*. Trans. by Philio Mairet. London: William Collins, Sons and Co. Ltd., 1963.

Wentzel, Johann Caspar. *Hymnographia, oder Historische Lebens-Beschreibung der berühmtesten Lieder-Dichter*. Herrnstadt, bey Samuel Roth-Scholten, 1719-1728.

Wentzlaff-Eggebert, Friedrich-Wilhelm. *Deutsche Mystik zwischen Mitte-lalter und Neuzeit*. Tübingen: J.C.B. Mohr (Paul Siebeck), 1947.

Wicks, Jared. *Man Yearning for Grace: Luther's Early Spiritual Teaching*. Washington and Cleveland: Corpus Books, 1968.

Wilken, Friedrich. *Geschichte der Königlichen Bibliothek zu Berlin*. Berlin: Duniker und Humblot, 1828.

Williams, George H. *The Radical Reformation*. Philadelphia, Pa.: The Westminster Press, 1962.

Willkomm, Bernhard. 'Gottfried Arnold als Professor historiarum in Giessen' *Mitteilungen des Oberhessischen Geschichtsvereins*, NF 9 (1900), 53-73.

Winkler, Eberhard. *Exegetische Methoden bei Meister Eckhart*. Tübingen: J.C.B. Mohr (Paul Siebeck), 1965.

Winkworth, Suzanna *The History and Life of the Reverend Doctor John Tauler*. London: H.R. Allenson, 1905.

Winter, F.J. 'Johann Arndt der Verfasser des *Wahres Christentums*' in *Schriften des Vereins für Reformationsgeschichte*, 28 (1910), 30ff.

Zöckler, Otto. *Askese und Mönchtum*. 2. Aufl.; Franckfurt a.M.: Heyder und Zimmer, 1897.

Zeeden, Ernst Walter. *The Legacy of Luther*. Trans. by Ruth Mary Bethell. London: Hollis and Carter, 1954.

Zeller, Winfried, hrsg. *Der Protestantismus des 17. Jahrhunderts.* Bremen: Carl Schünemann Verlag, 1962.

Zeller, Winfried. 'Rezension von Dörries: Geist und Geschichte bei Gottfried Arnold, (Göttingen, 1963),' *Zeitschrift für Religion in Geschichte und Gegenwart*, 18 (1966), 289f.

von Heinemann, Otto. *Die Handschriften der herzoglichen Bibliothek zu Wolfenbüttel.* Wolfenbüttel, 1884-1913.

von Loewenich, Walter. 'Zum Verständniss Meister Eckhards,' *Jahrbuch des Martin Luther Bundes*, 50 (1947), 68ff.

von Wegele, Franz X. *Geschichte der deutschen Historiographie.* München und Leipzig: Druck und Verlag von R. Oldenbourg, 1885.

Index